Windows Server 2016 Cookbook

Sauté your way through more than 100 hands-on recipes
designed to prepare any server administrator to work with
Windows Server 2016

Jordan Krause

Packt>

BIRMINGHAM - MUMBAI

Windows Server 2016 Cookbook

First published: January 2015

Second edition: November 2016

Production reference: 1151116

Published by Packt Publishing Ltd.
Livery Place
35 Livery Street
Birmingham
B3 2PB, UK.
ISBN 978-1-78588-383-5

www.packtpub.com

Credits

Author

Jordan Krause

Reviewer

Florian Klaffenbach

Commissioning Editor

Pratik Shah

Acquisition Editor

Vinay Argekar

Content Development Editor

Mayur Pawanikar

Technical Editor

Mohita Vyas

Copy Editors

Vikrant Phadke
Safis Editing

Project Coordinator

Nidhi Joshi

Proofreader

Safis Editing

Indexer

Aishwarya Gangawane

Graphics

Disha Haria

Production Coordinator

Nilesh Mohite

About the Author

Jordan Krause is a Microsoft MVP in the Cloud and Datacenter Management - enterprise security group. He has had the unique opportunity to work with the Microsoft networking technologies daily as a senior engineer at IVO Networks. Jordan specializes in Microsoft DirectAccess, and has authored one of the only books available worldwide on this subject. Additional writings include books on *Windows Server 2012 R2 Administrative Cookbook* and the new *Windows Server 2016 Cookbook*, both by *Packt Publishing*. He spends the majority of each workday planning, designing, and implementing DirectAccess and VPN solutions for companies around the world. Committed to continuous learning, Jordan holds Microsoft certifications as an MCP, MCTS, MCSA, and MCITP Enterprise Administrator. He regularly writes tech notes and articles reflecting his experiences with the Microsoft networking technologies; these can be found at: `http://www.ivonetworks.com/news`.

Jordan also strives to spend time helping the DirectAccess community, mostly by way of the Microsoft TechNet forums. Always open to direct contact, he encourages anyone who needs assistance to head over to the forums and find him personally. Jordan lives and works in the ever-changing climate, that is, Michigan.

About the Reviewer

Florian Klaffenbach started his IT carrier in 2004 as a first- and second-level IT support technician and IT salesman trainee for a B2B online shop. After that he changed to a small company working as an IT project manager for planning, implementing, and integration from industrial plants and laundries into enterprise IT. After spending some years, he joined Dell Germany. There he started from scratch as an enterprise technical support analyst and later worked on a project to start Dell technical Communities and support over social Media in Europe and outside of the U.S. Currently he is working as a solutions architect and consultant for Microsoft Infrastructure and cloud, specialized in Microsoft Hyper-V, Fileservices, System Center Virtual Machine Manager, and Microsoft Azure IaaS.

Additionally, he is an active Microsoft blogger and lecturer. He blogs for example on his own page at Datacenter-Flo.de or Brocade Germany Community. Together with a very good friend, he founded the Windows Server User Group Berlin to create a network of Microsoft IT Pros in Berlin. Florian is maintaining a very tight network to many vendors such as Cisco, Dell, and Microsoft as well as communities. That helps him to grow his experience and to get the best out of a solution for his customers. Since 2016 he is also a co-chairman of the Azure Community Germany. In April 2016, Microsoft awarded Florian the Microsoft Most Valuable Professional for Cloud and Datacenter Management.

He has worked for several companies such as Dell Germany, CGI Germany, and his first employer, TACK GmbH. Currently, he is working at MSG service AG as a senior consultant of Microsoft cloud infrastructure.

Here are some of the books that he has worked on: *Taking Control with System Center App Controller*, *Microsoft Azure Storage Essentials*, *Mastering Microsoft Azure Development*, and *Mastering Microsoft Deployment Toolkit 2013*, all by *Packt Publishing*.

www.PacktPub.com

For support files and downloads related to your book, please visit `www.PacktPub.com`.

Did you know that Packt offers eBook versions of every book published, with PDF and ePub files available? You can upgrade to the eBook version at `www.PacktPub.com` and as a print book customer, you are entitled to a discount on the eBook copy. Get in touch with us at `service@packtpub.com` for more details.

At `www.PacktPub.com`, you can also read a collection of free technical articles, sign up for a range of free newsletters and receive exclusive discounts and offers on Packt books and eBooks.

Mapt

`https://www.packtpub.com/mapt`

Get the most in-demand software skills with Mapt. Mapt gives you full access to all Packt books and video courses, as well as industry-leading tools to help you plan your personal development and advance your career.

Why subscribe?

- Fully searchable across every book published by Packt
- Copy and paste, print, and bookmark content
- On demand and accessible via a web browser

Table of Contents

Preface

Microsoft is the clear leader of server racks in enterprise data centers across the globe. Walk into any backroom or data center of any company and you are almost guaranteed to find the infrastructure of that organization being supported by the Windows Server operating system. We have been relying on Windows Server for more than 20 years, and rightfully so--nowhere else can you find such an enormous mix of capabilities all provided inside one installer disc. Windows Server 2016 continues to provide the core functionality that we have come to rely upon from all previous versions of Windows Server, but in better and more efficient ways. On top of that, we have some brand new capabilities in Server 2016 that are particularly mind-bending, new ways to accomplish more efficient and secure handling of our network traffic and data.

There is a relevant question mixed into all this server talk, "We hear so much about the cloud. Isn't everyone moving to the cloud? If so, why would we even need Windows Server 2016 in our company?" There are two different ways to answer this question, and both result in having huge benefits to knowing and understanding this newest version of Windows Server. First, there really aren't that many companies moving all of their equipment into the cloud. In fact, I have yet to meet any business with more than 10 employees who has gone *all-in* for the cloud. In almost all cases, it still makes sense that you would use at least one on premise server to manage local user account authentication, or DHCP, or print services, or for a local file server--the list goes on and on. Another reason companies aren't moving to the cloud like you might think they are is security. Sure, we might throw some data and some user accounts to the cloud to enable things like federation and ease of accessing that data, but what about sensitive or classified company data? You don't own your data if it resides in the cloud – you don't even have the capability to manage the backend servers that are actually storing that data alongside data from other companies. How can you be guaranteed of your data's security and survival? The ultimate answer is that you cannot. And this alone keeps many folks that I have talked to away from moving all of their information to the cloud. The second reason it is still important to build knowledge on the Windows Server platform is that even if you have made the decision to move everything to the cloud, what server platform will you be running in the cloud that you now have to log into and administer? If you are using Azure for cloud services, there is a very good chance that you will be logging into Windows Server 2016 instances in order to administer your environment, even if those Server 2016 boxes are sitting in the cloud. So whether you have on premise servers, or you are managing servers sitting in the cloud somewhere, learning all you can about the new Windows Server 2016 operating system will be beneficial to your day job in IT.

When I first learned of the opportunity to put together this book, it was a difficult task to assemble an outline of possible recipes. Where to begin? There are so many different roles that can be run in Windows Server 2016, and so many tasks within each role that could be displayed. It was a natural reaction to start looking for all of the things that are brand new in Server 2016, and to want to talk only about recipes that display the latest and greatest features. But then I realized that those recipes on their own won't accomplish anything helpful for someone who is trying to learn about Windows Server administration for the first time. It is critical that we provide a base understanding of the important infrastructural roles that are commonly provided by Windows Server, because without that baseline the newest features won't amount to a hill of beans.

So my hope is that you find a pleasant mix of both in this volume. There are recipes that tackle the core infrastructure tasks that we have been performing in previous versions of Windows Server, but now focusing on how to make them work in the new Windows Server 2016. Then we mix those core tasks with recipes that display some of the brand new features provided in 2016 that enhance the standard roles and services. Some recipes are clearly for the beginner, while others get deeper into the details so that someone already experienced with working inside Windows Server will gain some new knowledge out of reading this book. We will discuss the roles that are critically important to making any Microsoft network function: Active Directory, DNS, DHCP, certificate services, and so on. Then we will also bring some light to the new functions inside Windows Server 2016 like Nano Server and Storage Spaces Direct.

A primary goal of this cookbook is to be a reference guide that you can come back to time and again when you need to accomplish common tasks in your environment, but want to ensure that you are performing them the right way. I hope that through these chapters you are able to become comfortable enough with Windows Server 2016 that you will go out and install it today!

What this book covers

Chapter 1, *Learning the Interface,* starts us on our journey working with Windows Server 2016 as we figure out how to navigate the look and feel of this new operating system, and gain some tips and tricks to make our daily chores more efficient.

Chapter 2, *Core Infrastructure Tasks,* takes us through configuring and working with the core Microsoft technology stack. The recipes contained in this chapter are what I consider essential knowledge for any administrator who intends to work in a Windows network.

Chapter 3, *Security and Networking,* teaches us some methods for locking down access on our servers. We will also cover commands which can be very useful tools as you start monitoring network traffic.

Chapter 4, *Working with Certificates*, will start to get us comfortable with the creation and distribution of certificates within our network. PKI is an area that is becoming more and more prevalent, but the majority of server administrators have not yet had an opportunity to work hands-on with them.

Chapter 5, *Internet Information Services*, brings us into the configuration of a Windows Server 2016 box as a web server in our network. Strangely, in the field, I find a lot of Microsoft networks with Apache web servers floating around. Let's explore IIS as a better alternative.

Chapter 6, *Remote Access*, digs into using your Server 2016 as the connectivity platform which brings your remote computers into the corporate network. We discuss DirectAccess and VPN in this chapter.

Chapter 7, *Remote Desktop Services*, encourages you to look into using Server 2016 as a virtual session host or VDI solution. RDS can be an incredibly powerful tool for anyone interested in centralized computing.

Chapter 8, *Monitoring and Backup*, covers some of the capabilities included with Server 2016 to help keep tabs on the servers running in your infrastructure. From monitoring system performance and IP address management to backing up and restoring data using the tools baked into Windows, these recipes will walk you through some helpful tasks related to monitoring and backup.

Chapter 9, *Group Policy*, takes us into the incredibly powerful and far reaching management powers contained within Active Directory that are provided out of the box with Windows Server 2016.

Chapter 10, *File Services and Data Control*, provides us with information and step-by-step recipes on some of the lesser known ways that data can be managed on a Windows server. We will cover technologies like DFSR, iSCSI, and Server 2016 Work Folders. Also included is information about the new Storage Spaces Direct, and Storage Replica.

Chapter 11, *Nano Server and Server Core*, encourages us to shrink our servers! Most of us automatically deploy all of our servers with the full graphical interface, but often times we could make our servers more efficient and more secure by using one of the headless interfaces. Let's explore these capabilities together to see where they can fit into your environment.

Chapter 12, *Working with Hyper-V*, takes a look into the backend interface of our virtualization infrastructure. Many server administrators only ever access their virtual machines as if they were physical servers, but there may come a day when you need to get into that backend administration and create a new VM or adjust some settings.

What you need for this book

All the technologies and features that are discussed in the recipes of this book are included with Windows Server 2016! As long as you have access to the operating system installer disc and either a piece of hardware or a virtualization environment where you can spin up a new virtual machine, you will be able to install the operating system and follow along with our lessons.

Many of the tasks that we are going to accomplish together require a certain amount of base networking and infrastructure to be configured, in order to fully test the technologies that we are working with. The easiest method to working through all of these recipes will be to have access to a Hyper-V server upon which you can build multiple virtual machines that run Windows Server 2016. With this available, you will be able to build recipe upon recipe as we move through setting up the core infrastructure tasks, and then utilize those same servers to build upon in the later recipes. Building a baseline lab network running Server 2016 for the Microsoft infrastructure roles like Active Directory, DNS, DHCP, certificates, and web/file services will help you tremendously as you move throughout this book. If you are not familiar with building out a lab, do not be dismayed. Many of the recipes included here will help with building the structure of the lab itself.

Who this book is for

This book is for system administrators and IT professionals that may or may not have previous experience with Windows Server 2012 R2 or its predecessors. Since the start of this book, I have been contacted and asked many times whether the core, baseline information to beginning to work with Windows Server will be included. These requests have come from current desktop administrators wanting to get into the server world, and even from developers hoping to better understand the infrastructure upon which their applications run. Both will benefit from the information provided here. Anyone hoping to acquire the skills and knowledge necessary to manage and maintain the core infrastructure required for a Windows Server 2016 environment should find something interesting on the pages contained within.

Sections

In this book, you will find several headings that appear frequently (Getting ready, How to do it, How it works, There's more, and See also).

To give clear instructions on how to complete a recipe, we use these sections as follows.

Getting ready

This section tells you what to expect in the recipe, and describes how to set up any software or any preliminary settings required for the recipe.

How to do it...

This section contains the steps required to follow the recipe.

How it works...

This section usually consists of a detailed explanation of what happened in the previous section.

There's more...

This section consists of additional information about the recipe in order to make the reader more knowledgeable about the recipe.

See also

This section provides helpful links to other useful information for the recipe.

Conventions

In this book, you will find a number of text styles that distinguish between different kinds of information. Here are some examples of these styles and an explanation of their meaning.

Code words in text, database table names, folder names, filenames, file extensions, pathnames, dummy URLs, user input, and Twitter handles are shown as follows: "Then utilize the `shutdown` command to take care of the rest."

A block of code is set as follows:

```
Param(
   [Parameter(Mandatory=$true)][string]$ServerName
)
```

Any command-line input or output is written as follows:

```
hostname
shutdown /r /t 0
```

New terms and **important words** are shown in bold. Words that you see on the screen, for example, in menus or dialog boxes, appear in the text like this: "Click on **Tools** in the upper-right corner."

Warnings or important notes appear in a box like this.

Tips and tricks appear like this.

Reader feedback

Feedback from our readers is always welcome. Let us know what you think about this book-what you liked or disliked. Reader feedback is important for us as it helps us develop titles that you will really get the most out of.

To send us general feedback, simply e-mail feedback@packtpub.com, and mention the book's title in the subject of your message.

If there is a topic that you have expertise in and you are interested in either writing or contributing to a book, see our author guide at www.packtpub.com/authors .

Customer support

Now that you are the proud owner of a Packt book, we have a number of things to help you to get the most from your purchase.

Errata

Although we have taken every care to ensure the accuracy of our content, mistakes do happen. If you find a mistake in one of our books-maybe a mistake in the text or the code-we would be grateful if you could report this to us. By doing so, you can save other readers from frustration and help us improve subsequent versions of this book. If you find any errata, please report them by visiting http://www.packtpub.com/submit-errata, selecting your book, clicking on the **Errata Submission Form** link, and entering the details of your errata. Once your errata are verified, your submission will be accepted and the errata will be uploaded to our website or added to any list of existing errata under the Errata section of that title.

To view the previously submitted errata, go to https://www.packtpub.com/books/content/supportand enter the name of the book in the search field. The required information will appear under the **Errata** section.

Piracy

Piracy of copyrighted material on the Internet is an ongoing problem across all media. At Packt, we take the protection of our copyright and licenses very seriously. If you come across any illegal copies of our works in any form on the Internet, please provide us with the location address or website name immediately so that we can pursue a remedy.

Please contact us at copyright@packtpub.com with a link to the suspected pirated material.

We appreciate your help in protecting our authors and our ability to bring you valuable content.

Questions

If you have a problem with any aspect of this book, you can contact us at questions@packtpub.com, and we will do our best to address the problem.

1
Learning the Interface

In an effort to become familiar with the look and feel of Windows Server 2016, you will learn how to navigate through some daily tasks using the graphical interface. On our agenda in this chapter are the following recipes:

- Shutting down or restarting the server
- Launching Administrative Tools
- Using WinKey + X for quick admin tasks
- Using the search function to launch applications quickly
- Managing remote servers from a single pane with Server Manager
- Using PowerShell to accomplish any function in Windows Server
- Installing a role or feature
- Administering Server 2016 from a Windows 10 machine
- Identifying useful keyboard shortcuts in Server 2016
- Setting your PowerShell Execution Policy
- Building and executing your first PowerShell script
- Searching for PowerShell cmdlets with Get-Help

Introduction

Windows 8 and Server 2012 brought us a drastic change in the way that we interfaced with the Windows operating system, and most of us didn't think that change was for the better. By now I assume you have all seen, used, and are hopefully deploying Windows 10 on your client computers, which brings some relief with regard to the user interface. With Windows 10 we have kind of a mix between Windows 7 and Windows 8, and it fits the needs of most people in a better way. Just like the last couple of rollouts of the Microsoft Windows operating systems, the Server platform follows on the heels of the Desktop version, and the look and feel of Windows Server 2016 is very much like Windows 10. In fact, I would say that Windows 10 and Windows Server 2016 are more alike than the Windows 7/Server 2008 combination or the Windows 8/Server 2012 combination.

If you have been using Windows 10, you already have a good head start for successfully interfacing with Windows Server 2016. However, if you are still using older equipment and haven't had a chance to really dive into the latest and greatest operating systems, these big changes in the way that we interact with our servers can be a big stumbling block to successfully utilizing the new tools. Many differences exist when comparing Server 2016 to something like Server 2008, and when you are working within three levels of **Remote Desktop Protocol** (**RDP**), bouncing from one server to another, all of these little differences are compounded. It suddenly becomes difficult to know which server it is that you are working on or changing. Let's have a show of hands, how many of you have mistakenly rebooted the wrong server? Or even more likely, how many of you have rebooted your own computer while you were trying to reboot a remote server? I know I have! And not just once.

Hope is not lost! I promise you that, once you learn to manage the interface, rather than letting it manage you, some of these changes may start to seem like good ideas. They can increase productivity and the ease of accomplishing tasks—we just need some pointers on making the best use of the new interface.

The recipes in this chapter are dedicated to doing just that. Let's work together to gain a better understanding of why the interface was built the way it is, and learn to take advantage of these new screens and settings.

Shutting down or restarting the server

I just couldn't resist starting with this one. Yes, this seems trivial. Silly even. However, the number of times that I have watched a simple server restart consume more mouse clicks than creating a domain controller has convinced me that this needed to be in the book. Perhaps the shutdown and restart options were hidden away purposefully, because once your system is up and running, there is not often a need to accomplish either of these tasks. When first configuring the box, though, it is very common to have to reboot a couple of time or to shut down a machine to move it to another location. Let's face it, it doesn't seem to matter how many years computers have been around, many times the magical reboot is still the fix—all answer to most problems, even if we have no idea why.

Getting ready

To go through this recipe, you will need a Windows Server 2016 system online. There are no other prerequisites.

How to do it…

Let's take a look at three different ways to shut down or restart your system. The first is going to be the most commonly employed. The second is still being used by quite a few folks who had to work hard at getting this strange location in their heads during the Windows 8 rollout, and they have continued to use it from that point forward. The third is less commonly known but is by far my favorite when tasked with restarting a remote server.

The first option, thankfully, is in a location that actually makes sense. I say thankfully because when Server 2012 was released, this option didn't exist, and finding the restart function was much more difficult. Just like we had always been able to do prior to the Windows 8 rollout, we can simply click on the **Start** button, and see right there near the bottom that we have **Power** control options available to us.

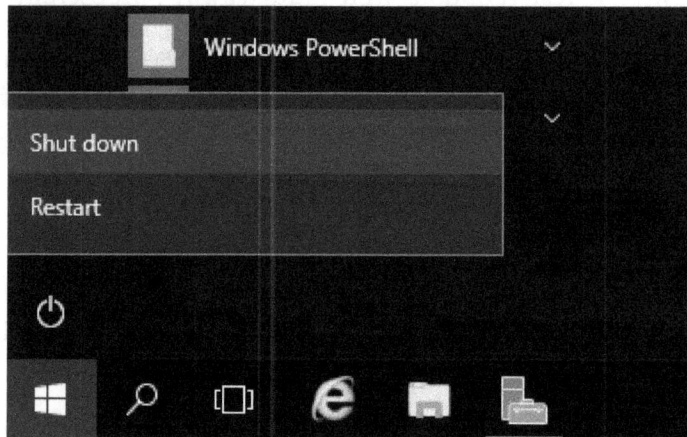

Now, when you click on **Shut down** or **Restart**, you are asked to supply a reason why you are restarting. Common sense tells us that if you are manually clicking on the **Restart** button, there is a pretty good chance you are actually intending to restart the server, right? A planned occurrence? But what is the default option that presents itself? **Other (Unplanned)**. Alas, this silly default option is certainly going to cause us log files full of unplanned restarts, even though all of those restarts were actually planned. Because let's be real—nobody takes the time to change that dropdown menu before they click **Continue**.

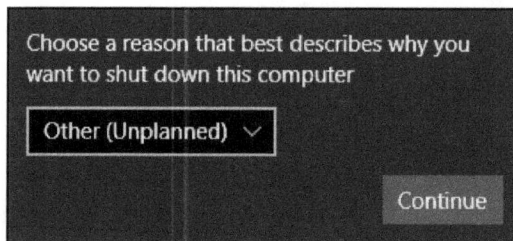

The second method to accomplish shutting down or restarting is by right-clicking on the Start button. We will discuss this little menu that is presented when right-clicking on **Start** in our next recipe, but for the sake of a quick shut down or restart, you can simply right-click on the **Start** button, and then choose **Shut down** or **Sign out**.

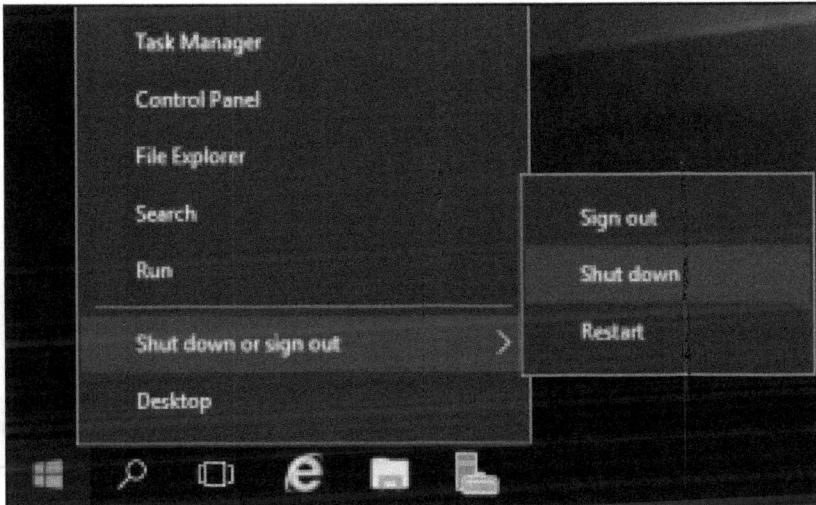

Each of the previous two examples runs the risk of rebooting the wrong system. Depending on how many layers of remote connections, such as RDP, you are using, it is fairly easy to reboot your own computer or the wrong server instead of the server you intended to reboot, because it is fairly easy to click on the **Start** button of a different system than the one you intended in the first place. The most definitive, and dare I say the most fun way of restarting your server is to utilize a Command Prompt. Doing this gives you the opportunity to double check that you are manipulating the correct machine. Open up a Command Prompt and run a quick hostname check to make sure you are restarting the one you really intend to. Then utilize the shutdown command to take care of the rest. This process can be especially helpful when logged into remote servers using RDP. Use the following commands to perform the explained operations:

```
hostname
shutdown /r /t 0
```

If you were to simply type shutdown, the server would shut itself down in 60 seconds. Using /r indicates a restart rather than a shutdown, and /t 0 is a timing flag that indicates the number of seconds the server should wait before restarting. Specifying slash zero here tells it to wait for zero seconds before initiating the restart.

```
C:\>hostname
DC1

C:\>shutdown /r /t 0
```

How it works...

Shutting down or restarting a server doesn't require a lot of explanation, but I hope that this small recipe gets some thought going about creative ways to do regular tasks. As you will see throughout this book, you can accomplish anything in Windows Server 2016 through the use of commands or scripts. You could easily turn the shutdown command, the last example that we tested in this recipe, into a batch file, and place it on the Desktop of each of your servers as a quick double-click option for accomplishing this task.

However, I work with RDP windows inside RDP windows very often. When you're bouncing around between a dozen servers that all have the same background image, I have decided that the only sure-fire way to make sure you are restarting the correct device is to do a quick hostname check before you initiate the restart. If you are interested in discovering all of the available flags that are available to use with the shutdown command, make sure to type in shutdown /? sometime to take a look at all of the available options.

> Using the Command Prompt is also an easy way to log off a server. Let's say you are layers-deep in RDP and want to log off from a single server (not all of them). Are you sure you clicked on the **Start** button of the right server? Instead, open up a prompt and simply type Logoff.

Launching Administrative Tools

Earlier versions of Windows Server placed all of the Administrative Tools in a self-named folder right inside the **Start** menu. This was always a quick and easy place to visit in order to see all of the Administrative Tools installed onto a particular server. This location for the tools disappeared as of Server 2012, because of the infamous Start Screen. I am glad to say that a more traditional-looking **Start** menu has returned in Windows Server 2016, and inside it once again is a link to the **Windows Administrative Tools**. However, as you also know there is this thing called Server Manager that loves to present itself every time that you log in to a server. Since Server Manager is already on your screen most of the time anyway, it is actually the fastest way to launch these Administrative Tools that you need to utilize so often. Let's take a look at launching your commonly used infrastructure tools right from inside the Server Manager interface.

Getting ready

All you really need is a Windows Server 2016 machine online. The more roles and services that you have running on it, the more options that you will see on your screen as we navigate these menus.

How to do it...

To launch Administrative Tools from your Desktop, perform the following steps:

1. Open up **Server Manager**. In fact, if you just logged into the server, it's probably already open for you.
2. Click on **Tools** in the upper-right corner.

There you go. A full list of all the Administrative Tools installed onto that server. Heading into this list is also a quick way of taking a look into what a particular server is doing, which you can take an educated guess at based on what roles and services are installed. By looking at the following screenshot, we can see that this server appears to be a domain controller that is also running DNS and DHCP, because all of the related tools are available to choose in this list. That is accurate, as this is my DC1 domain controller server. It is important to note that your server may be running components that do not show up in this list. For example, if you install a role via PowerShell and do not enter the parameter to also install the management tools for that role, it is possible that you could have a server where the role is up and running, but the management tools simply have not been installed. In that case, those tools would not show up in this list.

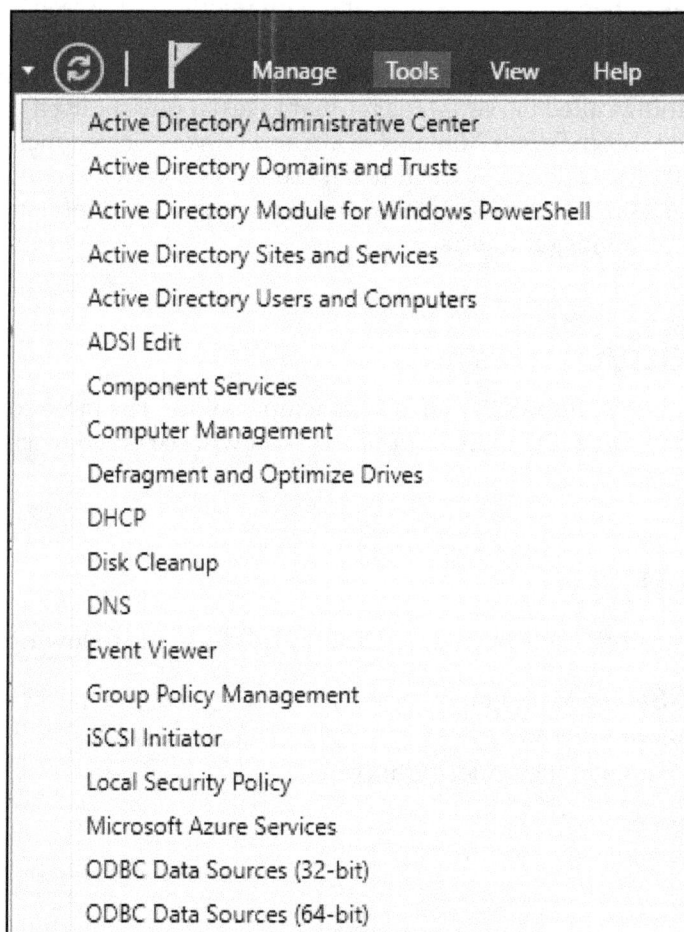

How it works...

Since Server Manager likes to open automatically when logging in, let's make quick use of it to open the tools that we need to do our jobs. Another way to have easy access to your tools from the Desktop is to create shortcuts or to pin each of them to your taskbar. Sometimes this isn't as easy as it sounds. In the past, these tools were all grouped together in the `Administrative Tools` folder, so you didn't have any reason to memorize the exact names of the tools. While you can access them that way again in Server 2016, that folder may or may not appear inside the Start menu depending on how the server is configured, because it appears as one of the live tiles. If you click on the **Start** button, you could try using the search function to find the tool you are looking for, but its name may not immediately come to you. If you're a consultant working on someone else's server, you may not want to pin anything to their Desktop anyway, and you certainly don't want to resort to using Bing in front of them to look up the name of the tool. So I like to stick with launching Administrative Tools from Server Manager since it always exists, and the tools will always be available inside that menu.

Using WinKey + X for quick admin tasks

There are some functions in Windows that a server administrator needs to use all the time. Instead of making shortcuts or pinning them all to the taskbar, let's get to know this hidden menu, which is extremely useful for launching these commonly used admin tools.

Getting ready

A running Windows Server 2016 machine is all we need to highlight this one. In fact, this menu also exists on any Windows 10 computer, so make use of it often!

How to do it...

There are two ways to open this little menu. While you are in the Server 2016 Desktop, you can perform either of these steps:

1. Hold down your Windows key (WinKey) on the keyboard and press X.

2. Hover your mouse over the Windows flag in the lower-left corner of the Desktop—the Start button—when you right-click on that button you will see a menu, shown in the following screenshot:

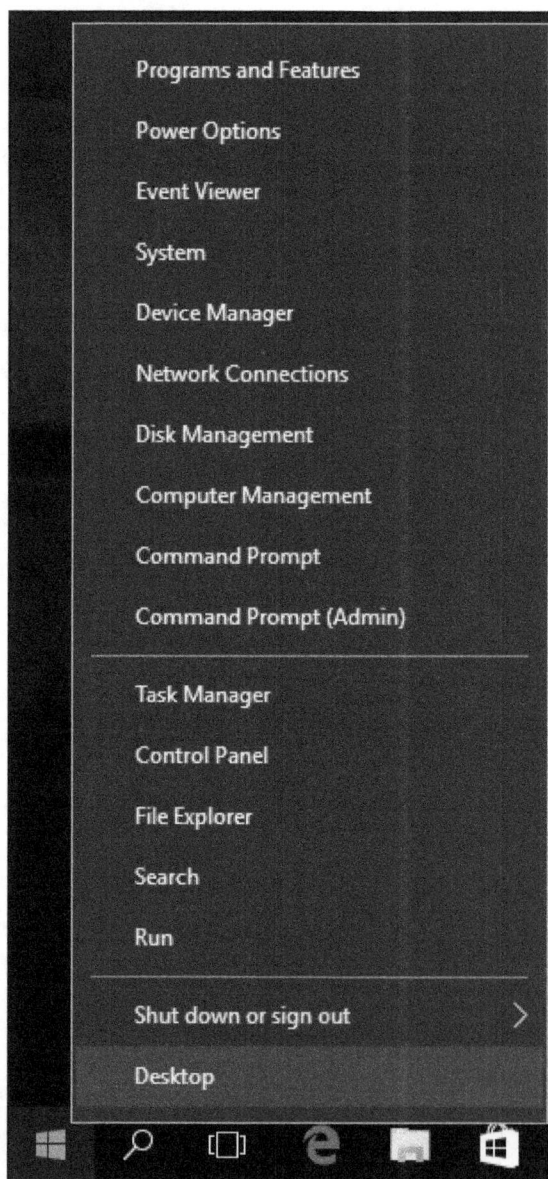

Programs and Features

Power Options

Event Viewer

System

Device Manager

Network Connections

Disk Management

Computer Management

Command Prompt

Command Prompt (Admin)

Task Manager

Control Panel

File Explorer

Search

Run

Shut down or sign out   >

Desktop

How it works...

This little quick-tasks admin menu is very easy to open and is very convenient for launching programs and settings that are accessed often. I won't talk too much about what particulars are in the menu as it's pretty self-explanatory, but I use this menu multiple times per day to open up the **System** properties and the **Command Prompt**, as it has an option to open an administrative Command Prompt right from the menu.

> Look at that, you can also shut down the server from here!

Using the search function to launch applications quickly

The Start screen in Windows Server 2012 was not the greatest idea to come out of Microsoft, and unfortunately what it did was train people to no longer click on the **Start** button, so that we didn't have to deal with the Start screen. Windows 10, and therefore Windows Server 2016, have moved back to a more traditional Start menu, but it is going to take a little bit of time to retrain ourselves to make use of it on a daily basis. I know it will for myself, anyway. Ever since Windows 7 was released, I have been using the Start menu for one critical function in my daily workflow: searching. Let's explore the search capabilities of Server 2016, which can be accessed with a single press of a button.

Getting ready

For this recipe, you will need a Windows Server 2016 system online.

How to do it...

There are two quick ways that you can search inside Server 2016, and they are right next to each other. If you take a look in the lower-left corner of your screen inside the taskbar, you will see a little magnifying glass next to the Start button. Looks like a search function to me. Click on that button, and you can start typing the name of whatever you would like to search for. In the following screenshot, you can see that I have clicked on my magnifying glass and typed cmd in order to find the Command Prompt application.

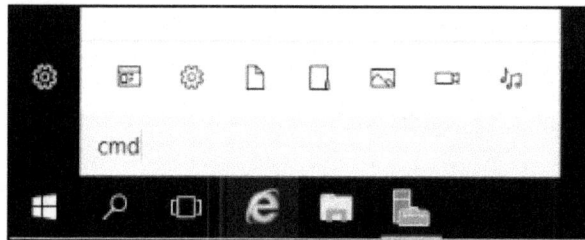

Search results are presented at the top of that screen, and you can choose what you are looking for accordingly. This is a quick, easy search—but I'm not a fan of it because I don't like using my mouse unless I have to. Grabbing my mouse in order to click on the magnifying glass slows down what I'm trying to do while my hands are on the keyboard, so let's take a look at a faster way to search. No matter where you are in Windows Server 2016, no matter what applications you have open, you can always press the WinKey on your keyboard to open up the Start menu, right? What you may not know is that as soon as your Start menu is open, you can immediately start typing anything in order to search for it. If you need to open Command Prompt, press WinKey and type cmd. If you need to search for a document called Text1, press WinKey and type Text1. I employ this method of opening applications all day every day. This way I don't have to pin anything, I don't have to create any shortcuts, and most importantly, I don't have to use my mouse in order to launch applications.

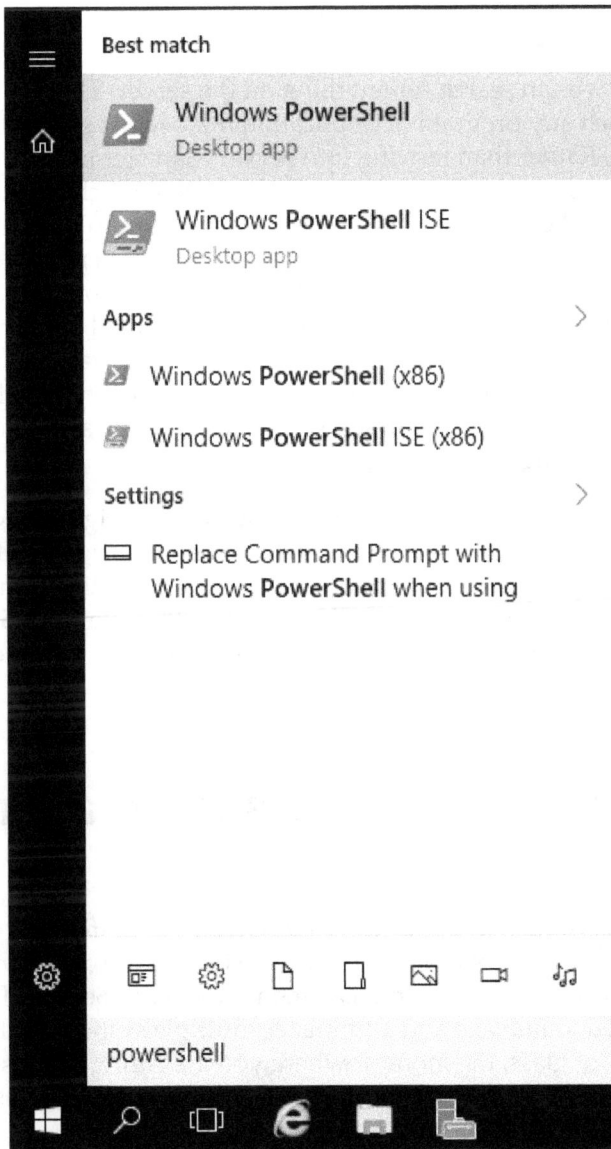

How it works...

From the Start menu, we can search for anything on the server. This gives us the ability to quickly find and launch any program or application that we have installed. This includes Administrative Tools. Rather than moving into Server Manager in order to launch your administrative consoles from the **Tools** menu, you can also search for them on the **Search** menu, and launch from there. It also gives us the ability to find files or documents by name. Another powerful way to use the search function in Windows Server 2016 is to open any kind of setting that you might want to change. In previous versions of Windows, you had to either memorize the way to get into the settings that you wanted to change or you had to open up Control Panel, where you had to poke and prod your way around until you stumbled upon the one that you were looking for. Now it is a very simple matter of pressing the Windows key, typing the first few characters of the setting or program you want to launch, and pressing Enter.

Another common task to perform from the **Search** screen is to right-click on the application that you are trying to launch and pin it somewhere. When you right-click on a program from the **Search** screen, you see options to pin the program to either your **Start** menu or to the taskbar. This will create a quick-launch shortcut on either the main **Start** menu or on the taskbar of the Desktop mode, giving you easier and faster access to launch those applications in the future.

Managing remote servers from a single pane with Server Manager

As you have already noticed, Server Manager has changed significantly over the past couple of versions of Windows Server. Part of these changes are a shift in mindset where the emphasis is now placed on remote management of servers. Server Manager in Windows Server 2016 can be used to manage and administer multiple systems at the same time, all from your single pane of glass, the monitor where you are sitting. In this recipe, you are going to learn how to manage both the local server we are logged into, as well as a remote server, from the same Server Manager window.

Getting ready

For this recipe, we need two servers. One is the machine we are physically logged into. Another is a server on the same network that we can contact from our primary server so that we can manage it from our local Server Manager.

How to do it...

To manage a local as well as a remote server from the same Server Manager window, perform the following instructions:

1. Log in to your primary server and launch **Server Manager**. You will see in the upper-left corner that the only server you have listed is the **Local Server** that we are logged into.

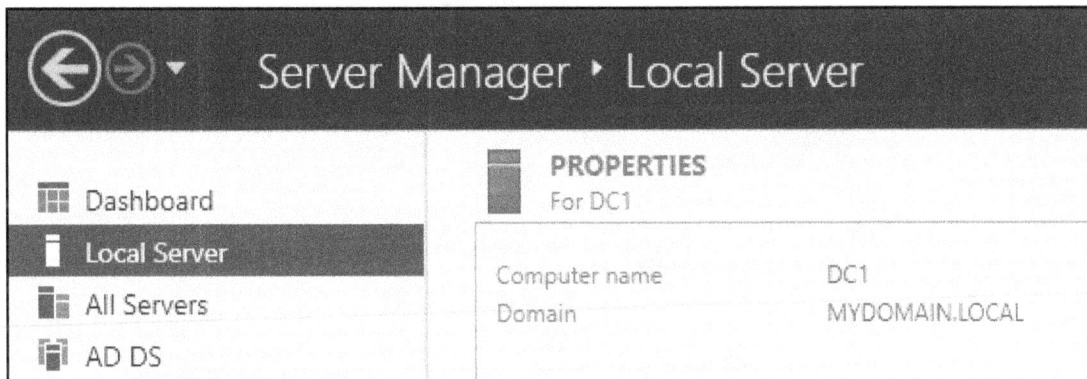

Server Manager ▸ Local Server	
▦ Dashboard	**PROPERTIES** For DC1
▮ Local Server	
▮▮ All Servers	Computer name DC1
▦ AD DS	Domain MYDOMAIN.LOCAL

2. Now head over toward the top-right of **Server Manager** and click on the **Manage** button. In this menu, click on **Add Servers**.

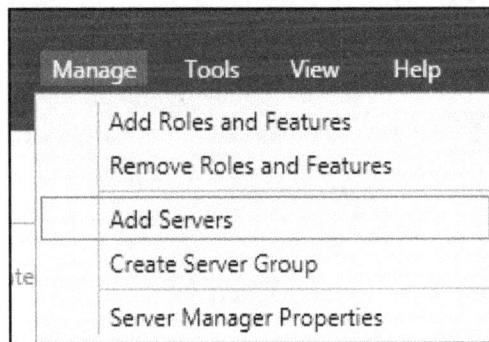

Manage	Tools	View	Help
Add Roles and Features			
Remove Roles and Features			
Add Servers			
Create Server Group			
Server Manager Properties			

3. If your servers are part of a domain, finding remote machines to manage is very easy by simply selecting them from the default **Active Directory** tab. If they are not yet joined to your domain, you simply click over to the tab labeled **DNS** and search for them from that screen.

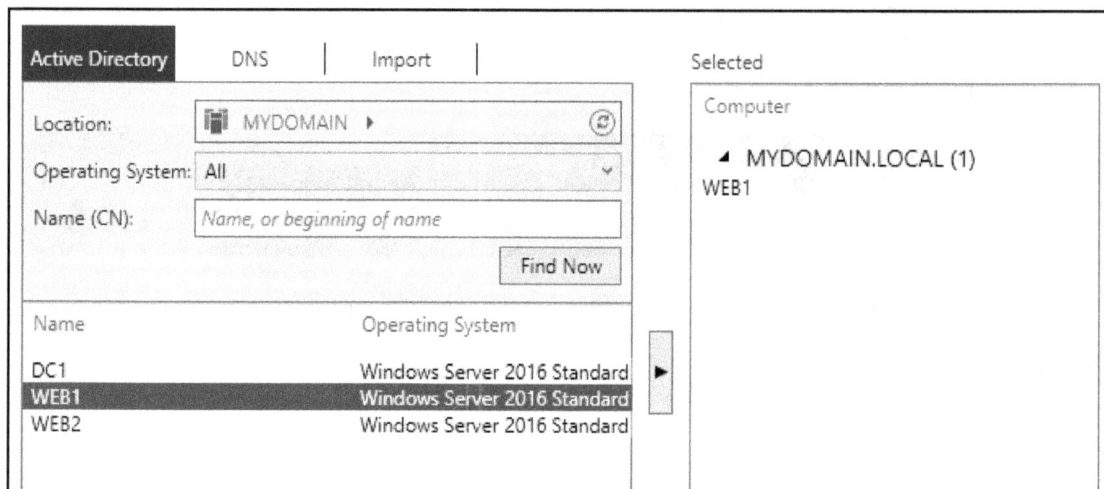

Active Directory	DNS	Import		Selected
				Computer
Location:	📇 MYDOMAIN ▸		⟳	◢ MYDOMAIN.LOCAL (1)
Operating System:	All		⌄	WEB1
Name (CN):	*Name, or beginning of name*			
		Find Now		
Name		Operating System		
DC1		Windows Server 2016 Standard	▶	
WEB1		Windows Server 2016 Standard		
WEB2		Windows Server 2016 Standard		

4. After adding the servers that you want to manage, if you go ahead and click on **All Servers** in the left window pane, you will see the additional servers listed that you have selected. If you double-click or right-click on those remote server names, you have many options available to you to remotely manage those machines without having to log into them.

Note that certain servers could resist being manipulated in this way. It is possible to restrict remote management on servers through Group Policy. If that has been done in your environment, you may find that remotely administering them from a centralized console is not possible, and you would have to lift those restrictions on your servers.

How it works...

Server Manager makes use of the **Windows Remote Management (WinRM)** tools to remotely manipulate servers. Historically, most of us who administer Windows Servers make extensive use of RDP, often having many windows and connections open simultaneously. This can cause confusion and can lead to tasks being accomplished on servers for which they are not intended. By using Server Manager from a single machine to manage multiple servers in your network, you will increase your administrative efficiency as well as minimize human error by having all management happen from a single pane of glass.

This recipe is written with the most common network scenario in mind, which is a domain environment where both servers have been joined to the domain. If you are working with standalone servers that are part of a workgroup, rather than being joined to a domain, you will have some additional considerations. In the workgroup scenario, WinRM will need to be enabled specifically, and the Windows Firewall will have to be adjusted in order to allow the right ports and protocols for that WinRM traffic flow to happen successfully. In general, though, most of you will be working within a Microsoft domain network, in which case these items are not necessary.

See also

- The*Administering Server 2016 from a Windows 10 machine* recipe

Using PowerShell to accomplish any function in Windows Server

An incredibly powerful tool in Windows Server 2016 is PowerShell. Think of PowerShell like a Command Prompt on steroids. It is a command-line interface from which you can manipulate almost anything inside Windows that you may care to. Better yet, any task that you may wish to accomplish can be scripted out in PowerShell and saved off as a `.ps1` script file, so that you can automate large tasks and schedule them for later, or at regular intervals. In this recipe, let's open up PowerShell and run some sample commands and tasks just to get a quick feel for the interface. In a later chapter of the book, we will do some more specific tasks with PowerShell to go even deeper into the technology.

Getting ready

To start using PowerShell, all you need is a server with Windows Server 2016 installed. PowerShell is installed and enabled by default.

How to do it...

To get a feel of using PowerShell, perform the following steps:

1. PowerShell used to exist in the taskbar by default, which was smart because we really should be pushing people to use it rather than Command Prompt, right? Unfortunately, PowerShell is not in the taskbar by default in Server 2016, but the Windows Store is...? Explain that one to me some day. So our first step to working in PowerShell is finding it. Thankfully, we know how to search for applications now, so I'll just press my WinKey and type `PowerShell`. Once my search result is displayed, I am going to right-click on **Windows PowerShell** and choose to **Run as administrator**.

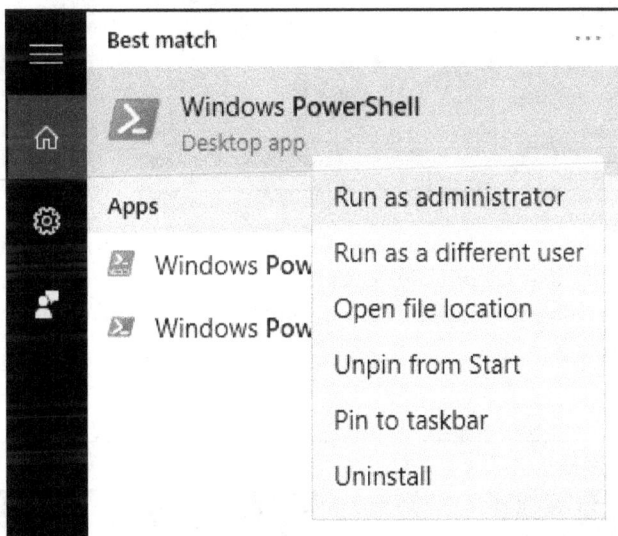

2. Test out some commands that you are familiar with from using the Command Prompt, such as `dir` and `cls`. Since you are able to make use of these familiar commands, PowerShell can really be your one and only command-line interface if you choose.

3. Now let's try some of the PowerShell secret sauce, one of its **cmdlets**. These are special commands that are built into Windows and allow us to do all kinds of information gathering, as well as manipulation of server components. Let's start by pulling some data. Maybe take a look at what IP addresses are on the system with `Get-NetIPAddress`.

```
Administrator: Windows PowerShell                           —   □   ×
PS C:\> Get-NetIPAddress

IPAddress            : fe80::79a1:f04f:406e:f589%2
ValidLifetime        : Infinite ([TimeSpan]::MaxValue)
PreferredLifetime    : Infinite ([TimeSpan]::MaxValue)
SkipAsSource         : False
PolicyStore          : ActiveStore

IPAddress            : fe80::5efe:10.0.0.85%4
InterfaceIndex       : 4
InterfaceAlias       : isatap.MYDOMAIN.LOCAL
AddressFamily        : IPv6
Type                 : Unicast
PrefixLength         : 128
PolicyStore          : ActiveStore
```

4. The previous command probably gave you a lot more information than you needed, since most companies don't make use of `IPv6` inside their network yet. Let's whittle this information down to the `IPv4`-specific info that you are most likely interested in. Enter `Get-NetIPAddress -AddressFamily IPv4` to attain it.

```
Administrator: Windows PowerShell                           —   □   ×
PS C:\> Get-NetIPAddress -AddressFamily IPv4

IPAddress            : 10.0.0.85
InterfaceIndex       : 2
InterfaceAlias       : Ethernet
AddressFamily        : IPv4
Type                 : Unicast
PrefixLength         : 24
PrefixOrigin         : Dhcp
SuffixOrigin         : Dhcp
AddressState         : Preferred
ValidLifetime        : 5.23:17:10
PreferredLifetime    : 5.23:17:10
SkipAsSource         : False
PolicyStore          : ActiveStore
```

How it works...

PowerShell has so many commands and cmdlets, we just wanted to get a feel for launching the program and pulling some data with this particular recipe. There are countless `Get` commands to query information from the server, and as you have seen those cmdlets have various parameters that can be appended to the cmdlets to pull more specific data to meet your needs. To make things even better, there are not only `Get` cmdlets, but also `Set` cmdlets, which will allow us to make use of the PowerShell prompt to configure many aspects of the configuration on our server, as well as remote servers. We will dive further into PowerShell in a later chapter.

Installing a role or feature

You've installed the Windows Server 2016 operating system onto a piece of hardware. Great! Now what? Without adding roles and features to your server, it makes a great paper weight. We're going to take the next steps here together. Let's install a role and a feature into Windows so that we can start making this server work for us.

Getting ready

As long as you have a Windows Server 2016 installed and running, you are ready to install roles and features onto that machine.

How to do it...

To install a role and a feature into Windows, perform the following steps:

1. Open **Server Manager**. In the middle of the screen, you'll see a link that says **Add roles and features**. Click on that link.
2. Click **Next** on the first summary screen and you will come to a choice on the second page. For most roles and features, we want to leave it set at the top bullet, which is **Role-based or feature-based installation**. If we were configuring Remote Desktop Services, which we will discuss in another chapter, then we would choose the second option.

3. Now we choose where we want to install a new role or feature. This is a neat page, as we can choose from any server that we have added into our Server Manager, or we can even choose to install a role or feature into a virtual hard disk. I am running the **Add Roles Wizard** from DC1, but I want to install the IIS role onto WEB1. Rather than having to log into WEB1 to accomplish this task, I will do it right from here. In the following screenshot, you can see WEB1 listed as a server that I can install a role onto, even though I am opening this console on the DC1 server.

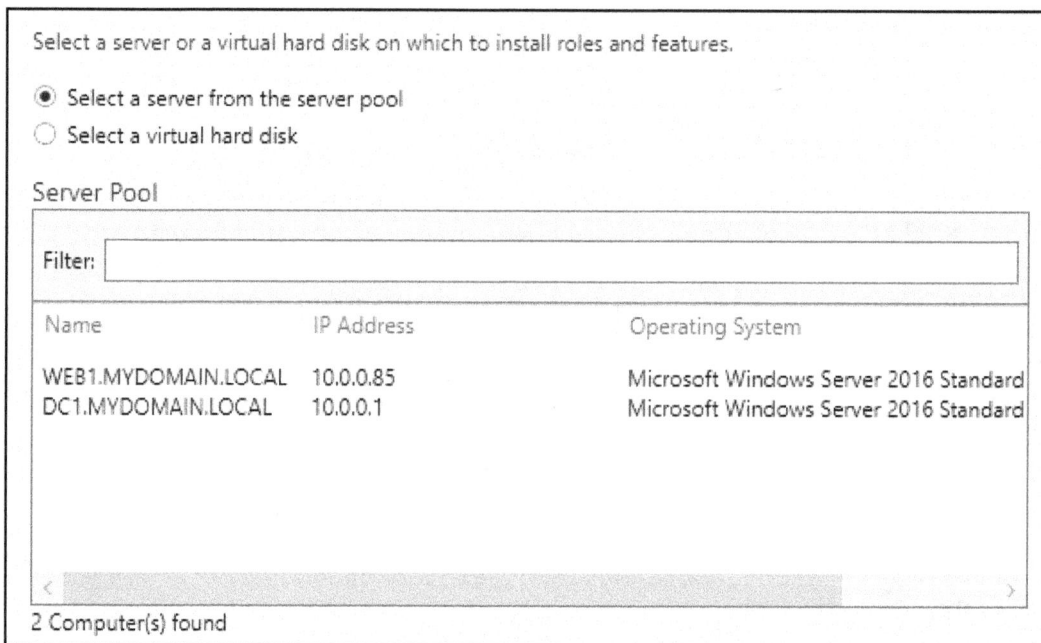

Select a server or a virtual hard disk on which to install roles and features.

◉ Select a server from the server pool
◯ Select a virtual hard disk

Server Pool

| Filter: | | |

Name	IP Address	Operating System
WEB1.MYDOMAIN.LOCAL	10.0.0.85	Microsoft Windows Server 2016 Standard
DC1.MYDOMAIN.LOCAL	10.0.0.1	Microsoft Windows Server 2016 Standard

2 Computer(s) found

4. Scroll down and choose the role that you want to install. For WEB1, I am choosing the **Web Server (IIS)** role. Then click **Next**.

You can install more than one role or feature at a time. Some roles require additional components to be installed for them to work properly. For example, when I chose to install the IIS role and clicked **Next**, I was prompted about needing to install some management tools. Simply click on the **Add Features** button to automatically add the items that it needs to perform correctly.

5. Now choose any features that you would like to install. For example, in order to do some network connectivity testing later, go ahead and select **Telnet Client** from the list.

6. Read and click **Next** through the informational messages that are displayed. These messages will vary depending on which roles and features you have installed.

7. The final screen is your installation summary. If everything looks correct, go ahead and click on **Install**.

After your roles and features have finished installing, the server may or may not have to reboot. This depends on whether or not the role installation requires it. Following installation, or following the reboot, if your new role needs any additional configuration or setting up to be completed, you will be notified at the top of the Server Manager screen.

How it works...

Adding roles and features to a Windows Server is something that every administrator will have to do sooner or later. These items are necessary to turn on the functions in the server that will perform tasks that need to be performed in your environment. Adding roles is quite straightforward. However, it is interesting to see the options that are available to add more than one role or feature at a time. Moreover, the ability to remotely install these items for servers in your network that you are not logged into is intriguing.

Administering Server 2016 from a Windows 10 machine

In the *Managing remote servers from a single pane with Server Manager* recipe, we discussed remotely administering another server by using Server Manager. Did you know we can accomplish the same remote management by using our day-to-day Windows 10 computer? We will install and use the **Remote Server Administration Tools** (**RSAT**) to take even more advantage of Server 2016's remote management ideology.

Getting ready

To test out the RSAT tools, we will need a Windows 10 client machine. We will then also need a Windows Server 2016 system online, and on the same network, which we can remotely control and manage.

How to do it...

To remotely manage a server using RSAT, follow these instructions:

1. First, we need to download the RSAT tools. You can use Bing to search for Remote Server Administration Tools for Windows 10, or use this link to download RSAT for Windows 10: `https://www.microsoft.com/en-us/download/details.aspx?id=45520`. Here is also the link for the same RSAT tools in the Windows 8.1 flavor: `http://www.microsoft.com/en-us/download/details.aspx?id=39296`. After you install these tools onto your Windows 10 or 8.1 computer, you should now have a copy of Server Manager installed onto your computer. Go ahead and launch that from the Start menu. You can pin it to your Taskbar for quicker launching in the future, of course. In the same fashion, as with Server 2016, you can use the Manage menu to add servers to Server Manager.

2. For this recipe, I do have the machines we are working with joined to a domain, so we will take a look at adding servers that are part of the domain.

3. Click on the **Find Now** button and you will see a list of server names that are remotely manageable.

Active Directory	DNS	Import	

Location: MYDOMAIN ▸

Operating System: All

Name (CN): *Name, or beginning of name*

Find Now

Name	Operating System
DC1	Windows Server 2016 Standard
WEB1	Windows Server 2016 Standard
WEB2	Windows Server 2016 Standard
Win10	Windows 10 Enterprise

4. Click on the server names that you want to administer and click on the arrow to move them over to the right side of the screen. Upon clicking on **OK**, you will see these new servers listed and ready for management inside your Server Manager console.

Dashboard

All Servers

AD DS

DHCP

DNS

File and Storage Services ▷

IIS

SERVERS
All servers | 2 total

Filter

Server Name	IPv4 Address
DC1	10.0.0.1
WEB1	10.0.0.85

How it works...

Server Manager in Windows Server 2016 is a powerful tool that can be used for the management of not only the local server but also remote servers that you want to manage. If we take this even a step further and install the RSAT tools on a Windows 10 computer, this gives us the ability to launch and use Server Manager from our everyday Windows 10 computer. In doing so, we enable ourselves to add roles, view events, and restart servers, all from our own desk. Managing servers using these tools will increase productivity and decrease errors because your entire infrastructure of servers can be available within a single window. This is much more efficient than using the RDP client to connect to many different servers, all in different windows. If you've never tried using RSAT to manage servers, give it a try!

See also

- The *Managing remote servers from a single pane with Server Manager* recipe

Identifying useful keyboard shortcuts in Server 2016

I prefer using a keyboard over a mouse any day, for almost any task. There are numerous keyboard shortcuts and tips and tricks that I employ on a daily basis and I want to test them out with you in this recipe. Some of these shortcuts have been around for years and will work with multiple versions of Windows Server; some are new in the Server 2016 operating system. They will all be useful to you as you start working with servers in your network.

Getting ready

We are going to run these commands and keyboard shortcuts while logged into a Windows Server 2016 machine.

How to do it...

- **Windows key**: Opens the **Start** menu, where you can immediately start typing to search for programs.

- **Windows key + X**: Opens the Quick Links menu, which we discussed in an earlier recipe.
- **Windows key + I**: Opens Windows **Settings** options.
- **Windows key + D**: Minimizes all open windows and brings you back to the Desktop.
- **Windows key + R**: Opens the **Run** box. Launching applications this way is often faster than using the Start menu, if you know the executable name of the application you are trying to launch.
- **Windows key + M**: Minimizes all windows.
- **Windows key + E**: Opens File Explorer.
- **Windows key + L**: Locks the computer.
- **Windows key + Tab**: Takes you into the new Task View options.
- **Window key + Ctrl + D**: Creates a new virtual Desktop from Task View.
- **Windows key + Ctrl + F4**: Closes the current virtual Desktop.
- **Windows key + Ctrl + Left or Right Arrow**: Move between different virtual Desktops.
- **Windows key + 1 or 2 or 3 or...**: Launches applications that are pinned to your taskbar, in order. So the first application pinned to the taskbar would open with WinKey + 1, for example.
- **Alt + F4**: Exits the program you are currently working in. This is especially helpful in full-screen apps—like those from the Windows Store – where it is not always obvious how to exit the program with your mouse.
- **Alt + Tab**: Displays a list of open programs so you can hop between them.
- **Shift + Delete**: Holding down *Shift* while pressing *Delete* deletes files without placing them into the Recycle Bin.
- **Using Tab inside Command Prompt or PowerShell**: I cannot believe that I went years without knowing about this one. When you are working inside Command Prompt, if you type the first letter of a file or folder that exists in the directory where you are working and then press the *Tab* key, it will auto-populate the rest of the filename. For example, you may be trying to launch a Microsoft update file with a filename that is 15 characters and comprises a mix of numbers and letters. No need to type out that filename! Let's say the file starts with KB. Simply navigate to the folder where your installer exists, type KB, and press *Tab*. The full filename is populated inside Command Prompt and you can press the *Enter* key to launch it.

How it works...

Keyboard shortcuts can greatly increase productivity once you are fluent with them. This is not an extensive list by any means, there are many more key combinations that you can use to launch apps, minimize and maximize windows, and do all sorts of other functions. This is a list to get you started with the most common ones that I employ often. Start using these with your daily tasks and I bet your mouse will start to feel lonely.

If you are interested in exploring more of the Windows Server 2016 key combinations available, this website is a great place to start: `http://technet.microsoft.com/en-us/lib rary/hh831491.aspx`.

Setting your PowerShell Execution Policy

To say that the Windows operating system can be manipulated by PowerShell is a gross understatement. They are fully intertwined, and PowerShell can be useful for so many tasks on your servers. However, the ability to run PowerShell scripts is disabled by default on many machines. The first stumbling block that many new PowerShell administrators bump into is the Execution Policy. It's quite simple: in order to allow PowerShell scripts to run on your server, the Execution Policy must be adjusted to allow that to happen. Let's introduce our first task in PowerShell by using some commands in this recipe that will set this policy for us.

This is also a good introduction to the idea of the verb-noun syntax that PowerShell utilizes. For example, we are going to make use of cmdlets called `Get-ExecutionPolicy` and `Set-ExecutionPolicy`. The `Get-(parameter name)` and `Set-(parameter name)` cmdlets are very common across all facets of cmdlets available in PowerShell. Wrap your mind around this verb-noun syntax and you will be well on your way to figuring out PowerShell on your machines.

Getting ready

We will be working within a PowerShell prompt on our Windows Server 2016 box.

How to do it...

Follow these steps to set the PowerShell Execution Policy:

1. Right-click on the PowerShell icon and choose **Run as administrator**.

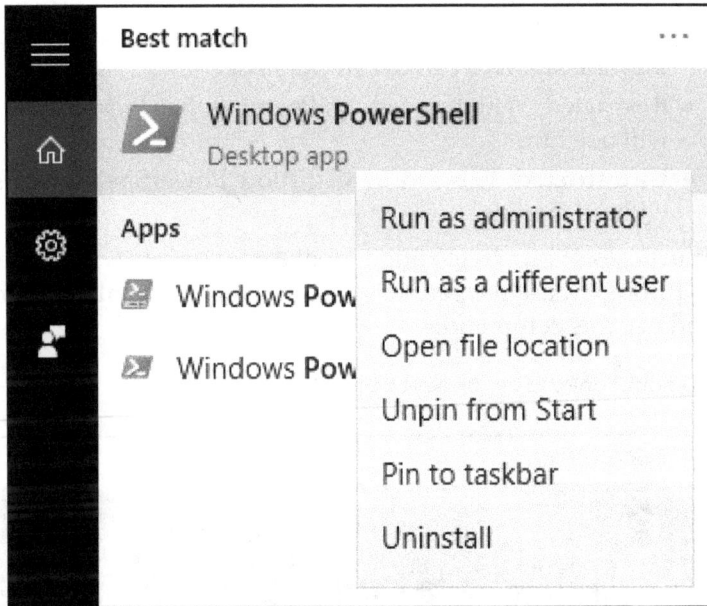

2. Type `Get-ExecutionPolicy` and press *Enter* in order to see the current setting of the PowerShell Execution Policy.

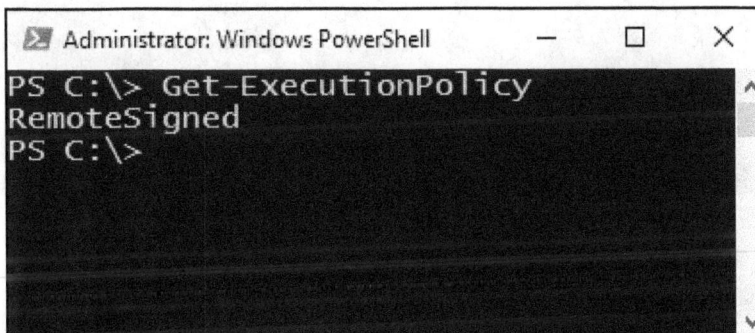

3. You can see that the current Execution Policy is set to **RemoteSigned**. Here is a short description of the different options for the policy:
   - **Remote Signed**: This is the default setting in Server 2016, which allows PowerShell scripts that are locally created to run. If you try running remote scripts, they must be signed by a trusted publisher in order to execute successfully.
   - **All Signed**: With this setting, all scripts will only be allowed to run if they are signed by a trusted publisher.
   - **Restricted**: With this setting, PowerShell is locked down so that scripts will not run.
   - **Unrestricted**: This setting will allow PowerShell to run scripts, with or without signing.

4. For the purposes of our recipe and to make sure scripts will run for us as we progress through these recipes, let's set our **Execution Policy** to **unrestricted**. Go ahead and use this command:

```
Set-ExecutionPolicy Unrestricted
```

How it works...

The PowerShell Execution Policy is a simple setting and easy to change, but can make a world of difference when it comes to running your first scripts. If configured to be more restrictive than you intend, you will have trouble getting your scripts to run and may think that you have mistyped something, when in fact the issue is only the policy. On the other hand, in an effort to make your servers as secure as possible, on machines where you don't need to execute PowerShell scripts, it makes sense to restrict this access. You may also want to read some additional information on the signing of scripts to see whether creating and executing signed scripts would make more sense in your own environment. There are some in-built server functions that rely on a certain level of security with your Execution Policy. Setting your policy to **unrestricted** on all of your servers could result in some functions not working properly, and you may have to increase that level of security back to **remote signed**.

Building and executing your first PowerShell script

Command Prompt and PowerShell are both great command-line interfaces that can acquire and configure information about our servers. Most of us are familiar with creating some simple batch files that are driven by Command Prompt, essentially programming out small tasks within these batch files to automate a series of commands. This saves time later as we do not have to type out the commands line by line, especially for common tasks or for items that we need to run during login.

PowerShell has similar functionality, the ability to write out multiple lines of PowerShell cmdlets inside a script file. We can then launch this script file as we would a batch file, automating tasks while taking advantage of the additional features that PowerShell brings to the table over Command Prompt. These PowerShell scripts are put together inside `.ps1` files; let's build a simple one together to get a feel for running these scripts.

Getting ready

Our work with PowerShell today will be accomplished from a Windows Server 2016 machine. PowerShell is installed by default with Windows, and there is nothing further that we need to install.

How to do it...

Follow these steps to build and execute our first PowerShell script:

1. Open the Start menu and type `Windows PowerShell ISE`. Right-click to launch this tool as an administrator. **Windows PowerShell ISE** is an editor for PowerShell scripts that is much more useful than opening a simple text editor such as Notepad in order to build our script.

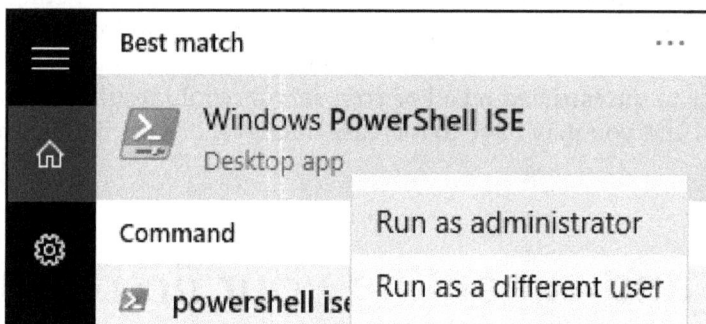

2. Navigate to **File** | **New** from the menus in order to open a blank `.ps1` script file.
3. In your first line, type the following: `Write-Host "Hello! Here is the current date and time:"`.
4. From the toolbar menu, click the green arrow that says Run Script. Alternatively, you can simply press the *F5* button. When you run the script, the command and output are displayed in the lower portion of the ISE window.

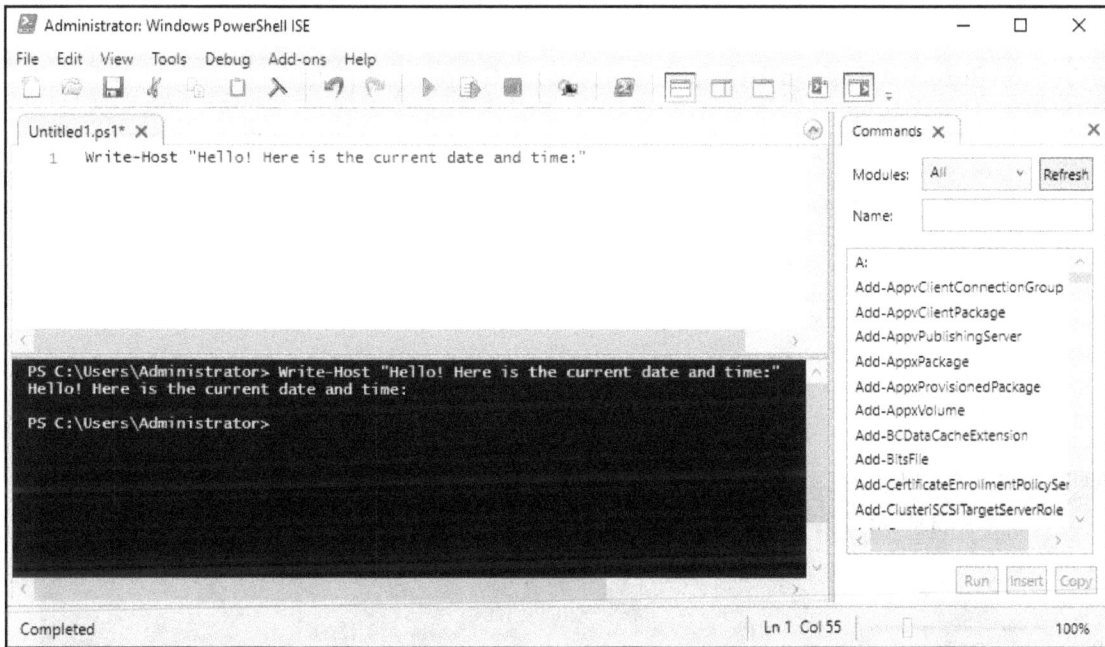

Cool! Okay, so far it's actually pretty lame. It's just reflecting the text that we told it to echo, but it worked. That is the nice thing about using the ISE editing tool rather than a generic text editor, you have the ability to quickly test run scripts as you make modifications.

5. Now let's add some additional lines into our script to give us the information we are looking for. You can see a list of available commands on the right side of the screen if you would like to browse through what is available, but for our example simply change your script to include the following:

```
Write-Host "Hello! Here is the current date and time:"
Get-Date
Write-Host "The name of your computer is:"
hostname
```

6. Press the **Run Script** button again to see the new output.

```
Untitled1.ps1* X
  1    Write-Host "Hello! Here is the current date and time:"
  2    Get-Date
  3    Write-Host "The name of your computer is:"
  4    hostname
```

```
Hello! Here is the current date and time:

Thursday, October 13, 2016 7:56:55 AM
The name of your computer is:
WEB1


PS C:\Users\Administrator>
```

7. Now navigate to **File | Save** and save your new `.ps1` PowerShell script out to the Desktop.
8. Let's test this script by launching it from within a real PowerShell command window. Right-click on your PowerShell icon in the Taskbar and choose **Run as administrator**.
9. Browse to the location of the script file, I placed mine on the Desktop. Then launch the script by inputting `.\filename`. In my case, it looks like this: `.\time.ps1`.

> **TIP**
>
> Remember that the *Tab* key can be our friend in this. When browsing to your Desktop, all you need to do is input the first letter of your script filename, and then press *Tab*. Since I named my script `Time.ps1`, all I had to do was press the *T* and then press *Tab*, then *Enter*.

How it works...

In this recipe, we created a very simple PowerShell script and saved it on our server for execution. While in practice getting time and date information from your server may come faster by using the standalone Get-Date cmdlet, we use this recipe to give a small taste of the ISE and to get your scripting juices flowing. Expanding upon the ideas presented here will start to save you valuable time and keystrokes as you identify more and more ways to automate the tasks and information gathering that are part of your daily routines. The possibilities of PowerShell are practically limitless, so make sure that you open it up and start becoming familiar with the interfaces and tools associated with it right away!

Searching for PowerShell cmdlets with Get-Help

With this recipe, let's take a minute to use Get-Help inside PowerShell in order to, well, get some help! I see both new and experienced PowerShell administrators going to the Web a lot in order to find commands and the parameters of those commands. The Internet is great, and there is a ton of data out there about how to use PowerShell, but in many cases the information that you are looking for resides right inside PowerShell itself. By using the Get-Help cmdlet combined with the functions you are running or searching for, you might not have to open that web browser after all.

Getting ready

We will be running some commands from inside PowerShell on a Windows Server 2016 machine.

How to do it...

To use the Get-Help function inside PowerShell, run the following steps:

1. Launch a PowerShell prompt.
2. Type Get-Help.
3. You're finished! No, I'm just kidding. Using Get-Help by itself will present you with some helpful data about the Get-Help command, but that's not really what we are looking for, is it? How about using Get-Help with a search parameter, like this:

```
Get-Help Computer
```

```
Administrator: Windows PowerShell                                   —    □    ×
PS C:\> Get-Help Computer

Name                               Category   Module                   Synopsis
----                               --------   ------                   --------
Add-Computer                       Cmdlet     Microsoft.PowerShell.M...  ...
Checkpoint-Computer                Cmdlet     Microsoft.PowerShell.M...  ...
Disable-ComputerRestore            Cmdlet     Microsoft.PowerShell.M...  ...
Enable-ComputerRestore             Cmdlet     Microsoft.PowerShell.M...  ...
Get-ComputerRestorePoint           Cmdlet     Microsoft.PowerShell.M...  ...
Remove-Computer                    Cmdlet     Microsoft.PowerShell.M...  ...
Rename-Computer                    Cmdlet     Microsoft.PowerShell.M...  ...
Reset-ComputerMachinePassword      Cmdlet     Microsoft.PowerShell.M...  ...
Restart-Computer                   Cmdlet     Microsoft.PowerShell.M...  ...
Restore-Computer                   Cmdlet     Microsoft.PowerShell.M...  ...
Stop-Computer                      Cmdlet     Microsoft.PowerShell.M...  ...
Test-ComputerSecureChannel         Cmdlet     Microsoft.PowerShell.M...  ...
Get-MpComputerStatus               Function   Defender                   ...
Get-SilComputer                    Function   SoftwareInventoryLogging   ...
Get-SilComputerIdentity            Function   SoftwareInventoryLogging   ...


PS C:\> _
```

Cool! That searched the available cmdlets and presented us with a list of the ones that contain the word Computer. Nice.

4. Now, what if we wanted to find out some more particular information about one of these cmdlets? Maybe about `Restart-Computer`; that sounds like something we might use often. Use the following command:

```
Get-Help Restart-Computer
```

```
Administrator: Windows PowerShell                                    —    □    ✕
PS C:\> Get-Help Restart-Computer

NAME
    Restart-Computer

SYNTAX
    Restart-Computer [[-ComputerName] <string[]>] [[-Credential]
    <pscredential>] [-DcomAuthentication {Default | None | Connect | Call |
    Packet | PacketIntegrity | PacketPrivacy | Unchanged}] [-Impersonation
    {Default | Anonymous | Identify | Impersonate | Delegate}]
    [-WsmanAuthentication {Default | Basic | Negotiate | CredSSP | Digest |
    Kerberos}] [-Protocol {DCOM | WSMan}] [-Force] [-Wait] [-Timeout <int>]
    [-For {Wmi | WinRM | PowerShell}] [-Delay <int16>] [-WhatIf] [-Confirm]
    [<CommonParameters>]

    Restart-Computer [[-ComputerName] <string[]>] [[-Credential]
    <pscredential>] [-AsJob] [-DcomAuthentication {Default | None | Connect |
    Call | Packet | PacketIntegrity | PacketPrivacy | Unchanged}]
    Delegate}] [-Force] [-ThrottleLimit <int>] [-WhatIf] [-Confirm]
    [<CommonParameters>]
```

Now we're really cooking! This is wonderful information. Basically, this is exactly what you would find if you were looking for information about the `Restart-Computer` cmdlet and went searching on TechNet for it.

How it works...

The `Get-Help` cmdlet in PowerShell can be used with virtually any command in order to find out more information about that particular function. I often use it when the specific name of a cmdlet that I want to use escapes my memory. By using `Get-Help` as a search function, it will present a list of available cmdlets that include the keyword you specified. This is a brilliant addition to PowerShell, and makes it so much more powerful than Command Prompt.

Also included with the `Get-Help` files are all of the special syntax and parameter options for each cmdlet that you might be working with. This saves you having to go to the Web in order to search for these functions, and it is just way more fun doing it at the command line than in a web browser.

2
Core Infrastructure Tasks

Windows Server 2016 has many roles and features that can be used to accomplish all sorts of different tasks in your network. This chapter reflects on the most common infrastructure tasks needed to create a successful Windows Active Directory environment by using Server 2016. In this chapter, we will cover the following recipes:

- Configuring a combination Domain Controller, DNS server, and DHCP server
- Adding a second Domain Controller
- Organizing your computers with Organizational Units
- Creating an A or AAAA record in DNS
- Creating and using a CNAME record in DNS
- Creating a DHCP scope to assign addresses to computers
- Creating a DHCP reservation for a specific server or resource
- Pre-staging a computer account in Active Directory
- Using PowerShell to create a new Active Directory user
- Using PowerShell to view system uptime

Introduction

There are a number of technologies in Windows Server 2016 that you *need to know* if you plan to ever work in a Windows environment. These are technologies such as **Active Directory Domain Services (AD DS)**, **Domain Name System (DNS)**, and **Dynamic Host Configuration Protocol (DHCP)**. If you haven't noticed already, everything in the Windows world has an acronym. In fact, you may only recognize these items by their acronyms, and that's okay.

Nobody calls DHCP the Dynamic Host Configuration Protocol anyway. But do you know how to build these services and bring a Windows Server infrastructure online from scratch, with only a piece of hardware and a Windows Server 2016 installation disk to guide your way? This is why we are here today. I would like to instruct you on taking your first server and turning it into everything that you need to run a Microsoft network.

Every company and network is different and has different requirements. Some will get by with a single server to host a myriad of roles, while others have thousands of servers at their disposal and will have every role split up into clusters of servers, each of which has a single purpose in life. Whatever your situation, this will get us back to the basics on setting up the core infrastructure technologies that are needed in any Microsoft-centric network.

Configuring a combination Domain Controller, DNS server, and DHCP server

The directory structure that Microsoft networks use to house their users and computer accounts is called **Active Directory** (**AD**), and the directory information is controlled and managed by **Domain Controller** (**DC**) servers. Two other server roles that almost always go hand-in-hand with Active Directory are DNS and DHCP, and in many networks these three roles are combined on each server where they reside. A lot of small businesses have always made do with a single server containing all three of these roles, but in recent years, virtualization has become so easy that almost everyone runs at least two DCs, for redundancy purposes. And if you are going to have two DCs, you may as well put the DNS and DHCP roles on them both to make those services redundant as well. But I'm getting ahead of myself. For this recipe, let's get started building these services by installing the roles and configuring them for the first time: the first DC/DNS/DHCP server in our network.

Getting ready

The only prerequisite here is an online Windows Server 2016 that we can use. We want it to be plugged into a network and have a static IP address assigned so that as you add new computers to this network, they have a way of communicating with the domain we are about to create. Also, make sure to set the hostname of the server now. Once you create a domain on this controller, you will not be able to change the name at a later date.

How to do it...

Let's configure our first DC/DNS/DHCP server by performing the following set of instructions:

1. Add the roles all at once. To do this, open up **Server Manager** and click on your link to add some new roles to this server. Now check all three: **Active Directory Domain Services**, **DHCP Server**, and **DNS Server:**

Roles

- ☐ Active Directory Certificate Services
- ☑ Active Directory Domain Services
- ☐ Active Directory Federation Services
- ☐ Active Directory Lightweight Directory Services
- ☐ Active Directory Rights Management Services
- ☐ Device Health Attestation
- ☑ DHCP Server
- ☑ DNS Server
- ☐ Fax Server

2. When you click on **Active Directory Domain Services**, you will be prompted whether you want to install some supporting items. Go ahead and click on the **Add Features** button to allow this:

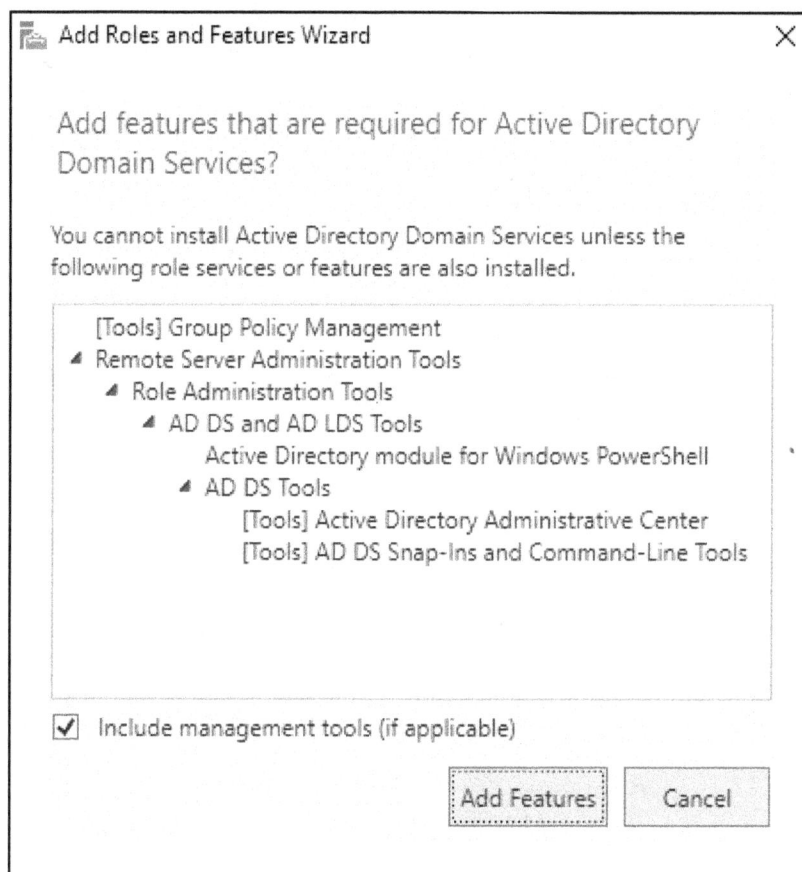

Add Roles and Features Wizard ✕

Add features that are required for Active Directory Domain Services?

You cannot install Active Directory Domain Services unless the following role services or features are also installed.

```
    [Tools] Group Policy Management
  ◢ Remote Server Administration Tools
     ◢ Role Administration Tools
        ◢ AD DS and AD LDS Tools
              Active Directory module for Windows PowerShell
           ◢ AD DS Tools
                 [Tools] Active Directory Administrative Center
                 [Tools] AD DS Snap-Ins and Command-Line Tools
```

☑ Include management tools (if applicable)

[Add Features]   [Cancel]

3. You are going to click **Next** through the following few screens. We don't have to add any additional features, so you can read and click through the informational screens that tell you about these new roles.
4. Once satisfied with the installation summary, press the **Install** button on the last page of the wizard.

5. Following installation, your progress summary screen shows a window with a
   couple of links on it. They are **Promote this server to a domain controller** and
   Complete DHCP configuration. We are going to click on the first link to promote
   this machine to be a DC.

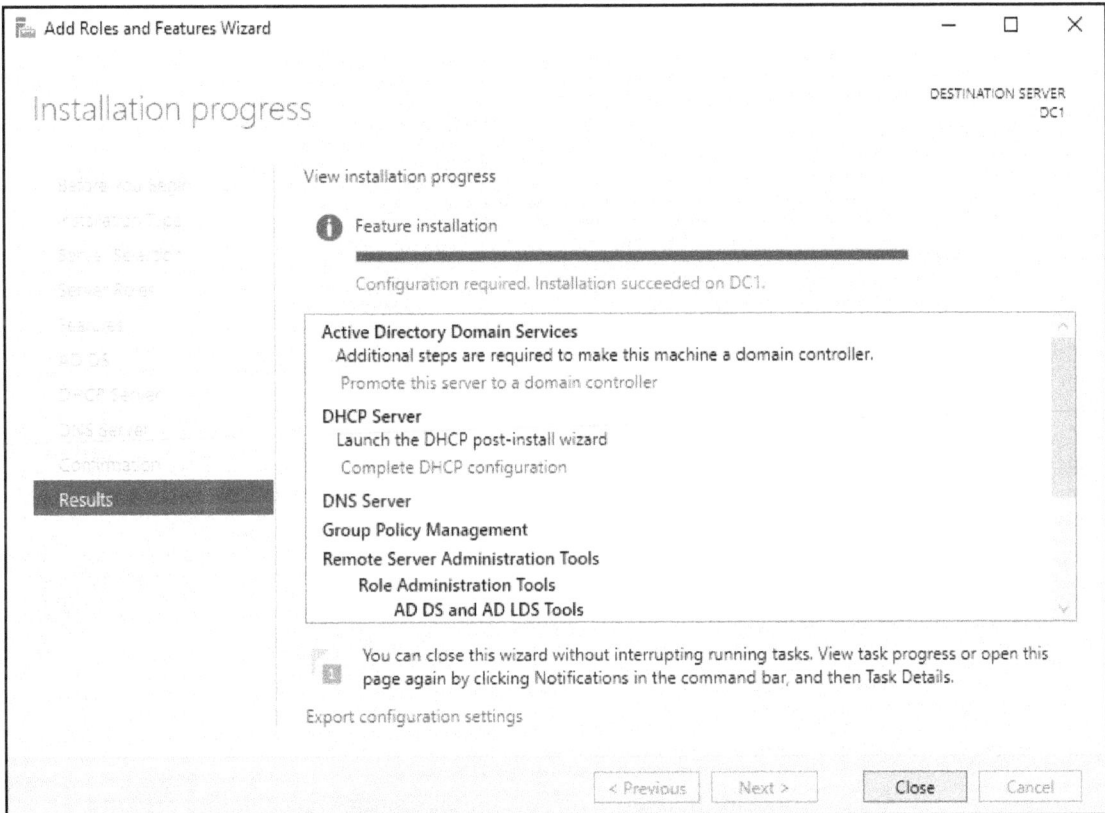

6. Now we are taken into the configuration of our DC. Since this is the very first DC in our entire network, we choose the option **Add a new forest**. At this point, we also have to specify a name for our root domain.

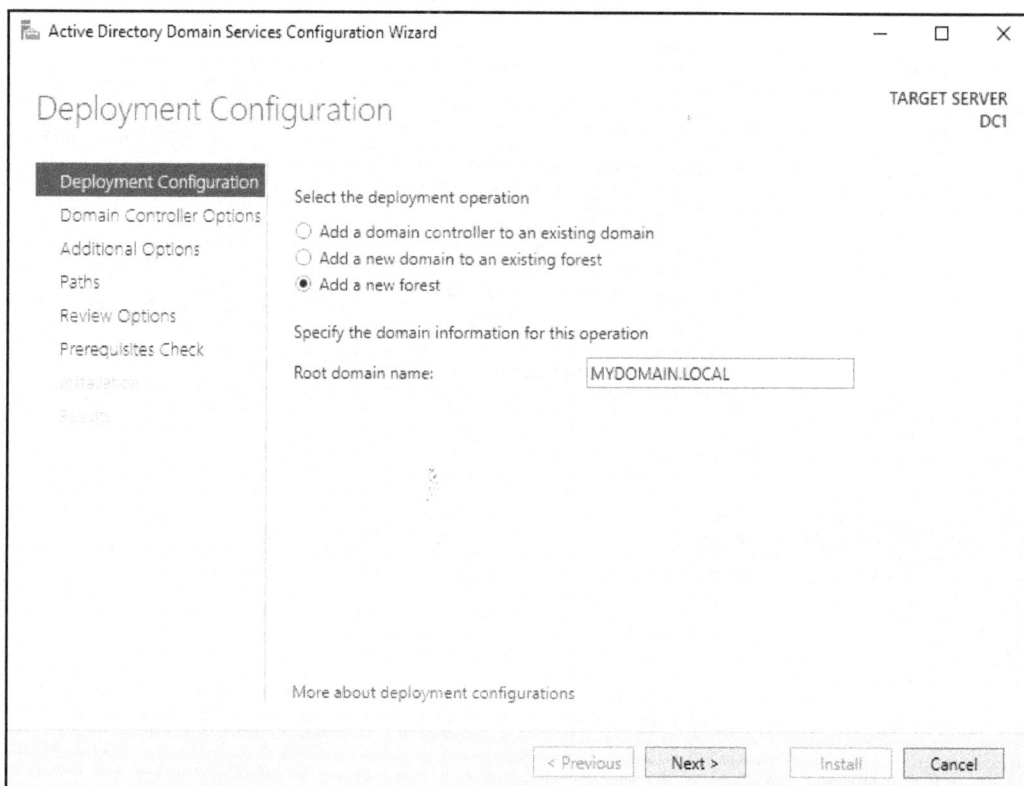

```
┌─────────────────────────────────────────────────────────────────────────────┐
│ ▣ Active Directory Domain Services Configuration Wizard        ─   □    ✕      │
├─────────────────────────────────────────────────────────────────────────────┤
│                                                              TARGET SERVER     │
│  Deployment Configuration                                         DC1          │
│                                                                               │
│  ┌─────────────────────────┐                                                  │
│  │ Deployment Configuration│   Select the deployment operation                │
│  │ Domain Controller Options│    ○ Add a domain controller to an existing domain│
│  │ Additional Options      │    ○ Add a new domain to an existing forest      │
│  │ Paths                   │    ● Add a new forest                            │
│  │ Review Options          │   Specify the domain information for this operation│
│  │ Prerequisites Check     │                                                  │
│  │ Installation            │   Root domain name:        MYDOMAIN.LOCAL         │
│  │ Results                 │                                                  │
│  └─────────────────────────┘                                                  │
│                                                                               │
│                              More about deployment configurations             │
│                                                                               │
│             < Previous │  Next >  │    Install    │   Cancel                   │
└─────────────────────────────────────────────────────────────────────────────┘
```

> **TIP**
>
> It is very important to choose a root domain name that you like and that makes sense for your installation. Whatever you enter here will more than likely be your domain name forever and always!!

7. This might be a good opportunity for a little side-bar of definitions and explanations. You can think of a *forest* as the top level of your Active Directory structure. Within that forest, you are setting up a *domain*, which is the container within your forest that contains your user, computer, and other accounts that will be joined to the domain. You can contain multiple domains within a forest, and multiple forests can share information and talk to each other by using something called a trust.

8. You can see that I have named my domain MYDOMAIN.LOCAL. The .local is important to discuss for a minute. It is really just a common specification that many companies use to clarify that this domain is an internal network, not a public one. However, I could have just as easily named it CONTOSO.COM, or JORDAN.PRIV, or many different things.

9. Another practice that I see often is for companies to use the same domain name inside their network as they do publicly. So basically, whatever their website ends in, that is their public domain name. You could certainly set up the internal domain name to be the same. This practice is commonly referred to as *split-brain DNS*. It used to be something that Microsoft warned against doing, but many companies do it this way, and all of the technology has evolved around this so that the Microsoft networking parts and pieces will all work just fine with split-brain DNS these days, though it does usually take additional consideration when setting up any new piece of technology.

> Once last important note: it is **not** recommended to set up your domain as a single label name, for example, if I had called it just MYDOMAIN. While this is technically possible, it presents many problems down the road and is not recommended by Microsoft.

10. On the **Domain Controller Options** screen, you can choose to lower the functional level of your forest or domain, but this is not recommended unless you have a specific reason to do so. You must also specify a DSRM password on this screen in case it is ever needed for recovery. You will receive a **DNS Options** warning message on the next page. This is normal, because we are turning on the first DC and DNS server in our environment.

11. The following two screens for **NetBIOS** and **Paths** can be left as the default unless you have a reason to change their settings.

12. Once you have reviewed the installation plan, go for it! There may be some informational and warning messages that show themselves, but you should see a green check mark telling you **All prerequisite checks passed successfully**, which means you are ready to proceed. When the server is finished being promoted to a DC, it will have to restart.

13. Following the restart, you will have noticed that you are now forced to log in to the server as a domain account. Once a server has been promoted to a DC, it no longer contains local user accounts on the system. All logins to the server from this point forward will have to be user accounts within the domain. Go ahead and log in as such.

14. Inside Server Manager you will have a notification up top to **Complete DHCP configuration**. Go ahead and click on that.

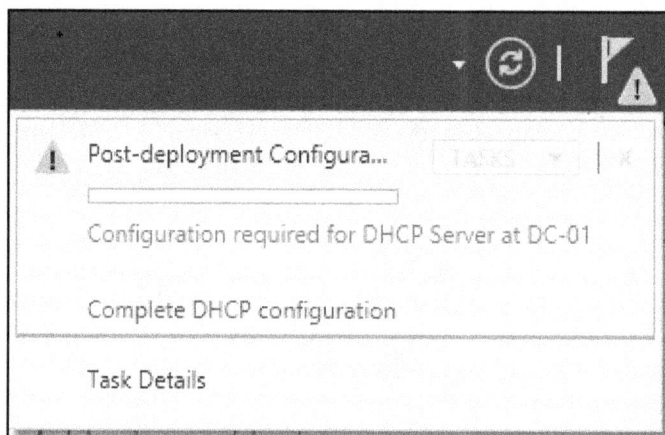

15. You don't have to specify anything in this wizard. Simply click through the steps.

How it works...

Configuring your first DC is essential to having a successful Microsoft Windows network. Now that the roles are installed for AD, DNS, and DHCP, we have the core infrastructure in place to start joining computers to the domain, adding users to the network, and shuttling around some network traffic! Each of these technologies has enough depth to warrant their own book, so there is no way that we can cover everything here. I hope that this tutorial will get you comfortable with enabling these system-critical functions in your own network. Having the ability to create a network from scratch is priceless ammunition to a server administrator.

See also

It is also possible to install Active Directory on your DCs through the use of PowerShell. Since we are discussing the use of PowerShell throughout this book to start utilizing it for some day-to-day tasks, make sure to check out the following links and try doing it this way on the next DC that you want to create:

- http://technet.microsoft.com/en-us/library/hh974719.aspx
- http://technet.microsoft.com/en-us/library/hh472162.aspx#BKMK_PS

Adding a second Domain Controller

AD is the core of your network. It has ties to everything! As such, it makes sense that you would want this to be as redundant as possible. In Windows Server 2016, creating a secondary DC is so easy that you really have no reason not to do it. Can you imagine rebuilding your directory following a single server hardware failure where you have 100 user accounts and computers that are all part of the domain that just failed? How about with 1,000 or even 10,000 users? That could take weeks to clean up, and you'll probably never get it back exactly the way it was before. Additionally, while you are stuck in the middle of this downtime, you will have all kinds of trouble inside your network since your user and computer accounts are relying on AD, which would then be offline. Here are the steps to take a second server in your network and join it to the existing domain that is running on the primary DC to create our redundant, secondary DC. The larger your network gets, the more domain controller servers you are going to have.

Getting ready

Two Server 2016 machines are needed for this. The first we will assume is running Active Directory and DNS already, like the one we set up in our previous recipe. The second server is online, plugged into the same network, and has been named DC2.

How to do it...

To create a redundant secondary DC, perform the following steps:

1. Open **Server Manager** on DC-02 and click the link to **Add roles and features**.

2. Click **Next** a few times until you get to the screen where we are selecting the role that we want to install. Let's choose both **Active Directory Domain Services** and **DNS Server**. It is very common for each DC to also run DNS so that you have redundancy for both services. Both of these roles will prompt for additional features, so make sure you press the **Add Features** button when it prompts you to allow the installation of those extra components.

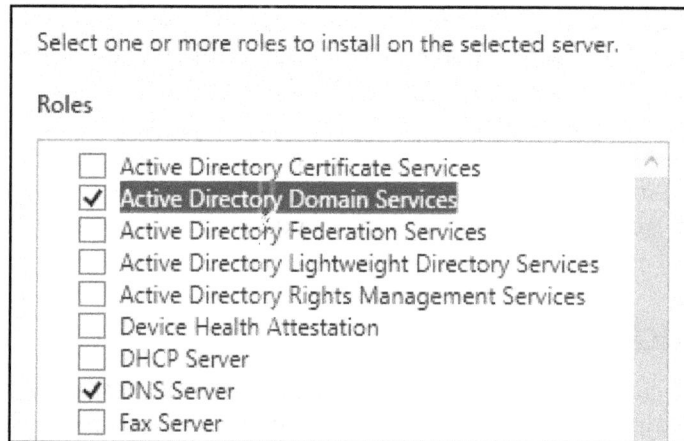

Select one or more roles to install on the selected server.

Roles

- [ ] Active Directory Certificate Services
- [x] Active Directory Domain Services
- [ ] Active Directory Federation Services
- [ ] Active Directory Lightweight Directory Services
- [ ] Active Directory Rights Management Services
- [ ] Device Health Attestation
- [ ] DHCP Server
- [x] DNS Server
- [ ] Fax Server

3. We do not require any other features, so click **Next** through the remaining screens and then click on **Install** on the last page.

4. Once the installation is finished, you have a link to click on that says **Promote this server to a domain controller**. Go ahead and click on that link.

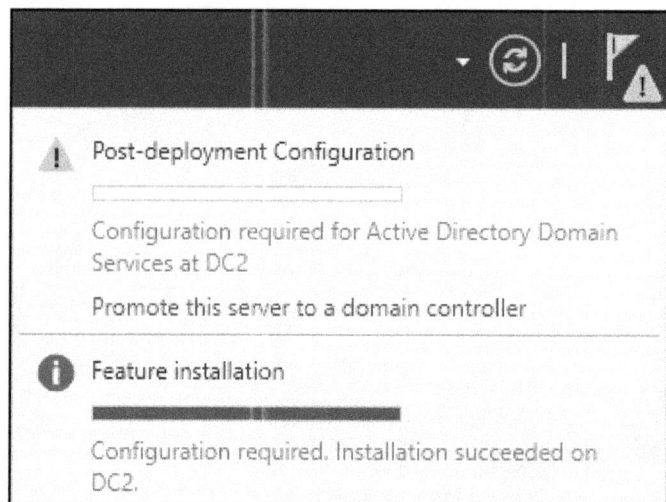

! Post-deployment Configuration

Configuration required for Active Directory Domain Services at DC2

Promote this server to a domain controller

ⓘ Feature installation

Configuration required. Installation succeeded on DC2.

5. For this second DC, we are going to choose the **Add a domain controller to an existing domain** option. Then in the **Domain** field, specify the name of the domain that is running on your primary DC. You must also specify a domain user account in the credentials field to validate against the domain.

Select the deployment operation

◉ Add a domain controller to an existing domain
◯ Add a new domain to an existing forest
◯ Add a new forest

Specify the domain information for this operation

Domain: MYDOMAIN.LOCAL| | Select... |

> **TIP**
>
> If you receive an error message that a DC for the domain could not be contacted, you probably haven't specified a DNS address in your TCP/IP settings. Add your primary DC's IP address in as your primary DNS server and it should work.

6. The rest of the steps reflect the same options we chose when creating our first DC in the previous recipe. Once you are finished stepping through the wizard, you will have a secondary DC and DNS server online and running.

How it works...

Creating redundancy for Active Directory is critical to the success of your network. Hardware fails, we all know it. A good practice for any company is to run two DCs so that everyone continues to work in the event of a server failure. An even better practice is to take this a step further and create more DCs, some of them in different sites perhaps, and maybe even make use of some **Read-Only Domain Controllers** (**RODC**) in your smaller, less secure sites. See the following link for some additional information on using an RODC in your environment: http://technet.microsoft.com/en-us/library/cc754719(v=ws.10).aspx.

Organizing your computers with Organizational Units

AD is the structure in which all of your user, computer, and server accounts reside. As you add new users and computers into your domain, they will be automatically placed into generic storage containers. You could get away with leaving all of your objects in their default locations, but there are a lot of advantages to putting a little time and effort into creating an organizational structure.

In this recipe, we will create some **Organizational Units** (**OUs**) inside Active Directory and move our existing objects into these OUs so that we can create some structure.

Getting ready

We will need a DC online for this recipe, which is a Server 2016 machine with the Active Directory Domain Services role installed. Specifically, I will be using the DC1 server that we prepped in the earlier *Configuring a combination Domain Controller, DNS server, and DHCP server* recipe.

How to do it...

Let's get comfortable working with OUs by creating some of our own, as follows:

1. Open **Active Directory Users and Computers**. This can be launched from the **Tools** menu inside Server Manager. As you can see, there are some pre-defined containers and OUs in here:

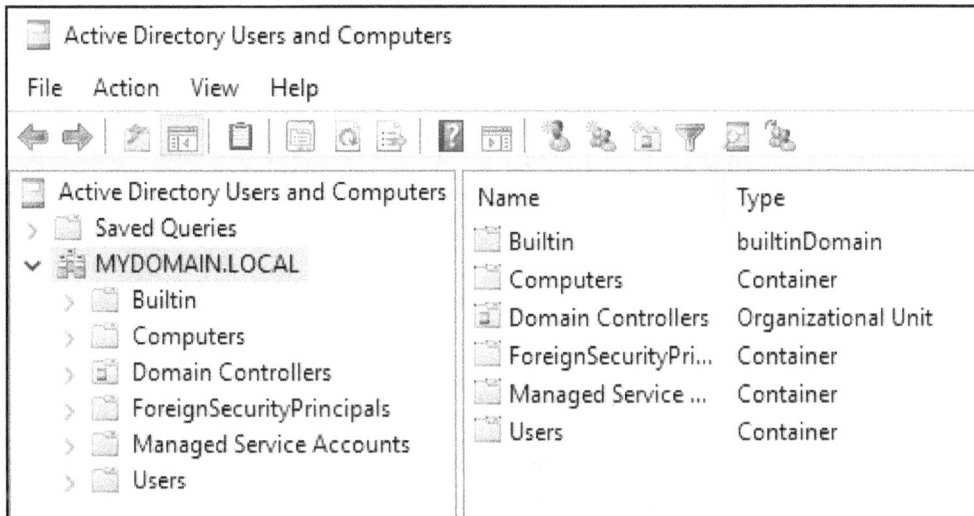

TIP

Alternatively, you can also open **Active Directory Users and Computers** by running `dsa.msc` from a command prompt or the Start screen.

2. We can already see that the DC servers have been segmented off into their own OU. If we look in our `Computers` folder, however, we can see that currently, all of the other systems we have joined to the domain have been lumped together:

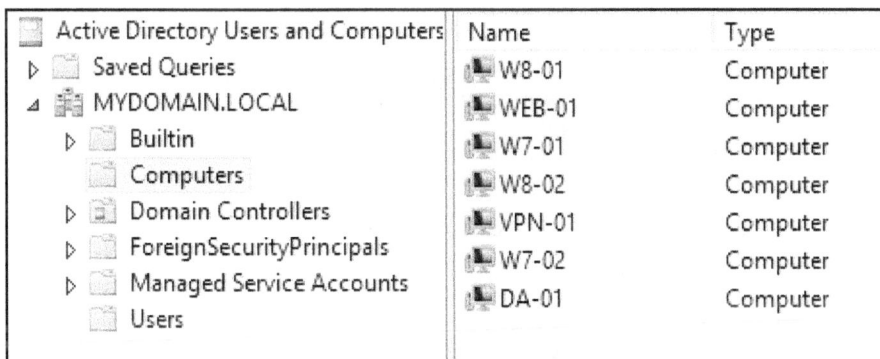

3. Currently, it's hard to tell which machine accomplishes what purpose. A better naming scheme might help, but what if you are working in an environment where there are hundreds of objects already? We want to break these machines up into appropriate groups so that we have better management over them in the future. Right-click on the name of your domain in the left-hand window pane, then navigate to **New | Organizational Unit**.

4. Input a name for your new OU and click **OK**. I am going to create a few new OUs called `Windows 7 Desktops`, `Windows 7 Laptops`, `Windows 8 Desktops`, `Windows 8 Laptops`, `Windows 10 Desktops`, `Windows 10 Laptops`, `Web Servers`, and `Remote Access Servers`.

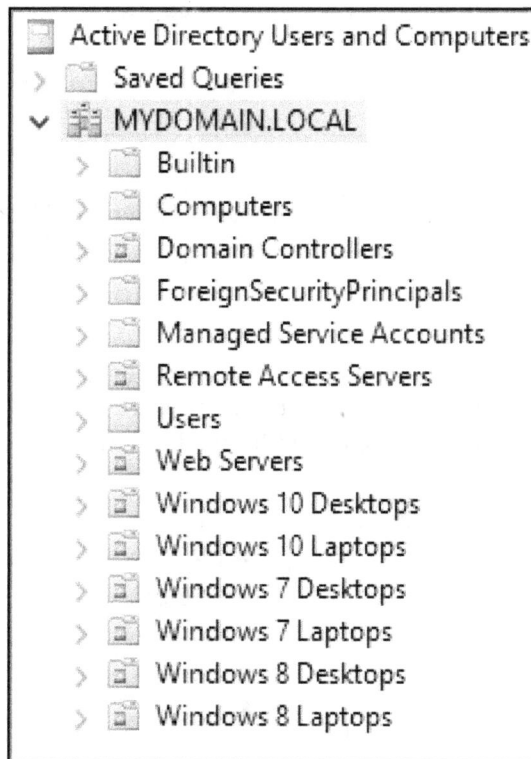

> - Active Directory Users and Computers
>   - > Saved Queries
>   - ∨ MYDOMAIN.LOCAL
>   - > Builtin
>   - > Computers
>   - > Domain Controllers
>   - > ForeignSecurityPrincipals
>   - > Managed Service Accounts
>   - > Remote Access Servers
>   - > Users
>   - > Web Servers
>   - > Windows 10 Desktops
>   - > Windows 10 Laptops
>   - > Windows 7 Desktops
>   - > Windows 7 Laptops
>   - > Windows 8 Desktops
>   - > Windows 8 Laptops

5. Now for each object that you want to move, simply find it, right-click on it, and then click on **Move…**.

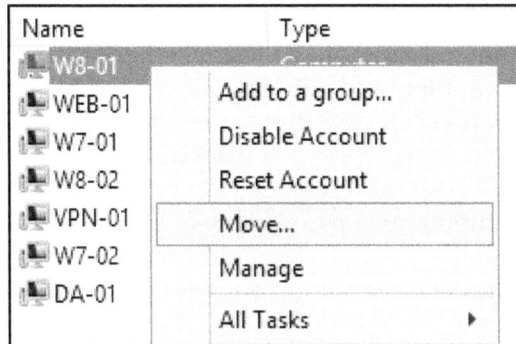

Name	Type
W8-01	
WEB-01	Add to a group…
W7-01	Disable Account
W8-02	Reset Account
VPN-01	Move…
W7-02	Manage
DA-01	All Tasks ▶

6. Choose which OU you would like this object to move into and click **OK**.

How it works…

The actual work involved with creating OUs and moving objects around between them isn't complicated at all. What is much more important about this recipe is prompting you to think about which way works best for you to set up these OUs to make the best organizational sense for your environment. By breaking our computer accounts out into pinpointed groups, we are able, in the future, to easily do things such as discover how many web servers we have running, or do some quick reporting on how many user accounts we have in the sales group. We could even apply different Group Policy settings to different computer sets based on what OU they are contained within. Both reporting and applying settings can be greatly improved upon by making good use of Organizational Units inside AD.

Creating an A or AAAA record in DNS

Most folks working in IT are familiar with using the `ping` command to test network connectivity. If you are trying to test the connection between your computer and another, you can ping it from a Command Prompt and test whether or not it replies. This assumes that the firewalls in your computers and network allow the ping to respond correctly, which generally is true. If you are inside a domain network and ping a device by its name, that name resolves to an IP address, which is the device's address on the network. But what tells your computer which IP address corresponds to which name? This is where DNS comes in. Any time your computer makes a request for a name, whether it is you pinging another computer or your Outlook e-mail client requesting the name of your Exchange Server, your computer always reaches out to your network's DNS servers and asks, "How do I get to this name?".

DNS contains a list of records that tell the computers in your network what IP addresses correspond to what names. By far the most common type of DNS record is called a **Host** record. When the Host record resolves to an IPv4 address, such as `192.168.0.1`, it is called an **A record**. When the Host record resolves to an IPv6 address, such as `2003:836b:2:8100::2`, it is called an **AAAA record**. This is usually pronounced *quad A*.

Understanding how to create and troubleshoot Host records in DNS is something that every Windows server administrator needs to know. Let's take a minute to create and test one of these DNS records so that we can experience firsthand how this all works together.

Getting ready

We have a DC online, which also has the DNS role installed. This is all we need to create the DNS record, but we will also make use of a Windows 10 client computer and a web server to do the name resolution testing.

How to do it...

To create and test a DNS record, perform these steps:

1. There is a new web server plugged into the network, but it is not yet joined to the domain and so it has not been registered to DNS. The name of this web server is `Web1`. Open up Command Prompt and type `ping web1`. As expected, because there is no Host record in DNS for this server yet, our ping request does not resolve to anything.

```
▣ Windows Command Processor                    —    □    ✕

C:\>ping web1
Ping request could not find host web1. Please check the name and try again.

C:\>
```

2. Now head into the DNS server and open up the **DNS** console from the **Tools** menu.

3. Inside **Forward Lookup Zones**, you should see your domain listed. Double-click on the name of your domain to see your existing DNS records.

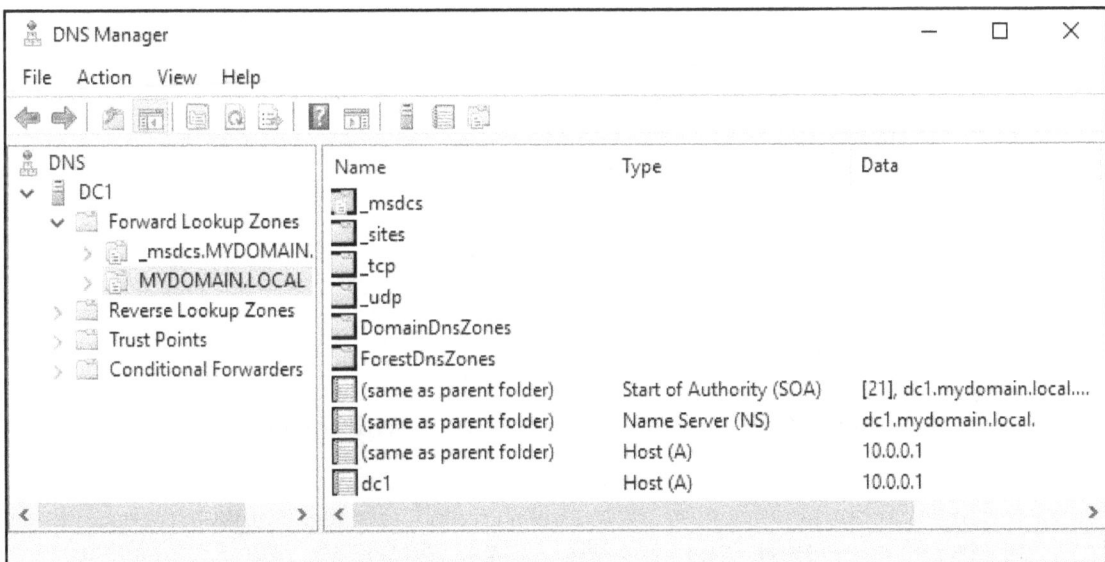

```
🖳 DNS Manager                                  —    □    ✕

File   Action   View   Help

🖳 DNS                    Name                Type                    Data
  DC1                   _msdcs
    Forward Lookup Zones  _sites
      _msdcs.MYDOMAIN.    _tcp
      MYDOMAIN.LOCAL      _udp
    Reverse Lookup Zones  DomainDnsZones
    Trust Points          ForestDnsZones
    Conditional Forwarders (same as parent folder)  Start of Authority (SOA)  [21], dc1.mydomain.local....
                          (same as parent folder)  Name Server (NS)          dc1.mydomain.local.
                          (same as parent folder)  Host (A)                  10.0.0.1
                          dc1                      Host (A)                  10.0.0.1
```

4. Right-click on your domain, then click on **New Host (A or AAAA)....**

5. Input the server name into the top field and the IP address where it is running into the bottom field. Then click **Add Host**.

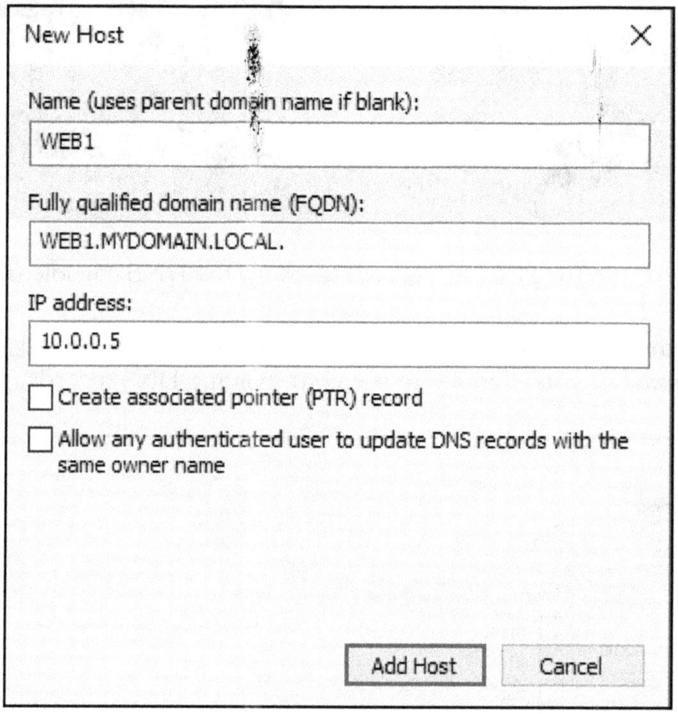

```
New Host                                              ×

Name (uses parent domain name if blank):

WEB1

Fully qualified domain name (FQDN):

WEB1.MYDOMAIN.LOCAL.

IP address:

10.0.0.5

☐ Create associated pointer (PTR) record
☐ Allow any authenticated user to update DNS records with the
   same owner name


                              Add Host        Cancel
```

If you are running IPv6 on your network and want to create a AAAA record instead, you use this exact same process. Simply enter the IPv6 address into the IP address field, instead of the IPv4 address.

6. Now that our new Host record has been created, let's test it out! Going back to our client computer, type `ping web1` again. You will see your output as shown in the following screenshot:

```
C:\>ping web1

Pinging web1.MYDOMAIN.LOCAL [10.0.0.5] with 32 bytes of data:
Reply from 10.0.0.5: bytes=32 time<1ms TTL=128
Reply from 10.0.0.5: bytes=32 time<1ms TTL=128
Reply from 10.0.0.5: bytes=32 time<1ms TTL=128
Reply from 10.0.0.5: bytes=32 time<1ms TTL=128

Ping statistics for 10.0.0.5:
    Packets: Sent = 4, Received = 4, Lost = 0 (0% loss),
Approximate round trip times in milli-seconds:
    Minimum = 0ms, Maximum = 0ms, Average = 0ms

C:\>_
```

How it works...

Any time a computer in a domain network requests to communicate with a hostname, DNS is the party responsible for pointing it in the right direction. If you or your applications are having trouble contacting the servers they need, this is one of the first places you will want to look into. Understanding DNS Host records is something that will be necessary when working with any networking technology. If you are working within an Active Directory integrated DNZ zone, which most of you will be, then any time you add a computer or server to the domain, their name will be automatically plugged into DNS for you. In these cases, you will not have to manually create them, but it is still important to understand how that works, in case you need to troubleshoot them later.

In this recipe, we have only talked about the most common form of DNS record, but there are others you may want to learn and test as well. In fact, take a look at our next recipe for information on another useful type of DNS record, the CNAME.

There are a couple of other name resolution functions in the Windows operating system that may cause resolution to happen before a hostname request gets to the DNS server. For example, if someone has created a static name and IP record inside a client computer's host file, it will resolve to the specified IP address, no matter what is in the DNS server. This is because the host file has priority over DNS. Also, there is a special table called the **Name Resolution Policy Table** (**NRPT**) that is used by DirectAccess client computers, and it works in a similar way. Name resolution requests pass through the host file and through the NRPT before making their way to DNS. If one of the former tables has an entry for the name that is being requested, they will resolve it before the computer sends the request to the DNS server for resolution. So if you are troubleshooting a name that doesn't resolve properly, keep those additional items in mind when looking for the answer to your problem.

See also

- The *Creating and using a CNAME record in DNS* recipe

Creating and using a CNAME record in DNS

Now that we are familiar with moving around a little bit inside the DNS management tool, we are going to create and test another type of record. This one is called a **CNAME**, and it is easiest to think of this one as an alias record. Rather than taking a DNS name and pointing it at an IP address, as we do with a host record, with a CNAME, we are going to take a DNS name and point it at another DNS name! Why would this be necessary? If you are hosting multiple services on a single server but want those services to be contacted by using different names, CNAME records can be your best friend.

Getting ready

We are going to make use of the same environment that we used to create our *A* records in the *Creating an A or AAAA record in DNS* recipe. There is a DC/DNS server online where we are going to create our records. Also running is WEB1, a server where we are hosting a website as well as some file shares. We will also use a Windows 10 client to test out our CNAME records after they have been created.

How to do it...

To create and test a CNAME record, perform the following instructions:

1. WEB1 is hosting a website and a file share. Currently, the only DNS record that exists for WEB1 is the primary *A* record, so users have to type in the WEB1 name to access both the website and the file shares. Our goal is to create aliases for these services by using CNAME records in DNS. First, we log into the DNS server and launch **DNS Manager**.

2. Once inside **DNS Manager**, expand **Forward Lookup Zones** and then your domain name so that we can see the list of DNS records that exist already.

3. Now right-click on your domain and select **New Alias (CNAME)....**

4. We would like our users to be able to browse the website by typing in http://intranet. So in our CNAME record, we want the **Alias name** to be INTRANET and the **FQDN for target host** to be WEB1.MYDOMAIN.LOCAL, which is the server where the website is being hosted.

```
Alias (CNAME)

Alias name (uses parent domain if left blank):
INTRANET

Fully qualified domain name (FQDN):
INTRANET.MYDOMAIN.LOCAL.

Fully qualified domain name (FQDN) for target host:
WEB1.MYDOMAIN.LOCAL                Browse...
```

5. We also want our file shares to be accessible by using \\FILESERVER\SHARE, so that the actual name of the server hosting this share is not visible to the users. Create another CNAME record with the **Alias name** field as FILESERVER, and the **FQDN for target host** field as WEB1.MYDOMAIN.LOCAL.

6. Log into the test client machine and give it a try. Users are now able to open up Internet Explorer and successfully browse to http://intranet. They are also able to open File Explorer and access \\fileserver\share.

How it works...

We have a server in our environment called **WEB1**. There is a website running on this server. It is also hosting a file share called **SHARE**. By creating a couple of quick CNAME records inside DNS, we are able to give users the ability to use some intuitive names to access these resources. By following the preceding instructions, we have masked the actual server name from the users, making knowledge of that name unnecessary. Masking internal hostnames of servers is also considered a security best practice in many organizations.

See also

- The *Creating an A or AAAA record in DNS* recipe

Creating a DHCP scope to assign addresses to computers

In the *Configuring a combination Domain Controller, DNS server, and DHCP server* recipes, we installed the DHCP role onto a server called DC1. Without some configuration, however, that role isn't doing anything. In most companies that I work with, all of the servers have statically assigned IP addresses, which are IPs entered by hand into the NIC properties. This way, those servers always retain the same IP address. But what about client machines that might move around, or even move in and out of the network? DHCP is a mechanism that the clients can reach out to in order to obtain IP addressing information for the network that they are currently plugged into.

This way, users or admins don't have to worry about configuring IP settings on the client machine, as they are configured automatically by the DHCP server. In order for our DHCP server to hand out IP addresses, we need to configure a scope.

Getting ready

We have a Server 2016 machine online with the DHCP role installed. We will also be testing using a Windows 10 client machine to ensure that it is able to acquire IP address information properly from the server.

How to do it...

Perform the following steps to create and configure a DHCP scope to assign addresses to client computers:

1. Drop down the **Tools** menu inside Server Manager, then click on **DHCP**. This opens the DHCP management console.

2. Expand the left-hand pane, where the name of your DHCP server is listed. You will see sections for **IPv4** and **IPv6**. For our network, we are sticking with IPv4, so we right-click on that and choose the option for **New Scope...**.

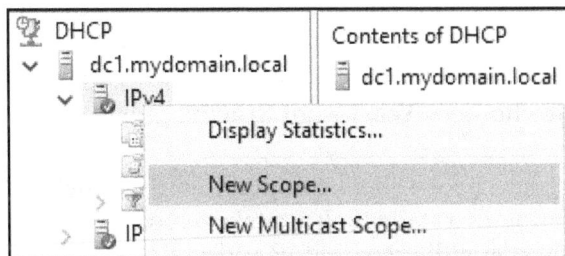

DHCP	Contents of DHCP
dc1.mydomain.local	dc1.mydomain.local
IPv4	
Display Statistics...	
New Scope...	
IP New Multicast Scope...	

3. Start the **New Scope Wizard** screen by creating a name for your scope. This can be anything you like.

4. Enter a range of IP addresses that you would like the DHCP server to hand out to computers. The **Subnet mask** field will likely populate automatically; just double-check to make sure it is accurate.

Configuration settings for DHCP Server

Enter the range of addresses that the scope distributes.

Start IP address:	10 . 0 . 0 . 50
End IP address:	10 . 0 . 0 . 99

Configuration settings that propagate to DHCP Client

Length:	24
Subnet mask:	255 . 255 . 255 . 0

5. On the **Add Exclusions and Delay** screen, if there are any IP addresses within the scope you just defined that you do not want handed out, specify them here. For example, if you are going to use .50 through .99, but you already have a print server running on .75, you could exclude .75 on this screen so that DHCP doesn't try to hand out the .75 address to a client computer.

6. Now set a time in your **Lease Duration** field. This is the amount of time in between DHCP *refreshes* for a client computer. If a particular computer leaves the network and comes back within its lease duration, it will be given the same IP address that it had last time. If you're not sure about this one, leave it set at the default and you can adjust it later.

7. Next, we will populate the rest of the IP information that the client computers need to receive on our network. Fill out fields for **Router (Default Gateway)**, **Domain Name and DNS Servers**, and **WINS Servers**, if necessary.

8. The last item to choose is **Yes, I want to activate this scope now**. We're in business!

9. As a quick test, let's boot a client computer onto this network whose NIC has not been configured with a static IP. If we take a look at its IP configuration, we can see that it has successfully received IP addressing information from our DHCP server automatically.

```
Ethernet adapter Ethernet:

   Connection-specific DNS Suffix  . : MYDOMAIN.LOCAL
   Link-local IPv6 Address . . . . . : fe80::5465:727f:ba9:a073%4
   IPv4 Address. . . . . . . . . . . : 10.0.0.50
   Subnet Mask . . . . . . . . . . . : 255.255.255.0
   Default Gateway . . . . . . . . . : 10.0.0.254
```

How it works...

DHCP is one of the core infrastructure roles that almost everyone uses inside their networks. While we have only scratched the surface here of what DHCP is capable of, the ability to automatically hand out IP addresses to connecting client computers is DHCP's core functionality. Installing the role and creating a scope are our primary steps to make use of DHCP. Take a look at our next recipe for one of the advanced functions that can be accomplished within your scope.

Creating a DHCP reservation for a specific server or resource

In a simple DHCP scope, any device that connects and asks for an IP address is handed whatever IP is next available within the scope. If you have a device for which you always want to keep the same IP address, you could manually configure the NIC properties with a static IP address. Otherwise, a more centralized way to assign a particular IP to the same device on a long-term basis is to use a **DHCP reservation**. Using a reservation in DHCP to assign an IP to a device makes a lot of sense, because you can see that reservation right in the DHCP console and you don't have to worry about keeping track of the static IP addresses that you have configured out in the field. Let's walk through configuring a quick reservation so that you are familiar with this process.

Getting ready

We will be using a Windows Server 2016 machine as our DHCP server where we will create the DHCP reservation. Additionally, we will use our WEB1 server to be the recipient of this reservation by assigning WEB1 to IP address 10.0.0.85.

How to do it...

To create a DHCP reservation for a specific server or resource, perform these instructions:

1. Open the **DHCP** manager tool.
2. Expand the left-hand pane down into the DHCP scope that we created earlier. Under this scope, you will see a folder called Reservations. Right-click on Reservations and click on **New Reservation...**.

3. Populate the fields. Your **Reservation name** field can contain anything descriptive. Fill out the **IP address** field with the IP address you want to reserve for this purpose. The last important piece of information is the **MAC address** field. This must be the MAC address of the device for which you want to receive this particular IP address. Since WEB1 is a Windows Server 2016 machine, we can get our MAC address by doing `ipconfig /all` on WEB1.

```
Ethernet adapter Ethernet:

   Connection-specific DNS Suffix  . :
   Description . . . . . . . . . . . : Microsoft Hyper-V Network Adapter
   Physical Address. . . . . . . . . : 00-15-5D-AC-20-01
```

4. You can see **Physical Address.........: 00-15-5D-AC-20-01** in Command Prompt—this is our MAC address for WEB1. Use it to finish populating the DHCP reservation.

New Reservation

Provide information for a reserved client.

Reservation name: WEB1
IP address: 10 . 0 . 0 . 85
MAC address: 00-15-5D-AC-20-01
Description: WEB1 web server

Supported types
- Both
- DHCP
- BOOTP

Add   Close

5. Click on **Add** and you will see your new reservation listed in the **DHCP** management console.

6. Now make sure that the NIC on WEB1 is set to **Obtain an IP address automatically**. When WEB1 reaches out to DHCP to grab an IP address, it will now always receive 10.0.0.85 because of the reservation, rather than getting whatever IP address is next available within the DHCP scope.

How it works...

Typically, whenever a client computer is set to obtain an IP address automatically, it reaches out and looks for a DHCP server that hands to the client whatever IP address is free and next in the list. This causes DHCP clients to change their IP addresses on a regular basis. For desktop computers, this is usually fine. In many cases, however, it is beneficial to reserve particular IP addresses for specific devices, thereby ensuring they always receive the same IP address. Creating DHCP reservations is a good practice for servers, and also for many static devices on the network, such as print server boxes and telephony equipment.

Pre-staging a computer account in Active Directory

Joining computers to your domain is going to be a very normal task for any IT professional, enough that all of you are probably familiar with the process of doing so. What you may not realize, though, is that when you join computers or servers to your domain, they get lumped automatically into a generic Computers container inside AD. Sometimes this doesn't present any problem at all and all of your machines can reside inside this Computers container folder forever. Most of the time, however, organizations will set up policies that filter down into the Computers container automatically. When this is the case, these policies and settings will immediately apply to all computers that you join to your domain. For a desktop computer, this might be desired behavior. When configuring a new server, though, this can present big problems.

Let's say you are interested in turning on a new remote access server that is going to be running DirectAccess. You have a domain policy in place that disables the Windows Firewall on computers that get added to the `Computers` container. In this case, if you turned on your new remote access server and simply joined it to the domain, it would immediately apply the policy to disable Windows Firewall, because it is no different than a regular client computer in your network. DirectAccess requires Windows Firewall to be enabled, and so you have effectively broken your server before you even finish configuring it! You would eventually realize this mistake and move the server into a different OU that doesn't have the firewall squash policy; however, this doesn't necessarily mean that all the changes the policy put into place will be reversed. You may still have trouble with that server on an ongoing basis.

The preceding example is the reason why we are going to follow this recipe. If we pre-stage the computer account for our new remote access server, we can choose where it will reside inside Active Directory even before we join it to the domain. **Pre-staging** is a way of creating the computer's object inside Active Directory before you go to the actual server and click **Join**. When you do this, as soon as the request to join the domain comes in, Active Directory already knows exactly where to place that computer account. This way, you can make sure that the account resides inside an OU that is not going to apply the firewall policy and keep your new server running properly.

Getting ready

We will use a Server 2016 DC to pre-stage the computer account. Following the preceding example, we will use a second server that we are going to join to our domain, which we plan to turn into a remote access server in the future.

How to do it...

To pre-stage a computer account so that it resides inside AD, perform the following steps:

1. Open the **Active Directory Users and Computers** tool on a DC.
2. Choose a location in which you want to place this new server. I am going to use an OU that I created called **RemoteAccessServers**.
3. Right-click on your OU and navigate to **New | Computer**.

4. Enter the name of your new server. Make sure this matches the hostname you are going to assign as you build this new server, so that when it joins the domain, it matches up with this entry in AD. Take note on this screen that you also have the ability to determine which user or group has permission to join this new machine to the domain, if you want to set a restriction here.

```
New Object - Computer                                          X

       [icon]   Create in:    MYDOMAIN.LOCAL/Remote Access Servers


       Computer name:
       ┌──────────────────────────────────────────────────────┐
       │ RA1                                                    │
       └──────────────────────────────────────────────────────┘
       Computer name (pre-Windows 2000):
       ┌──────────────────────────────────┐
       │ RA1                              │
       └──────────────────────────────────┘
       The following user or group can join this computer to a domain.


       User or group:
       ┌──────────────────────────────────────────┐  ┌──────────────┐
       │ Default: Domain Admins                    │  │  Change...   │
       └──────────────────────────────────────────┘  └──────────────┘
       ☐ Assign this computer account as a pre-Windows 2000 computer



                        ┌──────────┐   ┌──────────┐   ┌──────────┐
                        │    OK    │   │  Cancel  │   │   Help   │
                        └──────────┘   └──────────┘   └──────────┘
```

5. Click **OK**, and that's it! Your object for this new server is entered into AD, waiting for a computer account to join the domain that matches the name.
6. The last step is building the RA1 server and joining it to the domain, just like you would with any computer or server. When you do so, it will utilize this pre-existing account in the **Remote Access Servers** OU, instead of placing a new entry into the generic Computers container.

How it works...

Pre-staging computer accounts in Active Directory is an important function when building new servers. It is sometimes critical to the long-term health of these servers for them to steer clear of the default domain policies and settings that you apply to your regular computer accounts. By taking a quick 30 seconds prior to joining a new server to the domain to pre-stage its account in AD, you ensure the correct placement of the system so that it fits your organizational structure. This will keep the system running properly as you continue to configure it for whatever job you are trying to accomplish.

Using PowerShell to create a new Active Directory user

Creating new user accounts in Active Directory is pretty standard stuff, but doing it the traditional way requires a lot of mouse clicks. Since we know that PowerShell can be used to accomplish anything within Windows Server 2016, but not many people actually employ it regularly, let's use this common task as a recipe to be accomplished with PowerShell rather than the GUI.

Getting ready

We will use PowerShell on our Windows Server 2016 DC in order to create this new user account.

How to do it...

Follow along to create a new user account in Active Directory by using the PowerShell command prompt:

1. Launch a PowerShell command prompt as an Administrator.
2. Enter the following command in order to create a new user account with very simple parameters:

```
New-ADUser -Name "John Smith" -UserPrincipalName
"jsmith@mydomain.local" -SamAccountName "jsmith"
```

```
Administrator: Windows PowerShell                                    _  □  X
PS C:\Users\Administrator> New-ADUser -Name "John Smith" -UserPrincipalName "jsmith@mydomain.local" -SamAccountName "jsm
ith"
PS C:\Users\Administrator>
```

3. If you open up the GUI for **Active Directory Users and Computers**, you will see that **John Smith** has now been created as a **User** account. There aren't many properties that exist within this account, as it is pretty simple, but it will work in order to get a new user up and running.

Group Policy Creat...	Security Group - Global	Members in this group c...
Guest	User	Built-in account for gue...
IPAMUG	Security Group - Univer...	
John Smith	User	
Jordan Krause	User	

4. Now let's create another new user, this time adding some additional parameters to our code in order to populate more of the typical user information. You may have also noticed that our new **John Smith** user account is currently disabled—this happens automatically when you create a new user account but do not populate a password. So, we will add in some more information, up to the first name and surname. We will also specify a couple of additional parameters in order to make sure the account is enabled and to require that the user changes their password during their initial login:

```
New-ADUser - Name "Jase Robertson" -UserPrincipalName
"jrobertson@mydomain.local" - SamAccountName "jrobertson"  -
GivenName "Jase" -Surname "Robertson" -DisplayName  "Jase
Robertson" -AccountPassword (Read-Host -AsSecureString
"AccountPassword") -ChangePasswordAtLogon $true -Enabled $true
```

```
Administrator: Windows PowerShell                                    _  □  X
PS C:\Users\Administrator> New-ADUser -Name "Jase Robertson" -UserPrincipalName "jrobertson@mydomain.local" -SamAccountN
ame "jrobertson" -GivenName "Jase" -Surname "Robertson" -DisplayName "Jase Robertson" -AccountPassword (Read-Host -AsSec
ureString "AccountPassword") -ChangePasswordAtLogon $true -Enabled $true
AccountPassword: ********
PS C:\Users\Administrator>
```

5. Open up **Active Directory Users and Computers** again and take a look at our new **Jase Robertson** user account. You can see that the account is enabled and ready for use, and it has much more information populated inside the account.

General	Address	Account	Profile	Telephones	Organization

Jase Robertson

First name: Jase   Initials: |

Last name: Robertson

Display name: Jase Robertson

6. Move over to the **Account** tab and you will also see the box is now checked for **User must change password at next logon**, just like we specified in our PowerShell command:

General	Address	Account	Profile	Telephones	Organization

User logon name:

robertson   @MYDOMAIN.LOCAL

User logon name (pre-Windows 2000):

MYDOMAIN\   jrobertson

[Logon Hours...]   [Log On To...]

☐ Unlock account

Account options:

☑ User must change password at next logon

How it works...

By using PowerShell, we are able to create new Active Directory user accounts right from a command interface, rather than logging into a server and launching the graphical interface in order to accomplish this common task. Can your New-ADUser commands become extremely lengthy in order to populate all of the attributes you want to include? Yes. However, can saving and running a PowerShell script that utilizes New-ADUser cmdlet save you time in the long run? Absolutely! It might take a few minutes of thought and testing in order to get your script to the point where it populates the information that you would like, but once you have created and saved that script, it can be modified and run quickly in the future in order to create new accounts. There is even a way to utilize the New-ADUser cmdlet to copy properties from an existing user account while it sets up the new one, which may also help to save you some time and energy on new user account creations.

See also

Make sure to check out the following TechNet link. This page lists all of the possible parameters and syntax that you might want to run alongside your New-ADUser cmdlet script. There are a ton of options:

* http://technet.microsoft.com/en-us/library/ee617253.aspx

Using PowerShell to view system uptime

I find myself constantly checking servers to figure out what time they last restarted. Usually, this is part of troubleshooting something in order to figure out whether the server rebooted as a planned action or if something went wrong and it restarted on its own during a non-standard time. For years, I had launched Event Viewer, waited for the System logs to open, hoped that they weren't corrupted in some way, and then headed over to noon on the previous day to find the number of seconds that the system had been online. Then I'd pull out the calculator and do the math for how many days/hours that really was. Way too complicated! Thankfully, we can make calls into WMI objects with PowerShell, and there is an object in there that will tell us the last time the server started. With a few lines plugged into a .ps1 script, we can create ourselves a nice little tool that will output the last time that a server booted. Let's give it a try.

Getting ready

We are using a Windows Server 2016 machine to build this script.

How to do it...

To build a script that shows us the last system boot time, perform the following steps:

1. Launch PowerShell ISE as an Administrator.
2. Open up a new script file and input the following line:

```
Get-WmiObject -Class Win32_OperatingSystem -ComputerName
localhost | Select-Object -Property LastBootUpTime
```

```
Untitled1.ps1* X
   1   Get-WmiObject -Class Win32_OperatingSystem -ComputerName localhost |
   2   Select-Object -Property LastBootUpTime
```

```
PS C:\Users\Administrator> Get-WmiObject -Class Win32_OperatingSystem -Compu

LastBootUpTime
--------------
20160517122955.129194-420


PS C:\Users\Administrator>
```

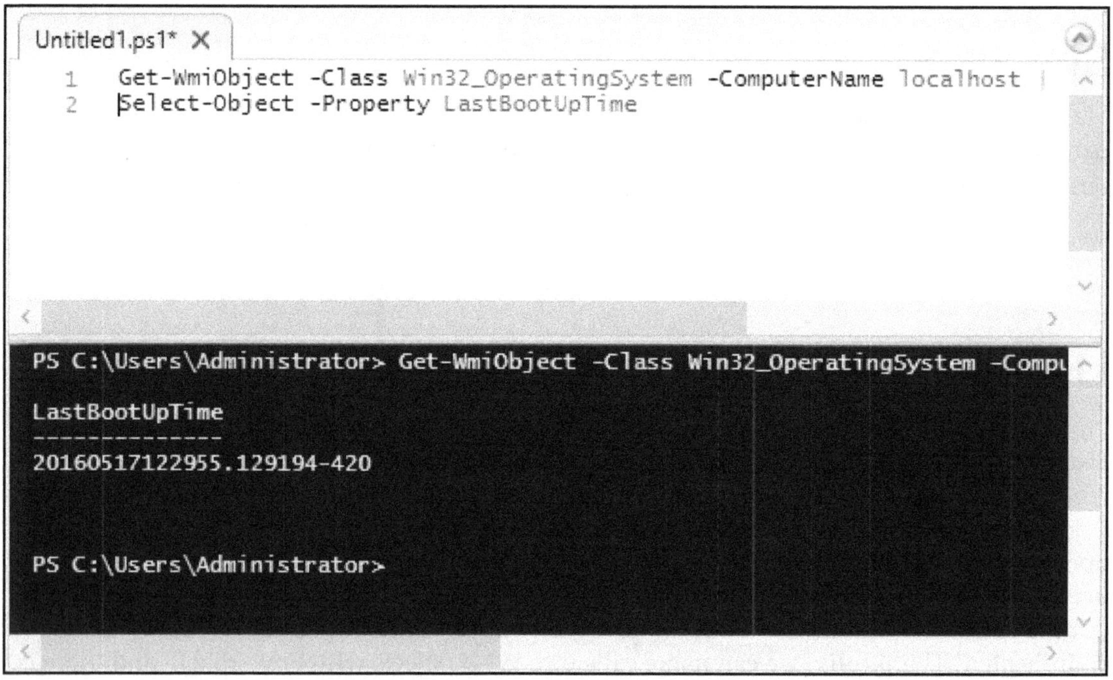

3. We have some data! It's kind of messy data, though. Maybe we can clean that up and make it a little more readable. With a couple of changes to our `Select-Object` code, we can change the header for this data to something more friendly, as well as changing the output of the date and time so it's way easier on the eyes:

```
Get-WmiObject -Class Win32_OperatingSystem -ComputerName
localhost | Select-Object -Property @{n="Last Boot Time";
e={ [Management.ManagementDateTimeConverter]::ToDateTime
($_.LastBootUpTime) }}
```

```
Untitled1.ps1* X
  1   Get-WmiObject -Class Win32_OperatingSystem -ComputerName localhost |
  2  Select-Object -Property @{n="Last Boot Time";
  3  e={[Management.ManagementDateTimeConverter]::ToDateTime($_.LastBootUpTime)}}
```

```
PS C:\Users\Administrator> Get-WmiObject -Class Win32_OperatingSystem -ComputerName localhos
Select-Object -Property @{n="Last Boot Time";
e={[Management.ManagementDateTimeConverter]::ToDateTime($_.LastBootUpTime)}}

Last Boot Time
--------------
5/17/2016 12:29:55 PM


PS C:\Users\Administrator>
```

That looks much better. At this point, I would say that this script is ready to be saved and used on any individual machine, and it would quickly give you the output you are looking for on that particular server. But, as you can see in the code, we are currently hardcoding the computer name to be `localhost`, the server or computer where we are currently running this script. What if we could change that so the user running this script could enter a different computer name? Maybe we could then use this script to execute a remote reach and find out when different servers last booted, without having to log into those servers? Here is an example of doing just that. With a few changes to our code, we can require that the user inputs a computer name as a flag while running the script, and outputs two properties now. We will place an additional property identifier in there for the computer name itself so that it is clear to us in the output that the last boot time we are looking at the server name that we actually enter.

1. Use this for your script code:

```
Param(
[Parameter(Mandatory=$true)][string]$ServerName
)
Get-WmiObject -Class Win32_OperatingSystem -ComputerName
$ServerName | Select-Object -Property CSName,@{n="Last Boot
    Time";
    e={[Management.ManagementDateTimeConverter]::
ToDateTime($_.LastBootUpTime)}}
```

2. Now when we run this script, we are asked to input the server name that we are trying to query.

```
Untitled1.ps1* ✕

1  ⊟param(
2  │    [Parameter(Mandatory=$true)][string]$ServerName
3  └    )
4
5       Get-WmiObject -Class Win32_OperatingSystem -ComputerName $ServerName |
6  ⊟    Select-Object -Property CSName,@{n="Last Boot Time";
7  └    e={[Management.ManagementDateTimeConverter]::ToDateTime($_.LastBootUpTime)}}
```

```
PS C:\Users\Administrator> param(
    [Parameter(Mandatory=$true)][string]$ServerName
)

    Get-WmiObject -Class Win32_OperatingSystem -ComputerName $ServerName |
    Select-Object -Property CSName,@{n="Last Boot Time";
    e={[Management.ManagementDateTimeConverter]::ToDateTime($_.LastBootUpTime)}}
cmdlet   at command pipeline position 1
Supply values for the following parameters:
ServerName: |
```

3. Go ahead and type `localhost` and you will receive the same boot time information as before, but now you see that we have a new column that shows us the server's name as well.

```
CSName Last Boot Time
------ --------------
DC1    5/17/2016 12:29:55 PM
```

4. Try running the script again, but this time enter the name of a remote server when it asks for **ServerName**. I will try to query our WEB1 web server. You should now see the last boot time output for that particular server with its name in the left column.

```
Untitled1.ps1* X
1  □param(
2          [Parameter(Mandatory=$true)][string]$ServerName
3      )
4
5          Get-WmiObject -Class Win32_OperatingSystem -ComputerName $ServerName |
6  □      Select-Object -Property CSName,@{n="Last Boot Time";
7          e={[Management.ManagementDateTimeConverter]::ToDateTime($_.LastBootUpTime)}}
```

```
      e={[Management.ManagementDateTimeConverter]::ToDateTime($_.LastBootUpTime)}}
cmdlet   at command pipeline position 1
Supply values for the following parameters:
ServerName: web1

CSName Last Boot Time
------ --------------
WEB1   5/17/2016 1:12:51 PM


PS C:\Users\Administrator> |
```

How it works...

In this recipe, we created a fun little script that asks for a server name and outputs the last boot information for the server entered. One of PowerShell's greatest attributes is its ability to grab information, both locally on the machine where you are running the script and on remote machines. This saves time, since you don't have to log into those servers to accomplish tasks, and makes your work environment more efficient.

One note on this particular script that we created, you don't have to run it as a first step and then take a second step in order to enter the server name. You are able to place the ServerName variable into your initial command when you launch the script. For example, open PowerShell and input the following command to launch the script:

```
.'Check Boot Time.ps1' -ServerName DC1
```

This will launch the script and automatically input **DC1** as the server that it is checking, instead of stopping to ask you for input.

3
Security and Networking

Various breaches and vulnerabilities over the past few years have brought security to the forefront of all IT Administrators' minds. In a Windows Server 2016 environment, there are many functions you can enable to lock down security on your own network. Let's explore some of these functions, as well as practice with some tools and tricks that can help us to better understand and navigate our own networks. We will also take a look at some common networking tasks that will help you out in your day-to-day work. In this chapter, we will look at the following recipes:

- Requiring complex passwords in your network
- Using Windows Firewall with Advanced Security to block unnecessary traffic
- Changing the RDP port on your server to hide access
- Multi-homing your Windows Server 2016
- Adding a static route into the Windows routing table
- Using Telnet to test a connection and network flow
- Using the Pathping command to trace network traffic
- Setting up NIC Teaming
- Renaming and domain joining via PowerShell
- Building your first Server Core

Introduction

In this chapter, we are going to tackle a number of tasks related to networking your Windows Server 2016 machines and locking down that environment a little bit by enabling some security functions. Some of the tools we are going to use can be very useful for daily tasks, and I hope that the steps we take will prompt you to start some gears spinning in your own mind to investigate deeper into taking full advantage of what Microsoft has to offer within this operating system.

Requiring complex passwords in your network

With the tools that attackers have available today, simple passwords should be outlawed by every company. Turning on the requirement for complex passwords in your network is pretty simple; the hard part is knowing where to find the setting. We are going to require complex passwords by making a change inside Group Policy. Further on in this book, we are going to do a lot of things inside Group Policy, but the requirement for complex passwords is so common that I felt it to be a general security item rather than something to be lumped alongside other Group Policy tasks. So, we will be using Group Policy in a step-by-step fashion, and combining this recipe with the chapter on Group Policy will give you even more creativity in the way that you could later change the implementation of this password policy.

Getting ready

We need to be working in a domain environment, as Group Policy is something that runs within Active Directory. The change that we are going to make in Group Policy is done from a Domain Controller, and we will utilize a client computer to test our policy once it has been implemented.

How to do it...

The following steps will help you enable complex passwords for your network:

1. On your Domain Controller, launch **Group Policy Management** from inside the **Tools** menu in **Server Manager**.

2. Expand your forest name and find the name of your domain inside the `Domains` folder. If you expand your domain name, you will see a **Group Policy Object (GPO)** in there called the **Default Domain Policy**. This policy is automatically configured in a new Active Directory environment to apply to all user accounts, so for this recipe, we will modify this GPO to require complex passwords for all of our users.

3. Right-click on **Default Domain Policy** and click **Edit...**.

Group Policy Management	Group Policy Objects in MYDOMAIN.LOCAL		
∨ Forest: MYDOMAIN.LOCAL	Contents Delegation		
∨ Domains	Name	GPO Status	WMI Filter
∨ MYDOMAIN.LOCAL	Default Domain Controller...	Enabled	None
Default Domain Policy	:y	Enabled	None
Domain Controll — Edit...			
Remote Access S — Enforced			
Web Servers — ✓ Link Enabled			
Windows 10 Desl			
Windows 10 Lapt — Save Report...			

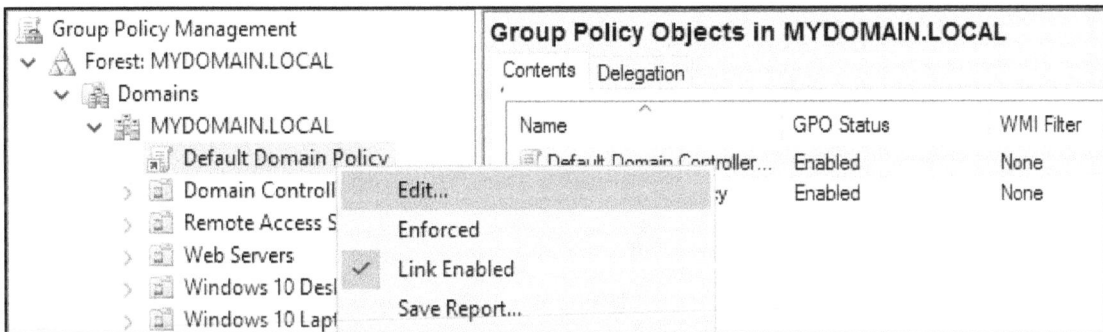

> **TIP**
>
> You can easily create a new GPO and use it instead of modifying the built-in default policy. This will give you better control over who or what gets the settings applied to them. See `Chapter 9`, *Group Policy*, for more detail on managing the GPOs themselves. We use the **Default Domain Policy** in this recipe for the sake of shortening the number of steps you need to take, but it really is recommended never to use the **Default Domain Policy** to make actual changes in a production environment.

4. Browse to the following location by navigating to **Computer Configuration | Policies | Windows Settings | Security Settings | Account Policies | Password Policy**.

5. Here are the configurable options that you can set for password requirements in your network. I am going to set **Maximum password age** to 30 days so that everyone needs to change their password monthly, and I will increase **Minimum password length** to 8 characters. I will also enable the complexity requirements setting, which sets a number of different requirements. If you double-click on that setting and browse to the **Explain** tab, you will see a list of all the items that are now required.

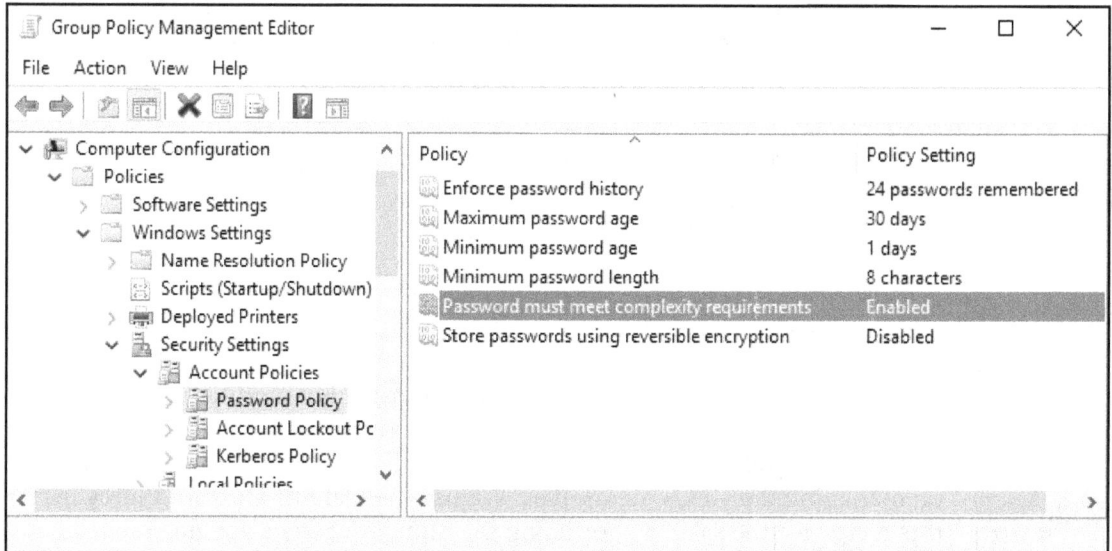

6. Now go ahead and try logging into a computer with a domain user account and come to discover that our password no longer meets the criteria and we have to change it accordingly.

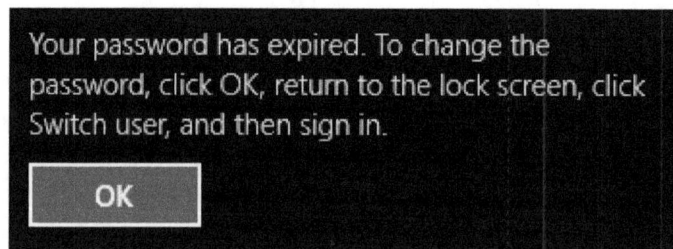

How it works...

Because we set requirements for password complexity in the Default Domain Policy, that requirement flows across our whole network. A solid password policy is very important in today's networks and just scratches the surface of Group Policy's abilities. These simple setting changes can make the difference in whether or not your company is compromised as a result of a brute force password attack.

Using Windows Firewall with Advanced Security to block unnecessary traffic

I encounter far too many networks with policies in place that disable the built-in **Windows Firewall with Advanced Security (WFAS)** by default on all of their machines. Usually, if I ask about this, the reason is either unknown or "It's always been that way." I think this is a carry-over from the Windows XP/Server 2003 days, or maybe even older, when the Windows Firewall was less than desirable. Believe me when I tell you that WFAS in today's operating systems is very advanced, stable, and beneficial. If you want to stop unnecessary or malicious traffic from getting to your server, look no further than this built-in tool.

Getting ready

We are going to use two Windows Server 2016 machines for this task. We will test connectivity between the two to set our baseline and then create a rule that blocks the functions we just tested. Next, we will test again to ensure that our changes did what we expected them to, blocking the traffic that we attempt to generate. It is important to set up a baseline of tests and run those same tests following each change to ensure the rules are working exactly as you want them to.

How to do it...

If you want to stop unnecessary traffic from getting to your server, execute the following instructions:

1. First, we want to test the existing connectivity. I log into my DC2 server, and from there I am able to successfully execute the `ping web1` command and get a reply. I can also open up File Explorer and browse to \\WEB1 and see a folder shared there. This baseline test tells me that both ICMP (ping) traffic and file access are currently open and allowed by WFAS on WEB1. We want to stop these functions from happening.

2. Log in to WEB1 and open **Windows Firewall with Advanced Security**. You can open this either from the **Start** screen and typing it in, or by opening a **Run** prompt and typing `wf.msc`.

3. Inside WFAS, your two best friends when trying to control traffic are the **Inbound Rules** and **Outbound Rules** sections on the left. You need to think of Inbound and Outbound from the server's perspective. Inbound Rules manipulate traffic that is flowing in toward your server, and Outbound Rules handle traffic flowing out of your server toward the rest of the network. If you click on **Inbound Rules**, you will see the list of preconfigured rules that exist already.

4. Right-click on **Inbound Rules** and click on **New Rule....**

5. First, let's make a rule to block the file access from happening. Choose **Port** and on the next screen, enter the value for port **TCP** as `445`. Then you realize that you might as well also block RDP access since that is also currently enabled. No problem! Simply comma separate these numbers as follows:

Does this rule apply to all local ports or specific local ports?

○ **All local ports**

◉ **Specific local ports:**   445, 3389

                    Example: 80, 443, 5000-5010

---

6. Choose **Block the connection**.

7. On the next screen where you choose which firewall profile the rule applies to, you can leave it set to all three checked as the default. This will ensure that the rule will apply to any NIC that has any firewall profile assigned. If you only have a single NIC on your server and it is joined to the domain, then you could get away with only selecting the domain profile if you wanted to deselect the other two. For our recipe, I'm going to leave them all checked.

8. Type any kind of descriptive name for your rule—something like `Block File` and `RDP Access`.

9. You did it! You will see that the new rule exists, and it is immediately put into action. If you head over to your other server, you will now find that you can no longer RDP or browse the file shares at all on WEB1.

10. We can still successfully ping WEB1, though, and we wanted to put a stop to that as well. To stop ICMP traffic, you simply need to create another rule. This one is a little bit more complicated, though. First, go ahead and create a second Inbound Rule, and use the exact same settings that you used for your `RDP` file rule. You can enter anything into the **Port** field; it doesn't matter because we will be invalidating it in a minute, so maybe use port 445 for our example.

11. Great, now you have two rules in there that are both blocking port 445. That doesn't do us much good. Right-click on the newest rule that we just created, head into **Properties**, and let's improve this rule a little bit.

12. Inside the **Protocols and Ports** tab, drop down the **Protocol** type and choose **ICMPv4**. That's all you have to do! You have now modified this rule so that it is no longer blocking TCP port 445, but rather this rule is now blocking ICMPv4 traffic.

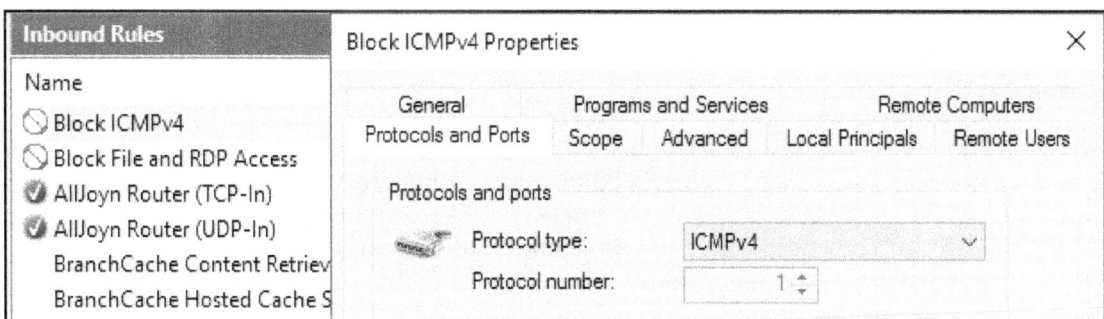

Inbound Rules	Block ICMPv4 Properties					✕
Name						
◌ Block ICMPv4	General		Programs and Services		Remote Computers	
◌ Block File and RDP Access	Protocols and Ports	Scope	Advanced	Local Principals	Remote Users	
⚫ AllJoyn Router (TCP-In)						
⚫ AllJoyn Router (UDP-In)	Protocols and ports					
BranchCache Content Retriev	Protocol type:		ICMPv4	⌄		
BranchCache Hosted Cache S	Protocol number:		1 ⌄			

13. If you log back into DC2, we no longer receive ping replies when trying to contact the WEB1 server.

Take some time to play around inside the **Scope** tab. This section of a WFAS rule allows you to scope the rule down so that it only applies to particular IP addresses or ranges. Maybe you only want to block file share access from a particular subnet or only for the external NIC of an edge server. Requirements like these are easy to accomplish!

How it works...

We used the Windows Firewall with Advanced Security to create a couple of simple rules to block unwanted traffic coming into our server. These rules are put into place immediately and are very easy to generate. What is even greater is that our WFAS rules can be created centrally by making use of Group Policy so that you don't even have to touch the individual servers to apply connection rules to them. WFAS is very different than the Windows Firewall of 10 years ago, and if you are not making use of it today I seriously recommend that you reconsider.

Changing the RDP port on your server to hide access

Everybody uses RDP. Attackers and bots, curiously, also know that *everybody* uses RDP. If you are working with perimeter servers that are potentially connected to the Internet, having RDP enabled can be especially dangerous because it is quite easy to leave your server in a state where it is open from outside of your network. This gives anyone the ability to start guessing passwords or trying to brute force their way into your server, or just a way to give you some denial-of-service headaches by throwing thousands of login attempts at that server.

Even aside from the worries of potential access from the public Internet, you may want to ensure that regular users aren't trying to poke around where they shouldn't be by opening up RDP connections to servers within your network. There are a few ways that you could restrict this access. You could come up with some creative firewall rules that only allow RDP access from certain subnets, and try to contain your IT computers to those subnets. Or maybe you could configure RDP on your destination servers to require certificates as part of the authentication process, thus only allowing users with those certificates to have access. These are both fairly complicated. I like to employ a much simpler solution to keep unwanted eyes from seeing my RDP login screens.

Change the port that RDP runs on! What? Can you do that? Yes, RDP by default listens and connects on TCP port 3389. The Remote Desktop Client that is installed on almost every client machine everywhere automatically assumes that the server they are connecting to is listening on 3389, and so you don't even have to specify a port when you try to connect. There isn't even a field for it in the client. So it's pretty rare that I talk to people (even IT people) who know that 3389 is the default. Given that, if we were able to change that 3389 to something different, something of our own choosing, I think that would do a grand job of keeping people out of our systems. Let's say we have a sensitive server and want to keep access to a minimum. Let's change the RDP port on that to something only we know, maybe port 4822. That'll keep 'em guessing for a while.

Getting ready

Any Windows Server 2016 machine will do for this task. We are going to set our custom RDP port on WEB1, and then we are going to test accessing it from a Windows 10 client machine.

How to do it...

Go through the following steps to change the RDP port to one of your liking:

1. Open **Registry Editor**. You can do this by going to either the **Start** screen or Command Prompt and typing `regedit`.
2. Browse to:
   `HKEY_LOCAL_MACHINE\SYSTEM\CurrentControlSet\Control\Terminal Server\WinStations\RDP-Tcp`.
3. Find the value called **PortNumber** and change it to `4822`.

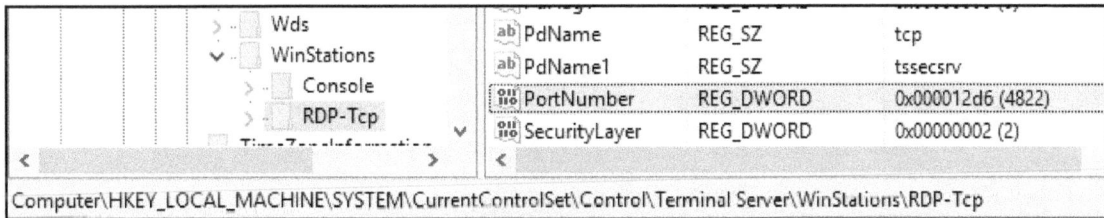

> Wds	ab PdName	REG_SZ	tcp	
∨ WinStations	ab PdName1	REG_SZ	tssecsrv	
> Console	PortNumber	REG_DWORD	0x000012d6 (4822)	
> RDP-Tcp	SecurityLayer	REG_DWORD	0x00000002 (2)	

Computer\HKEY_LOCAL_MACHINE\SYSTEM\CurrentControlSet\Control\Terminal Server\WinStations\RDP-Tcp

4. Restart the server.

5. Now log into your client computer and open up **Remote Desktop Connection** by typing that name into your **Start** screen. You can also type mstsc in Command Prompt to open this program. If you try to connect directly to WEB1, your connection will fail as the server is no longer listening on the standard port 3389.

6. Enter in WEB1:4822 and you connect successfully.

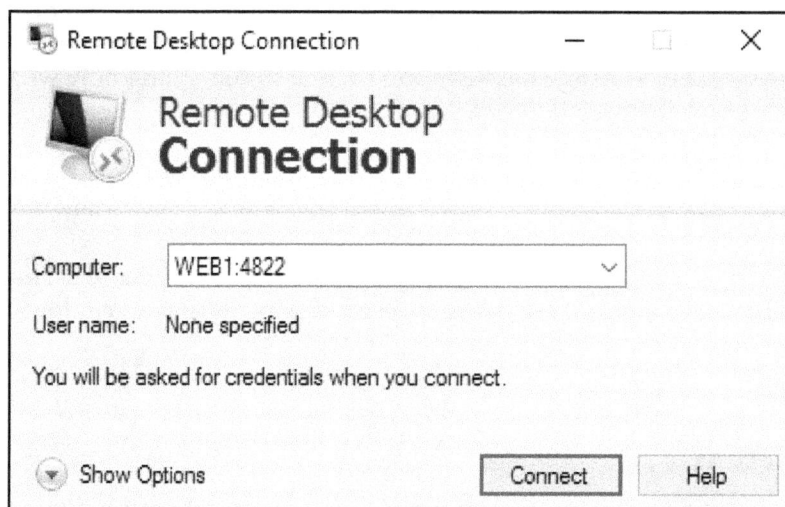

If at first you cannot connect, make sure to check your Windows Firewall settings. It is possible that you may need to add a rule to WFAS on the server to allow port 4822.

How it works...

With a simple registry change, we can adjust the RDP listener port on servers. This will help keep unwanted RDP connections from being made, which can be useful both inside and outside the corporate network. After making this change, the only people who will be able to reach the RDP login screen would be those who know your new RDP port, and who know how to utilize that custom port within the Remote Desktop Connection tool.

Multi-homing your Windows Server 2016

Historically, there haven't been many scenarios that require Windows servers to have more than a single network card. This is because most of the roles that they were accomplishing were done on whatever single network they were plugged into. There was no need for a server to have direct connections to multiple networks because that was the router and switch's job, right? In today's Windows Server world, there are numerous roles that can take advantage of multi-homing, which simply means having multiple NICs connected to different networks at the same time. There are some proxy roles that can use multiple NICs; Remote Access roles such as DirectAccess and VPN recommend a dual-NIC setup, and you can even use a Windows Server as a general router if you want to.

I work a lot with DirectAccess and I find many multi-homed servers with incorrect network configurations. This recipe is a collection of points that need to be followed when configuring a Windows Server with multiple NICs to make sure it behaves and flows traffic as you expect it to.

Getting ready

You just need a Windows Server 2016 online for this one. We have two NICs installed on this server and they are plugged into different networks. I am prepping a Remote Access server that will sit on the edge, so I have one NIC plugged into the corporate internal network, while the other NIC is connected to the Internet.

How to do it...

To configure a Windows Server with multiple NICs, perform the following process:

- **Only one Default Gateway**: In your NIC properties, you need to make sure that you only have a Default Gateway identified on *one* of your NICs. This is the most common mistake that I find in the field. If you have two NICs, it would seem logical that you would simply populate their IP address settings just like you would with any server or computer, right? Nope. The purpose of a Default Gateway is to be the fallback or the route of last resort. Whenever your server tries to send out network traffic, it will search the local routing table for information on how to send out that traffic. If it does not find a specific route that corresponds to the IP address that you are sending to, then it will default that traffic over to the Default Gateway address. Therefore, you only ever want to have one Default Gateway assigned on a server, no matter how many NICs are connected. On all other NICs installed on the system, simply leave the Default Gateway field unpopulated inside the TCP/IP properties. By the way, for a DirectAccess server or for pretty much any other server that faces the Internet, the Default Gateway needs to be on the External NIC, so I will be leaving that field empty in the properties of my Internal NIC.

- **Limit your DNS servers**: Another common configuration that I have seen is to have DNS server addresses defined for every network adapter installed on the system. While this doesn't usually break anything like multiple Default Gateways can, it does cause unnecessary slowness when the system is trying to resolve DNS names. Try to have DNS server addresses configured on only one NIC. Once again, using our example DirectAccess server setup, I will be configuring DNS server addresses on my Internal NIC because that is necessary for DA to work. I will not be putting my public DNS server specifications into the External NIC; instead, I will leave those fields empty.

- **Use static IP addresses**: The roles and functions you may perform on a Windows Server that requires multiple NICs will be best served by having static IP address information assigned to those network cards. If you let one or more of the NICs pull information from DHCP, you could easily create a situation where you have too many DNS servers defined, or where you have multiple Default Gateways on your system. As we already know, neither of these scenarios is desirable.

- **Prioritize the NIC binding**: It is a good practice to set a priority for your NICs so you can place the card that you expect to have the most network traffic as #1 in the list. For our DirectAccess server, we always want the Internal NIC to be placed on the top, so let's make sure that is set correctly using the following steps:
  1. Open up **Network and Sharing Center** and click on **Change adapter settings** so that you are in the **Network Connections** screen where you can see the network cards installed on your system.
  2. Now press the *Alt* key on your keyboard and you will see the menus at the top of this window.
  3. Head into the **Advanced** menu and click on **Advanced Settings...**. Now simply make sure that your **Internal** NIC is listed on top.

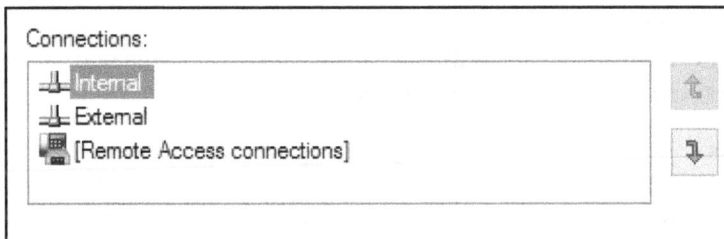

- **Add static routes**: A couple of minutes ago, you probably started thinking "Hey, if I don't have a Default Gateway on my Internal NIC, what tells the server how to get packets into the subnets of my internal network?" Great question! Because you only have one Default Gateway, when you need to send traffic out one of the other NICs, you need to make sure that a static route exists in the Windows routing table. This ensures that the server knows which interface gets traffic for each subnet. Make sure to check out our next recipe for specific information on how to add those routes.

How it works...

Anybody can multi-home their server by simply plugging two NICs into two different networks. The tricky part is making sure that you configure those NICs and the operating system appropriately so that network traffic flows in the right directions at the right times. Following this list of rules will give you a solid foundation so that you can build out these types of scenarios and know that you are doing so in the correct fashion. Deviating from these rules will result in unexpected behavior, which sometimes is not immediately obvious. This can make for some very frustrating troubleshooting down the road.

See also

- The *Adding a static route into the Windows routing table* recipe

Adding a static route into the Windows routing table

This recipe follows right on the heels of our previous topic. If you have never worked on a server that is making use of more than one NIC, then you have probably never had a reason to poke around in the Windows routing table. The minute that you are tasked with setting up a new server that needs to be connected to multiple networks, or that you get thrown into a situation where you need to troubleshoot such a system, this suddenly becomes critical information to have in your back pocket.

On a server that is connected to multiple networks, you only have one Default Gateway address defined. This means any subnets that need to be reached by flowing through one of the other NICs, the ones that do not contain the Default Gateway, need to be specifically defined inside the routing table. Otherwise, Windows simply does not know how to get to those subnets and it will attempt to push all traffic through the Default Gateway. This traffic will never make it to its destination and communications will fail.

Today, we are setting up a new VPN server. This server has a NIC plugged into the Internet where remote clients will come in, and another NIC plugged into the internal network so that the client traffic can make its way to the application servers that the users need to access. In this scenario, the Default Gateway must be populated on the External NIC. There will be no Default Gateway address defined on the Internal NIC, and without some assistance, Windows will have no idea how to properly route traffic toward the servers inside the network.

For our example, the Internal NIC is plugged into the 10.0.0.x network. Since it has a direct physical connection to this network, it is automatically able to properly contact other servers that reside on this subnet. So if the VPN server was 10.0.0.5 and we had a Domain Controller running on 10.0.0.2, we would be able to contact that Domain Controller without any additional configuration. But most companies have multiple subnets inside their network. So what if our VPN users needed to contact a web server that is sitting on the 10.0.1.x network? When traffic comes into the VPN server looking for a destination of 10.0.1.8 (the web server), the VPN server will check its local routing table and find that it does not have an entry for the 10.0.1.x network. Since it doesn't know what to do with this request, it sends it to the Default Gateway, which sends the packets back out the External NIC. Those packets don't have a valid destination to reach through the External NIC, which is plugged into the Internet, and so the traffic simply fails.

We need to define a static route in the routing table of our VPN server, so that when VPN clients request resources inside the 10.0.1.x network, then that traffic makes its way to the destination network successfully. We need to bind this route to our Internal NIC so that the VPN server knows it has to send these packets through that physical network interface.

Getting ready

We are setting up a new Windows Server 2016 VPN server. This server has two NICs installed, one plugged into the Internet and the other plugged into the internal network. Inside our corporate network, there are two subnets. 10.0.0.x (/24), which our Internal NIC is plugged into, and 10.0.1.x (/24), where our web server resides. There is, of course, a router between the two internal subnets, which is how traffic physically flows between the two. The IP address of that router is 10.0.0.254. If we were able to configure a Default Gateway on the Internal NIC of our VPN server, it would be set to 10.0.0.254, and all traffic would work without any further input. However, since our VPN server is multi-homed and there can only be a Default Gateway configured on the External NIC, we need to tell the server that it has to push 10.0.1.x traffic through 10.0.0.254 by using the Internal NIC.

How to do it...

So basically, we need to do the following to create a static route in our VPN server:

- Identify the subnet that we want to contact. In our example, it is 10.0.1.0
- Identify the subnet mask, which is 255.255.255.0
- Identify the IP address of the router that will get us to that network, which is 10.0.0.254

- Identify the Interface ID number of the physical NIC that needs to carry this traffic, which can be attained as follows:

    1. Discovering this NIC ID is going to take us a minute. First, open up **Network Connections** and expand the fields so that you can see the device name of each NIC.

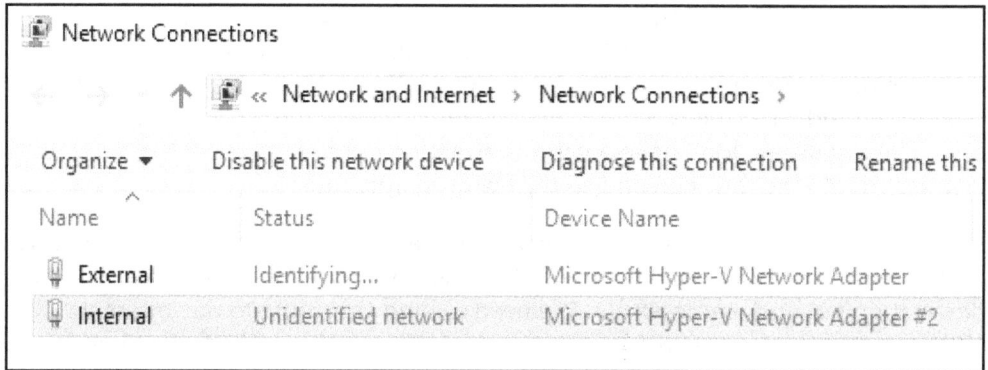

Network Connections		

↑ « Network and Internet › Network Connections ›

Name	Status	Device Name	
Organize ▼	Disable this network device	Diagnose this connection	Rename this
External	Identifying...	Microsoft Hyper-V Network Adapter
Internal	Unidentified network	Microsoft Hyper-V Network Adapter #2

   2. Now open Command Prompt and type `route print`. This is a print of your entire routing table. Scroll back up to the very top and you will see the Interface ID numbers of your NICs listed.

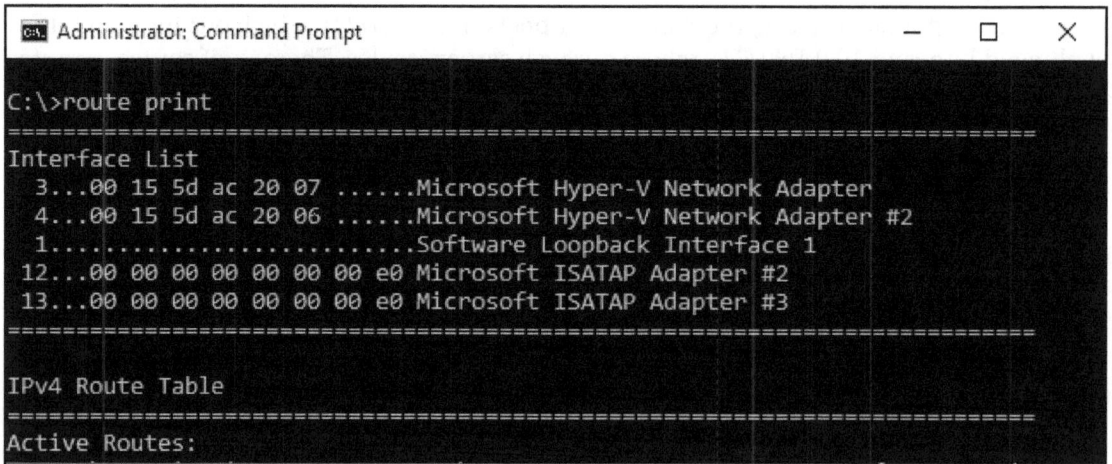

```
Administrator: Command Prompt                                    —    □    ×

C:\>route print
===========================================================================
Interface List
  3...00 15 5d ac 20 07 ......Microsoft Hyper-V Network Adapter
  4...00 15 5d ac 20 06 ......Microsoft Hyper-V Network Adapter #2
  1...........................Software Loopback Interface 1
 12...00 00 00 00 00 00 00 e0 Microsoft ISATAP Adapter #2
 13...00 00 00 00 00 00 00 e0 Microsoft ISATAP Adapter #3
===========================================================================

IPv4 Route Table
===========================================================================
Active Routes:
```

We can see that our Internal NIC is the second NIC, named `Microsoft Hyper-V Network Adapter #2`. Looking at that entry in the route print, there is a number over to the left of that name. This is our Internal NIC's Interface ID number, which is 4 in this example.

We now have all the information needed to put together our route statement and bind it to our Internal NIC. The general format that our route add statement needs to take is `route add -p <subnet> mask <mask> <gateway> if <interfaceID>`. The -p part of the command is very important as it makes this route persistent. Without the -p part, our new route would disappear after the reboot.

So, in order to tell our VPN server how to send traffic into the new 10.0.1.x subnet that we have been talking about, our specific command is as follows:

```
route add -p 10.0.1.0 mask 255.255.255.0 10.0.0.254 if 4
```

```
C:\>route add -p 10.0.1.0 mask 255.255.255.0 10.0.0.254 if 4
 OK!

C:\>_
```

This command tells the server to add a new persistent route for the 10.0.1.0/24 network, flow this network traffic through the 10.0.0.254 gateway and bind this route to NIC ID 4, which is our internal network interface.

How it works...

With a multi-homed server, only one NIC will have a Default Gateway. Therefore, any subnets that we need to access through the other interfaces have to be specifically defined. Before we added this new route, the server was completely unable to contact the 10.0.1.x network. This is because the routing table did not have any information about this subnet, so any traffic trying to get there was being sent out the Default Gateway, which is on the External NIC plugged into the Internet. By adding a static route to our server, we have now defined a routing path for the server to take whenever it has traffic that needs to get to 10.0.1.x.

If you have many subnets in your network, you may be able to cover them all with a blanket route statement. A **blanket route** is also known as an aggregate or supernet route. This could save you the time of having to set up a new route statement for each and every one of your networks. For example, if we had many *10.something* networks and we wanted to flow all of them through our Internal NIC, we could do that with a single route statement, as follows:

```
Route add -p 10.0.0.0 mask 255.0.0.0 10.0.0.254 if 4
```

This route would send any 10.x.x.x traffic through the Internal NIC. Whether you blanket your routes like this or set each one up individually doesn't make a difference to the server as long as its routing table contains information about where to send the packets that it needs to process.

Using Telnet to test a connection and network flow

The `ping` command has always been an IT person's best friend to do quick network connection checks. How many of you are the family and neighborhood go-to guy to fix anything with buttons? I'm guessing most of you. And as such, if someone told you they were having trouble accessing the Internet from their laptop at home, what is the first thing you would do when you showed up? Try to ping their router, a website, or another computer in their network. You know you would! This has always been a wonderfully quick and easy way to test whether or not you have network traffic flowing between two endpoints. The same troubleshooting procedure exists in all workplaces and corporations. I have even seen many monitoring tools and scripts utilize the results of whether or not a ping replies to report on whether or not a particular service is up and running. If you get a ping reply, it's working, and if it times out, it's down, right?

Not necessarily. The problem we are here to address today is that more and more networks and routers are starting to block ICMP traffic by default. We can say Pings = ICMP. This means that you can no longer take your ping test results to the bank. If your network connection traverses a router or firewall that blocks ICMP, your ping test will time out, even if the service is up and running. Windows Firewall even blocks ICMP by default now. So if you bring a new server online in your network and give it an IP address, you may notice that attempting to ping that new server results in timeouts. There is nothing wrong with the server, and it is capable of sending and receiving network traffic, but the local firewall on that server is blocking the incoming ping request.

I only lay out this information to let you know that `ping` is no longer the best tool for determining a connection between machines. Today's recipe will introduce a tool that has been around for a long time, but that I don't find many administrators taking advantage of. This is the **Telnet Client**, which I use on a daily basis. I hope that you will too!

Getting ready

We have a Server 2016 web server that has a website running. It is also enabled for RDP access and file sharing, but ICMP is being blocked by the local Windows Firewall. We are going to run some tests with a client machine against this server to try to determine which services are up and running.

How to do it...

To start working with Telnet Client, have a look at these instructions:

1. First, just to prove our point here, let's open up Command Prompt on our testing client machine and try to ping WEB1 using the `ping web1` command. Because ICMP is being blocked by the firewall, all we get is a series of timeouts.

```
Administrator: Command Prompt                          —    □    ✕

Pinging web1.MYDOMAIN.LOCAL [10.0.0.85] with 32 bytes of data:
Request timed out.
Request timed out.
Request timed out.
Request timed out.

Ping statistics for 10.0.0.85:
    Packets: Sent = 4, Received = 0, Lost = 4 (100% loss),

C:\>
```

2. Now let's use the `Telnet` command to accomplish some more intuitive digging into whether or not WEB1 is online and functional. Note that Telnet Client is not available inside Command Prompt by default; it is a Windows feature that must be installed. On the client machine we are using to test, head into **Control Panel | Programs | Turn Windows features on or off** (or **Server Manager** if your testing machine is a server) and choose to add roles or features. We want to install the **feature** called **Telnet Client**. Alternatively, you can install the **Telnet Client** feature with a simple PowerShell command:

```
Install-WindowsFeature Telnet-Client
```

3. Now we have the `telnet` command available to use inside Command Prompt. The general format of the command goes like this: `telnet <server> <port>`. When you run this command, you are effectively saying "Let's try to create a connection to this server name, on this particular port."

4. Even though we cannot ping WEB1, let's try to use `telnet` to open a connection to port 80, which is the website that we have running. The command is as follows:

```
telnet web1 80
```

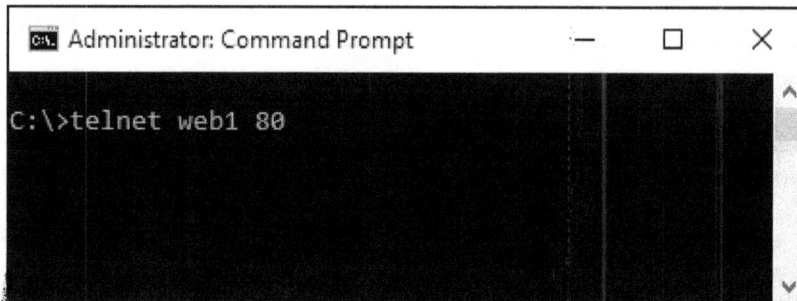

5. When we press *Enter*, the Command Prompt window changes to a flashing cursor. This is your confirmation that Telnet was able to open a successful connection to port 80 on the WEB1 server.

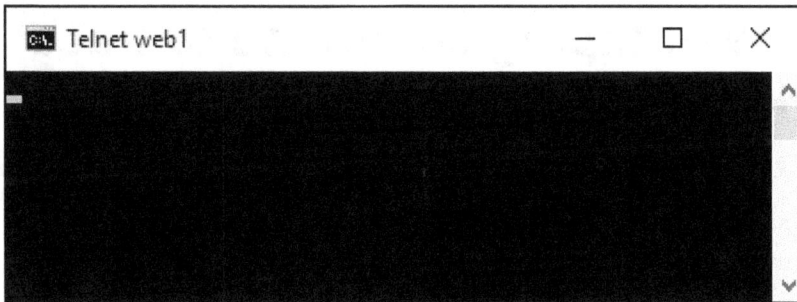

6. Now try using the `telnet 10.0.0.85 3389` command. This also results in a flashing cursor, indicating that we successfully connected to port 3389 (RDP) on IP address 10.0.0.85. This is the IP address of WEB1. I wanted to show this to point out that you can use either names or IP addresses with your `telnet` commands.

7. And finally, how about `telnet web1 53`? This one results in a timeout, and we do not see our flashing cursor. So it appears that port 53 is not responding on the WEB1 server, which makes sense because port 53 is commonly used by DNS, and this is a web server, not a DNS server. If we were to query one of our Domain Controllers that is also running DNS, we would be able to make a successful telnet connection to port 53 on those guys.

> Telnet queries work with TCP traffic, which covers most services that you will be polling for. Telnet does not have a connector for UDP ports.

How it works...

Telnet is a simple but powerful command that can be run to query against particular ports and services on your servers. When trying to determine whether or not a particular service is available, or when trying to troubleshoot some form of network connectivity problem, it is a much more reliable tool than using a simple `ping` request. If you have been thinking about building some kind of script that programmatically reaches out and checks against servers to report whether they are online or offline, consider using `telnet` rather than `ping` so that you can query the individual service that the system is providing by using its particular port number.

Using the Pathping command to trace network traffic

When building or troubleshooting a network connection, it is often very beneficial to be able to watch the path that your packets take as they make their way from source to destination. Or perhaps they never make it to the destination and you want to figure out how far they do travel before stopping so that you can focus your work efforts in that area.

One command that has been used by network admins for years is traceroute (`tracert`), but the output contains some information that is often unnecessary, and the output is missing one large key ingredient. Namely, traceroute shows the first hop as the first router that you traverse and does not show you what physical NIC the packets are flowing out of. Granted, many times you only have one NIC, so this is obvious information, but what if you are working with a multi-homed server and you are simply checking to make sure packets for a particular destination are flowing out the correct NIC? What if we just want to double-check that some route statements we added are working properly? Cue `Pathping`. This command has been around for a long time but is virtually unknown. It shows the same information that `tracert` does, except it saves the information about the time between hops and some other details until the end of the output. This allows you to focus on the physical hops themselves in a clear, concise manner. More importantly, it shows you our key ingredient right away—the NIC that your packets are flowing out of! Once I discovered this, I left `tracert` behind and have never looked back. `Pathping` is the way to go.

Getting ready

Not much to get ready for this one. All we need is a server with a network connection and a Command Prompt window. `Pathping` is a command that is already available to any Windows Server; we just need to start using it.

How to do it...

The following two steps get you started with `Pathping`:

1. Open **Command Prompt** on your server.
2. Type `pathping <servername or IP>`. Your output will be as follows:

```
Administrator: Command Prompt                          —    □    ×

C:\>pathping dc1

Tracing route to DC1.MYDOMAIN.LOCAL [10.0.0.1]
over a maximum of 30 hops:
  0  WEB1.MYDOMAIN.LOCAL [10.0.0.85]
  1  DC1 [10.0.0.1]

Computing statistics for 25 seconds...
             Source to Here    This Node/Link
Hop  RTT     Lost/Sent = Pct   Lost/Sent = Pct  Address
  0                                              WEB1.MYDOMAIN.LOCAL [10.0.0.85]
                               0/ 100 =   0%    |
  1   0ms    0/ 100 =   0%     0/ 100 =   0%  DC1 [10.0.0.1]

Trace complete.

C:\>
```

How it works...

Pathping is a networking tool that allows you to watch the path that your packets are taking as they make their way to the destination. Similar to traceroute, it is much less commonly known, but in my opinion gives a better layout of the same data. It is a command that should be added to your regular tool bag and vocabulary, right alongside ping and telnet.

Setting up NIC Teaming

Teaming your network cards basically means installing two NICs onto the same server, plugging them both into the same network, and joining them together in a *team*. This gives you NIC redundancy in case of a failure, and redundancy is always a great thing! Sounds simple, right? Well, with Windows Server 2016, it finally is. This seemingly easy task has always been challenging to put into practice with previous versions of the operating system, but with 2016 we can finally do it properly from a single interface and actually count on it to work as we expect it to.

Getting ready

We are going to set up a NIC team on a Windows Server 2016 machine. There are two NICs installed onto this server, neither of which have yet been configured.

How to do it...

With the following steps, start teaming up:

1. Open up **Server Manager**, and in the left-hand pane go ahead and click on **Local Server**.
2. Near the middle of the screen, you will see a section marked **NIC Teaming**. Go ahead and click on the word **Disabled** in order to launch the NIC Teaming screen as follows:

Windows Firewall	Domain: On
Remote management	Enabled
Remote Desktop	Disabled
NIC Teaming	Disabled
NIC1	IPv4 address assigned by DHCP, IPv6 enabled
NIC2	IPv4 address assigned by DHCP, IPv6 enabled

3. Down in the **TEAMS** section, drop down the **TASKS** menu, and click on **New Team**.

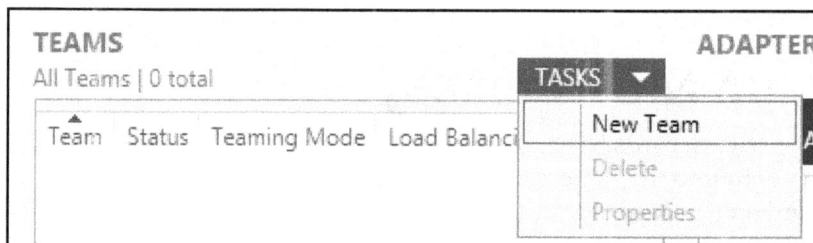

TEAMS					ADAPTER
All Teams | 0 total				TASKS ▼	
Team	Status	Teaming Mode	Load Balanci	New Team	A
				Delete	
				Properties	

4. Define a name for your new team and choose the two NICs that you want to be a part of it.

Team name:

Internal NIC Team

Member adapters:

In Team	Adapter	Speed	State	Reason
✓	Ethernet	10 Gbps		
✓	Ethernet 2	10 Gbps		

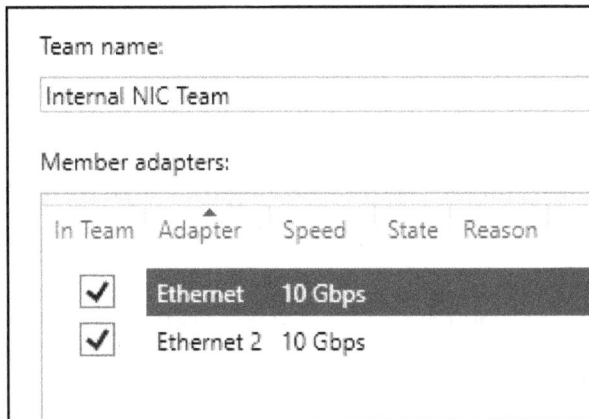

5. That's it! NIC1 and NIC2 are now successfully joined together in a team and will work in tandem to make sure you are still connected in the event of a failure.

6. If you make your way to the regular **Network Connections** screen, where you define IP address information, you will see that you now have a new item listed beneath your physical network cards. This new item is the place where you will go to define the IP address information that you want the server to use.

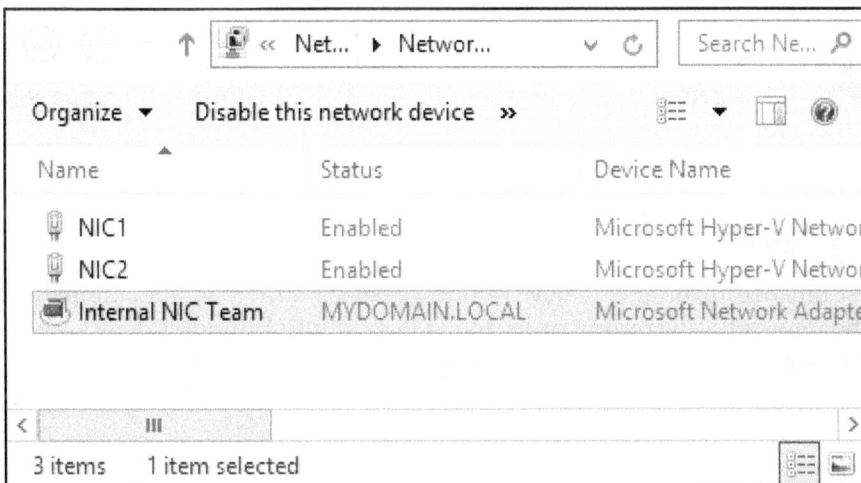

Name	Status	Device Name
NIC1	Enabled	Microsoft Hyper-V Networ
NIC2	Enabled	Microsoft Hyper-V Networ
Internal NIC Team	MYDOMAIN.LOCAL	Microsoft Network Adapte

3 items   1 item selected

> You can create more than one team on a server! When setting up a multi-homed server with two network connections, you could easily make use of four NICs and create two teams, each containing two physical network cards.

How it works...

Creating NIC teams is a pretty easy process that you should practice as time permits. This option for redundancy has never been very popular because, I believe, it had some stability problems in earlier versions of the server operating systems. Now that we have Windows Server 2016 available to us, and the process to configure it is so straightforward, I fully expect that NIC Teaming will become a standard procedure for administrators as they build every new server.

Another benefit of, and the reason, for setting up NIC teaming is additional bandwidth. This may be yet another reason for which you start setting up your own servers with NIC teams. Keep in mind that if you are looking to implement teaming on a large scale, there is a limit of 32 NICs that can be joined to a team, and an additional limit of 32 teams that can be created on a single server.

Renaming and domain joining via PowerShell

Every server that you build will need a hostname, and most likely will need to be joined to your domain. We are all familiar with doing these things with the mouse using system properties, but have you ever thought of using a command interface to do these tasks quickly? Let's work together to discover how PowerShell can once again help make these necessary tasks more efficient.

Getting ready

We have just finished turning on a new Windows Server 2016 machine. Immediately following the mini-setup wizard in order to get logged into Windows, let's now use PowerShell to set our hostname and join the system to our domain.

How to do it...

Follow these steps to rename and domain join this new server with PowerShell:

1. Right-click on your PowerShell icon on the Taskbar and choose **Run as administrator**:

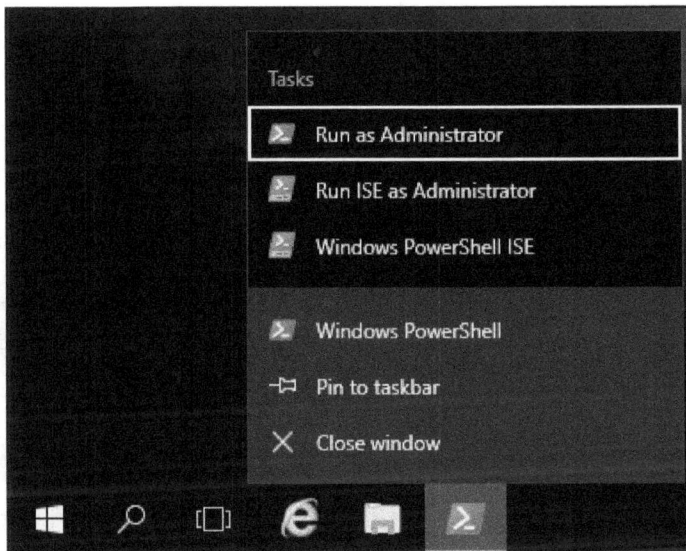

2. In order to rename our new server WEB2, input the following command. Using the -Restart flag will ensure that our server reboots following the name change:

```
Rename-Computer -NewName WEB2 -Restart
```

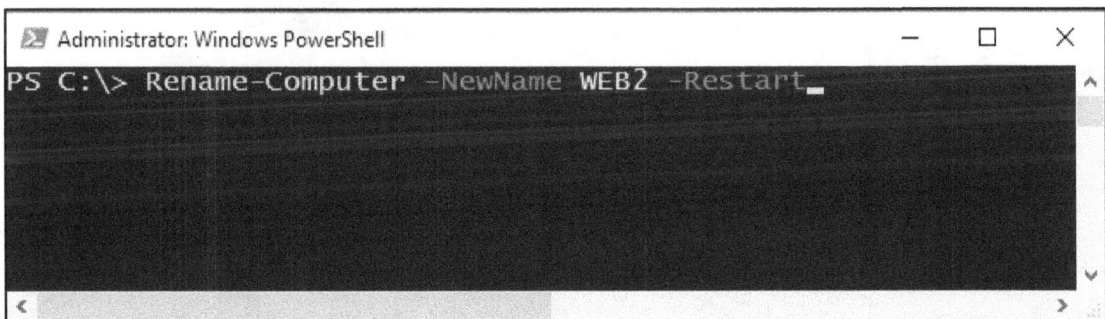

3. That's it for renaming! Now that our WEB2 server has rebooted, open PowerShell again and use the `Add-Computer` command in order to join it to our domain:

```
Add-Computer -DomainName MYDOMAIN.LOCAL -Credential
MYDOMAIN.LOCAL\Administrator -Restart
```

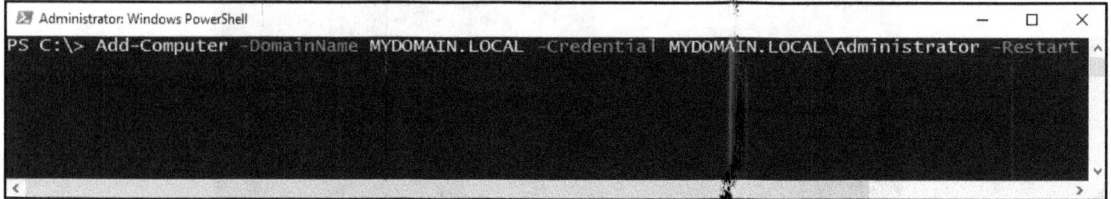

```
Administrator: Windows PowerShell
PS C:\> Add-Computer -DomainName MYDOMAIN.LOCAL -Credential MYDOMAIN.LOCAL\Administrator -Restart
```

4. Since we specified an account to use as credentials when joining the domain, we are prompted to supply the password. As soon as you enter the password, the server will be joined to the domain and will immediately restart to complete the process.

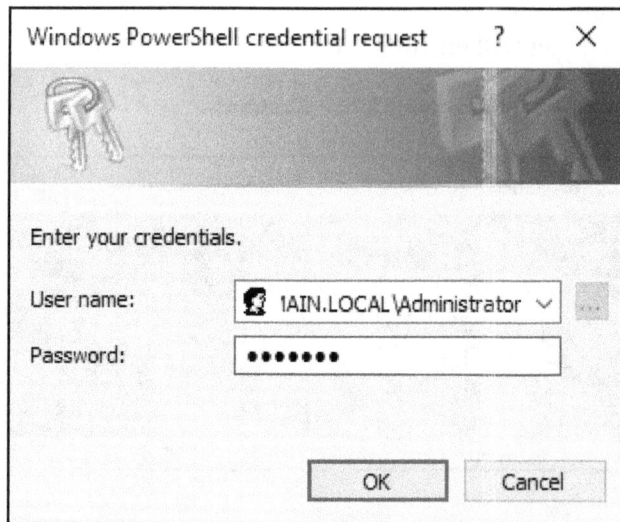

```
Windows PowerShell credential request        ?    X

Enter your credentials.

User name:    1AIN.LOCAL\Administrator  v

Password:     •••••••

              OK            Cancel
```

5. Following the reboot, you can see in system properties that our server is now appropriately named and domain joined.

Computer name, domain, and workgroup settings

Computer name:	WEB2
Full computer name:	WEB2.MYDOMAIN.LOCAL
Computer description:	
Domain:	MYDOMAIN.LOCAL

How it works...

Through a couple of quick PowerShell cmdlets, we can rename computers and join them to our domain. In fact, these functions are even possible without ever logging into the console of the server. There are parameters that can be added to these cmdlets that allow you to run them remotely. For example, you could run the PowerShell commands from a local desktop computer, specifying that you want to run them against the remote server's IP address or name. By performing the functions this way, you never even have to log into the server itself in order to name and join it. See the links in the following section for additional information on these parameters.

See also

Take a look at the following links for even more detailed information about the `Rename-Computer` and `Add-Computer` cmdlets that we used in this recipe:

- http://technet.microsoft.com/en-us/library/hh849792.aspx
- http://technet.microsoft.com/en-us/library/hh849798.aspx

Building your first Server Core

Perhaps the most important way to increase security in your organization is to lower the security threshold, or footprint, of your servers and infrastructure. In other words, if there are any services running or ports open on your servers that aren't actually being used purposefully, you should disable or turn that particular service off. Now, hardening a Windows Server by disabling services and uninstalling things isn't an easy job; you can quickly turn something off that is important to the operating system and cause all kinds of problems on that server. Thankfully, there is a much safer and more secure way to harden your servers, but it requires planning from the beginning of your server build.

Server Core is a version of Windows Server 2016 that is essentially a headless operating system; all of your interaction with it is either command-line driven or done remotely from other servers or systems. Server Core is an alternate installation method to the full Windows desktop version of Server 2016. It installs the necessary technical componentry to behave as a Windows Server, join to your domain, and host the roles and services you need it to host, but it does all of that without a graphical desktop interface. This dramatically lowers the security vulnerability footprint and attack vectors on the server, but does mean you have to re-wire your brain in how you interact with these servers. We will work more with Server Core and the even newer Nano Server coming up in `Chapter 11`, *Nano Server and Server Core*, but since Server Core is a big leap forward for security in many companies, it is appropriate that we start working with it here in our chapter regarding security. Let's take a quick look at the installation process for it, and an initial glance at the interface, so you get familiar with the console you will be looking at on these new, hardened servers you are going to start using.

Getting ready

We are going to build a new instance of Windows Server 2016 but will be making sure to choose the appropriate options for installing Server Core and not the full desktop experience version of the operating system. Our new server will be a VM; it doesn't have to be actual hardware.

How to do it...

Here is a procedure that will get you started rolling out your first instance of Windows Server 2016, Server Core:

1. Create your new VM—or physical server—and insert the Windows Server 2016 installation media, just like you would if you were installing the full version of the operating system. Walk through the installation steps, the only difference being that you want to make sure and choose the default option for **Windows Server 2016 Standard**. Or you can, of course, choose the Datacenter installation option, but the important part here is that you do *NOT* choose the **(Desktop Experience)** version of the operating system, as that would give us a regular old desktop interface just like any other server. By choosing the top option, and notice that it is now the default installation option, we are telling it that we want the more secure Server Core version of Windows Server 2016.

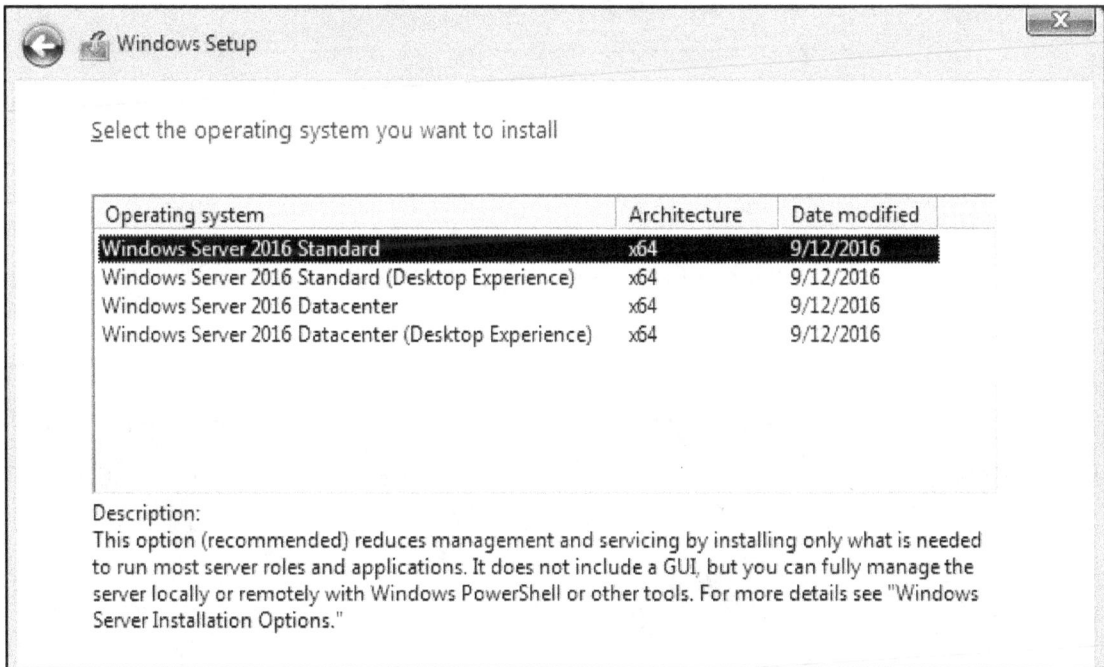

Operating system	Architecture	Date modified
Windows Server 2016 Standard	x64	9/12/2016
Windows Server 2016 Standard (Desktop Experience)	x64	9/12/2016
Windows Server 2016 Datacenter	x64	9/12/2016
Windows Server 2016 Datacenter (Desktop Experience)	x64	9/12/2016

Windows Setup

Select the operating system you want to install

Description:
This option (recommended) reduces management and servicing by installing only what is needed to run most server roles and applications. It does not include a GUI, but you can fully manage the server locally or remotely with Windows PowerShell or other tools. For more details see "Windows Server Installation Options."

2. Finish walking through the installation wizard, and when your new server has booted, instead of being presented with the standard Windows mini-setup wizard in order to start configuring your server, you will simply be presented with the following screen:

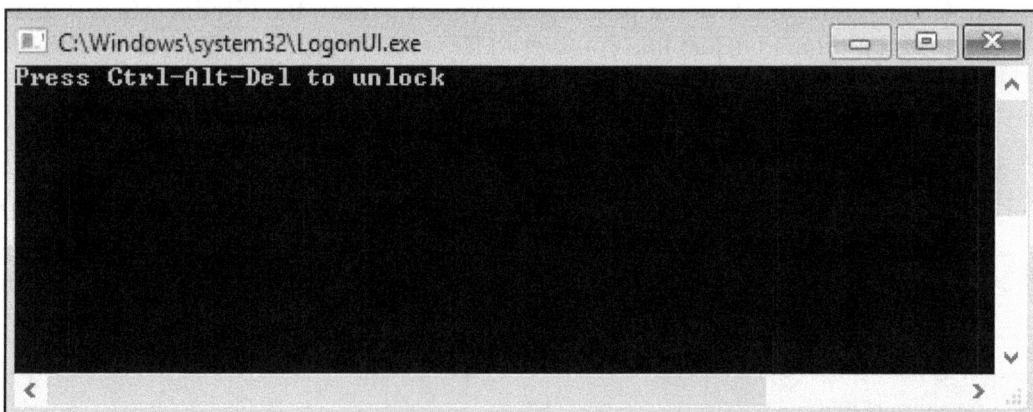

```
C:\Windows\system32\LogonUI.exe
Press Ctrl-Alt-Del to unlock
```

3. Upon pressing *Ctrl* + *Alt* + *Delete* you are prompted to set a password for the local administrator account, after which you will find yourself sitting at a traditional Command Prompt interface. From this interface, you can interact with your new server by using Command Prompt commands, or you can even type powershell in order to move over into the PowerShell interface and start working from there, just like you would with PowerShell on any Windows Server 2016.

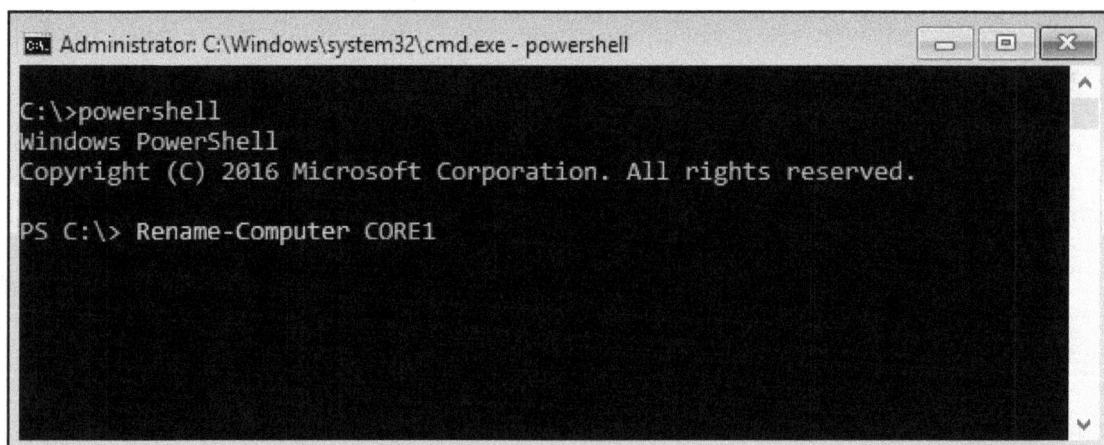

```
Administrator: C:\Windows\system32\cmd.exe - powershell

C:\>powershell
Windows PowerShell
Copyright (C) 2016 Microsoft Corporation. All rights reserved.

PS C:\> Rename-Computer CORE1
```

4. The Server Core Shell is not limited to command-line interfacing. If you were to type `notepad.exe` and press *Enter*, the Notepad application will appear, within which you can utilize your mouse as well as the keyboard.

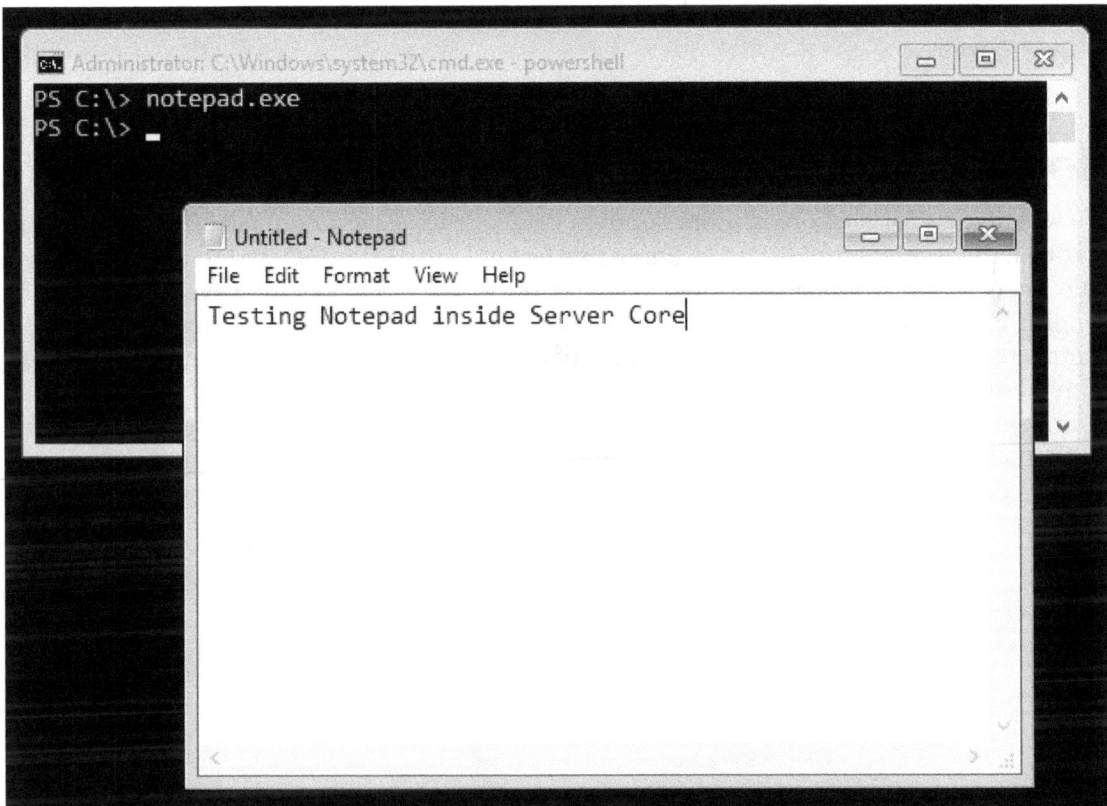

5. From this point, the most common tasks are going to be the same as the things you would do in a desktop experience version of Windows Server 2016. You can use the Command Prompt or PowerShell interfaces to set IP addresses, set a hostname for your server, and even join it to your domain. There are cmdlets that will allow you to install the Windows roles that you need to run on this server as well.

How it works...

We will discuss Server Core in more depth in `Chapter 11`, *Nano Server and Server Core*, but it is critical that server administrators know this technology exists, and start to use it in their day-to-day server workloads. A quick recipe in order to get the operating system up and running is a good start, but working with Server Core regularly and learning the common commands that you will need to use is essential information to really get started interacting with these headless versions of the operating system. Make sure to follow up with the information later in this book so that you can make Server Core a reality in your infrastructure, and not just one of those things you know you should be doing but don't, simply because you are not familiar with it. Server Core can be an enormous security benefit; all you need to do is start using it!

See also

`Chapter 11`, *Nano Server and Server Core*

4
Working with Certificates

Understanding certificates is something that I avoided for many years in my technology career. For many facets of IT, you never had to deal with them. That was for the networking guys, not anybody doing development or desktop support. Times have changed, and a solid understanding of the common certificate types is quickly becoming an ability that anyone in support should possess. More and more security is becoming focused on certificates, and with the exponential increase in the amount of applications that are served via the Web, understanding the certificates that protect these services is more important than ever.

Almost anyone who has set up a website has dealt with SSL certificates from a public **Certification Authority (CA)**, but did you know that you can be your own CA? That you can issue certificates to the machines in your network right from your own CA server? Follow along as we explore some of the capabilities of Windows Server 2016 running as a CA server in your network. Our work in this chapter will cover the following topics:

- Setting up the first Certification Authority server in a network
- Building a Subordinate Certification Authority server
- Creating a certificate template to prepare for issuing machine certificates to your clients
- Publishing a certificate template to allow enrollment
- Using MMC to request a new certificate
- Using the web interface to request a new certificate
- Configuring Autoenrollment to issue certificates to all domain joined systems
- Renewing your root certificate

Introduction

When getting to know a new customer and network as part of my day job, I generally find that one of two things are true. Either they don't have a CA server, or they do, but it isn't being used for anything yet. Most folks know that certificates are upcoming and in demand and that new technologies are released all the time that require a fairly large use of certificates. Technologies such as Lync, SharePoint, System Center, DirectAccess, or even just building a website almost always require the use of a certificate in today's world. Jumping into a project to deploy almost any new system these days will quickly bring you to the realization that a knowledge of certificates is becoming mandatory. Even in places where they aren't required, they are usually still recommended in order to make the solution more secure or to adhere to best practices.

Together, we are going to build a **Public Key Infrastructure** (**PKI**) environment inside our network and use it for some common certificate issuing tasks. By the end of this chapter, you should be comfortable with creating a PKI in your own environment, which will prepare you for any requirements you may encounter when working with certificate-based technologies.

Setting up the first Certification Authority server in a network

The first hurdle to overcome when you want to start certificate work is putting the server into place. There are many valid questions to be answered. Do I need a dedicated server for this task? Can I co-locate this role on an existing server? Do I need to install an Enterprise or stand-alone CA? I've heard the term offline root, but what does that mean? Let's start with the basics and assume that you need to build the first CA server in your environment.

In an AD domain network, the most useful CA servers are of the Enterprise variety. Enterprise CA servers integrate with AD, making them visible to machines in the network and automatically trusted by computers that you join to your domain. There are differing opinions on the matter of best practices when setting up a series of CA servers. For example, there is a good test lab guide (referenced at the end of this recipe) published by Microsoft, which walks you through setting up a stand-alone Root CA, a Subordinate Enterprise CA, and then taking the stand-alone root offline. An advantage of this is that certificates are issued from the subordinate, not directly from the root, and so if certificate keys are somehow compromised in the environment, the Root CA is completely offline and unavailable so that it cannot be compromised. In this situation, you could wipe out the subordinate and the certificates it has published, bring up the offline root, build out a new subordinate, and be back in business publishing certificates without having to regenerate a new Root CA server.

Given the preceding best practice, or as defined by some anyway, it is surprising that I quite rarely see offline Root CAs in the field. Almost never, in fact. And in some of the cases where I have, the existence of an offline Root CA has caused problems. Just as an example, when deploying a DirectAccess infrastructure with one-time-password (OTP) capabilities in a customer environment, it was discovered that in order to make the OTP work correctly, the offline Root CA had to be brought back online. This wasn't in the best interests of the way the PKI had been established, and so instead we had to implement a second certificate environment to be a stand-alone root with two intermediaries in order to maintain an online Root CA for the purpose of the OTP certificates. This caused big delays in the project, as we had to build the three new servers necessary just to get the certificates published in the correct way, which caused a much more complex certificate infrastructure to support afterward.

If the preceding description confused you, good—because it's kind of a messy setup. If the company had instead been running on the online Root CA server in the first place, none of this extra work would have been necessary. I'm not advocating that an Enterprise Root CA that remains online all the time is the best way to do certificates, but it will cause you the fewest problems, and there are many companies that operate their production CA environments in exactly this way.

Another field observation is that most small- or medium-sized companies do not take the offline Root CA approach. In fact, I find that many small businesses need to co-host servers in order to save resources and have their CA role installed onto a server that is also performing some other task. Many times, the CA role is installed onto a Domain Controller. While at the surface level this appears to make sense, because the Enterprise CA services are so tightly integrated with AD, it is actually a bad idea. Microsoft recommends that you never co-host the CA role onto a Domain Controller, so stay away from that scenario if you can. That being said, I have seen dozens of companies that do exactly this and have never had a problem with it, so I suppose it's just your call on how closely you want to adhere to the *Microsoft way*. Make sure to do some reading from the links provided at the end of this recipe, as they should provide you with information that is helpful to make the right decisions about which certificate server setup is best suited for your network.

Getting ready

I have created a new Windows Server 2016 named CA1, a domain member upon which we will be enabling our new certificate infrastructure.

How to do it…

To install Active Directory Certificate Services onto your Server 2016, use the following set of instructions:

1. Open **Server Manager** and click the **Add roles and features** link.
2. Walk through the steps, choosing the default settings. When you come to the **Server Roles** screen, select **Active Directory Certificate Services**.

3. Upon selecting the role, you will be prompted to confirm the installation of additional features. Go ahead and click on **Add Features**.

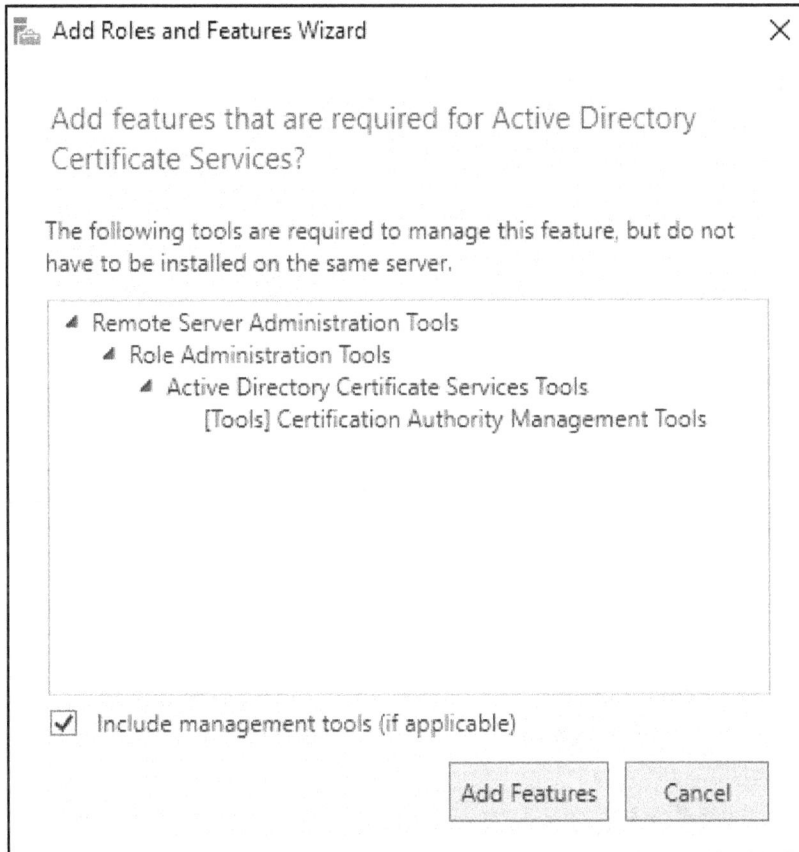

4. Click **Next** a couple of times until you come to the **Role Services** screen. Here you will see a few different options that can be used on your CA server. Since we would like to be able to request certificates from a web interface on the CA, I am going to check the additional box for **Certification Authority Web Enrollment**. After selecting this box, you will receive an additional pop-up box asking you to add features. Make sure to allow those features to be installed.

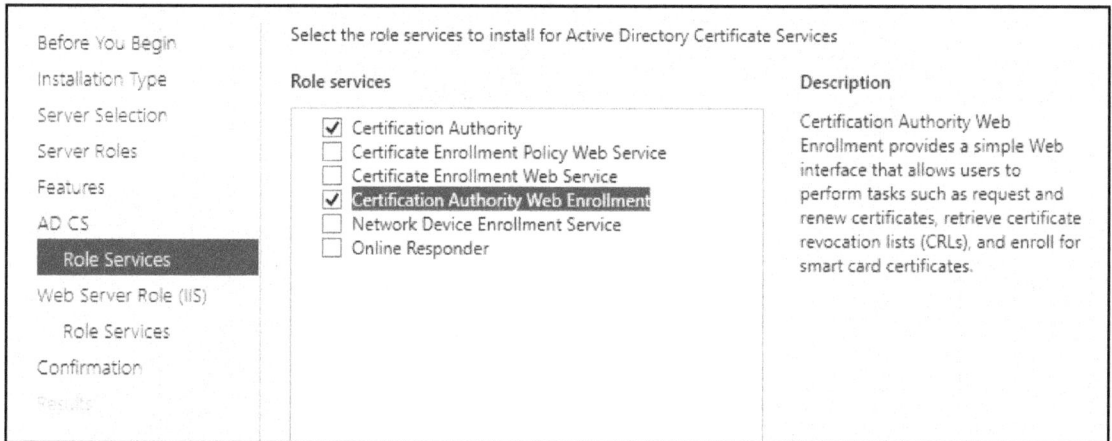

5. Click **Next** through the remaining screens until you reach the last page, where you click on the **Install** button to start the installation of the role.

6. Once completed, you will see a link inside your installation summary screen that says **Configure Active Directory Certificate Services on the destination server**. You can click either on this link or on the Server Manager notifications yellow exclamation mark near the top of the Server Manager screen in order to continue configuring the CA role. On the first configuration screen, the wizard will probably auto-insert the username of the currently logged-in user. As stated in the text on that screen, make sure the user you are logged in as has Enterprise Admin rights on the domain, as we are planning to set this CA server up as an Enterprise Root CA.

You can click on **More about AD CS Server Roles** at any time to read more information about the different types of CA roles and features available. For the purposes of this recipe, we will not discuss them all, but rather focus on creating our Enterprise Root CA.

7. To get certificate services rolling on our server, go ahead and check the top two options to configure **Certification Authority** and **Certification Authority Web Enrollment**.

Credentials	Select Role Services to configure
Role Services	
Setup Type	☑ Certification Authority
CA Type	☑ Certification Authority Web Enrollment
	☐ Online Responder
Private Key	☐ Network Device Enrollment Service
Cryptography	☐ Certificate Enrollment Web Service
CA Name	☐ Certificate Enrollment Policy Web Service

8. Choose **Enterprise CA**.
9. Choose **Root CA;** because this is our first CA server, we need to implement a root before we can think about a subordinate.
10. Choose **Create a new private key**.

11. On the **Cryptography** screen, you have the ability to choose the kind of crypto options you can provide on your CA server. Typically, the default options will work best if you're unsure of these settings. Just make sure that the **Key length** field is set to **2048** as a minimum. This is the new industry standard for the minimum key length. Similarly, hash standards have changed recently to SHA256, you should really no longer be using SHA1 for any of your certificates as it has now been estimated that SHA1 could be compromised in the next couple of years.

Specify the cryptographic options

Select a cryptographic provider: Key length:

| RSA#Microsoft Software Key Storage Provider | ⌄ | 2048 | ⌄ |

Select the hash algorithm for signing certificates issued by this CA:

SHA256	^
SHA384	
SHA512	
SHA1	
MD5	⌄

☐ Allow administrator interaction when the private key is accessed by the CA.

12. If desired, you may modify the **Common name for this CA**. Keep in mind, this does not have to match the hostname of the server in any way. This is the name of the CA that will show up inside Active Directory as well as inside the certificates that you issue from this CA. Typically, I find that admins leave the **Distinguished name suffix** field alone.

Common name for this CA:

MyDomain-CertServer

Distinguished name suffix:

DC=MYDOMAIN,DC=LOCAL

Preview of distinguished name:

CN=MyDomain-CertServer,DC=MYDOMAIN,DC=LOCAL

13. Change the **Validity Period** of your root certificate if desired. Often admins blow through this screen and leave it set at the default five years, but that means in just five short years you will suddenly invalidate every single certificate that you have ever issued from this CA server. I recommend increasing that number to 10 or even 20 years so you don't have to worry about this level of certificate expiry for a long time. The validity period will determine how often the root certificate has to be renewed.

14. Continue through the remaining screens, leaving the default options set in place. When this wizard finishes, your CA server is now live.

15. It is generally a good idea to schedule a reboot for this server after such a significant role installation. Go ahead and reboot when time permits.

The following roles, role services, or features were configured:

(∧) **Active Directory Certificate Services**

Certification Authority   ✓ Configuration succeeded
More about CA Configuration

Certification Authority Web Enrollment   ✓ Configuration succeeded
More about Web Enrollment Configuration

How it works...

In this recipe, we installed the first CA server into our network. As we discussed, you will want to make sure you read over some of the following links to help determine how many CAs you require and where they should be installed. This is one of those answers that can be different for every organization, and so I cannot make any blanket statements here that will apply for everyone. You may decide that your primary Root CA should be stand-alone rather than enterprise, and that is fine as long as it fits your needs. We also installed the web services piece of the role onto our primary CA because we plan to use this in upcoming recipes to issue certificates. If you are building an environment with multiple CA servers, you might determine that your root authority doesn't need the web interface...maybe only a particular subordinate CA will do that job for you. There are numerous ways that our design could play out, but through this recipe, I hope that enough information is provided so that you are comfortable with the actual process once those decisions have been made.

There are a couple of items that we did not cover in this recipe that should be pointed out. Following the preceding steps will get you a CA server up and running that is ready to issue certificates, there is no doubt about that. The remainder of the recipes in this chapter reflect CAs built exactly as shown here. However, there are additional steps that can be taken in order to further customize your CA settings if you have the need. If you plan to issue SSL certificate for websites, especially if you plan to install these certificates onto web servers which are facing the Internet, then you need to familiarize yourself with the **Certificate Revocation List (CRL)** settings. Whenever a certificate is accessed, the client computer checks in with the CRL in order to make sure the certificate is still valid. If the certificate is not valid or is fraudulent in some way, the CRL check will identify that compromise and disallow the connection. Particularly when publishing websites to the Internet that use certificates issued by your internal PKI, you will need to plan the publishing of your CRL so that external client computers can access it in a clean, secure fashion. Here is a great link to get you started on CRL information: `http://technet.micro soft.com/en-us/library/cc771079.aspx`.

The second piece of information I would like to reference is the `CAPolicy.inf` file. This is a file that can be populated with various customization settings for your CA server, such as the validity period of your root certificate, information about your CRL, and whether or not you want the default certificate templates to be loaded during CA role installation. If any of these settings are of interest to you, you simply create a `CAPolicy.inf` file with the appropriate configurations and place it inside `C:\Windows` on your CA server prior to role installation. The role installation wizard will then utilize the settings inside this file during role installation and incorporate your customizations. If you do not use one of these files, it is fine, and the role will be installed with some default settings in place just like we did in this recipe. But if you are interested in changing some of them, check out this link for more detailed information on the `CAPolicy.inf` file: `http://technet.microsoft.com/en-us/library/jj125373.aspx`.

Neither of these items, tweaking the CRL or using a `CAPolicy.inf` file, are required in order to get a certificate environment up and running. Thus, they are not included in the step-by-step configuration of the recipe itself. But I am always a fan of having all knowledge available to me on a particular subject, and so I strongly encourage you to read over these additional links provided to round out your understanding of possible functionality.

See also

Here are some links that make for good additional reading on this subject. In order to make an informed decision about what sequence of CA servers is right for your environment, I encourage you to do as much reading on the subject as possible before proceeding in the production network:

- `http://technet.microsoft.com/en-us/library/dn786443.aspx`
- `http://technet.microsoft.com/en-us/library/dn786436.aspx`
- `http://technet.microsoft.com/en-us/library/hh831348.aspx`

Building a Subordinate Certification Authority server

We build Subordinate CAs not really for the purposes of redundancy, like with many other kinds of servers, but because there are specific tasks that you may want to perform on a subordinate CA rather than a Root CA. If you issue a lot of certificates or different kinds of certificates, you may want to differentiate between CA servers when issuing. Perhaps you want machine certificates that are used for IPsec to be issued from IPSEC-CA, but the SSL website certificates that you issue should show as being issued from WEB-CA. Rather than building out two independent Root CAs that both have top-level rights, you should consider creating a single Root CA, maybe called ROOT-CA, and placing these two CA servers in a subordinate role under the Root CA in the chain. This can also be useful for geographically dispersed networks, having Subordinate CA servers dedicated to assigning certificates for different offices or regions.

As we discussed in the previous recipe, there are certainly some best practice standards that would suggest you only utilize Subordinate CAs to accomplish your certificate issuance. I don't always find that this is feasible for companies, particularly smaller ones, but it is a good idea if you can swing it. With Subordinate CA servers online, you have the option of bringing your Root CA offline, and using the Subordinates to issue all of your certificates.

Getting ready

We are inside a domain network and have a single Enterprise Root CA online and running. We now require an additional server that will be joined to the CA environment as a new Subordinate CA.

How to do it...

To implement our new Subordinate CA server, the process will be very similar to the *Setting up the first Certification Authority server in a network* recipe. However, there are a few key differences, and that is where we will focus. Some of the specific steps may be shortened here; please refer the previous recipe for more detailed information on the specific steps and settings with regards to installation of the role:

1. Log in to our new server, which has already been joined to the domain.
2. Follow the steps to add the Active Directory Certificate Services role to this server.

3. When we implemented our Root CA server, we chose to install the web services as well. This will enable us to request and issue certificates from a browser inside our network. You have the option of installing these web services on the new Subordinate CA, which you would definitely do if you planned on using an offline Root CA, but for our situation, we are not going to do this. We will stick with only **Certification Authority** in our list of available role services.

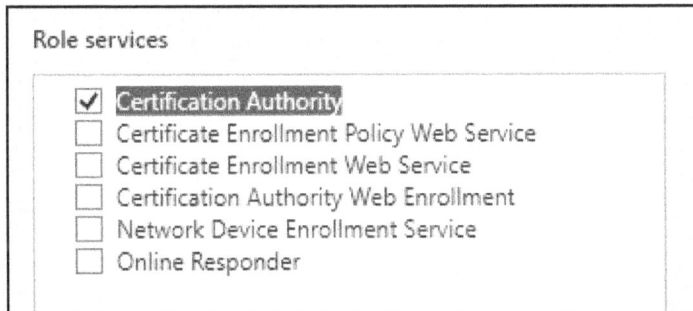

Role services

- ☑ Certification Authority
- ☐ Certificate Enrollment Policy Web Service
- ☐ Certificate Enrollment Web Service
- ☐ Certification Authority Web Enrollment
- ☐ Network Device Enrollment Service
- ☐ Online Responder

4. After the role has finished installing, go ahead and click on your link for **Configure Active Directory Certificate Services on the destination server**.

5. Input credentials as needed and choose the only option we have in the list to configure, **Certificate Authority**.

6. Here is where we start to detour from the path that we took with our Root CA creation. We are still choosing to set up an **Enterprise CA** because we still want it to be domain-integrated.

- ⦿ Enterprise CA

  Enterprise CAs must be domain members and are typically online to issue certificates or certificate policies.

- ○ Standalone CA

  Standalone CAs can be members or a workgroup or domain. Standalone CAs do not require AD DS and can be used without a network connection (offline).

7. But instead of choosing to install a new Root CA, we are going to choose the option for **Subordinate CA**. In fact, it was already chosen for us as the default, because it recognizes that a Root CA already exists in the network. We could install another Root CA, but that is not our purpose in this recipe.

○ Root CA

Root CAs are the first and may be the only CAs configured in a PKI hierarchy.

◉ Subordinate CA

Subordinate CAs require an established PKI hierarchy and are authorized to issue certificates by the CA above them in the hierarchy.

8. Choose **Create a new private key**. The only time we would typically want to use an existing private key is when rebuilding a CA server.
9. Choose your cryptography settings. These are typically going to be the same that you configured on the Root CA.
10. Name your new Subordinate CA appropriately. If you have a specific function in mind for this CA, it will be helpful to you in the future to name it accordingly. For example, I intend to use this subordinate CA to issue all of the SSL certificates that I will need for internal webpages, so I have included *SSL* in the name.

Common name for this CA:

MyDomain-SSLCertServer

11. Now we come to a new screen. We need to acquire a certificate from our parent CA server in order to issue certificates from this new one. Choose the option for **Send a certificate request to a parent CA**, and use the **Select…** button to choose your Root CA.

Send a certificate request to a parent CA:

Select:

⦿ CA name

◯ Computer name

Parent CA: `CA1.MYDOMAIN.LOCAL\MyDomain-CertServer`   Select...

12. On the following screen, adjust the location of the certificate database files if required; otherwise, click **Next**, then **Configure**.

How it works...

Installing a Subordinate CA server in a network is very similar to implementing our first Root CA server. In our case, we simplified the installation by not having the requirement for the web services to run on the Subordinate, we will do all of those requests from the Root CA. We now have a Root CA running and a Subordinate CA running under it. For our installation, we are going to leave both online and running as we intend to issue certificates from both. We could easily run through this same process again with another new server in order to create another Subordinate CA, maybe to issue a different kind of certificate or for a different division of the company to utilize.

See also

- The *Setting up the first Certification Authority server in a network* recipe.

Creating a certificate template to prepare for issuing machine certificates to your clients

This recipe is the first hurdle that many new certificate admins bump into. You may have a CA server up and running, but what's next? Before you can start granting certificates to computers and users, you need to establish certificate templates that you are going to publish. You will configure these templates with particular settings, and when a certificate is requested against the template, that new certificate will be built based on the information in the template combined with the information provided by the certificate requestor.

There are some built-in certificate templates that preinstall when you add the CA role to your server. Some companies utilize these built-in templates for issuing certificates, but it is a better practice to create your own templates. There is no need to start from scratch, though. You can take one of the built-in templates, find one that comes close to meeting your needs, and tweak it to do your bidding with your particular certificate needs. This is the process we are going to be taking. We need to issue machine certificates to each of our systems in the network to authenticate some IPsec tunnels. There are a few criteria we need to meet in these certificates, and the built-in Computer template comes close to checking all the options that we need. So we will take that template, copy it, and modify it to meet our requirements.

Getting ready

This is a Server 2016 domain environment with a new CA server running. We will utilize the CA console on our CA server to accomplish this work today. The new template that we create will be automatically replicated with other CA servers in the domain.

How to do it…

The following steps will help you build a new certificate template:

1. Launch the **Certification Authority** management tool from inside Server Manager.
2. Expand the name of your CA and click on **Certificate Templates**. You will see a list of the built-in templates available to us.
3. Right-click on **Certificate Templates** and choose **Manage**.

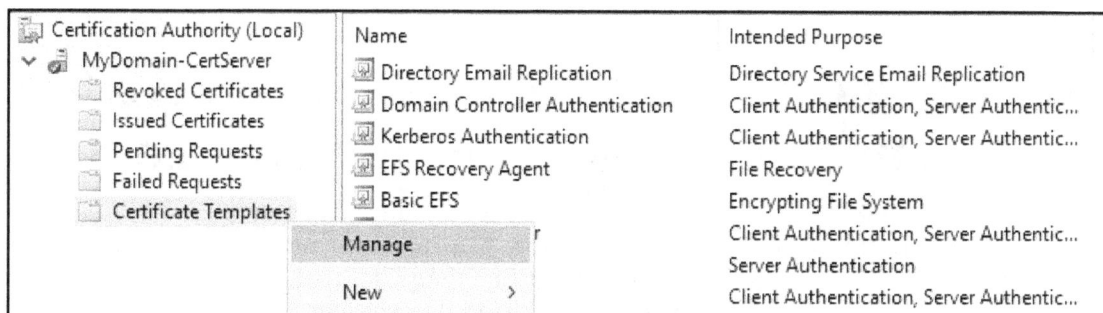

Certification Authority (Local)	Name	Intended Purpose
✓ MyDomain-CertServer	Directory Email Replication	Directory Service Email Replication
Revoked Certificates	Domain Controller Authentication	Client Authentication, Server Authentic…
Issued Certificates	Kerberos Authentication	Client Authentication, Server Authentic…
Pending Requests	EFS Recovery Agent	File Recovery
Failed Requests	Basic EFS	Encrypting File System
Certificate Templates		Client Authentication, Server Authentic…
Manage	r	Server Authentication
New >		Client Authentication, Server Authentic…

4. Right-click on the **Computer** template and choose **Duplicate Template**.

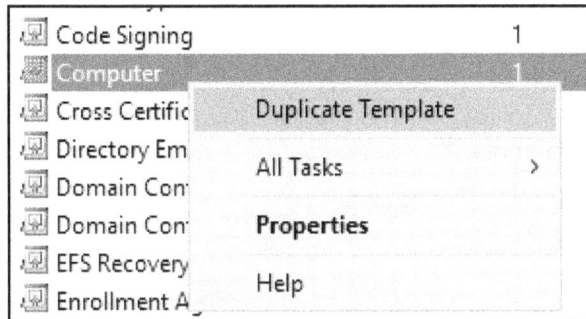

5. Now we adjust options within the certificate template. Any attributes that your certificates must have, you set here in the template properties. As an example, let's configure a few items that our new IPsec certificates must contain to be valid.

6. Go to the **General** tab and set the **Template display name** so that you can identify this new template we are building.

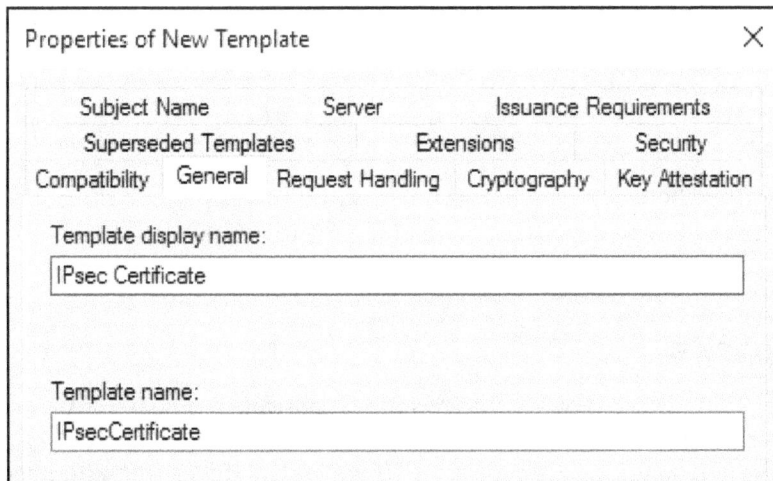

7. On the same tab, adjust the **Validity period** field to 2 years.

8. Browse to the **Subject Name** tab and set **Common name** as the **Subject name format** field. This will cause the subject name of the certificate to reflect the hostname of the computer that is requesting the certificate. Using the DNS name as the alternate subject name is another requirement that we have been given for our new certificates. You can see it checked in the screenshot below. Since we used the built-in Computer template as our starting point, this checkbox, as well as other requirements that we needed covered, were already taken care of for us.

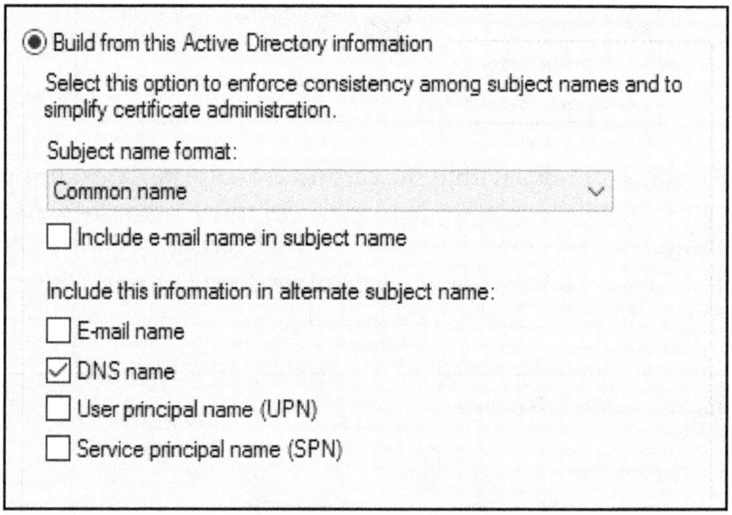

9. Click **OK**. There is now a brand new certificate template in the list called `IPsec Certificate` (or whatever name you gave to yours).

How it works...

When installing any new technology that requires certificates to be issued, your first stop should be the certificate templates on your CA server. You need to make sure that you have a template configured with the appropriate settings and switches that you need in your new certificates. By duplicating one of the built-in templates that came with our CA server, we were able to build a new template without having to configure every single option from the ground up.

Publishing a certificate template to allow enrollment

One of the most common certificate troubleshooting tasks I encounter is figuring out why a particular certificate template is not available when the user or computer tries to request a certificate. Having created a new certificate template does not necessarily mean that you are ready to start issuing certificates based on that template. We also need to publish our new template so that the CA server knows that it is ready to publish out to computers and users. There is also a security section of the template properties, where you need to define who or what has access to request certificates based on that template. In this recipe, we will find those settings and configure our new certificate template so that any domain joined workstation is allowed to request a certificate from our new template.

Getting ready

We are going to use the Windows Server 2016 machine that is our Enterprise Root CA.

How to do it...

In order to issue certificates based on a particular template, we need to take steps to publish and adjust the security properties of that template:

1. Launch the **Certification Authority** management tool from inside Server Manager.
2. Expand the name of your CA server in the left-hand tree.

3. Right-click on **Certificate Templates** and navigate to **New** | **Certificate Template to Issue**.

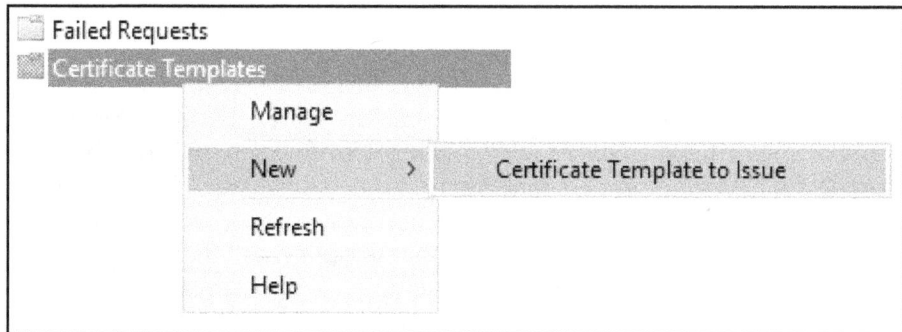

Failed Requests		
Certificate Templates		
	Manage	
	New >	Certificate Template to Issue
	Refresh	
	Help	

4. Select your new template from the list and click on **OK**.
5. Now right-click on **Certificate Templates** and choose **Manage**.
6. Find the template that you want to modify. For our recipe, we are modifying the new template called IPsec Certificate.
7. Right-click on the template and choose **Properties**.
8. Browse to the **Security** tab.
9. Now we need to set up permissions according to your requirements. For our particular example, we want to issue IPsec certificates to all domain joined computers so that they can later be used during IPsec negotiations inside our network. Therefore, in our permissions, we add **Domain Computers** and we check the box to allow **Enroll** permissions.

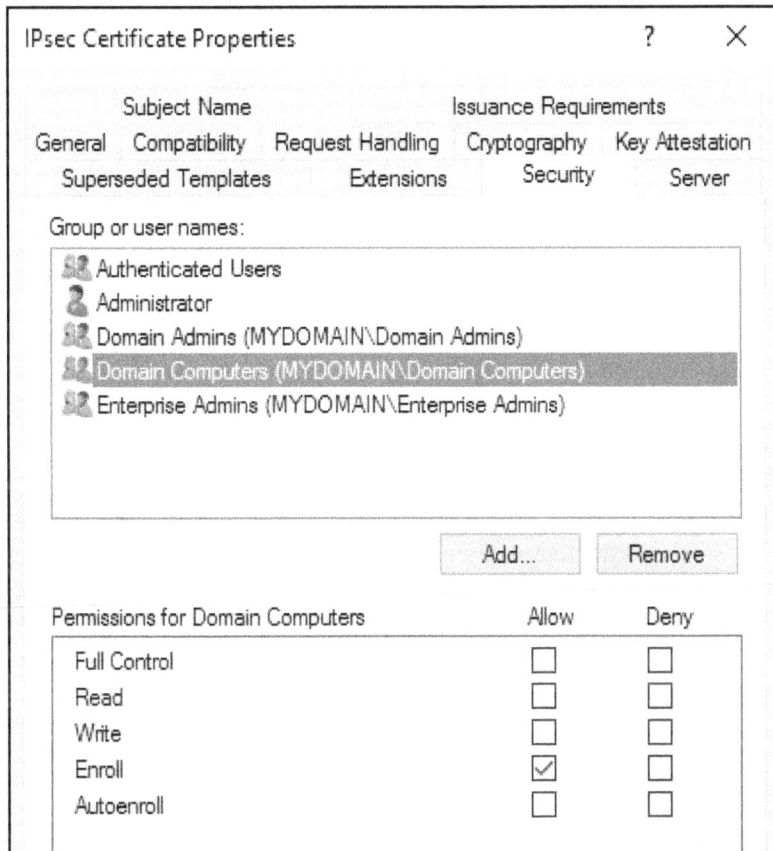

IPsec Certificate Properties   ?   ✕

Subject Name		Issuance Requirements	
General Compatibility Request Handling Cryptography Key Attestation			
Superseded Templates Extensions Security Server			

Group or user names:

- Authenticated Users
- Administrator
- Domain Admins (MYDOMAIN\Domain Admins)
- **Domain Computers (MYDOMAIN\Domain Computers)**
- Enterprise Admins (MYDOMAIN\Enterprise Admins)

[Add...]   [Remove]

Permissions for Domain Computers   Allow   Deny

	Allow	Deny
Full Control	☐	☐
Read	☐	☐
Write	☐	☐
Enroll	☑	☐
Autoenroll	☐	☐

How it works...

A new certificate template doesn't do us any good without a couple of extra steps to publish that template. We need to walk through the process of specifying our new template to be issued, which is a simple option to accomplish but one that isn't immediately obvious inside the CA management console. Also, we need to make sure that the permissions we have set on our certificate template line up with the purpose for which our certificate is intended. If your user accounts are going to be requesting certificates, then you will have to add users or user groups and grant them enroll permissions. If computer accounts are going to be the ones making the requests, then make sure that the appropriate groups are entered in there with enrolling rights as well.

Using MMC to request a new certificate

The most common way that I see administrators interface with the certificates on their systems is through the MMC snap-in tool. **MMC** is short for **Microsoft Management Console**, and by using MMC, you can administer just about anything in the operating system. Though this is perhaps a greatly underutilized tool, I only generally see it being opened for a few select tasks. Requesting certificates is one of those tasks.

We are going to use the MMC console on a new server that we have in our network. There is a new certificate template that has been created, and we would like to issue one of these certificates to our new web server.

Getting ready

A Server 2016 Enterprise Root CA server is online and running in our network. On it, we have configured a new certificate template called `IPsec Certificate`. The steps have been taken to publish this template so that it may be requested from computers in our network. We are now working from a brand new web server that is also running Server 2016 and joined to our domain, where we are going to accomplish the work of manually requesting a certificate from the CA server.

How to do it...

Follow these steps to request a new certificate using the MMC console:

1. Open Command Prompt on our new web server and type `mmc`. Then press *Enter*. Alternatively, you could open MMC from the **Start** screen.
2. Now inside the MMC console, click on the **File** menu, then on **Add/Remove Snap-in...**.
3. Choose **Certificates** from the list of available snap-ins and click on the **Add** button. This will bring a new window with some more choices about the certificates snap-in.
4. First, we need to choose whether we are opening the user certificate repository or the Computer certificate repository. I don't generally see service account used in the field. The selection here will depend on what type of certificate you are requesting. For our example, we are looking for an IPsec certificate, which needs to go in the Computer container. Choose **Computer account** and click **Finish**.

This snap-in will always manage certificates for:

○ My user account

○ Service account

● Computer account

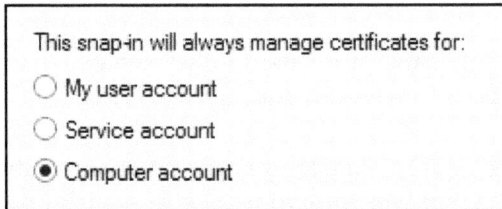

5. Leave the next option set on the **Local computer** and click **Finish** again.
6. Click **OK**.
7. There are also MSC launchers that can be utilized to bring you into the certificate stores even faster. Make use of these by navigating to **Start** | **Run** or Command Prompt and type the following commands:

    • CERTMGR.MSC opens user certificates

    • CERTLM.MSC opens computer certificates

8. Now back inside the main MMC console, expand **Certificates (Local Computer)** and select the Personal folder. You can see that there are currently no certificates installed here.
9. Right-click on the Personal folder and navigate to **All Tasks** | **Request New Certificate...**.

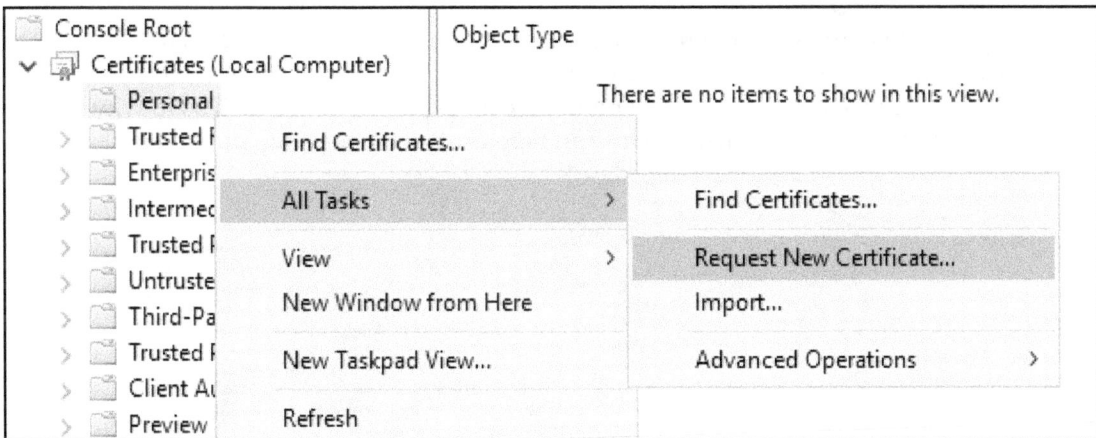

Console Root			Object Type	
✓ Certificates (Local Computer)				
Personal			There are no items to show in this view.	
> Trusted F	Find Certificates...			
> Enterpris				
> Intermec	All Tasks	>	Find Certificates...	
> Trusted F	View	>	Request New Certificate...	
> Untruste	New Window from Here		Import...	
> Third-Pa				
> Trusted F	New Taskpad View...		Advanced Operations	>
> Client Au				
> Preview	Refresh			

10. Click **Next**.

11. On the **Select Certificate Enrollment Policy** screen, **Active Directory Enrollment Policy** is automatically selected. Simply click **Next** again to go on to the next screen.

12. Now we see a list of certificate templates that are available to us. Check the boxes for the certificates that you want to request and click **Enroll**.

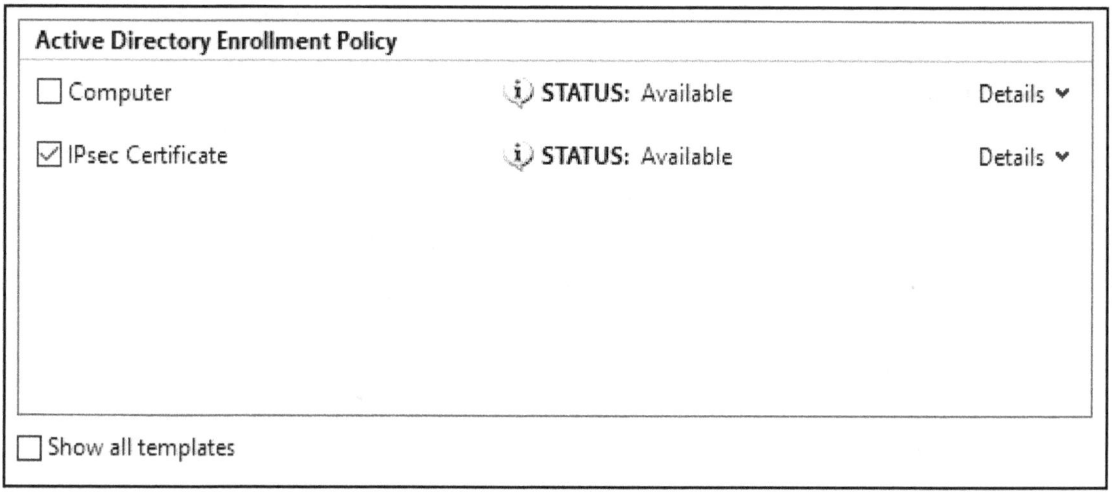

Active Directory Enrollment Policy

☐ Computer   ⓘ **STATUS:** Available   Details ∨

☑ IPsec Certificate   ⓘ **STATUS:** Available   Details ∨

☐ Show all templates

TIP

If you are expecting to see a particular template here but it doesn't show up in the list, click on **Show all templates**. This will display a list of all templates on the CA server and give an explanation for each as to why it is not currently available. This can help for troubleshooting purposes.

How it works...

Utilizing the MMC console is a quick and easy way to request new certificates to be issued manually. In an Active Directory environment, any certificate template on the CA server that you have permissions to enroll will be visible and easy to enroll. Our example today displayed the enrollment process for a machine certificate that we are planning to use in the future for IPsec authentication. However, there are many cases where you may want to issue user-level certificates, rather than computer certificates. In those cases, you would want to snap-in the User account certificates, where in our example, we defined computer account certificates.

Using the web interface to request a new certificate

Sometimes when requesting a new certificate, you may not have access to query certificate services directly by using a tool such as the MMC snap-in. Or perhaps you want to provide a way for users to be able to request certificates even while outside the office. By enabling the web services portion of the CA role, we turn on a website that runs on our CA server. This website can be accessed from inside the corporate network and could potentially even be published out to the Internet with some kind of a reverse proxy solution.

For our recipe today, let's access the web interface that is now running on the CA server where we installed the web services part of the CA role. We will use this website to request and acquire a certificate on our client computer.

Getting ready

Our Enterprise Root CA is a Windows Server 2016 that has the Active Directory Certificate Services role installed. When we installed and configured the role, we made sure to select the option for the web service so that we could make use of it to request a new certificate.

How to do it...

We do not have to be logged into the CA server directly to accomplish this work. Instead, we are logged into a new web server in our environment. From this web server, we take the following steps:

1. Open Internet Explorer and browse to `https://<CAServerName>/CertSrv/`. In our case, it is `https://CA1/CertSrv/`.

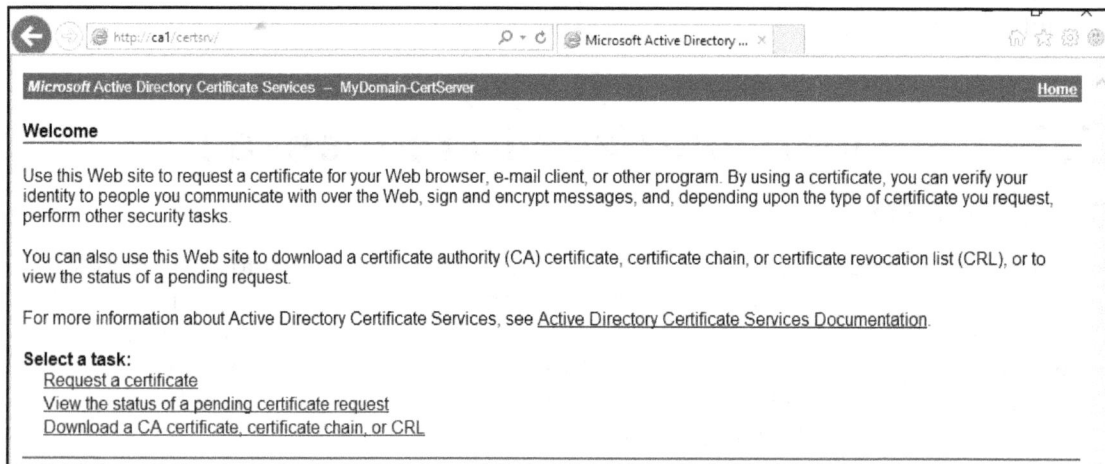

---

http://ca1/certsrv/   🔍 ▾ ⭮ 🌐 Microsoft Active Directory ... ✕   ⌂ ☆ ⚙ ⚙

Microsoft Active Directory Certificate Services — MyDomain-CertServer   Home

Welcome

Use this Web site to request a certificate for your Web browser, e-mail client, or other program. By using a certificate, you can verify your identity to people you communicate with over the Web, sign and encrypt messages, and, depending upon the type of certificate you request, perform other security tasks.

You can also use this Web site to download a certificate authority (CA) certificate, certificate chain, or certificate revocation list (CRL), or to view the status of a pending request.

For more information about Active Directory Certificate Services, see Active Directory Certificate Services Documentation.

Select a task:
Request a certificate
View the status of a pending certificate request
Download a CA certificate, certificate chain, or CRL

> **TIP**
>
> Make sure you specify to access the site using HTTPS or you will not be allowed to finish requesting a certificate later during the wizard.

2. Click on **Request a certificate**.

---

3. You will see there is a pre-built request in there for acquiring a user certificate. For one of those, you simply click on that link, then click Submit on the next screen. However, to dig a little deeper with our recipe, we are going to request an SSL certificate, not a user certificate. To start the process, click on **advanced certificate request**.

4. Choose **Create and submit a request to this CA**.

5. Click **Yes** if prompted with the following message:

Web Access Confirmation   ✕

   ⚠   This Web site is attempting to perform a digital certificate operation on
         your behalf:

         https://ca1/certsrv/certrqma.asp

         You should only allow known Web sites to perform digital certificate
         operations on your behalf.
         Do you want to allow this operation?

                                   Yes   No

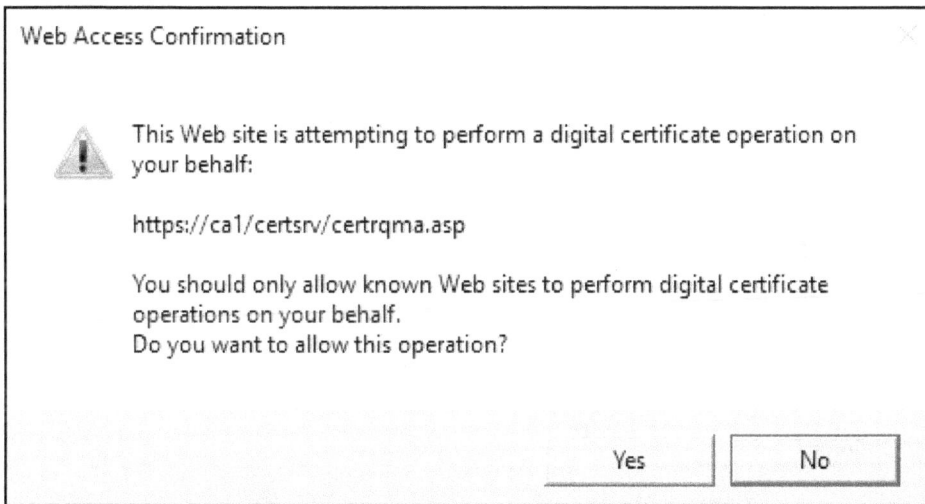

6. Choose the **Certificate Template** that you would like to use in order to accomplish your certificate request. On my Root CA server where the web services are installed, I set up a new template, which I duplicated from the Web Server template with my specific certificate requirements. I called this template **Custom Web Server** and have published it to be available for enrollment.

7. Because this is an SSL certificate, I need to populate the regularly requested information. My website name and company contact info is entered here.

8. The rest of the options available to change are already configured as I want them to be. This is because when I set up my Custom Web Server template, I already specified all of these item defaults. Here is my request:

Advanced Certificate Request

Certificate Template:

> Custom Web Server ▼

Identifying Information For Offline Template:

Name:	sharepoint.mydomain.local
E-Mail:	
Company:	Your Company name
Department:	Web
City:	YourCity
State:	YourState
Country/Region:	US

Key Options:

◉ Create new key set   ○ Use existing key set

CSP: Microsoft RSA SChannel Cryptographic Provider ▼

Key Usage: ◉ Exchange

Key Size: 2048   Min: 2048 Max:16384   (common key sizes: 2048 4096 8192 16384)

◉ Automatic key container name   ○ User specified key container name

☑ Mark keys as exportable

☐ Enable strong private key protection

---

9. Click **Submit**.
10. Your browser will spin for a minute while the CA server creates the new certificate based on the information that you entered. When it is finished, you should have a link to click on called **Install this certificate**. Go ahead and click that link.

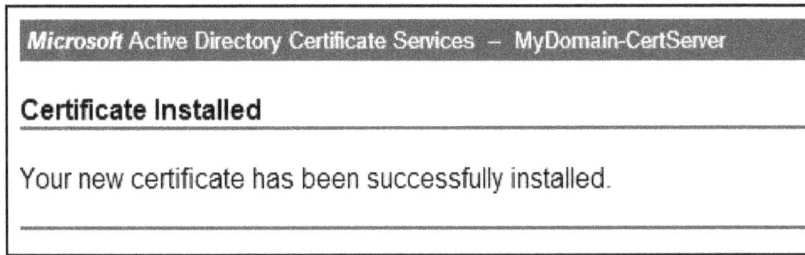

```
Microsoft Active Directory Certificate Services  —  MyDomain-CertServer

Certificate Installed

Your new certificate has been successfully installed.
```

How it works...

Running the web service on your CA server can be beneficial because it allows another method of requesting certificates. In this recipe, we were able to very quickly pull open our CA certificate requesting webpage and walk through some simple steps. This enabled us to download a new certificate that we are planning to use with our new web server's SharePoint site.

Because our web server is inside the corporate network, we could have also accomplished this request right from the Certificates MMC console. However, if our web server had been in a different building separated by networking equipment and firewalls, this may not have been an option for us. Or if we were trying to acquire a certificate from another machine that didn't have the MMC access for one reason or another, this web service is a nice way to accomplish the same task.

Configuring Autoenrollment to issue certificates to all domain joined systems

A lot of the new technologies requiring certificates to be used for authentication require those certificates to be distributed on a large scale. For example, if we want to use the Computer certificate for DirectAccess authentication, we need to issue a certificate to every DirectAccess client computer. This could be thousands of laptops in your network. If we want to start encrypting traffic inside the network with IPsec and require certificates to be distributed for that purpose, you would potentially need to issue some kind of machine certificate to every computer inside your network. While you could certainly issue each by hand using either the MMC console or the CA web interface, that doesn't sound like very much fun.

Enter **Autoenrollment**. We can turn on this feature, which is sort of like flipping a switch in Active Directory, and in doing so we can tell AD to issue certificates automatically to the computers, even if we need to get them to every single domain joined the system. Let's work together through this recipe to turn on this option and test it out.

Getting ready

We are working inside a Windows Server 2016 based Active Directory domain. We also have a Server 2016 Enterprise Root CA running in this network. The work that we will be accomplishing is a combination of work on the CA server and work inside Group Policy on a Domain Controller.

How to do it...

To enable Autoenrollment in your domain, take a look at these instructions:

1. Log into your CA server and open up **Certification Authority**. Expand the name of your CA, then right-click on **Certificate Templates** and choose **Manage**.
2. Now choose which certificate template that you want to be set up for Autoenrollment. I have a template called **DA Cert** that I want issued to every computer in my network. Right-click on **DA Cert** and head into **Properties**.
3. Click on the **Security** tab. Here you need to configure whatever users, computers, or other objects that you want to have Autoenroll permissions to this template. I am going to **Allow** the **Autoenroll** permission for all **Domain Computers** in my network, as shown in the following screenshot:

DA Cert Properties   ?   ✕

Subject Name		Issuance Requirements	
General	Compatibility	Request Handling	Cryptography	Key Attestation
Superseded Templates		Extensions	Security	Server

Group or user names:

- Authenticated Users
- Administrator
- Domain Admins (MYDOMAIN\Domain Admins)
- Domain Computers (MYDOMAIN\Domain Computers)
- Enterprise Admins (MYDOMAIN\Enterprise Admins)

Add...   Remove

Permissions for Domain Computers	Allow	Deny
Full Control	☐	☐
Read	☑	☐
Write	☐	☐
Enroll	☑	☐
Autoenroll	☑	☐

For special permissions or advanced settings, click Advanced.   Advanced

OK   Cancel   Apply   Help

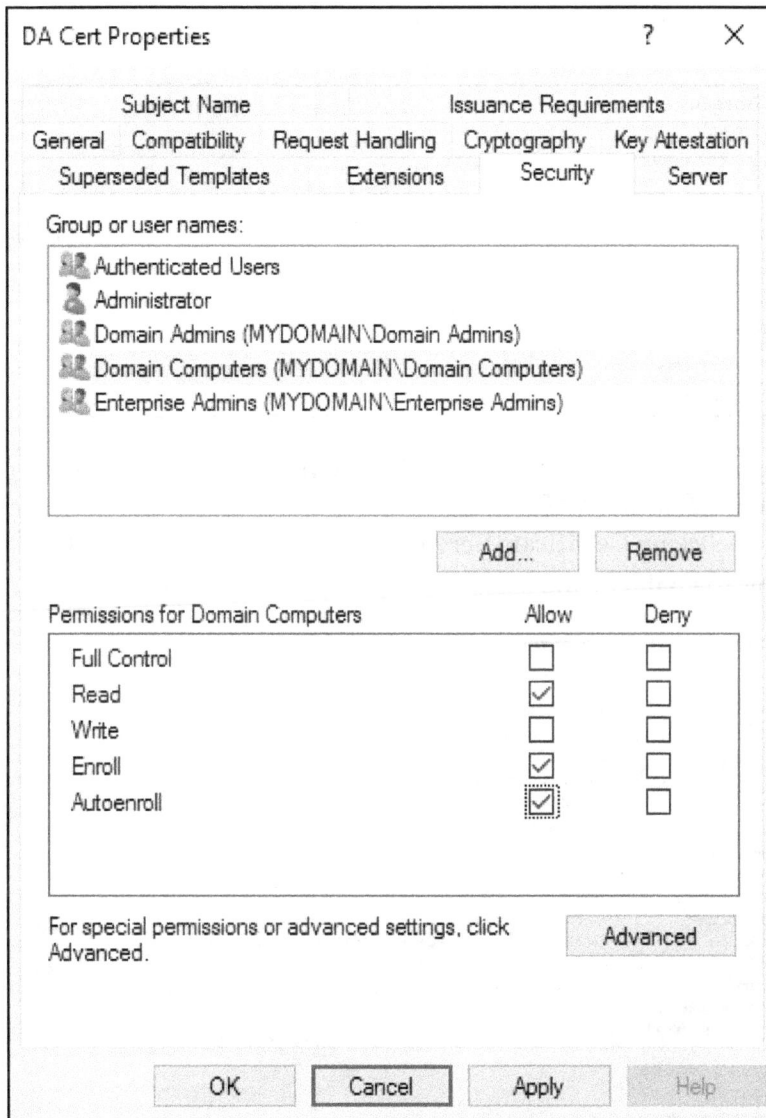

4. Click **OK**, and now we need to head over to Group Policy. Log into a Domain Controller and open the **Group Policy Management Console**.

5. I have created a new GPO for this task called **Certificate Autoenrollment Policy**. This new GPO is linked to the top of my domain so that it applies to all machines that are joined to the domain. If you didn't need your policy to be so broad, you could of course pare down the access here by limiting the link or filtering associated with your GPO.

6. Right-click on the **Certificate Autoenrollment Policy** GPO and choose **Edit....**

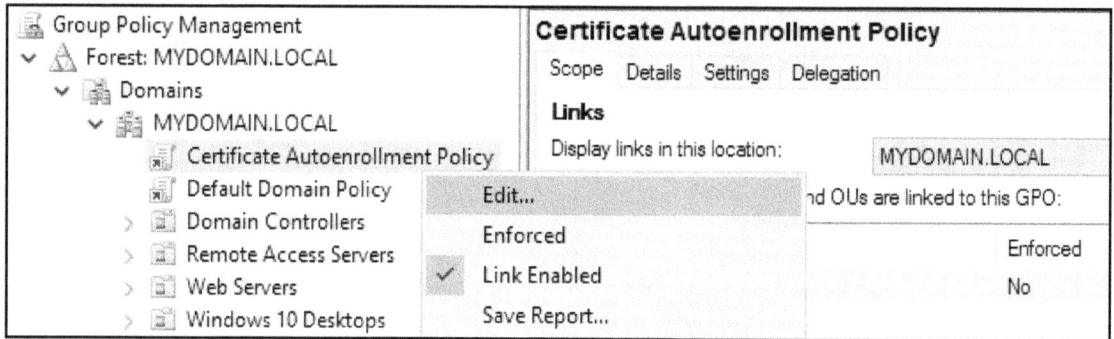

7. Navigate to **Computer Configuration | Policies | Windows Settings | Security Settings | Public Key Policies**.
8. Double-click on **Certificate Services Client – Auto-Enrollment**.
9. Set this to **Enabled**, and select both of the checkboxes on the screen.

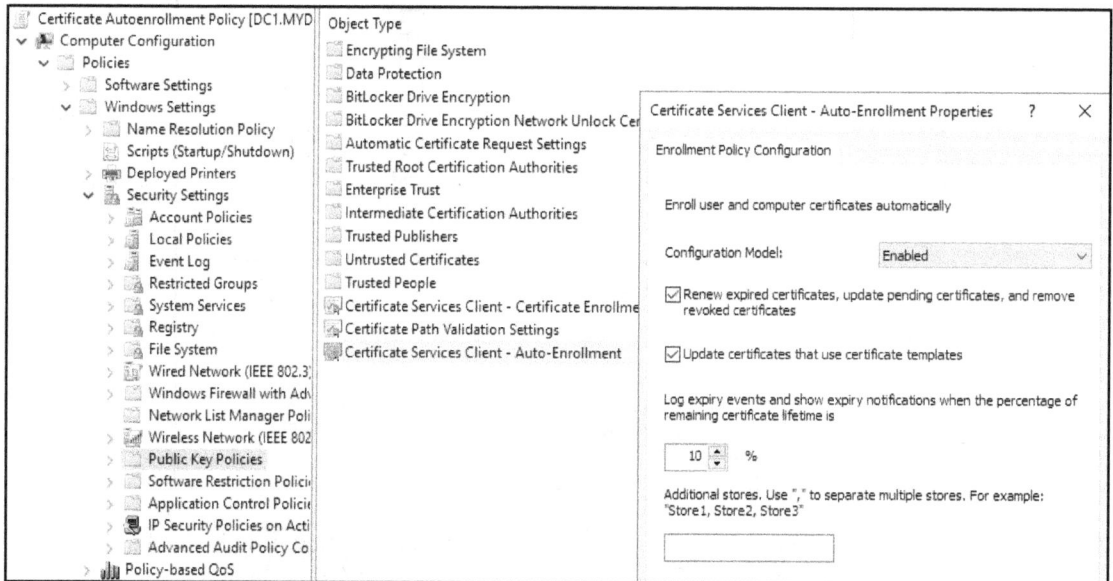

10. As soon as you click **OK**, this new GPO will start taking effect. Machines will check in with Group Policy and realize they need these new settings from the GPO. Upon putting this new option into place, the computers will then check in with the CA server and ask it for a copy of any certificate for which it has autoenroll permissions. Since we configured all Domain Computers to have autoenroll permission to our DA Cert template, our workstations and servers should immediately start receiving a copy of this new certificate. Here is a screenshot from my CA server just a few minutes after configuring this GPO. You can see that it is starting to issue certificates to my domain-joined systems:

7	MYDOMAIN\DC1$	-----BEGIN C...	Directory Email Repli...
8	MYDOMAIN\WEB1$	-----BEGIN C...	DA Cert (1.3.6.1.4.1.3...
9	MYDOMAIN\CA2$	-----BEGIN C...	DA Cert (1.3.6.1.4.1.3...

How it works...

We make use of Group Policy in order to flip our autoenrollment on-switch and immediately start the autoenrollment of certificates to our domain-joined systems. There are a couple of different ways that autoenrollment can be regulated. You can decide who gets the autoenrollment policy applied to them through Group Policy links and filtering, meaning that you can define in the GPO properties which users or computers are going to be subject to autoenrollment in the first place. Alternatively, or additionally, you can also specify permissions inside each certificate template on the CA server so that you can better determine which users or computers in your environment will receive copies of each template once autoenrollment is enabled.

Planning is essential to this task. You need to build a clear definition for what certificates you need to publish, and to which devices or people you need that certificate to roll itself out to. Follow the steps incorrectly and it may not work, or worse yet, you may end up with a thousand certificates being issued all over your network that you did not intend to be distributed. Group Policy is extremely powerful, and tapping into that power comes with great responsibility.

After configuring these settings, if you reboot a few domain joined machines in your network, you will notice that when they come back online, there will be a new certificate sitting in the computer's personal certificate store. Sit back and wait a few hours, and they will have rolled around to everybody automatically. If you don't like waiting for Group Policy to refresh, you can open Command Prompt on some of those computers and issue the `gpupdate /force` command to manually refresh the policies and pull down the certificate.

Renewing your root certificate

Remember a few pages back, when we configured the first CA server in our environment, the Enterprise Root? We left many of the default options in place, and that means that our root certificate is set automatically with a validity period of five years. This seems like a long time, but five years can flash by in an instant, especially if you have kids. So what happens when that root certificate finally does expire? Bad things happen. You will definitely want to keep track of the expiration date on your root certificates, and make sure to renew them before they expire!

Getting ready

We just built this new CA server, so we are not in danger of our root certificate expiring anytime soon. However, it is important to understand how to accomplish this task, so we are going to walk through the process of renewing the root authority certificate. We will accomplish this task right from our CA server itself.

How to do it...

To renew your CA's root certificate, take the following steps:

1. Log into the Enterprise Root CA server and open the **Certification Authority** management console.
2. Right-click on the name of your CA, navigate to **All Tasks** and then choose **Renew CA Certificate...**

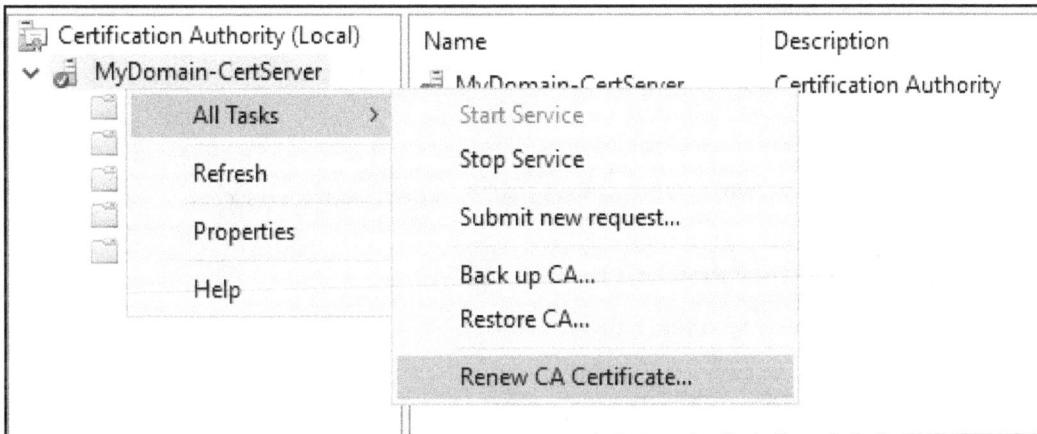

Certification Authority (Local)	Name	Description
MyDomain-CertServer	MyDomain-CertServer	Certification Authority

All Tasks >

    Start Service

Refresh

    Stop Service

Properties

    Submit new request...

Help

    Back up CA...

    Restore CA...

    Renew CA Certificate...

If you haven't stopped ADCS during this process, you will be prompted to do so. Go ahead and click **Yes** in order to stop the certificate processes temporarily.

3. On the **Renew CA Certificate** screen, you only have one option to worry about. You need to choose whether you want to generate a new key pair for the new root certificate or re-use the existing one. If you have published many certificates from this CA, it is generally easier to say **No** to this and let it re-use the existing key pair. As you can see on the screen, there are some situations where you would want to choose **Yes** and create a new key pair, so the correct answer to this question is going to depend on your situation and your needs.

Renew CA Certificate ☐ ✕

In addition to obtaining a new certificate for your certification authority (CA), you also have the option of generating a new signing key.

You need a new certificate for your CA when:

The lifetime of the certificates you are currently issuing is reduced.

You need a new signing key when:

The signing key is compromised.

You have a program that requires a new signing key to be used with a new CA certificate.

The current certificate revocation list (CRL) is too big, and you want to move some of the information to a new CRL.

Do you want to generate a new public and private key pair? The cryptographic service provider and hash algorithm settings will be preserved. If the existing key length is less than 1024 bits, it may be increased.

○ Yes
◉ No

[OK] [Cancel]

---

4. Click **OK**, and the new root certificate is immediately created and starts being distributed via Group Policy.

How it works...

Your top-level root certificate is critical to the overall health of your PKI infrastructure. If this certificate expires, every single certificate that has ever been issued from your CA servers will immediately become invalid. Fortunately, renewing this root certificate is generally pretty easy. Simply follow our steps and you're back in business for another 5 or 10 years. When you renew the root authority certificate, it places the new copy of that certificate into Group Policy's Trusted Root Authorities location. All systems joined to a domain keep this list updated automatically through Group Policy so that whenever you add a new CA server or renew an existing root certificate, the new trusts associated with that new certificate are automatically distributed to all of your client machines and servers. Therefore, generally, all you have to do is renew the certificate and sit back and relax, because Group Policy will start pushing that new certificate into place all across your network.

However—and this is a BIG however—if you let your root authority certificate expire and you have issued certificates that are being used by clients and servers for network authentication, the root certificate expiry will cause those systems to no longer be connected to the network. You can easily renew the root certificate and get the backend up and running, but without having a valid way to authenticate to the network, your systems that are relying on a valid certificate to connect to that network will be dead in the water. You will need to figure out an alternative way to connect them to the network and update their Group Policy before they will learn how to trust the newly refreshed root authority certificate. This warning comes to mind for me because I just helped a company combat exactly this issue. Their root certificate expired, and they had whole offices, worth of people who were connecting to the data center and the domain solely through the DirectAccess remote connectivity technology. DirectAccess relies on certificates as part of its authentication process, so those remote systems were completely unable to communicate with the network once their root cert expired. We had to connect them to the network in a different way in order to pull down GPO settings and a new copy of the new root certificate before they could start connecting remotely again.

Moral of the story: make sure you mark your calendars to renew certificates BEFORE they expire!

5
Internet Information Services

Websites and web services are used for everything these days. With the evolution of Cloud, we are accessing more and more via web browsers than we ever have before. The cloud can mean very different things to different people, but what I see most commonly in Enterprise is the creation of private clouds. This generally means a collection of web servers that are being used to serve up web applications for the company's user population to work from. Sometimes, the private cloud is onsite in a company's data center; sometimes it is in a co-location; and sometimes it is a combination of local data center and a true cloud web service provider such as Azure. Whatever defines a private cloud for you, one variable is the same. Your cloud includes web servers that need to be managed and administered.

For any Microsoft-centric shop, your web servers should be running Windows Server with the **Internet Information Services (IIS)** role installed. IIS is the website platform in Windows Server 2016, and with it we can run any kind of website or web service that we need. The hope for this collection of recipes is to give you a solid foundation to understand the way that websites work within IIS. Even if you don't normally set up new web services, you may very well have to troubleshoot one. Becoming familiar with the console and options, and just understanding the parts and pieces, can be hugely beneficial to anyone administering servers in a Windows environment. In this chapter, we will cover following recipes:

- Installing the Web Server role with PowerShell
- Launching your first website
- Changing the port on which your website runs
- Adding encryption to your website
- Using a Certificate Signing Request to acquire your SSL certificate
- Moving an SSL certificate from one server to another

- Rebinding your renewed certificates automatically
- Hosting multiple websites on your IIS server
- Using host headers to manage multiple websites on a single IP address

Introduction

If you have been reading through this recipe book from start to finish, you probably noticed that we utilize our new web server a lot when testing or rounding out tasks in our infrastructure. So our web server has a whole bunch of things on it that have been pushed down as a result of regular network tasks that we have done, but we aren't doing any actual web serving with it yet!

We are going to assume, for most tasks in this chapter, that the role for IIS is already installed on the web server. This role is specifically called Web Server (IIS) in the list of roles, and there are numerous additional features that we can add to IIS. For all of our recipes, we only need the defaults added, the ones that are selected automatically when installing the role. That role installation is the only thing a Windows Server 2016 box needs in order to serve up web pages to users, other than a little bit of knowledge of how to get the site doing what you want it to do. In order to get the role installed properly, make sure to stop by the *Installing the Web Server role with PowerShell* recipe in order to put that component into place. Let's get familiar with some of the common tasks in IIS.

Installing the Web Server role with PowerShell

If you haven't started using PowerShell to accomplish some of your regular Windows Server tasks, do it now! PowerShell can be used in Windows Server 2016 to accomplish any task or configuration inside the operating system. I am a huge fan of using the keyboard instead of the mouse in any circumstance, and saving scripts that can be used over and over to save time in the future.

In this recipe, we are going to explore the `Install-WindowsFeature` cmdlet, which can be used to add a role or roles to your Server 2016. Since we are discussing IIS in this chapter, let's take our newly created web server and use PowerShell to place the Web Server (IIS) role onto it.

Getting ready

There is a new Windows Server 2016 web server in our environment called WEB2. Let's use PowerShell on this machine in order to install the IIS role.

How to do it...

To add the Web Server (IIS) role to WEB2 via PowerShell, follow these steps:

1. Log in to WEB2 and open a PowerShell prompt; make sure to run it as administrator.

2. All we have to do is run the proper cmdlet specifying the role name, but the specific name of our role evades me. Well, not really, but I thought this would be a good opportunity to explore another command that will help us see a list of the available roles to be installed. Type the following command to see the list of roles:

`Get-WindowsFeature`

3. Whoa! There's a big list of all the roles and features that can be installed on this server. Scrolling up, I can see `Web Server (IIS)` in the list, and it looks like the role name is `Web-Server`. I am going to keep that name in mind, and since we have the ability to install multiple items at the same time, I am also going to note `Web-Common-Http` in order to install the common HTTP features when I install the role.

```
[ ] Volume Activation Services              VolumeActivation
[ ] Web Server (IIS)                        Web-Server
    [ ] Web Server                          Web-WebServer
        [ ] Common HTTP Features            Web-Common-Http
            [ ] Default Document            Web-Default-Doc
            [ ] Directory Browsing          Web-Dir-Browsing
            [ ] HTTP Errors                 Web-Http-Errors
            [ ] Static Content              Web-Static-Content
            [ ] HTTP Redirection            Web-Http-Redirect
            [ ] WebDAV Publishing           Web-DAV-Publishing
        [ ] Health and Diagnostics          Web-Health
```

4. Now we need to build out the PowerShell command to install these two items:

```
Install-WindowsFeature Web-Server,Web-Common-Http,Web-Mgmt-
Console -Restart
```

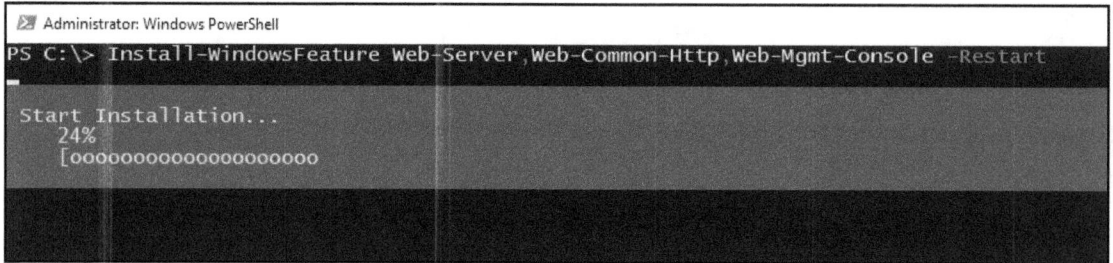

```
Administrator: Windows PowerShell
PS C:\> Install-WindowsFeature Web-Server,Web-Common-Http,Web-Mgmt-Console -Restart


Start Installation...
    24%
    [oooooooooooooooooooooo
```

5. Installation succeeded! Just to double-check it for the sake of our recipe, if we navigate through the GUI to see the installed roles and features, we can see that the items we configured via PowerShell are fully installed.

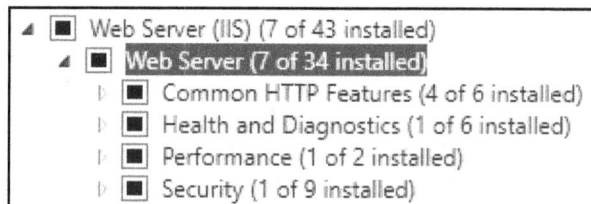

```
◢ ■ Web Server (IIS) (7 of 43 installed)
    ◢ ■ Web Server (7 of 34 installed)
        ▷ ■ Common HTTP Features (4 of 6 installed)
        ▷ ■ Health and Diagnostics (1 of 6 installed)
        ▷ ■ Performance (1 of 2 installed)
        ▷ ■ Security (1 of 9 installed)
```

How it works...

We can use the `Install-WindowsFeature` cmdlet in PowerShell to easily add roles and features to our servers. This one can save a lot of time compared to running through these options in the graphical wizards. For example, if you had a group of new servers that all needed to accomplish the same task, and therefore needed the same set of roles installed, you could build out one single command to install those roles and run it on each server. No need to launch Server Manager at all.

See also

Here are some links to additional TechNet documentation on adding roles to servers, and specifically for the `Install-WindowsFeature` cmdlet. Make sure to familiarize yourself with all of the available options. Once you start using this command, I doubt you will go back to Server Manager!

- `http://technet.microsoft.com/en-us/library/cc732263.aspx#BKMK_powershell`
- `http://technet.microsoft.com/en-us/library/jj205467.aspx`

Launching your first website

Seems like a pretty logical first step; let's get a website started! Actually, you already have one, but it's pretty useless at the moment. As soon as you finished installing the IIS role, a standard website was started automatically so that you can verify everything is working as it should. Now we want to replace that default website with one of our own so that we can make some real use of this new server.

Getting ready

We will be accomplishing all work from our new Server 2016 web server. This one does happen to be domain joined, but that is not a requirement. You would be able to launch a website on a standalone, workgroup joined server just as easily.

How to do it...

Follow these steps to start your first website on this new IIS web server:

1. Open **Server Manager** and drop down the **Tools** menu. Then click on **Internet Information Services (IIS) Manager**.
2. In the left-hand window pane, expand the name of your server and click on the **Sites** folder.

3. Right-click on **Default Web Site** and navigate to **Manage Website** | **Stop**. This will stop that automatically created website from running and getting in the way of the new website that we are about to create.

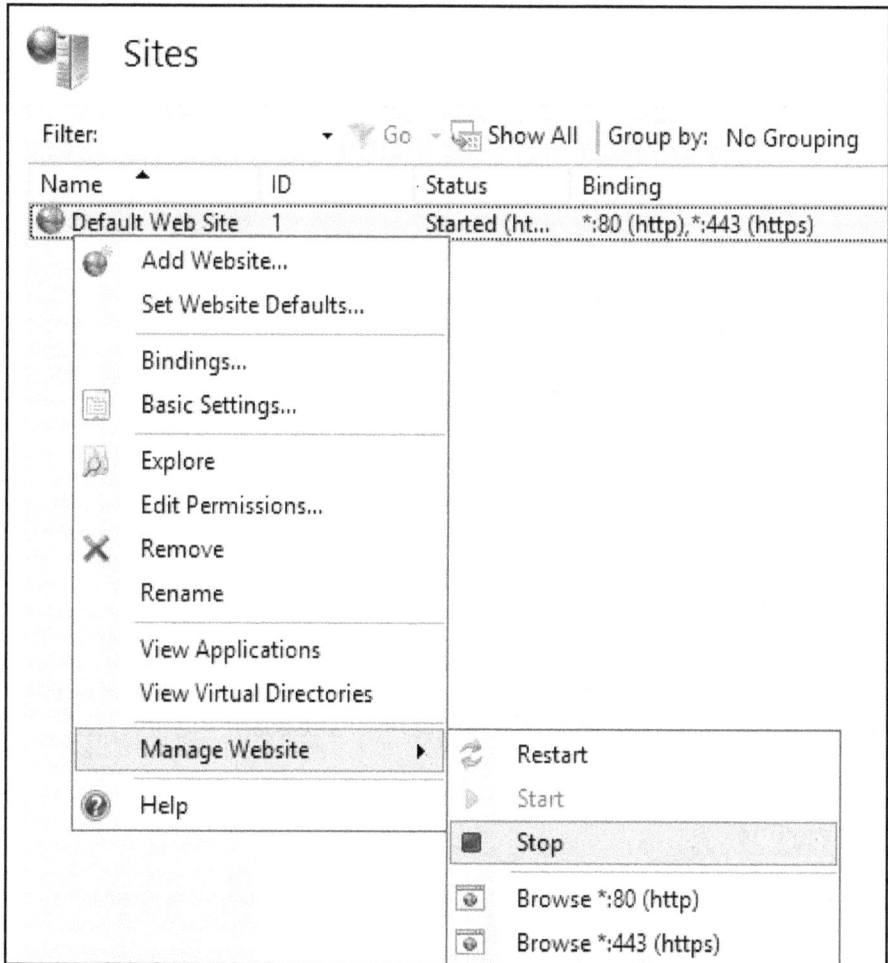

4. Before we create our new website, we will need to create an HTML webpage file that will run when users browse to the new site. Let's leave IIS Manager open for a minute and switch over to File Explorer. Browse to `C:\inetpub`. This is sort of the home folder that IIS creates and can be a good starting point for building your website. You do not have to create your new page within this folder, you could certainly set one up in another location, or even on a different drive altogether.

5. Create a new folder called `NewWebsite`, or whatever you want it to be called.

6. Inside this new folder, we are going to create a new file called `Default.htm`. To do this, I usually right-click and choose to create a new text file, and name this file `Default.txt`. Then I either adjust **Folder Options** so that I can see and modify file extensions, or I simply open up a **Command Prompt** window and rename the file that way. However you do it, make sure that your `Default.txt` gets changed to `Default.htm` as the final filename.

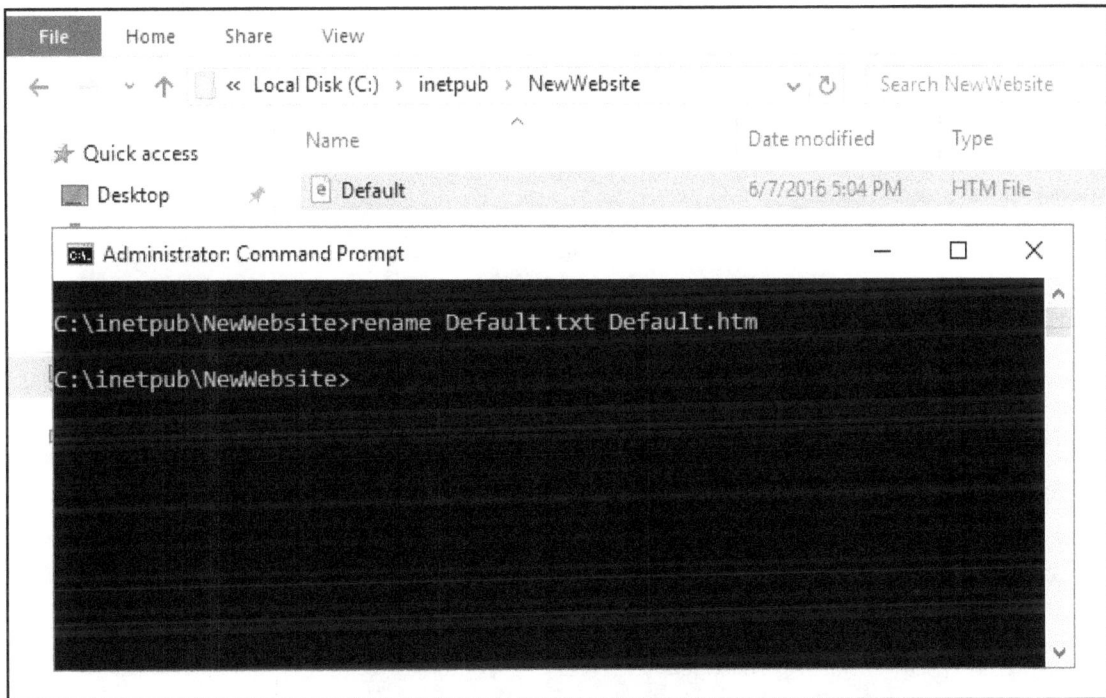

File	Home	Share	View

« Local Disk (C:) › inetpub › NewWebsite   ∨ ↻   Search NewWebsite

Name	Date modified	Type
Quick access		
Desktop e Default	6/7/2016 5:04 PM	HTM File

Administrator: Command Prompt   — □ ✕

```
C:\inetpub\NewWebsite>rename Default.txt Default.htm

C:\inetpub\NewWebsite>
```

7. Now edit your new `Default.htm` file with Notepad or another text editing tool and enter some text. Thankfully, modern web browsers will properly display a page based on some plain text, so that we don't have to input valid HTML code. If you know how to program in HTML, even better, though I doubt you would be reading this particular recipe. Or maybe you have a preconfigured webpage file or set of files from a software installation; you could place those into this folder as well. I am going to simply enter some text in that file, which says, `Congratulations, you are viewing our new website!`.

8. Head back over to IIS, and let's get our site rolling. Right-click on the `Sites` folder and choose **Add Website....**

9. Input a site name, which is just a descriptive name for your own purposes to identify the site in IIS.

10. For the **Physical path**, choose our new website location, which is as follows: `C:\inetpub\NewWebsite`.

11. If you are running multiple IP addresses on this web server and want to dedicate this new site to only run on a particular IP address, you can choose it from the **IP address** field. Otherwise, if you are running a single IP or if you want our new site to work on all IPs configured on this system, leave it set to **All Unassigned**.

Site name:		Application pool:		
NewWebsite		NewWebsite		Select...

Content Directory

Physical path:

C:\inetpub\NewWebsite	...

Pass-through authentication

Connect as...	Test Settings...

Binding

Type:	IP address:	Port:
http ∨	All Unassigned ∨	80

Host name:

Example: www.contoso.com or marketing.contoso.com

12. Click **OK**.

13. From another computer on the network, open up Internet Explorer and browse to `http://<webserver>`. For our particular example, we will go to `http://web2`.

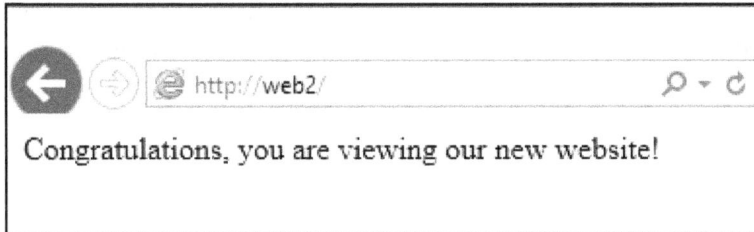

Congratulations, you are viewing our new website!

How it works...

Starting a new website is perhaps the simplest task that can be accomplished in IIS, but it portrays the core functionality of this role. The purpose of running IIS in the first place is to publish websites. It is important to understand the location of this task and the places that you may have to reach inside the filesystem in order to modify or create websites of your own. Not everything is done from within the IIS Management window.

Changing the port on which your website runs

Normally, whenever you access a website, it is running on port 80 or 443. Any normal HTTP request travels over port 80, and the encrypted HTTPS uses port 443. Inside IIS, it is very easy to change the port that a website is listening on if you need to do so. Probably the most common reason to institute a port change on a website is to keep it hidden. Maybe you have an administrative site of some kind and want to make sure that nobody stumbles across it, or perhaps your web server is limited on IP addresses, and you need to turn on another web page but all of your IPs are already running sites. You could utilize a different port for the new site and then have the opportunity to run two (or more) sites using the same IP address, one site on each port.

Whatever your reason for wanting to change the port that a website runs on, let's walk through the steps to accomplish this task so that it can be one more tool added to your belt.

Getting ready

We have a Windows Server 2016 server online that has the IIS role installed. There is already a website running on this server. Currently, it is using port 80 by default, but we want to change that port to 81 and test accessing it from a client computer.

How to do it...

Here are the steps needed to change your website listener port:

1. Open **Internet Information Services (IIS) Manager** from inside the **Tools** menu of Server Manager.
2. In the left-hand window pane, expand the name of your web server and click on the **Sites** folder.
3. Right-click on your website and choose **Bindings....**

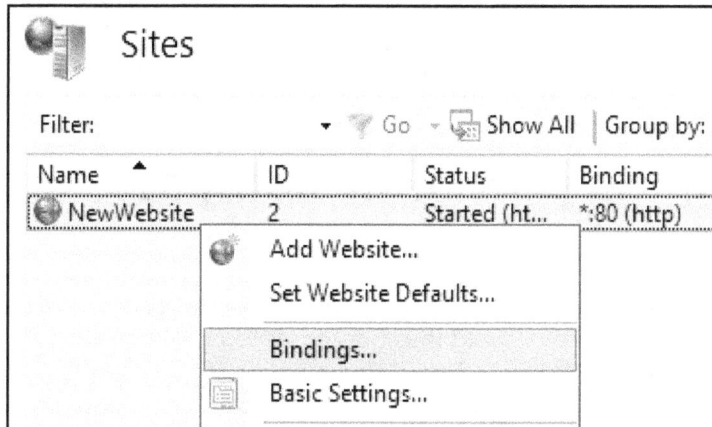

4. Choose the **http** binding that currently displays port **80** and click on the **Edit...** button.
5. Change the **Port** field to 81. This is just for our example, of course. You could enter any valid port number in this field that isn't otherwise in use on this server.
6. Click **OK**, then **Close**.
7. The port is immediately changed on your website. It is no longer listening on port 80. Let's test this by moving to a client computer on our network and opening Internet Explorer.

8. Try browsing to the old website address, `http://web2`.

This page can't be displayed

9. Whoops! I guess that isn't going to work anymore. Instead, we need to include our specific port in the URL from now on. Let's try `http://web2:81`.

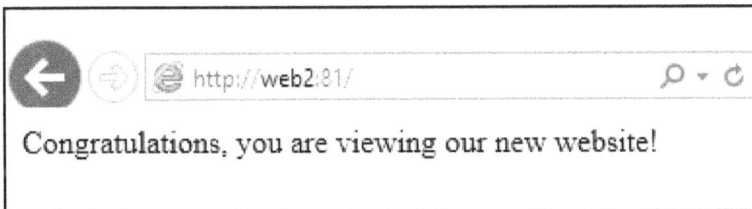
Congratulations, you are viewing our new website!

How it works...

We can easily adjust the port that is used to access a website inside IIS by making one simple adjustment. After changing the port number in our website's bindings, the site immediately changes over to listening on the new port and is no longer active on the old port. Instead of changing the port, you could also add an additional binding into that same screen in order to get the website to respond from multiple ports at the same time. For example, if you wanted your website to run both HTTP for regular access and HTTPS for encrypted access to pages with sensitive information, you could create bindings for both port 80 and port 443.

One note of importance when changing your website port; doing so means your web links for accessing the website will now have to include that specific port number at the end. Also, if you are running firewalls in your network or on the web server itself, it is possible that you will need to adjust settings on those firewalls to allow the new port to be allowed safe passage.

Adding encryption to your website

Using websites to pass data around the Internet is a staple of technology as we know it today. Installing even the simplest new tool or system will probably require you to download software or an update, or to register your information with a website. As an IT professional, I hope that you are familiar with HTTP versus HTTPS websites and the importance of distinguishing between the two. But now that we have a website running, how can we enable HTTPS on it so that we can protect this data that is traversing back and forth between our web server and the client computers?

It is typically the web developer's job to tell a website when to call for HTTPS, so you shouldn't have to worry too much about the actual content of the website. As the server administrator, however, you need to make sure that once HTTPS is called for on the website, your web server is capable of processing that traffic appropriately.

Getting ready

We are running a Server 2016 web server from which we will accomplish this task. There is a simple website currently running inside IIS on this server. Part of our recipe will be choosing an SSL certificate that we want to run on our website, so this recipe assumes that the certificate is already installed on your server. If you need assistance with the acquisition of the certificate itself, please refer to the *Using a Certificate Signing Request to acquire your SSL certificate* recipe.

How to do it...

To configure your website for HTTPS traffic, follow these steps:

1. Launch **Internet Information Services (IIS) Manager** from the **Tools** menu inside Server Manager.
2. In the left-hand window pane, expand your web server name and click on the **Sites** folder.
3. Right-click on your website and choose **Bindings...**.

Filter:		▼ ⟡ Go ▾ ⟨ Show All	Group by:
Name	ID	Status	Binding
⊕ NewWebsite	2	Started (ht...	*:80 (http)

⊕ Add Website...
   Set Website Defaults...

   Bindings...
▣ Basic Settings...

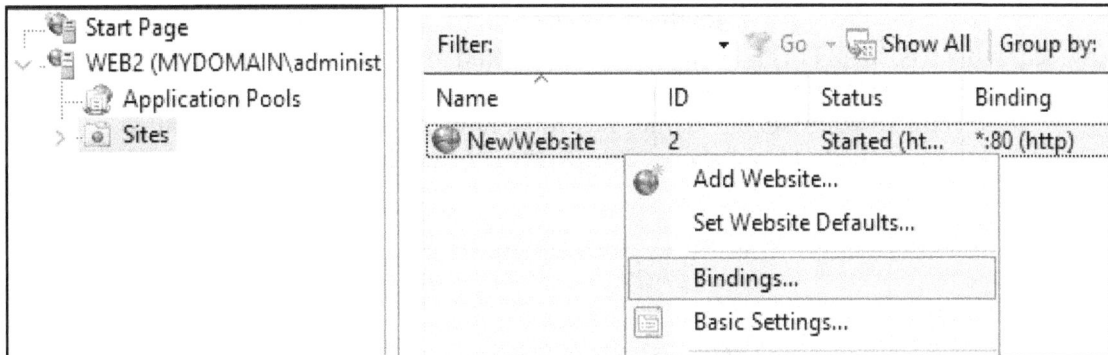

Since it is a new website, you can see that there is only one binding listed currently. This binding is for port 80, which makes it an HTTP-only website. If you currently tried to access this site via HTTPS, it would fail. The port for HTTPS is 443, and so we need to add a new binding that uses port 443. A mistake that I have watched new admins make is to edit this existing binding and change it from 80 to 443. This will cause the website to only listen on port 443, or rather to only accept requests via HTTPS. This may be desirable in some instances, but not most. You generally want the website to respond to both HTTP and HTTPS requests.

4. Go ahead and click the **Add...** button.
5. Change the **Type** field to **https**. You will notice that the **Port** field changes to 443 automatically.
6. If you only want this new binding to work on a particular IP address, choose it now. Otherwise, leave it set to **All Unassigned** to cause this new listener to be active on all IP addresses that exist on our server.

7. Select the **SSL certificate** that you want IIS to use for authenticating requests to this website. HTTPS traffic is only encrypted and guaranteed to be safe from prying eyes because the tunnel is being validated by an SSL certificate that is specific to your website name. You must have an SSL certificate installed on the server so that you can choose it from the list here in order to create an HTTPS binding.

```
┌─────────────────────────────────────────────────────────────────────────┐
│                        Add Site Binding                       [ ? ] [ X ] │
│                                                                           │
│   Type:                  IP address:                    Port:             │
│   ┌──────────────┬─┐     ┌──────────────────────────┬─┐ ┌─────────────┐   │
│   │ https        │v│     │ All Unassigned           │v│ │ 443         │   │
│   └──────────────┴─┘     └──────────────────────────┴─┘ └─────────────┘   │
│   Host name:                                                              │
│   ┌───────────────────────────────────────────────────────┐              │
│   │                                                         │              │
│   └───────────────────────────────────────────────────────┘              │
│                                                                           │
│   [ ] Require Server Name Indication                                      │
│                                                                           │
│                                                                           │
│   SSL certificate:                                                        │
│   ┌──────────────────────────────────────────┬─┐  ┌──────────┐ ┌───────┐ │
│   │ sharepoint.mydomain.local                │v│  │ Select...│ │View...│ │
│   └──────────────────────────────────────────┴─┘  └──────────┘ └───────┘ │
│                                                                           │
│                                            ┌──────────┐  ┌──────────┐     │
│                                            │    OK    │  │  Cancel  │     │
│                                            └──────────┘  └──────────┘     │
└─────────────────────────────────────────────────────────────────────────┘
```

8. Click **OK**, then click **Close**. Your HTTPS binding is now active on this website.

How it works...

In this recipe, we used the IIS management console to add a second binding to our new website. This new binding is for accepting HTTPS traffic. We intend to run parts of this website as HTTP, and some more sensitive pages as HTTPS. Therefore, we created a second binding, enabling both HTTP and HTTPS traffic to flow successfully to and from this site. During the course of this recipe, we needed to choose the SSL certificate that the website is going to use in order to validate the HTTPS traffic that is coming in. There was already an SSL certificate installed on the server for our website; we simply had to choose it from the list.

Using a Certificate Signing Request to acquire your SSL certificate

When publishing a website to the Internet, it is generally a best practice to use an SSL certificate on the website that you acquired from a public Certification Authority (CA). These are the big certificate issuing entities such as Entrust, Verisign, GoDaddy, and so on. It is possible to use your own internal PKI infrastructure to issue SSL certificates that can be exposed to the outside world, but it can be difficult to set up the certificate infrastructure appropriately and securely. As cheap as SSL certificates are, it is worth the investment to have the security of knowing that the certificate you are running on your website is the one and only certificate of its kind, and that nobody else has a chance to get their hands on a copy of your certificate and spoof your website. Modern browsers also have a pre-built list of the public CAs that they trust; this makes using a certificate from one of those public entities even more beneficial, because your user's browsers will automatically trust those certificates without any additional work on the client side.

It is easy enough to log in to one of these CA's websites and purchase a new certificate, but then comes the tricky part. Once purchased, you need to walk through some steps and enter information about your certificate. Easy enough; it asks you for some company information and the name that you plan to use for your site, of course. Then it asks for your **Certificate Signing Request (CSR)** and gives you either a very large empty text box to paste it into or an upload function where you can upload your CSR directly to them. This is the place where I have watched many new admins struggle to find traction on their next step.

A CSR is a file that must be created on your web server. It contains information that the CA uses when it creates your certificate. When they do this, it binds the certificate to the information in the CSR, ensuring that your certificate is built specifically for your web server. Here, we are going to generate a CSR together, so that you are prepared to handle that screen when you come across it.

Getting ready

We are going to use IIS that is running on our Server 2016 web server to generate a CSR. This server is the only piece of infrastructure that we need running for this task.

How to do it...

In order to request a new certificate from a public CA, you will need to spin out a CSR on your web server. Here are the steps to do so:

1. Open **Internet Information Services (IIS) Manager**.
2. Click on the name of your server in the left-hand window pane.
3. Double-click on the **Server Certificates** applet. This will display currently installed certificates on your server.

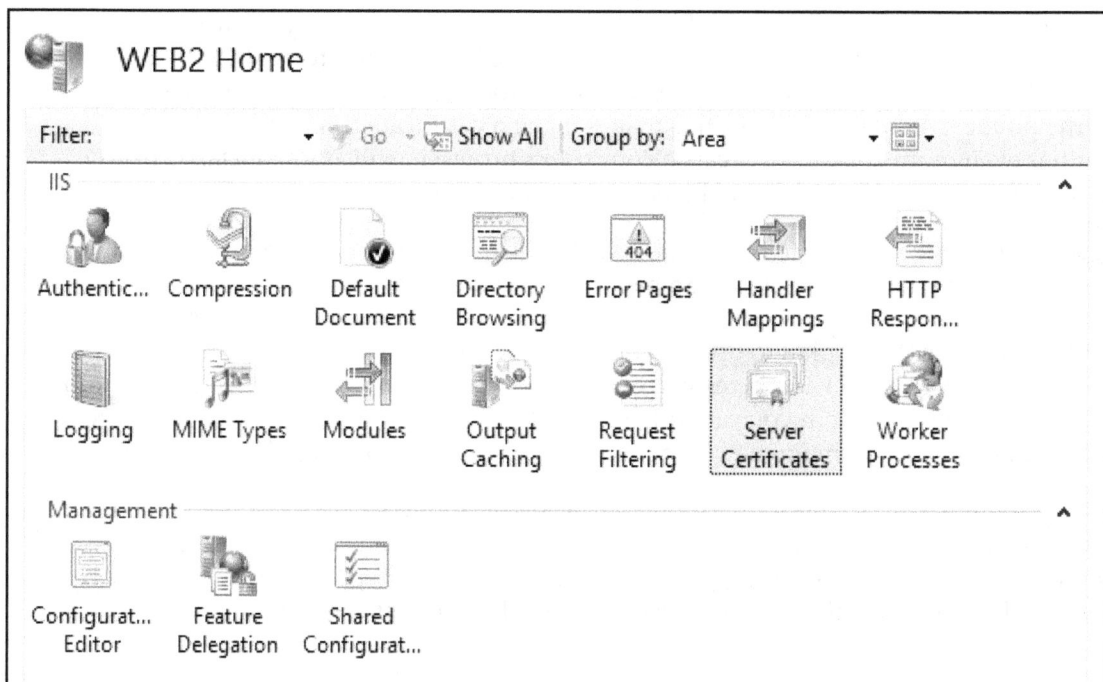

4. Click on the action near the right of your screen that says **Create Certificate Request...**.
5. Populate **Common name** with the DNS name that your website will be running on. This is the name that users will type into their browsers in order to access this site.
6. **Organization** is the name of your company or organization. Typically, this information needs to match whatever is on file with the CA, so take a minute to check another certificate that you might have already and make sure to type in the same info.

7. The **Organizational unit** can be anything you desire. I often just type the word
   `Web`.

8. Type in your **City/locality** and **State/province** to finish out this screen. Make sure
   to spell out the whole word of your state, for example, California. They tend to
   dislike abbreviations.

Common name:	www.contoso.com
Organization:	Your Company Name
Organizational unit:	Web
City/locality	Dallas
State/province:	Texas
Country/region:	US

9. Click **Next**.

10. Increase your **Bit length** to at least **2048**. This is typically considered to be the
    new minimum standard in the industry.

Cryptographic service provider:
Microsoft RSA SChannel Cryptographic Provider
Bit length:
2048

11. Click **Next**.

12. Type a location and name where you want to store your new CSR. Usually, you
    set this into a text (`.txt`) file. Make sure to specify the full filename, including the
    extension. I have found that if you do not, the file disappears into neverland.

Specify a file name for the certificate request:
C:\Users\administrator.MYDOMAIN\Desktop\mycsr.txt

13. Click **Finish** and go take a look at that new file. It will look like a big mess of letters and numbers, which is normal!

14. Now you can proceed to your public CA's web interface and use this new CSR during the official request for a new SSL certificate. When prompted, paste the contents of the CSR file into their system. This is the last time you will need that CSR.

> **TIP**
>
> Each authority handles this process differently, but they are all generally done through a website, with a series of steps that you walk through. Many CAs will allow you to generate a 15 or 30-day trial certificate so that you can test this without cost.

15. After the CA validates your request and your CSR, they will issue you a link where you can download your new certificate. Go ahead and download that file, and copy it onto your web server.

16. Once the certificate file is on your server, you need to import it into IIS. Head back into the **Server Certificates** section and this time click on **Complete Certificate Request...**.

17. Specify the newly downloaded certificate file and input the **Friendly name** field if you choose. This is a descriptive name that you can give to this new certificate inside IIS so that you can easily identify it later when assigning it to a website binding. You typically want to store these certificates in the **Personal** store, as is set by default.

File name containing the certification authority's response:

C:\Users\administrator.MYDOMAIN\Desktop\NewCert.crt

Friendly name:

SSL Certificate for main website

Select a certificate store for the new certificate:

Personal

18. Click **OK**, and that's it! Your new certificate is installed and ready to use.

How it works...

In this recipe, we requested a new SSL certificate from our favorite public Certification Authority. In order to receive a certificate from them, we had to issue a CSR from our web server. Once we have our CSR generated, we simply copy and paste it into the web interface for our CA entity and they give us a new certificate based on that CSR. Once downloaded, the new certificate file can be imported back into the web server, where it is ready for use by our own website.

> One note of importance; after you install the new certificate on your server, double-click on the certificate to open it up. You want to make sure that you have a message displaying on the main page of your certificate properties that says **You have a private key that corresponds to this certificate**. This will display near the bottom of the **General** tab of the certificate. If you do not see this message, something did not work correctly with the CSR and you will probably have to start the process over to request another new copy of the certificate. Having a private key that corresponds to your SSL certificate is critical to getting your website working properly.

Moving an SSL certificate from one server to another

There are multiple reasons why you may need to move or copy an SSL certificate from one web server to another. If you have purchased a wildcard certificate for your network, you are probably going to use that same certificate on a lot of different servers, as it can be used to validate multiple websites and DNS names. Even if you are using singularly named certificates, you may be turning on multiple web servers to host the same site, to be set up in some sort of load-balanced fashion. In this case, you will also need the same SSL certificate on each of the web servers, as they could all potentially be accepting traffic from clients.

When moving or copying a certificate from one server to another, there is definitely a right way and a wrong way to go about it. Let's spend a little bit of time copying a certificate from one server to another so that you can become familiar with this task.

Getting ready

We have two Server 2016 boxes online in our environment. These are both destined to be web servers hosting the same website. IIS has been installed on both. The SSL certificate that we require has been installed on the primary server. We now need to export the certificate from there and import it successfully onto our second server.

How to do it...

Follow these steps to copy a certificate from one server to another:

1. On your primary web server, launch **Internet Information Services (IIS) Manager** from the **Tools** menu of Server Manager.
2. Click on the name of your server in the left-hand window pane.
3. Double-click on the **Server Certificates** applet to view the certificates currently installed on this system.
4. For our example, I am using a wildcard certificate that has been installed on this server. Right-click on the certificate and choose **Export...**.

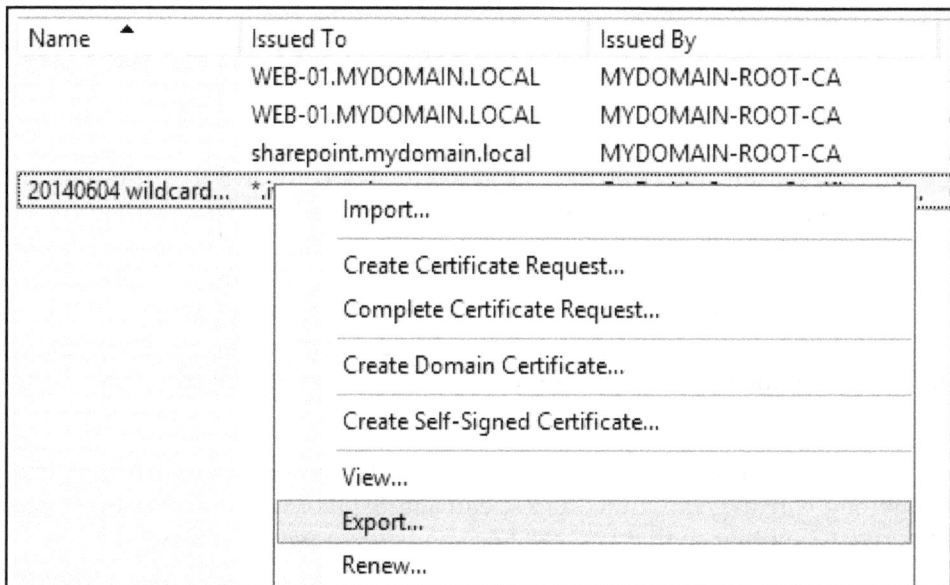

Name ▲	Issued To	Issued By
	WEB-01.MYDOMAIN.LOCAL	MYDOMAIN-ROOT-CA
	WEB-01.MYDOMAIN.LOCAL	MYDOMAIN-ROOT-CA
	sharepoint.mydomain.local	MYDOMAIN-ROOT-CA
20140604 wildcard...	*.i	

Import...

Create Certificate Request...
Complete Certificate Request...

Create Domain Certificate...

Create Self-Signed Certificate...

View...

Export...

Renew...

5. Choose a location to store this exported file and enter a password that will be used to protect the file.

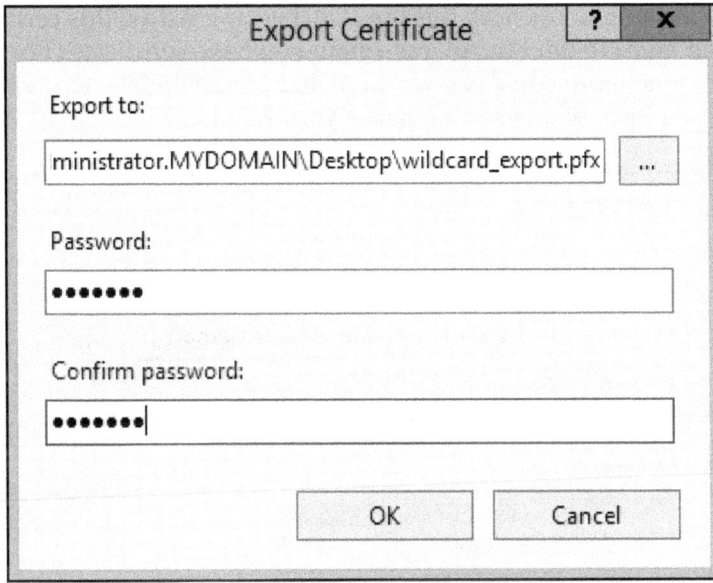

Export Certificate ? X

Export to:

ministrator.MYDOMAIN\Desktop\wildcard_export.pfx ...

Password:

••••••••

Confirm password:

••••••••

OK Cancel

6. Clicking **OK** will create a PFX file and place it onto your Desktop (or wherever you told it to save). Now copy this PFX file over to your secondary web server.

7. Open up the IIS Management console on the second server and navigate to the same **Server Certificates** location.

8. Right-click in the center pane and choose **Import....** Alternatively, you could choose the **Import...** action from the right-hand window pane.

9. Browse to the location of your certificate and input the password that you used to protect the PFX file.

10. Before clicking **OK**, decide whether or not you want this certificate to be exportable from this secondary server. Sometimes this is desirable if you plan to have to export the certificate again in the future. If you do not have a reason to do that, go ahead and uncheck this box. Unchecking **Allow this certificate to be exported** helps to limit the places where you have certificates floating around the network. The more you have out there that are potentially exportable, the more chance you have of one getting out of your hands.

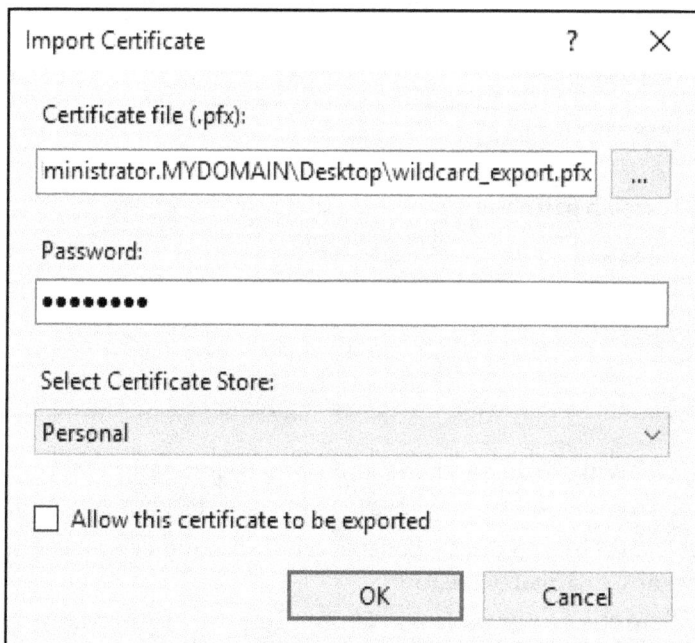

11. Once you click **OK**, your certificate should now be installed and visible inside the IIS window.

12. Double-click on the certificate and check over the properties to make sure everything looks correct. Make sure that you see the message across the bottom that says **You have a private key that corresponds to this certificate**. If that message is missing, something didn't work properly during your export and the private key was somehow not included in the certificate export that you did. You will have to revisit the primary server and export again to make sure that the certificate on the secondary server does contain private key information, or it will not work properly.

Valid from 6/6/2016 **to** 6/6/2018

You have a private key that corresponds to this certificate.

How it works…

We used the IIS management console to export and import an SSL certificate, which is a pretty straightforward and simple task to do once you understand the process. The critical part is making sure that your export includes the private key information. If it does not, the certificate will not be able to validate traffic properly. Using IIS to accomplish this task is the best way to move certificates. You could also make use of the MMC snap-in for certificates, but it is a little more complicated. If you try to use that console, you will be asked whether or not you want to export the private key. The default option is set to **No, do not export the private key**. It is a common mistake to leave that setting in place and wonder later why the certificate doesn't work properly on other servers where you have installed it. You must make sure to select the option **Yes, export the private key**.

Rebinding your renewed certificates automatically

Certificates expire; this is just a simple fact of life. Most often, I find that companies purchase SSL certificates on a short-term basis, usually for only one year. This means that every year, each certificate needs to be renewed. However, downloading a new copy of the certificate and installing it onto your web server is not enough to make it continue working. Simply putting the new certificate into place on the server does not mean that IIS is going to start using the new one to validate traffic on your website. Even if you delete the old certificate, there is no action that has been taken inside IIS to tell it that this new certificate that suddenly appeared is the one that it should start using as the binding for your site. So we have always had to make this additional change manually. Every time you replace a certificate, you also go into IIS and change the binding on the website. This seems particularly painful when you have the certificate renewal automated through something such as Autoenrollment. You may mistakenly think that you are covered in the future and no longer have to do anything to renew your certificates because they will be renewed at the server level automatically. But alas, this is not true; up until now we have still always had to go into IIS and change the binding by hand. Fear not, the future is here…

The IIS team has made a simple but powerful change to help this problem in the new version of IIS that ships with Windows Server 2016. In fact, this function was available in Server 2012 R2 in its first iteration, but I still haven't seen anybody use it in the field, so for most folks, this is going to be brand new. This new feature called **Certificate Rebind**, when enabled, causes IIS to automatically recognize a new certificate installation, and to automatically rebind the appropriate website to use the new copy of the certificate instead of the expiring one. Let's take a look at the interface so that you know how to turn this option on and off. We will also take a little look under the hood so that you can understand how this functionality works.

Getting ready

This work will be accomplished on our Windows Server 2016 web server. We have IIS installed and have an HTTPS website running with an SSL certificate already bound to the site.

How to do it...

Follow these steps to enable Certificate Rebind on your IIS web server:

1. Open **Internet Information Services (IIS) Manager** from inside the **Tools** menu of Server Manager.
2. In the left-hand window pane, click on the name of your web server.
3. Double-click on the **Server Certificates** applet.
4. In the right-hand window pane, click on the action called **Enable Automatic Rebind of Renewed Certificate**.

5. That's it! IIS has now been configured so that it will recognize the installation of a renewed certificate, and will rebind your website automatically to make use of the new certificate. Now let's take a little look at how this process actually works.

6. Use either Command Prompt or the **Start** screen to launch `Taskschd.msc`. This is the **Windows Task Scheduler**.

7. In the left-hand pane, navigate to **Task Scheduler Library | Microsoft | Windows | CertificateServicesClient**.

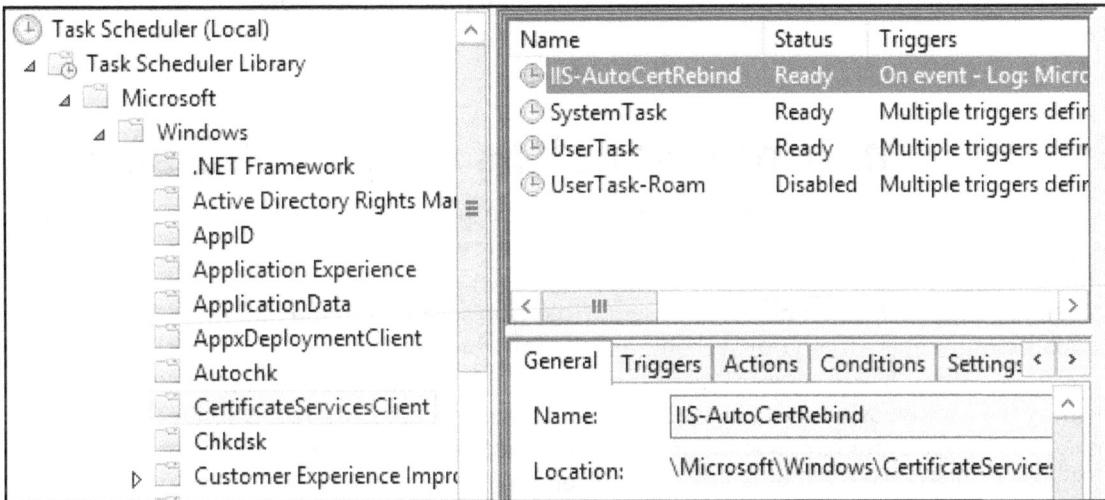

8. You can see a scheduled task listed here that is called **IIS-AutoCertRebind**. This is the magic of Certificate Rebind. When a certificate gets added or renewed on your Server 2016 system, an event is logged. When this event is logged, this scheduled task picks it up and uses the information that it has from IIS about the certificates to rebind the websites onto the new certificates.

9. If you head back into IIS and click on the **Action** for **Disable Automatic Rebind of Renewed Certificate**, you will notice that our scheduled task disappears from the list.

How it works...

Certificate Rebind is a really simple action to enable inside IIS, but it can make all the difference to whether you have a good or bad day at the office. When enabled, this feature builds a scheduled task inside Windows that triggers the commands to bind our IIS website to its new certificate. This task is triggered by an event that is logged in Windows when our new certificate is installed or renewed. With Certificate Rebind enabled and the configuration of your certificate distribution set to happen automatically through Autoenrollment, you can now have a truly automated certificate renewal system inside your network!

Hosting multiple websites on your IIS server

Spinning up a web server, implementing the IIS role, and hosting a website are great first steps. Depending on the size and importance of your website, you may even require multiple web servers running that will serve up exact copies of the same website and have load balancing configured between the multiple web servers. On the other hand, it is probably more likely that your website will actually be an underutilization of your server's resources, rather than an overutilization, and so you have now created a new web server hosting a single website, and it's really not being taxed at all. Is there a way that we can make use of that extra hardware that is currently sitting idle? Perhaps you have additional websites or web services that need to be turned on, for which you were planning to spin up multiple servers. The good news is that IIS is capable of hosting many different websites at the same time. We can take that underutilized server and create additional website listeners on it so that you can serve up multiple web pages from the same physical server.

There are a couple of different ways that we can host multiple websites on the same IIS server at the same time, through the use of multiple ports or multiple IP addresses. Let's take a minute and test both avenues.

Getting ready

We are going to use IIS on our WEB1 server today in order to host multiple websites. We will also need access to DNS in order to create names for these websites.

How to do it...

Follow these steps to host multiple websites on the same IIS server:

1. First, we need to create some sites that will be served up by IIS. Inside my c:\inetpub folder, I am simply creating four new folders. Inside each folder will be a simple Default.htm file that contains some text. This way I can serve up these different web pages on different sites inside IIS, and later browse to them individually to prove that IIS is serving up all of the different web pages.

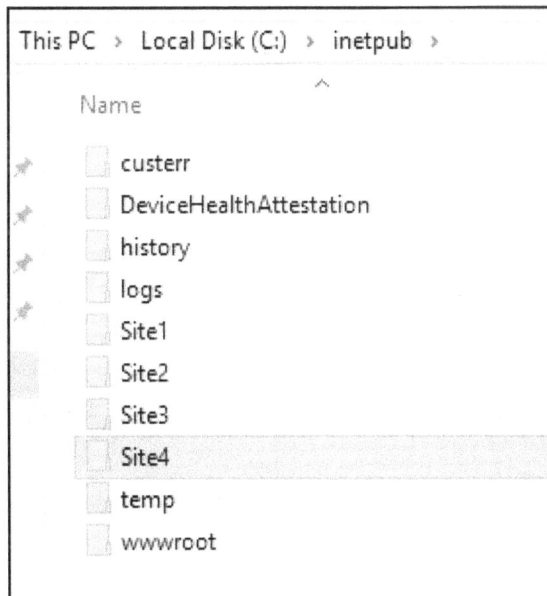

This PC › Local Disk (C:) › inetpub ›
Name
custerr
DeviceHealthAttestation
history
logs
Site1
Site2
Site3
Site4
temp
wwwroot

2. Now open up **Internet Information Services (IIS) Manager** and browse to the **Sites** folder. Right-click on **Sites** and choose **Add Website...** four different times to walk through the process of creating your four new websites. For each site, make sure to choose the appropriate folder on the hard drive for serving up the correct page.

3. At this point in time, we only have one IP address on our web server. So in order to allow IIS to host multiple websites on this single IP address, we are going to take the approach of having each website run on its own port number. When you configure the **Add Website** screen, identify a unique port number under the **Binding** session for each site. This will permit all four websites to run at the same time using the same IP address, because each site will be running on a unique port number.

Site name: Application pool:

[Site4]   [Site4]   [Select...]

Content Directory

  Physical path:

  [C:\inetpub\Site4]   [...]

  Pass-through authentication

  [Connect as...]   [Test Settings...]

Binding

  Type: IP address: Port:

  [http ⌄]   [All Unassigned ⌄]   [84]

  Host name:

  [   ]

  Example: www.contoso.com or marketing.contoso.com

---

5. Now you can see that all four of our websites are started, and each is running on its own port number.

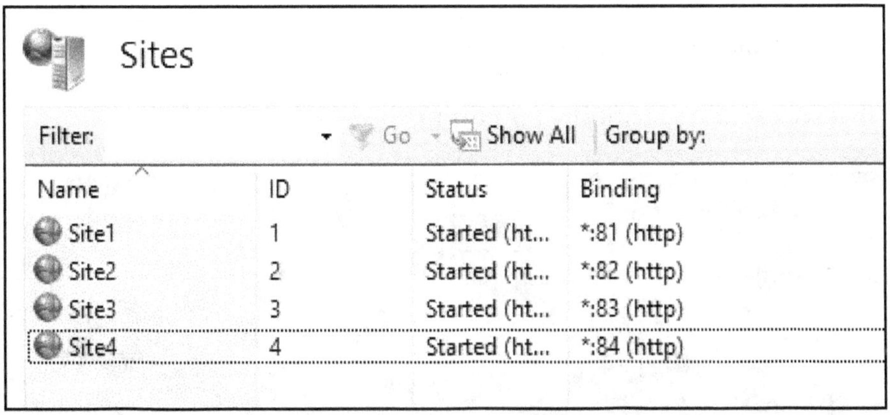

6. Client computers in the network can now browse the following links and successfully see the four different web pages being served up by our IIS server:

- `http://web1:81`
- `http://web1:82`
- `http://web1:83`
- `http://web1:84`

7. Requiring the users to type in a specific port number when they want to access websites isn't something they are going to appreciate, so let's try hosting these four different websites on our WEB1 server in a different fashion. Instead of using different port numbers, we are now going to take the approach of hosting each website on its own unique IP address. In order to start that process, open up the NIC properties of the WEB1 server and plug in three additional IP addresses that we can use specifically for hosting these websites.

```
Ethernet adapter Ethernet:

   Connection-specific DNS Suffix  . :
   Link-local IPv6 Address . . . . . : fe80::79a1:f04f:406e:f589%3
   IPv4 Address. . . . . . . . . . . : 10.0.0.21
   Subnet Mask . . . . . . . . . . . : 255.255.255.0
   IPv4 Address. . . . . . . . . . . : 10.0.0.22
   Subnet Mask . . . . . . . . . . . : 255.255.255.0
   IPv4 Address. . . . . . . . . . . : 10.0.0.23
   Subnet Mask . . . . . . . . . . . : 255.255.255.0
   IPv4 Address. . . . . . . . . . . : 10.0.0.24
   Subnet Mask . . . . . . . . . . . : 255.255.255.0
   Default Gateway . . . . . . . . . :
```

8. Now back inside IIS, right-click on each of your websites and modify **Bindings...** so that each website is once again using the default port 80, but it is also running on its own unique IP address.

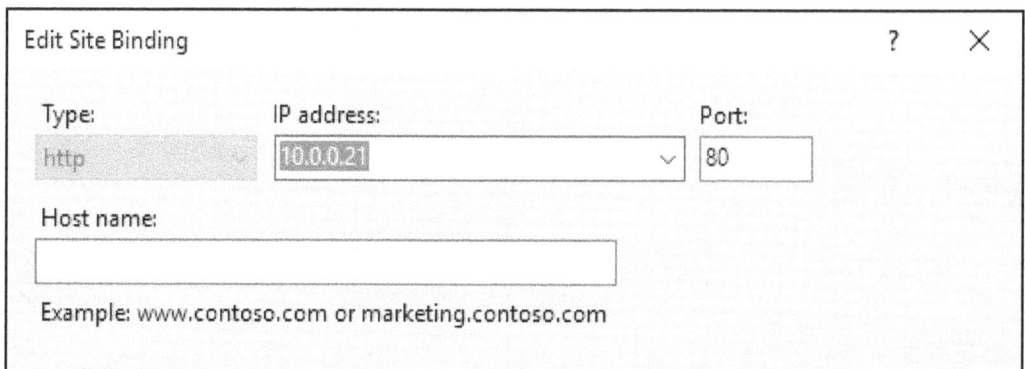

Edit Site Binding		? ✕
Type:	**IP address:**	**Port:**
http	10.0.0.21	80
Host name:		
Example: www.contoso.com or marketing.contoso.com		

9. Once the four websites are each running on their own IP addresses, you can create DNS host records so that each site has a unique DNS name on the network as well. Simply point these four new DNS names to the corresponding IP address where the site is running, and your client computers can now access the websites via individual hostnames on the network:

   - http://site1.mydomain.local
   - http://site2.mydomain.local
   - http://site3.mydomain.local
   - http://site4.mydomain.local

Site1	Host (A)	10.0.0.21
Site2	Host (A)	10.0.0.22
Site3	Host (A)	10.0.0.23
Site4	Host (A)	10.0.0.24

How it works...

Whether you decide to host multiple websites on a single web server by splitting up access at the port level or the IP address level, it is important to know that you can push the limits of your web server a little bit by hosting multiple things at the same time. IIS is more than capable of handling this division of resources, and as long as your hardware is keeping up with the task, you can continue to grow vertically in this way and save the number of servers you have running, rather than having to grow out horizontally by installing server after server after server, as you begin to need additional web resources.

Using host headers to manage multiple websites on a single IP address

As we just saw, it is pretty straightforward to configure multiple websites inside IIS by assigning individual IP addresses for each site. It is common to run more than one site on a single web server, and so this sometimes means that your web servers have numerous IP addresses configured on them. However, sometimes this is not possible. For example, you may be working on a web server that is Internet facing and there is a restriction on the amount of available public IP addresses that can be used. In this case, you may run across the need to host multiple websites on a single IP address, but you don't want to force the users into having to type in specific port numbers in order to gain access to the right website.

This is where host headers come into play. Host headers can be configured on your websites so that the site responds to a particular request coming in from the client. These header requests can help the web server distinguish between traffic, directing users calling for websites to their appropriate site inside IIS. Let's work together to set up two websites inside IIS and force them to utilize the same IP address and port. We want everything to remain standard as far as the port goes, so we want them to both be able to utilize port 80, but we only have one IP address available to install on our web server.

Getting ready

The work will be accomplished from inside IIS on our Server 2016 web server. We will also utilize a client computer to test connectivity to the websites once we are finished setting them up.

How to do it...

To create two websites that share the same IP address and split traffic by using host headers, follow these steps:

1. On your web server, open up File Explorer and create a new folder called `C:\Websites`. Inside this folder, create two new folders and call them `Site1` and `Site2`.

2. Inside each folder, create a new `Default.htm` file. You should now have two different `Default.htm` files, one sitting inside the `Site1` folder, and one sitting inside the `Site2` folder. These will be our example websites.

3. Put some text inside each of those `Default.htm` files. Make sure that whatever text you write in them distinguishes between the websites so that we can know it is working properly when we test in a few minutes.

4. Open **Internet Information Services (IIS) Manager** from the **Tools** menu of Server Manager.

5. In the left-hand window pane, expand the name of your web server. Then right-click on the `Sites` folder, and choose **Add Website...**.

6. We are going to name our site `Site1` and choose our `C:\Websites\Site1` folder as the location for this website. I am also going to drop down the **IP address** field and specify the one and only IP address on this system so that we can prove host headers are working as they should. Remember, our intention is to get two websites running on this same IP address and port combination.

7. Here's the part that may be new territory for you, the **Host name** field. This is the DNS name that requests for this website will be coming in with. So whatever DNS name your users are going to type into their browser is the name that you need to enter here. We are going to use `mysite1.mydomain.local`.

Site name:		Application pool:	
Site1		Site1	Select...

Content Directory

Physical path:

C:\Websites\Site1	...

Pass-through authentication

Connect as...	Test Settings...

Binding

Type:	IP address:	Port:
http ⌄	10.0.0.6 ⌄	80

Host name:

mysite1.mydomain.local

Example: www.contoso.com or marketing.contoso.com

8. Click **OK**, and you have the first website up and running on the web server.

9. Now walk through the same process as above, but this time specify all of the information for `Site2`. We are going to choose the same **IP address** and **Port**, but we are going to specify a different name in the **Host name** field:

Site name: Application pool:

| Site2 | | Site2 | | Select... |

Content Directory

  Physical path:

  C:\Websites\Site2   ...

  Pass-through authentication

  | Connect as... | | Test Settings... |

Binding

  Type: IP address: Port:

  | http ⌄ | | 10.0.0.6   ⌄ | | 80 |

  Host name:

  | mysite2.mydomain.local |

  Example: www.contoso.com or marketing.contoso.com

---

10. We now have two websites, both running on the same IP address and port on the same web server. Let's test to find out whether or not IIS is smart enough to distinguish between the sites when we try to browse these websites from our client computer.

> **TIP**
>
> Remember to create DNS records for these websites! You will need host records created for `mysite1.mydomain.local` and `mysite2.mydomain.local`, and they both need to be pointed at the IP address of the web server, which in our case is `10.0.0.6`.

11. On a client computer, browse to `http://mysite1.mydomain.local`. You should see the text from the `Default.htm` file that we put into the `Site1` folder on the web server.

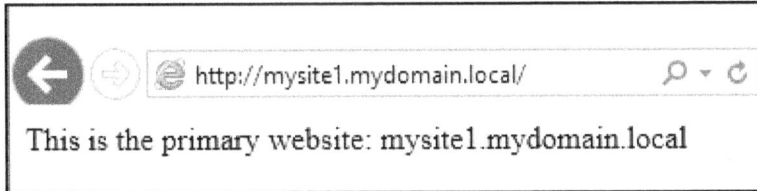

> **←** → 🌐 http://mysite1.mydomain.local/ 🔍 ▾ ↻
>
> This is the primary website: mysite1.mydomain.local

12. Now browse to `http://mysite2.mydomain.local`. We can see that the web server recognizes our request for the second site, and even though they are running on the same IP address, our request is sent over to the second website.

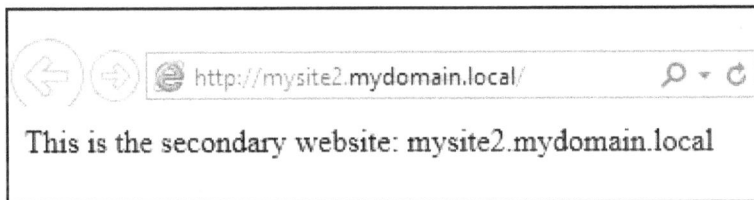

> ← → 🌐 http://mysite2.mydomain.local/ 🔍 ▾ ↻
>
> This is the secondary website: mysite2.mydomain.local

How it works...

When we set up websites inside IIS to utilize different host headers, it gives us the ability to publish multiple sites on the same IP address and port numbers. This can be very useful in cases where IP addresses are limited or where you don't want to configure multiple addresses onto the web server for any reason. IIS is capable of listening on the same IP and port for web requests coming into different host names and forwarding those requests on to the appropriate website based on the host header name that was requested by the client computer. It is important to note that requests for these web pages must come by the name for this to work properly; you cannot type the IP address of the website into the browser and expect it to work, since we are now sharing that IP address between two or more different sites.

6
Remote Access

With Windows Server 2016, Microsoft brings a whole new way of looking at remote access. Companies have historically relied on third-party tools to connect remote users to the network, such as traditional and SSL VPN provided by appliances from large networking vendors. I'm here to tell you those days are gone. Those of us running Microsoft-centric shops can now rely on Microsoft technologies to connect our remote workforce. Better yet is that these technologies are included with the Server 2016 operating system, and have functionality that is much improved over anything that a traditional VPN can provide.

Regular VPN does still have a place in the remote access space, and the great news is that you can also provide it with Server 2016. We have some recipes on setting up VPN, but our primary focus for this chapter will be **DirectAccess (DA)**. DA is kind of like *automatic VPN*. There is nothing the user needs to do in order to be connected to work. Whenever they are on the Internet, they are connected automatically to the corporate network. DirectAccess is an amazing way to have your Windows 7, Windows 8, and Windows 10 domain joined systems connected back to the network for data access and for the management of those traveling machines. DA has actually been around since 2008, but the first version came with some steep infrastructure requirements and was not widely used. Server 2016 brings a whole new set of advantages and makes implementation much easier than in the past. I still find many server and networking admins who have never heard of DirectAccess, so let's spend some time together exploring some of the common tasks associated with it.

In this chapter, we will cover the following recipes:

- DirectAccess planning question and answers
- Configuring DirectAccess, VPN, or a combination of the two
- Pre-staging Group Policy Objects to be used by DirectAccess
- Enhancing the security of DirectAccess by requiring certificate authentication
- Building your Network Location Server on its own system
- Enabling Network Load Balancing on your DirectAccess servers

- Adding VPN to your existing DirectAccess server
- Replacing your expiring IP-HTTPS certificate
- Reporting on DirectAccess and VPN connections

Introduction

There are two flavors of remote access available in Windows Server 2016. The most common way to implement the Remote Access role is to provide DirectAccess for your Windows 7, 8, and 10 domain-joined client computers and a VPN for the rest. The DA machines are typically your company-owned corporate assets. One of the primary reasons why DirectAccess is usually only for company assets is that the client machines must be joined to your domain because the DA configuration settings are brought down to the client through a GPO. I doubt you want the home and personal computers joining your domain.

VPN is therefore used for down-level clients such as Windows XP or non-domain-joined Windows 7/8/10, and for home and personal devices that want to access the network. Since this is a traditional VPN listener with all regular protocols available such as PPTP, L2TP, and SSTP, it can even work to connect devices such as smartphones and tablets to your network.

There is a third function available within the Server 2016 Remote Access role called the **Web Application Proxy** (**WAP**). This function is not used for connecting remote computers fully into the network, unlike DirectAccess and VPN; rather, WAP is used for publishing internal web resources out to the Internet. For example, if you are running Exchange and SharePoint Server inside your network and want to publish access to these web-based resources to the Internet for external users to connect to, WAP would be a mechanism that could publish access to these resources. The term for publishing to the Internet like this is Reverse Proxy, and WAP can act as such. It can also behave as an ADFS Proxy.

For further information on the WAP role, please visit `http://technet.microsoft.com/en-us/library/dn584107.aspx`.

DirectAccess planning question and answers

One of the most confusing parts about setting up DirectAccess is that there are many different ways to do it. Some are good ideas, while others are not. Before we get rolling with recipes, we are going to cover a series of questions and answers to help guide you towards a successful DA deployment. One of the first questions that always presents itself when setting up DirectAccess is "How do I assign IP addresses to my DA server?". This is quite a loaded question because the answer depends on how you plan to implement DA, which features you plan to utilize, and even upon how secure you believe your DA server to be. Let me ask you some questions, pose potential answers to those questions, and discuss the effects of making each decision.

- Which client operating systems can connect using DirectAccess?

  Windows 7 Ultimate, Windows 7 Enterprise, Windows 8.x Enterprise, and Windows 10 Enterprise or Education. You'll notice that the Professional SKU is missing from this list. That is correct; Windows 7, Windows 8, and Windows 10 Pro do *not* contain the DirectAccess connectivity components. Yes, this does mean that Surface Pro tablets cannot utilize DirectAccess out-of-the-box. However, I have seen many companies now install Windows 10 Enterprise onto their Surface tablets, effectively turning them into *Surface Enterprises*. This works well and does indeed enable them to be DA clients. In fact, I am currently typing this text on a DirectAccess connected Surface *Pro turned Enterprise* tablet.

- Do I need one or two NICs on my DirectAccess server?

  Technically, you could set up either way. In practice, however, it really is designed for dual-NIC implementation. Single NIC DirectAccess works okay sometimes to establish a proof-of-concept to test out the technology, but I have seen too many problems with single NIC implementations in the field to ever recommend it for production use. Stick with two network cards, one facing the internal network and one facing the Internet.

- Do my DirectAccess servers have to be joined to the domain?

  Yes.

- Does DirectAccess have site-to-site failover capabilities?

  Yes, though only Windows 8.x and 10 client computers can take advantage of it. This functionality is called Multi-Site DirectAccess. Multiple DA servers that are spread out geographically can be joined together in a multi-site array. Windows 8 and 10 client computers keep track of each individual entry point and are able to swing between them as needed or at user preference. Windows 7 clients do not have this capability and will always connect through their primary site.

- What are these things called 6to4, Teredo, and IP-HTTPS that I have seen in the Microsoft documentation?

  6to4, Teredo, and IP-HTTPS are all IPv6 transition tunneling protocols. All DirectAccess packets that are moving across the Internet between a DA client and DA server are IPv6 packets. If your internal network is IPv4, then when those packets reach the DirectAccess server they get turned down into IPv4 packets by some special components called DNS64 and NAT64. While these functions handle the translation of packets from IPv6 into IPv4 when necessary inside the corporate network, the key point here is that all DirectAccess packets that are traveling over the Internet part of the connection are always IPv6. Since the majority of the Internet is still IPv4, this means that we must tunnel those IPv6 packets inside something to get them across the Internet. That is the job of 6to4, Teredo, and IP-HTTPS. 6to4 encapsulates IPv6 packets into IPv4 headers and shuttles them around the Internet using protocol 41. Teredo similarly encapsulates IPv6 packets inside IPv4 headers, but then uses UDP port 3544 to transport them. IP-HTTPS encapsulates IPv6 inside IPv4 and then inside HTTP encrypted with TLS, essentially creating an HTTPS stream across the Internet. This, like any HTTPS traffic, utilizes TCP port 443. The DirectAccess traffic traveling inside either kind of tunnel is always encrypted since DirectAccess itself is protected by IPsec.

- Do I want to enable my clients to connect using Teredo?

  Most of the time, the answer here is yes. Probably the biggest factor that weighs on this decision is whether or not you are still running Windows 7 clients. When Teredo is enabled in an environment, this gives the client computers an opportunity to connect using Teredo, rather than all clients connecting in over the IP-HTTPS protocol. IP-HTTPS is sort of the catch-all for connections, but Teredo will be preferred by clients if it is available. For Windows 7 clients, Teredo is quite a bit faster than IP-HTTPS. So enabling Teredo on the server side means your Windows 7 clients (the ones connecting via Teredo) will have quicker response times, and the load on your DirectAccess server will be lessened. This is because Windows 7 clients connecting over IP-HTTPS are encrypting all of the traffic twice. This also means that the DA server is encrypting/decrypting everything that comes and goes twice. In Windows 8 and 10, there is an enhancement that brings IP-HTTPS performance almost on a par with Teredo, and so environments that are fully upgraded to Windows 8 and higher will receive less benefit from the extra work that goes into making sure Teredo works.

- Can I place my DirectAccess server behind a NAT?

  Yes, though there is a downside. Teredo cannot work if the DirectAccess server is sitting behind a NAT. For Teredo to be available, the DA server must have an External NIC with two consecutive *public* IP addresses. True public addresses. If you place your DA server behind any kind of NAT, Teredo will not be available and all clients will connect using the IP-HTTPS protocol. Again, if you are using Windows 7 clients, this will decrease their speed and increase the load on your DirectAccess server.

- How many IP addresses do I need on a standalone DirectAccess server?

    I am going to leave single NIC implementation out of this answer since I don't recommend it anyway. For scenarios where you are sitting the External NIC behind a NAT or, for any other reason, are limiting your DA to IP-HTTPS only, then we need one external address and one internal address. The external address can be a true public address or a private NATed DMZ address. Same with the internal; it could be a true internal IP or a DMZ IP. Make sure both NICs are not plugged into the same DMZ, however. For a better installation scenario that allows Teredo connections to be possible, you would need two consecutive public IP addresses on the External NIC and a single internal IP on the Internal NIC. This internal IP could be either a true internal or DMZ, but the public IPs really have to be public for Teredo to work.

- Do I need an internal PKI?

    Maybe. If you want to connect Windows 7 clients, then the answer is yes. If you are completely Windows 8 and above, then technically you do not need an internal PKI. But you really should use it anyway. Using an internal PKI, which can be a single, simple Windows CA server, greatly increases the security of your DirectAccess infrastructure. You'll find out during this chapter just how easy it is to implement certificates as part of the tunnel building authentication process, making your connections stronger and more secure.

Configuring DirectAccess, VPN, or a combination of the two

Now that we have some general ideas about how we want to implement our remote access technologies, where do we begin? Most services that you want to run on a Windows Server begin with a role installation, but the implementation of remote access begins before that. Let's walk through the process of taking a new server and turning it into a Microsoft Remote Access server.

Getting ready

All of our work will be accomplished on a new Windows Server 2016. We are taking the two-NIC approach to networking, and so we have two NICs installed on this server. The Internal NIC is plugged into the corporate network and the External NIC is plugged into the Internet for the sake of simplicity. The External NIC could just as well be plugged into a DMZ.

How to do it...

Follow these steps to turn your new server into a Remote Access server:

1. Assign IP addresses to your server. Since this is a multi-homed system with both internal and external networks connected, make sure you follow the steps in the *Multi-homing your Windows Server 2016* recipe in `Chapter 3`, *Security and Networking*. Remember, the most important part is making sure that the Default Gateway goes on the External NIC only.

2. Join the new server to your domain.

3. Install an SSL certificate onto your DirectAccess server, which you plan to use for the IP-HTTPS listener. This is typically a certificate purchased from a public CA.

4. If you're planning to use client certificates for authentication, make sure to pull down a copy of the certificate from your internal CA to your DirectAccess server.

> You want to make sure certificates are in place before you start the configuration of DirectAccess. This way the wizards will be able to automatically pull in information about those certificates in the first run. If you don't, DA will set itself up to use self-signed certificates, which are a security no-no.

5. Use Server Manager to install the **Remote Access** role. You should only do this after completing the previous steps.

6. If you plan to load balance multiple DirectAccess servers together at a later time, make sure to also install the feature called **Network Load Balancing**.

7. After selecting your role and feature, you will be asked which Remote Access role services you want to install. For our purposes of getting the remote workforce connected back into the corporate network, we want to choose **DirectAccess and VPN (RAS)**.

Select the role services to install for Remote Access

Role services

☑ DirectAccess and VPN (RAS)
☐ Routing
☐ Web Application Proxy

---

8. Now that the role has been successfully installed, you will see a yellow exclamation mark notification near the top of Server Manager indicating that you have some **Post-deployment Configuration** that needs to be done.

> Do *not* click on **Open the Getting Started Wizard!**

9. Unfortunately, Server Manager leads you to believe that launching the **Getting Started Wizard (GSW)** is the logical next step. However, using the GSW as the mechanism for configuring your DirectAccess settings is kind of like roasting a marshmallow with a pair of tweezers. In order to ensure you have the full range of options available to you as you configure your remote access settings and that you don't get burned later, make sure to launch the configuration this way:

10. Click on the **Tools** menu from inside Server Manager and launch the **Remote Access Management Console**.

11. In the left window pane, navigate to **Configuration | DirectAccess and VPN**.

12. Click on the second link, the one that says **Run the Remote Access Setup Wizard**. Please note that once again the top option is to run that pesky Getting Started Wizard. Don't do it! I'll explain why in the *How it works...* section of this recipe.

➜ Run the Remote Access Setup Wizard

Use this wizard to configure DirectAccess and VPN with custom settings.

---

13. Now you have a choice that you will have to answer for yourself. Are you configuring only DirectAccess, only VPN, or a combination of the two? Simply click on the option that you want to deploy. Following your choice, you will see a series of steps (Steps 1 through 4) that need to be accomplished. This series of mini-wizards will guide you through the remainder of the DirectAccess and VPN particulars. This recipe isn't large enough to cover every specific option included in those wizards, but at least you now know the correct way to bring a DA/VPN server into operation.

How it works...

The remote access technologies included in Server 2016 have great functionality, but their initial configuration can be confusing. Following the procedure listed in this recipe will set you on the right path to be successful in your deployment, and prevent you from running into issues down the road. The reasons that I absolutely recommend you stay away from using the shortcut deployment method provided by the Getting Started Wizard are twofold:

- GSW skips a lot of options as it sets up DirectAccess, so you don't really have any understanding of how it works after finishing. You may have DA up-and-running, but have no idea how it's authenticating or working under the hood. This holds so much potential for problems later, should anything suddenly stop working.

- GSW employs a number of bad security practices in order to save time and effort in the setup process. For example, using the GSW usually means that your DirectAccess server will be authenticating users without client certificates, which is not a best practice. Also, it will co-host something called the NLS website on itself, which is also not a best practice. Those who utilize the GSW to configure DirectAccess will find that their GPO, which contains the client connectivity settings, will be security-filtered to the Domain Computers group. Even though it also contains a WMI filter that is supposed to limit that policy application to only mobile hardware like laptops, this is a terribly scary thing to see inside GPO filtering settings. You probably don't want all of your laptops to immediately start getting DA connectivity settings, but that is exactly what the GSW does for you. Perhaps worst, the GSW will create and make use of self-signed SSL certificates to validate its web traffic, even the traffic coming in from the Internet! This is a terrible practice and is the number one reason that should convince you that clicking on the Getting Started Wizard is not in your best interests.

Pre-staging Group Policy Objects to be used by DirectAccess

One of the great things about DirectAccess is that all of the connectivity settings the client computers need in order to connect are contained within a **Group Policy Objects** (**GPO**). This means that you can turn new client computers into DirectAccess-connected clients without ever touching that system. Once configured properly, all you need to do is add the new computer account to an Active Directory security group and, during the next automatic Group Policy refresh cycle (usually within 90 minutes), that new laptop will be connecting via DirectAccess whenever outside the corporate network.

You can certainly choose not to pre-stage anything with the GPOs and DirectAccess will still work. When you get to the end of the DA configuration wizard, it will inform you that two new GPOs are about to be created inside Active Directory. One GPO is used to contain the DirectAccess server settings, and the other GPO is used to contain the DirectAccess client settings. If you allow the wizard to handle the generation of these GPOs, it will create them, link them, filter them, and populate them with settings automatically. About half of the time, I see folks do it this way and are forever happy with letting the wizard manage those GPOs now and in the future.

The other half of the time, it is desired that we maintain a little more personal control over the GPOs. If you are setting up a new DA environment but your credentials don't have permission to create GPOs, the wizard is not going to be able to create them either. In this case, you will need to work with someone on your Active Directory team to get them created. Another reason to manage the GPOs manually is to have better control over placement of these policies. When you let the DA wizard create the GPOs, it will link them to the top level of your domain. It also sets Security Filtering on those GPOs so they are not going to be applied to everything in your domain, but when you open up the **Group Policy Management** console you will always see those DA policies listed right up there at the top level of the domain. Sometimes this is simply not desirable. So for this reason as well, you may want to choose to create and manage the GPOs by hand, so that we can secure placement and links where we specifically want them to be located.

Getting ready

While the DirectAccess wizards themselves are run from the DA server, our work with this recipe is not. The Group Policy settings that we will be configuring are all accomplished within Active Directory, and we will be doing the work from a Domain Controller in our environment.

How to do it...

To pre-stage GPOs for use with DirectAccess, follow these steps:

1. In your Domain Controller, launch the **Group Policy Management Console**.
2. Navigate to **Forest | Domains | Your Domain Name**. There should be a listing here called **Group Policy Objects**. Right-click on that and choose **New**.
3. Name your new GPO something like `DirectAccess Server Settings`.
4. Click on the new **DirectAccess Server Settings** GPO and it should open up automatically to the **Scope** tab. We need to adjust the **Security Filtering** section so that this GPO only applies to our DirectAccess server. This is a critical step for each GPO to ensure the settings that are going to be placed here do not get applied to the wrong computers.
5. Remove **Authenticated Users** that are prepopulated in that list. The list should now be empty.
6. Click the **Add...** button and search for the computer account of your DirectAccess server. Mine is called `RA1`. By default, this window will only search user accounts, so you will need to adjust **Object Types** to include **Computers** before it will allow you to add your server to this filtering list.
7. Your **Security Filtering** list should now look like this:

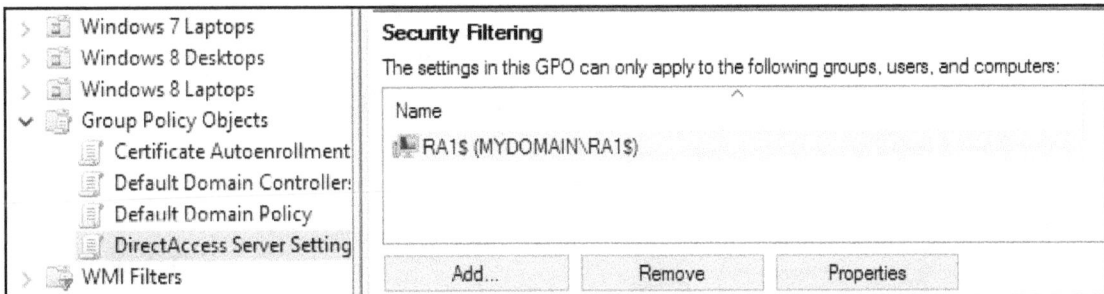

8. Now click on the **Details** tab of your GPO.

9. Change the **GPO Status** to **User configuration settings disabled**. We do this because our GPO is only going to contain computer-level settings, nothing at the user level.

10. The last thing to do is link your GPO to an appropriate container. Since we have Security Filtering enabled, our GPO is only ever going to apply its settings to the RA1 server but, without creating a link, the GPO will not even attempt to apply itself to anything. My RA1 server is sitting inside the OU called **Remote Access Servers**, so I will right-click on my **Remote Access Servers** OU and choose **Link an Existing GPO...**.

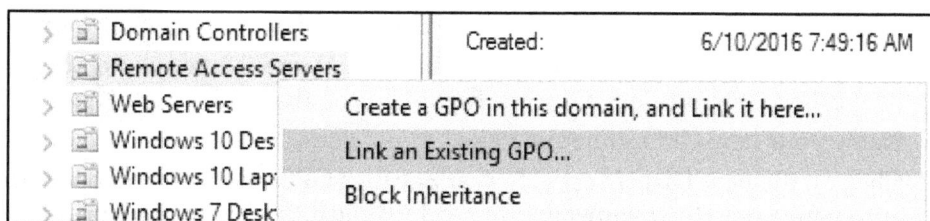

11. Choose the new **DirectAccess Server Settings** from the list of available GPOs and click on the **OK** button. This creates the link and puts the GPO into action. Since there are not yet any settings inside the GPO, it won't actually make any changes on the server. The DA configuration wizards take care of populating the GPO with the settings that are needed.

12. Now we simply need to rinse and repeat all of these steps to create another GPO, something like **DirectAccess Client Settings**. You want to set up the client settings GPO in the same way. Make sure that it is filtering to only the Active Directory Security Group that you created to contain your DirectAccess client computers. And make sure to link it to an appropriate container that will include those computer accounts. So maybe your client's GPO will look something like this:

```
DirectAccess Client Settings

Scope   Details   Settings   Delegation   Status

Links

Display links in this location:        MYDOMAIN.LOCAL                                    ∨

The following sites, domains, and OUs are linked to this GPO:

┌──────────────────────────────────────────────────────────────────────────────────┐
│ Location                        Enforced    Link Enabled    Path                   │
│  ▦ Windows 10 Laptops             No           Yes          MYDOMAIN.LOCAL/Wind     │
│  ▦ Windows 7 Laptops              No           Yes          MYDOMAIN.LOCAL/Wind     │
│  ▦ Windows 8 Laptops              No           Yes          MYDOMAIN.LOCAL/Wind     │
│  ‹                                                                              ›   │
└──────────────────────────────────────────────────────────────────────────────────┘

Security Filtering

The settings in this GPO can only apply to the following groups, users, and computers:

┌──────────────────────────────────────────────────────────────────────────────────┐
│ Name                                                                               │
│  ⚇ DirectAccess Computers (MYDOMAIN\DirectAccess Computers)                         │
│                                                                                    │
│                                                                                    │
└──────────────────────────────────────────────────────────────────────────────────┘

    [ Add... ]          [ Remove ]          [ Properties ]
```

How it works...

Creating GPOs in Active Directory is a simple enough task, but it is critical that you
configure the Links and Security Filtering correctly. If you do not take care to ensure that
these DirectAccess connection settings are only going to apply to the machines that actually
need the settings, you could create a world of trouble with internal servers getting remote
access connection settings and causing them issues with connection while inside the
network.

The key factors here are to make sure your DirectAccess Server Settings GPO applies to only the DA server or servers in your environment, and that the DirectAccess Client Settings GPO applies to only the DA client computers that you plan to enable in your network. The best practice here is to specify this GPO to only apply to a specific Active Directory security group so that you have full control over which computer accounts are in that group. I have seen some folks do it based only on the OU links and include whole OUs in the filtering for the clients GPO (foregoing the use of an AD group at all), but doing it this way makes it quite a bit more difficult to add or remove machines from the access list in the future.

Enhancing the security of DirectAccess by requiring certificate authentication

When a DirectAccess client computer builds its IPsec tunnels back to the corporate network, it has the ability to require a certificate as part of that authentication process. In earlier versions of DirectAccess, the one in Server 2008 R2 and the one provided by **Unified Access Gateway** (**UAG**), these certificates were required in order to make DirectAccess work. Setting up the certificates really isn't a big deal at all. As long as there is a CA server in your network, you are already prepared to issue the necessary certificates at no cost. Unfortunately, though, there must have been enough complaints back to Microsoft in order for them to make these certificates recommended instead of required, and they created a new mechanism in Windows 8 and Server 2012 called KerberosProxy that can be used to authenticate the tunnels instead. This allows the DirectAccess tunnels to build without the computer certificate, making that authentication process easier to set up initially, but less secure overall.

I'm here to strongly recommend that you still utilize certificates in your installs! They are not difficult to set up, and using them makes your tunnel authentication stronger. Further, many of you may not have a choice and will still be required to install these certificates. Only simple DirectAccess scenarios that are all Windows 8 or higher on the client side can get away with the shortcut method of foregoing certificates. Anybody who still wants to connect Windows 7 via DirectAccess will need to use certificates as part of their implementation. In addition to Windows 7 access, anyone who intends to use the advanced features of DirectAccess, such as load balancing, multi-site, or two-factor authentication, will also need to utilize these certificates. With any of these scenarios, certificates become a requirement again, not a recommendation.

In my experience, almost everyone still has Windows 7 clients that would benefit from being DirectAccess-connected, and it's always a good idea to make your DA environment redundant by having load-balanced servers. This further emphasizes the point that you should just set up certificate authentication right out of the gate, whether or not you need it initially. You might decide to make a change later that would require certificates, and it would be easier to have them installed from the get-go than trying to incorporate them later into a running DA environment.

Getting ready

In order to distribute certificates, you will need a CA server running in your network. Once certificates are distributed to the appropriate places, the rest of our work will be accomplished from our Server 2016 DirectAccess server.

How to do it...

Follow these steps to make use of certificates as part of the DirectAccess tunnel authentication process:

1. The first thing that you need to do is distribute certificates to your DA servers and all DA client computers. The easiest way to do this is by building a new template on the CA server that is duplicated from the in-built Computer template. Whenever I create a custom template for use with DirectAccess, I try to make sure that it meets the following criteria:
   - The **Subject Name** of the certificate should match the **Common Name** of the computer (which is also the FQDN of the computer)
   - The **Subject Alternative Name** (**SAN**) of the certificate should match the **DNS Name** of the computer (which is also the FQDN of the computer)
   - The certificate should serve the **Intended Purposes** of both **Client Authentication** and **Server Authentication**

2. For the actual distribution of these certificates, I'm going to direct you to review a couple of other recipes in this book. You can issue these certificates manually using **Microsoft Management Console** (**MMC**), as described in the *Using MMC to request a new certificate* recipe in `Chapter 4`, *Working with Certificates*. Otherwise, you can lessen your hands-on administrative duties by enabling Autoenrollment, which is discussed in the *Configuring Autoenrollment to issue certificates to all domain joined systems* recipe in `Chapter 4`, *Working with Certificates*.

3. Now that we have certificates distributed to our DirectAccess clients and servers, log-in to your primary DirectAccess server and open up the **Remote Access Management Console**.

4. Click on **Configuration** in the top-left corner. You should now see steps 1 through 4 listed.

5. Click **Edit...** listed under step 2.

6. Now you can either click **Next** twice or click on the word **Authentication** to jump directly to the authentication screen.

7. Check the box that says **Use computer certificates**.

8. Now we have to specify the Certification Authority server that issued our client certificates. If you used an intermediary CA to issue your certificates, make sure to check the appropriate checkbox. Otherwise, most of the time, certificates are issued from a root CA, and in this case you would simply click on the **Browse...** button and look for your CA in the list.

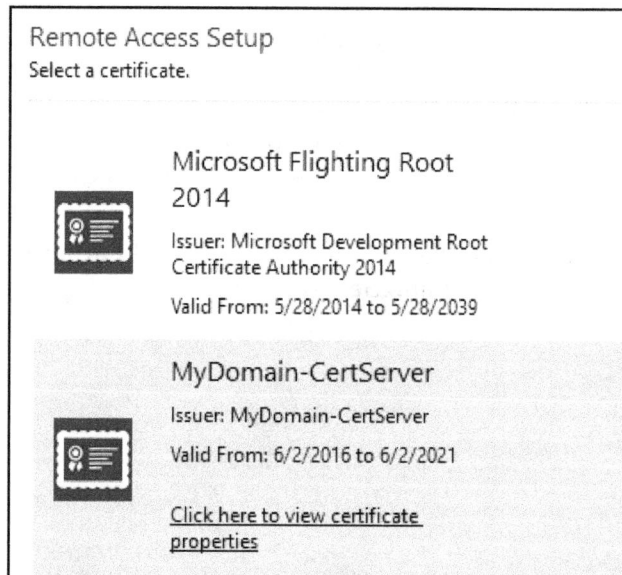

Remote Access Setup
Select a certificate.

Microsoft Flighting Root 2014

Issuer: Microsoft Development Root Certificate Authority 2014

Valid From: 5/28/2014 to 5/28/2039

MyDomain-CertServer

Issuer: MyDomain-CertServer

Valid From: 6/2/2016 to 6/2/2021

Click here to view certificate properties

This screen is sometimes confusing because people expect to have to choose the certificate itself from the list. This is not the case. What you are actually choosing from this list is the CA server that issued the certificates.

9. Make any other appropriate selections on the **Authentication** screen. For example, many times when we require client certificates for authentication, it is because we have Windows 7 computers that we want to connect via DirectAccess. If that is the case for you, select the checkbox for **Enable Windows 7 client computers to connect via DirectAccess**.

Remote Access Setup ✕

Remote Access Server Setup
Configure DirectAccess and VPN settings.

Network Topology
Network Adapters
Authentication

Specify how DirectAccess clients authenticate. If computer certificates are not used for authentication, DirectAccess acts as a Kerberos proxy on behalf of the client. Enable support for Windows 7 clients.

User Authentication
- ● Active Directory credentials (username/password)
- ○ Two-factor authentication (smart card or one-time password (OTP))
  - ☐ Use OTP

☑ Use computer certificates

Select the root or intermediate certification authority (CA) that issues the certificates.
☐ Use an intermediate certificate

CN=MyDomain-CertServer, DC=MYDOMAIN, DC=LOCAL   Browse...

☑ Enable Windows 7 client computers to connect via DirectAccess

< Back   Next >   Finish   Cancel

How it works...

Requiring certificates as part of your DirectAccess tunnel authentication process is a good idea in any environment. It makes the solution more secure, and enables advanced functionality. The primary driver for most companies to require these certificates is the enablement of Windows 7 clients to connect via DirectAccess, but I suggest that anyone using DirectAccess in any capacity make use of these certs. They are simple to deploy, easy to configure, and give you some extra peace of mind knowing that only computers with a certificate issued directly to them from your own internal CA server are going to be able to connect through your DirectAccess entry point.

Building your Network Location Server on its own system

If you zipped through the default settings when configuring DirectAccess, or worse, used the Getting Started Wizard, chances are that your **Network Location Server** (**NLS**) is running right on the DirectAccess server itself. This is not the recommended method for using NLS; it really should be running on a separate web server. In fact, if you want to do something more advanced later, such as setting up load-balanced DirectAccess servers, you're going to have to move NLS onto a different server anyway, so you might as well do it right the first time.

NLS is a very simple requirement, but a critical one. It is just a website, it doesn't matter what content the site has, and it only has to run inside your network. Nothing has to be externally available. In fact, nothing should be externally available, because you only want this site accessed internally. This NLS website is a large part of the mechanism by which DirectAccess client computers figure out when they are inside the office and when they are outside. If they can see the NLS website, they know they are inside the network and will disable DirectAccess name resolution, effectively turning off DA. If they do not see the NLS website, they will assume they are outside the corporate network and enable DirectAccess name resolution.

There are two *gotchas* with setting up an NLS website:

- The first is that it must be HTTPS, so it does need a valid SSL certificate. Since this website is only running inside the network and being accessed from domain-joined computers, this SSL certificate can easily be one that has been issued from your internal CA server. So there's no cost associated there.
- The second catch that I have encountered a number of times is that for some reason the default IIS splash screen page doesn't make for a very good NLS website. If you set up a standard IIS web server and use the default site as NLS, sometimes it works to validate the connections and sometimes it doesn't. Given that, I always set up a specific site that I create myself, just to be on the safe side.

So let's work together to follow the exact process I always take when setting up NLS websites in a new DirectAccess environment.

Getting ready

Our NLS website will be hosted on an IIS server that runs Server 2016. Most of the work will be accomplished from this web server, but we will also be creating a DNS record and will utilize a Domain Controller for that task.

How to do it...

Let's work together to set up our new Network Location Server website:

1. First, decide on an internal DNS name to use for this website and set it up in DNS of your domain. I am going to use `nls.mydomain.local` and am creating a regular Host (A) record, which points `nls.mydomain.local` to the IP address of my web server.
2. Now log in to that web server and let's create some simple content for this new website. Create a new folder called `C:\NLS`.
3. Inside your new folder, create a new `Default.htm` file.

4. Edit this file and throw some simple text in there. I usually say something like `This is the NLS website used by DirectAccess. Please do not delete or modify me!`.

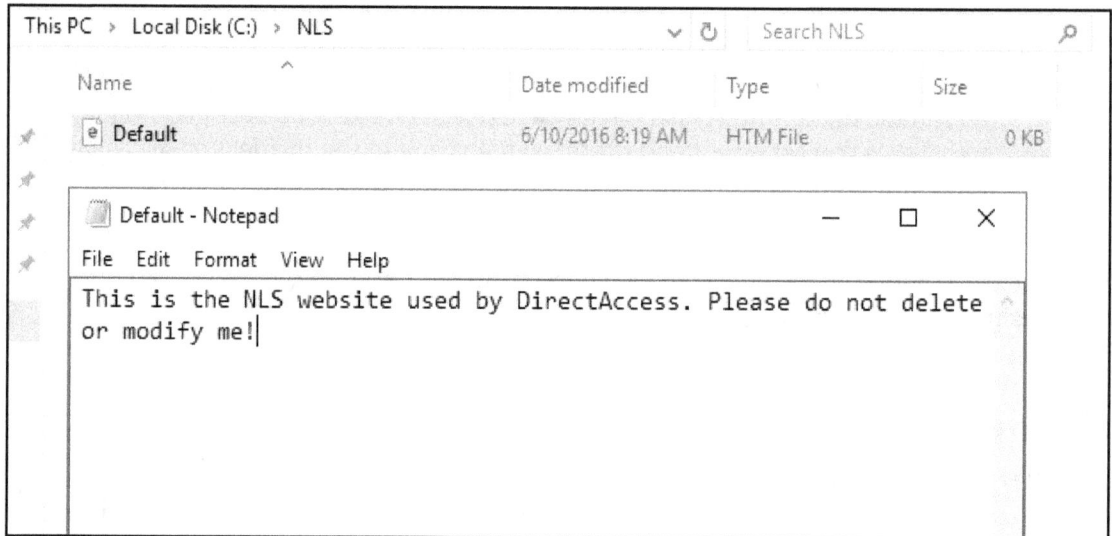

This PC › Local Disk (C:) › NLS				
Name	Date modified	Type	Size	
e Default	6/10/2016 8:19 AM	HTM File	0 KB	

```
Default - Notepad                                    —    □    ✕
File  Edit  Format  View  Help
This is the NLS website used by DirectAccess. Please do not delete
or modify me!
```

5. Remember, this needs to be an HTTPS website, so before we try setting up the actual website, we should acquire the SSL certificate that we need to use with this site. Since this certificate is coming from my internal CA server, I'm going to open up MMC on my web server to accomplish this task.

6. Once MMC is opened, snap in the **Certificates** module. Make sure to choose **Computer account** and then **Local computer** when it prompts you for which certificate store you want to open.

7. Navigate to **Certificates (Local Computer)** | **Personal** | **Certificates**.

8. Right-click on this **Certificates** folder and choose **All Tasks** | **Request New Certificate…**.

9. Click **Next** twice and you should see your list of certificate templates that are available on your internal CA server. If you do not see one that looks appropriate for requesting a website certificate, you may need to check over the settings on your CA server to make sure the correct templates are configured for issuance.

10. My template is called **Custom Web Server**. Since this is a web server certificate, there is some additional information that I need to provide in my request in order to successfully issue a certificate. So I go ahead and click on the link that says **More information is required to enroll for this certificate. Click here to configure settings.**

Active Directory Enrollment Policy

☐ Computer   (i) **STATUS:** Available   Details ⌄

☑ Custom Web Server   (i) **STATUS:** Available   Details ⌄
   ⚠ More information is required to enroll for this certificate. Click here to configure settings.

☐ DA Cert   (i) **STATUS:** Available   Details ⌄

☐ IPsec Certificate   (i) **STATUS:** Available   Details ⌄

---

11. Drop down the **Subject name** | **Type** menu and choose the **Common name** option.
12. Enter a common name for our website into the **Value** field, which in my case is `nls.mydomain.local`.
13. Click the **Add** button, and your CN should move over to the right side of the screen like this:

Subject name:

Type: CN=nls.mydomain.local

Common name   ⌄   Add >

Value: < Remove

14. Click on **OK** then click on the **Enroll** button. You should now have an SSL certificate sitting in your certificates store that can be used to authenticate traffic moving to our `nls.mydomain.local name`.
15. Open up **Internet Information Services (IIS) Manager** and browse to the **Sites** folder. Go ahead and remove the default website that IIS had automatically set up so that we can create our own NLS website without any fear of conflict.
16. Click on the **Add Website...** button.

17. Populate the information as shown in the following screenshot. Make sure to choose your own IP address and SSL certificate from the lists, of course:

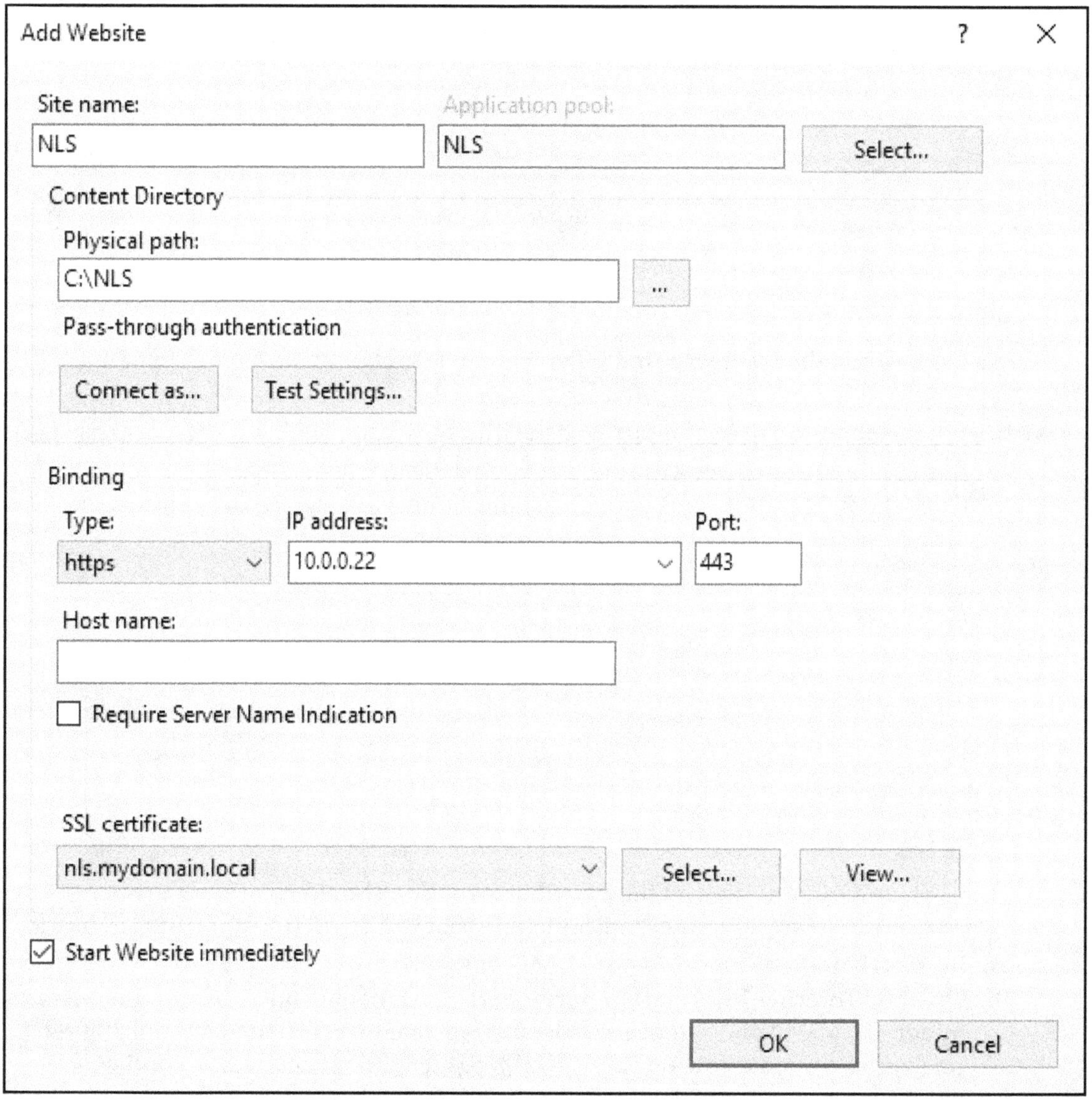

Add Website ? ✕

Site name:
`NLS`

Application pool:
`NLS` Select...

Content Directory

Physical path:
`C:\NLS` ...

Pass-through authentication

Connect as... Test Settings...

Binding

Type: | IP address: | Port:
https ∨ | 10.0.0.22 ∨ | 443

Host name:

☐ Require Server Name Indication

SSL certificate:
nls.mydomain.local ∨ Select... View...

☑ Start Website immediately

OK Cancel

18. Click the **OK** button, and you now have an NLS website running successfully in your network. You should be able to open up a browser on a client computer sitting inside the network and successfully browse to `https://nls.mydomain.local`.

How it works...

In this recipe, we configured a basic Network Location Server website for use with our DirectAccess environment. This site will do exactly what we need it to when our DA client computers try to validate whether they are inside or outside the corporate network. While this recipe meets our requirements for NLS, and in fact puts us into the good practice of installing with NLS being hosted on its own web server, there is yet another step you could take to make it even better. Currently, this web server is a single point of failure for NLS. If this web server goes down or has a problem, we will have DirectAccess client computers inside the office thinking they are outside, and they will have some major name resolution problems until we sort out the NLS problem. Given that, it is a great idea to make NLS redundant. You could cluster servers together, use **Microsoft Network Load Balancing (NLB)**, or even use some kind of hardware load balancer if you have one available in your network. This way you could run the same NLS website on multiple web servers and know that your clients will still work properly in the event of a web server failure.

Enabling Network Load Balancing on your DirectAccess servers

DirectAccess is designed so that you always get a single server environment up-and-running first before you start tinkering with arrays or load balancing. This way you can validate that all of the environmental factors are in place and working and that you can successfully build DA tunnels from your client computers before introducing any further complexity into the design. Once established, however, it is a common next step to look into turning up another new server and creating some redundancy for your new remote access solution.

While joining two similar servers together to share the load is commonly called clustering, and sometimes I hear admins refer to it as such in the DirectAccess world, load balancing DA servers together actually has nothing to do with Windows Clustering. When you install both the remote access role and the Network Load Balancing feature onto your remote access servers, you have already equipped them with all the parts and pieces they need in order to communicate with each other and run an Active/Active sharing configuration. The operating system will make use of Windows NLB to shuttle traffic to the appropriate destinations, but everything inside NLB gets configured from the remote access Management Console. This gives you a nice visual console that can be used to administer and manage those NLB settings right alongside your other remote access settings.

Once DirectAccess is established and running on a single server, there really are just a couple of quick wizards to run through to configure this NLB. However, the verbiage in these options can be quite confusing, especially if you're not overly familiar with the way that DirectAccess transmits packets. So let's take some time to walk through creating an array from our existing DA server and adding a second node to that array.

Getting ready

We are going to use our existing RA1 server, which is already running DirectAccess. This, and our new server, RA2, are both running Windows Server 2016. They both have the Remote Access role and the Network Load Balancing feature installed. Both are joined to our domain and have their required certificates (SSL and IPsec) installed for use with DirectAccess. The same SSL certificate has been installed to both servers; since they are going to be sharing the load and all requests to both systems will be coming in from the same public DNS name, they are able to share that certificate.

If your DirectAccess servers are virtual machines, there is one very important prerequisite. You must go into your VM's NIC settings and choose the **Enable spoofing of MAC addresses** option. Without this box checked for each of the NICs, your network traffic will stop working altogether when you create a load balanced array.

How to do it...

For the purposes of this recipe, we are going to assume that RA1 has been configured for use with Teredo, meaning that it has two public IP addresses assigned on the External NIC. We are using this as an example because it is the most complex configuration to walk through when setting up NLB. The same procedure applies for a single IP on the External NIC; it would simply mean that you are only configuring one **Virtual IP** (**VIP**) instead of two.

1. First, we need to have a clear understanding of which IP addresses are going to be used where. This is critical information to possess and understand before trying to start any kind of configuration. The current RA1 IP addresses are as follows:
   - **External IPs**: 1.1.1.10 and 1.1.1.11
   - **Internal IP**: 10.0.0.7

2. These three IP addresses that are currently running on RA1 are going to turn into our **Virtual IPs** (**VIPs**). These are the IP addresses that are going to be shared between both DirectAccess servers. Since we are changing the roles of these IPs, this means that we need to dedicate new **Dedicated IPs** (**DIPs**), both internally and externally, to both RA1 and RA2.

3. New IP address assignments are shown as follows:
   - **External VIPs (shared)**: 1.1.1.10 and 1.1.1.11
   - **Internal VIP (shared)**: 10.0.0.7
   - **RA1 External DIP**: 1.1.1.12
   - **RA1 Internal DIP**: 10.0.0.8
   - **RA2 External DIP**: 1.1.1.13
   - **RA2 Internal DIP**: 10.0.0.9

4. So, to summarize, when using Teredo (dual public IPs) and creating a two-node DirectAccess server load balanced array, you will need a total of four public IP addresses and three internal IP addresses.

5. On RA1, we are going to leave the VIPs in place for now. The DirectAccess wizards will change them for us later.

6. On the new RA2 server, set its final DIP addresses on the NICs. So in our example, the External NIC gets 1.1.1.13 and the Internal NIC gets 10.0.0.9.

7. There are only four steps to take on a DirectAccess array node server such as RA2, or any additional DA server that you want to add to the array in the future:
   - Assign IP addresses.
   - Join it to the domain.
   - Install the certificates.
   - Add the Remote Access role and Network Load Balancing feature.

8. The remainder of its configuration is accomplished from the Remote Access Management Console on RA1.

9. On RA1, your primary DirectAccess server, open **Remote Access Management Console**.

10. In the left window pane, navigate to **Configuration** | **DirectAccess and VPN**.

11. Now, over in the right-hand **Tasks** pane, down at the bottom, choose **Enable Load Balancing**.

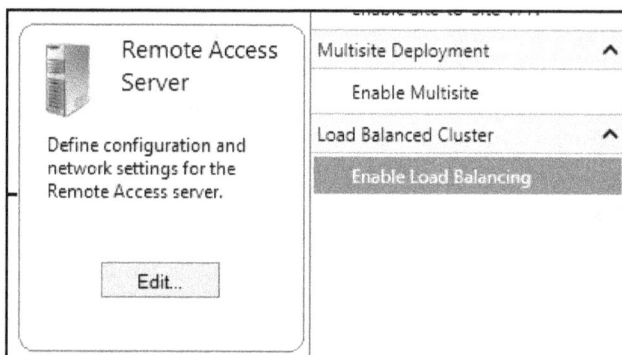

12. Click **Next**.

13. Choose **Use Windows Network Load Balancing (NLB)**. You can see there is also an option for using an external load balancer, if you have one available to you. I find that the majority of customers utilize the built-in NLB, even when hardware load balancers are available.

14. The next screen is **External Dedicated IP Addresses**. This is where things start to get confusing and mistakes are often made. If you read the text on this screen, it is telling you that the current IP addresses assigned to the NICs are now going to be used as VIPs. You do not need to specify anything about the VIPs on this screen. Instead, what we are doing on this screen and the next is specifying what *new* DIPs are now going to be assigned to the physical NICs on this server. First, since this is the external screen, we specify our new public IP that will be used by RA1:

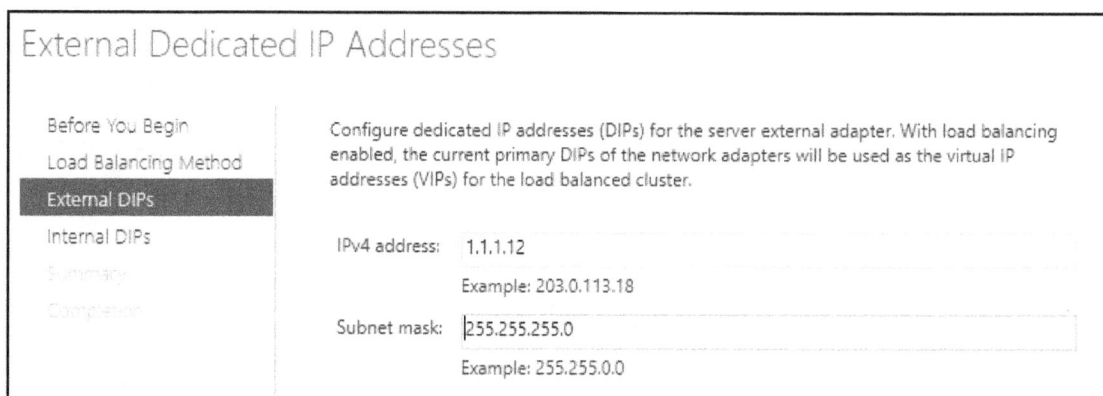

15. On the following screen, do the same thing but this time for the Internal NIC. The current IP address of 10.0.0.7 is going to be converted over into a shared VIP, and so we need to specify the new Internal DIP that is going to be assigned to RA1's Internal NIC.

Internal Dedicated IP Addresses

Before You Begin

Load Balancing Method

External DIPs

Internal DIPs

Summary

Completion

Configure dedicated IP addresses (DIPs) for the server internal adapter. With load balancing enabled, the current primary DIPs of the network adapters will be used as the virtual IP addresses (VIPs) for the load balanced cluster.

IPv4 address: 10.0.0.8

Example: 10.0.0.18

Subnet mask: 255.255.255.0

Example: 255.255.0.0

> Now you can see why having a definitive list of IP addresses before starting this wizard is important!

16. Click **Next**, then if everything looks correct in the **Summary** screen, go ahead and click on the **Commit** button. This will roll the changes into the GPO settings and apply the changes to our RA1 server. Remember, nothing has been done to RA2 yet as we haven't specified anything about it in these screens. We now have an active array, but so far there is only one member, RA1.

17. Now that you are back inside the main **Configuration** screen, go ahead and navigate to **Load Balanced Cluster | Add or Remove Servers**.

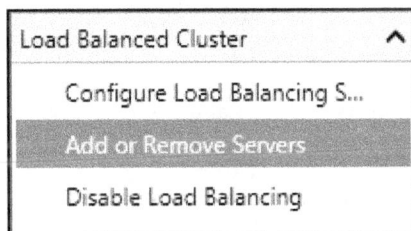

Load Balanced Cluster ⌃

Configure Load Balancing S...

Add or Remove Servers

Disable Load Balancing

18. Click on the **Add Server...** button.

19. Input the FQDN of your second server. Mine is `RA2.MYDOMAIN.LOCAL`. Then click **Next**.

20. If you have appropriately configured your second remote access server with correct IP address information and the certificates that it needs, the **Network Adapters** screen should self-populate all of the necessary information. Double-check this info to make sure it looks correct and click **Next**.

Network Adapters

Select Server	Select the network adapters that connect to the external and internal network.
Network Adapters	
Summary	
Completion	

External adapter:

External	▼		Internal	▼
1.1.1.13	:	Details	192.168.0.27	Details

Internal adapter:

Select the certificate used to authenticate IP-HTTPS connections.

☐ Use a self-signed certificate

CN=directaccess.my [_____] Browse...

21. If the **Summary** page all looks correct, click on the **Add** button.

22. Click **Close**. Then back in the **Add or Remove Servers** screen, you should now see both of your remote access servers in the list. Go ahead and click on the **Commit** button to finalize the addition of this second node.

Add or Remove Servers

Add or remove servers from a load balanced cluster. The cluster must contain at least one server.

Server Name	External Adapter	Internal Adapter	VPN Static Pool
RA-01.MYDOMAIN.LOCAL	External	Internal	
RA-02.MYDOMAIN.LOCAL	External	Internal	

Following the addition of the second node, I always go back into the NIC properties of both NICs on both servers and make sure that all of the expected IP addresses got added correctly. Sometimes I find that the wizard is not able to successfully populate all of the VIPs and DIPs, and that I have to add them manually afterwards. Each NIC now has a specific DIP, as listed at the beginning of this recipe. In addition to those DIPs, the External NIC on each server should also list both External VIPs, and the Internal NIC on each server should list the Internal VIP. The TCP/IPv4 properties of the NICs sure look to be overly-populated with IP addresses, but this is all normal and well for a successfully load-balanced DirectAccess array.

How it works...

The ability to load balance DA servers together right out of the box with Windows Server 2016 is an incredibly nice feature. Redundancy is key for any good solution, and configuring this array for an Active/Active failover situation is a no-brainer. While the wizards for enabling NLB are centralized right alongside all the other DirectAccess settings, they can certainly be confusing when running through them for the first time. As with any system whose job is to shuttle network traffic around, planning correctly for IP addressing and routing is key to the success of your DirectAccess NLB deployment. Hopefully, this recipe helps to clear up questions surrounding this commonly requested task on our remote access servers.

Following the creation of your array, you will notice that navigation through some of the screens inside the Remote Access Management Console has changed slightly. When you access screens such as **Configuration** to make changes, **Operations Status** to check on the status of your servers, or **Remote Client Status** to see what clients are connected, you will now notice that the nodes are listed separately. You can now click on the individual node name to see information on those screens that is specific to one particular server in the array, or you can click on the words **Load Balanced Cluster** in order to see information that is shared among all of the array members.

One other important note. Now that we have a load balanced array up-and-running, it is easy to add a third node to this array as well! Your DirectAccess array can grow as your company grows, up to eight node servers if required. Simply add additional servers to this array by navigating to **Load Balanced Cluster | Add or Remove Servers** task.

Adding VPN to your existing DirectAccess server

It is fairly common when starting work with the new Remote Access role for administrators to choose the *Deploy DirectAccess only* option. Maybe you initially thought this box was only going to be used for DA, or that all of your client connections would be handled by only the DA role. While this is true for some organizations, it is pretty common to get some benefit from having both DirectAccess and VPN configured on your remote access entry point. Maybe you have some mobile phones or personal tablets that you want connected to the corporate network. Or perhaps you want to give the ability for home computers, or even Macs, to connect remotely. These are scenarios that are outside the scope of DirectAccess and require some other form of VPN connectivity.

Making significant changes on a production server can be intimidating, and you want to make sure that you select the right options. Also, IP addressing remote access servers isn't always a cakewalk, and so it would be natural to assume that turning a DirectAccess server into a DirectAccess plus VPN server would involve some additional IP addressing. You would actually be wrong about that last one. VPN can share the public IP address already configured and running for your DA clients, so thankfully when you decide to add VPN to your server, you don't have to reconfigure the NICs in any way. Since we don't have to make networking changes first, let's jump right into taking our production DA server and adding the VPN role to it.

Getting ready

We are working today from our new DirectAccess server, which is a Windows Server 2016 that has the Remote Access role installed.

How to do it...

To add VPN functionality to your existing 2016 DirectAccess server, follow these steps:

1. Open **Remote Access Management Console** from the **Tools** menu inside Server Manager.
2. In the left window pane, navigate to **Configuration | DirectAccess and VPN**. This is the screen where you see the four setup steps listed in the middle.
3. Now over on the right, you see a section of buttons related to **VPN**. Go ahead and click on **Enable VPN**.

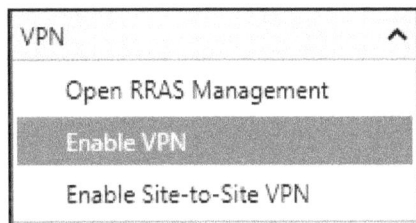

4. You will receive a pop-up message asking you to make sure you intend to configure VPN settings on this server. Go ahead and click **OK**. This will cause your remote access server to spin through some processes, reaching out to the GPOs and reconfiguring the necessary settings so that they include VPN connectivity.
5. VPN is now enabled on our server, but we have yet to configure IP addressing that will be handed out to the client computers. Once you are back at the main **Configuration** screen, click the **Edit...** button listed under step 2.
6. There is now a fourth screen available inside this mini-wizard called **VPN Configuration**. Go ahead and click on that.

7. If you want VPN clients to pull IP addresses from an internal DHCP server, leave the radio button set to the top option. If you would rather specify a particular range of IP addresses that should be handed out to client computers, choose **Assign addresses from a static address pool** and specify the range of addresses in the given fields.

IP Address Assignment   Authentication

Address assignment method:

○ Assign addresses automatically

   With this option enabled, addresses are assigned by a DHCP server.

◉ Assign addresses from a static address pool

   Add IP address ranges to the static pool. Addresses are assigned from the first range before continuing to the next.

From	To	Number
10.0.1.1	10.0.1.254	254

When you specify a static range like this, your remote access server will start handing out these addresses to the client computers that connect using VPN. However, these client computers will most likely not be able to connect to any internal resources without a little additional networking consideration. When you create a static address pool for assigning IP addresses to VPN clients, there are two rules you need to keep in mind:

- The pool of addresses to be handed out to clients should come from a subnet that does not exist in the remote access server's internal routing table. For example, my network is 10.0.0.x and I am going to assign VPN client licenses from 10.0.1.x.
- You need to set the default route for this other subnet so that it points back to the internal IP address of the remote access server. Without doing this, traffic from the VPN clients might make its way into the 10.0.1.x subnet, but responses from that subnet aren't going to know how to get back to the VPN client computers. By setting a default route on the 10.0.1.x subnet to point back to the Internal NIC of the remote access server, you fix this.

How it works...

The act of enabling VPN on a DirectAccess server is a single action, but without a couple of extra configuration steps, that VPN enablement isn't going to do much for you. With this recipe, you should now have the information you need to enable and configure a VPN on your remote access server and get those machines connected that do not meet the requirements to be DirectAccess-connected. In the field, I find that most companies try to get all the computers they can connected via DirectAccess, because it is a much easier technology to deal with on the client side and is better for managing domain joined systems. When faced with the need to connect computers that aren't Windows 7, 8, or 10, or are not domain joined, it is nice to know that traditional VPN connectivity options exist right in our Server 2016 operating system.

Replacing your expiring IP-HTTPS certificate

DirectAccess has the ability to utilize certificates in a couple of different ways. Depending on how you configure DA, there are different places that certificates may or may not be used, but one common variable in all DirectAccess implementations is **IP-HTTPS**. This is a transition technology that is always enabled on a DA server, and it requires an SSL certificate to work properly. IP-HTTPS traffic comes in from the Internet, and so I always recommend that the SSL certificate used for the IP-HTTPS listener should be one purchased from a public CA entity.

As with any SSL certificate, they are only valid for a certain time period. Typically, these certificates are purchased on a one-, two-, or three-year basis. This means that eventually, you will have to renew that certificate and figure out how to make DirectAccess recognize and utilize the new one. IP-HTTPS makes use of a web listener inside IIS, and so it is a natural assumption that, when you need to change your certificate, you do so inside IIS. This is an incorrect assumption. What's worse is that you can actually dig into the site inside IIS and change the certificate binding, and cause it to work for a while. This is not the correct place to change the certificate! If you simply change the binding inside IIS, your change will eventually be reversed and it will go back to using the old certificate. Unfortunately, I get calls quite regularly from customers who do this and then have all sorts of users unable to connect remotely because the DA server has reverted to using the old, now expired, certificate.

Let's work through this recipe together to configure our DirectAccess to utilize a new certificate that was recently purchased and installed onto our server.

Getting ready

We have DirectAccess up-and-running on our Windows Server 2016 Remote Access server. Our SSL certificate that we use for IP-HTTPS is about to expire and we have renewed it with our CA. The new copy of the certificate has already been downloaded and installed onto the server itself, so now we just need to figure out where it needs to be adjusted for DirectAccess to start using it.

How to do it...

To adjust the DirectAccess configuration to start using a new certificate for the IP-HTTPS listener, follow these steps:

1. Open **Remote Access Management Console** on your DirectAccess server.
2. In the left window pane, browse to **Configuration** | **DirectAccess and VPN**.
3. Under **Step 2** of the configuration, click on **Edit...**.

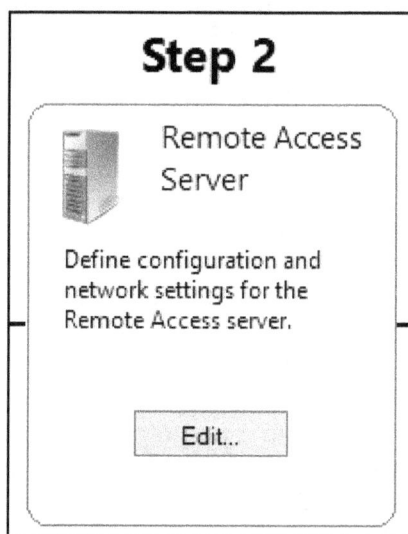

Step 2

Remote Access Server

Define configuration and network settings for the Remote Access server.

Edit...

4. Click **Next**.
5. You will now see the currently assigned certificate for IP-HTTPS. This is the certificate that is about to expire. Go ahead and click on the **Browse...** button.

Select the certificate used to authenticate IP-HTTPS connections:

☐ Use a self-signed certificate created automatically by DirectAccess

| CN=directaccess. | Browse... |

6. Now simply choose the new certificate with the new expiration date from the newly opnened list of available certificates.
7. Click **Next** a couple more times to finish up the **Step 2** wizard.

> 💡 **TIP**
>
> Keep in mind that the IP-HTTPS certificate is a per-node setting. If you have an array of multiple DirectAccess servers, you make all changes from the primary server's console, but you must install the certificate on each server and then make the certificate change on each node separately within the configuration.

8. At this point, nothing has actually been changed with the live configuration. To make this change active, you need to press the **Finish...** button, which is near the bottom of **Remote Access Management Console**.

> ⚠ Some configuration changes have not been applied. Click Finish to apply the changes. | Finish... |

9. If everything in the review looks good, click on **Apply**, and this will push your changes into action. The new certificate is now in place and working to validate those IP-HTTPS connections.

How it works...

Replacing the SSL certificate that is used by IP-HTTPS is a regular and necessary task for any DirectAccess server administrator, but one that only comes maybe once per year. This generally means that, by the time your certificate expiration date rolls around, you have probably forgotten where this setting is in the configuration. I hope this recipe can be a quick reference to alleviate that worry.

I always check the certificate from outside the network after making the change to ensure the new certificate is really the one that is now live on the system. If you take a computer outside of your network on the Internet, try browsing to a dummy site from your public DNS record on your DirectAccess server. For example, if the public DNS record that you are using on your server is `directaccess.contoso.com`, try browsing to `https://directaccess.contoso.com/test`. You can expect to get a 404 error because the page we are requesting doesn't actually exist, but when you get the 404 error you have the ability (depending on what browser you are using; I tend to prefer Chrome for this task) to view which certificate is being used to validate your web traffic. Click to view the certificate details and make sure that it is your new certificate with the newest validity dates. Further, if you encounter any kind of certificate warning message when you are trying to browse to this test website, this probably indicates that there is some kind of problem with the certificate and you may need to investigate it further.

Reporting on DirectAccess and VPN connections

One of the big benefits that Microsoft brought to the table in these newer versions of the remote access role is reporting. In the past, it was difficult to tell who was connected and even harder to find out what they were doing or when they had been connected previously. Historical reporting on remote sessions was kind of absent. All of that changes in the newer editions, as we now have a nice interface to show us who is connecting, how often they are connecting, and even some information on what things they are doing while they are connected. Here, we'll take a look into those interfaces and explore some of the information that is available to consume. We will also make sure you know how to turn on the historical reporting, as it is not enabled by default.

Getting ready

All work with this recipe will be accomplished from our Windows Server 2016 Remote Access server that is servicing both DirectAccess and VPN clients.

How to do it...

Follow these steps to get familiar with the remote access reporting options available in Server 2016:

1. Open **Remote Access Management Console** from the **Tools** menu inside Server Manager.
2. In the left window pane, browse to **Remote Client Status**. Here, you will see a list of all currently connected devices and users. This shows both DirectAccess connections and VPN connections.
3. If you click on a particular connection, you will see some additional data displayed below. You can easily find out whether the user is connected using DirectAccess or VPN, and some more specific information about their connection.

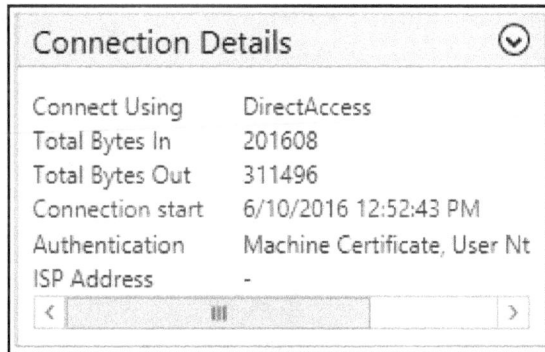

Connection Details	⌄
Connect Using	DirectAccess
Total Bytes In	201608
Total Bytes Out	311496
Connection start	6/10/2016 12:52:43 PM
Authentication	Machine Certificate, User Nt
ISP Address	-

4. Look over toward the left a little where is says **Access Details** and you can even see what internal resources have been accessed by the user and computer.

Access Details			⌄
Protocol	Port	IP Address	
6	80	192.168.250.45	
6	445	192.168.250.18	
17	389	192.168.250.2	

5. Once your environment is large enough that this screen becomes filled with connections, the **Search** box at the top comes in very handy. You simply type in any information you want to search for, and the results in the window will filter down to your search criteria.

6. If you would like to display more data on the screen, you can right-click on any of the existing column names and select additional columns to show or hide.

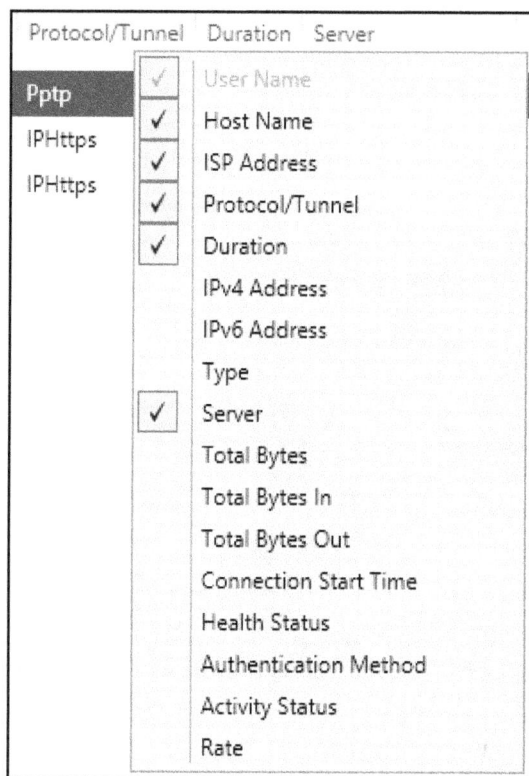

Protocol/Tunnel	Duration	Server		
Pptp	✓		User Name	
IPHttps	✓		Host Name	
IPHttps	✓		ISP Address	
	✓		Protocol/Tunnel	
	✓		Duration	
			IPv4 Address	
			IPv6 Address	
			Type	
	✓		Server	
			Total Bytes	
			Total Bytes In	
			Total Bytes Out	
			Connection Start Time	
			Health Status	
			Authentication Method	
			Activity Status	
			Rate	

7. All of this information is great! But what if we want to look back and view this data historically? Maybe you want to view connections from the past day, or week. Maybe you need to come up with some kind of report on how many connections happened over the past month. In the left window pane, click on **Reporting** to get started with that.

8. Since reporting is not enabled by default, we don't have any data here yet. Instead, you will see a message indicating that you need to configure accounting. Go ahead and click on this link.

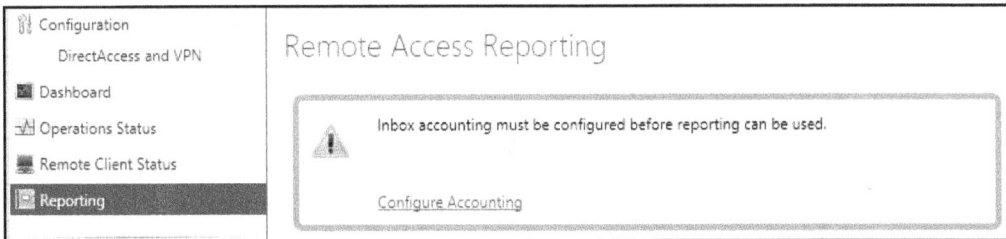

9. Now you have options for **Use RADIUS accounting**, **Use inbox accounting**, or both. RADIUS accounting implies that you have a RADIUS server set up and ready to accept this kind of data. I don't see many customers using this option. Instead, most select **Use inbox accounting**, which writes all of the data right to the **Windows Internal Database** (**WID**) on the DirectAccess server itself.

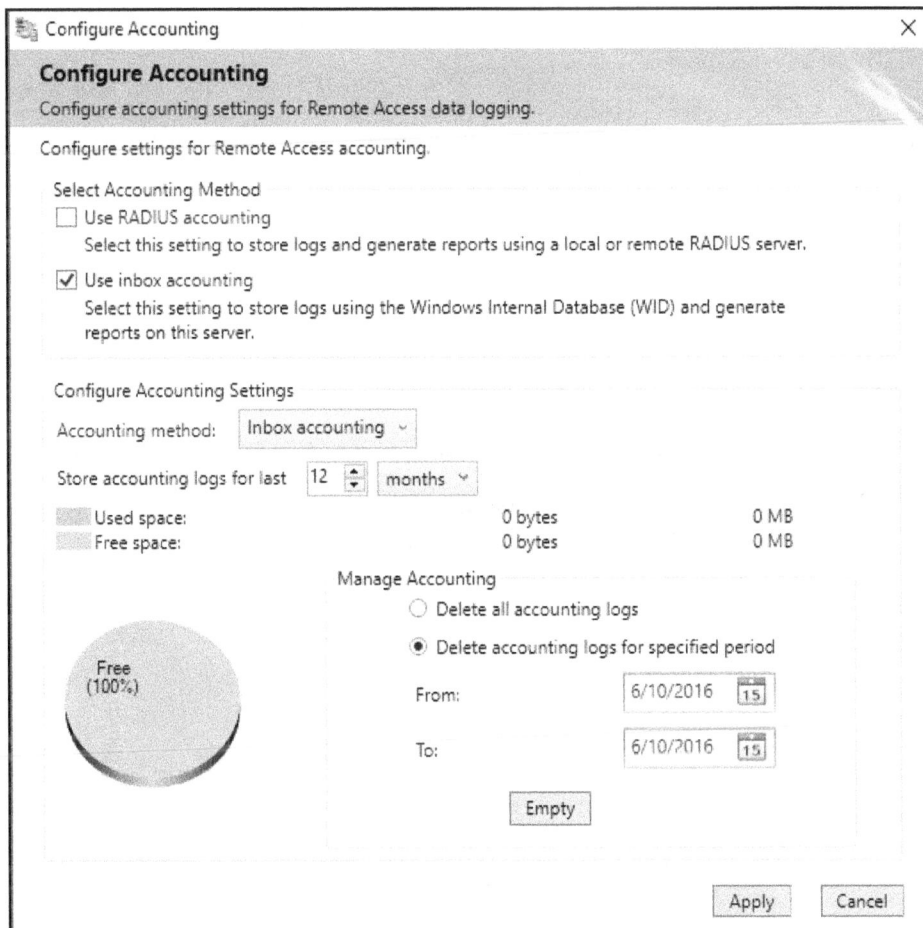

10. Once you have made your selection, click **Apply**. You will see that the **Reporting** screen now looks a lot more like the **Remote Client Status** screen, except that inside **Reporting**, you have additional options to select date ranges and pull historical information.

How it works...

The reporting of user connection data is critical to most remote access systems. The inclusion of this data, particularly for historical connections, is a great feature addition that I am sure every remote access administrator is going to make use of. With a simple configuration change, we set up our Windows Remote Access server to keep track of these DirectAccess and VPN connections so that we can run and save reports on that data in the future.

7
Remote Desktop Services

Remote Desktop Services (RDS) is an outstanding way to provide users with access to applications and data, without those applications and data needing to reside on their local workstations. Formerly known as Terminal Services, this technology enables companies to retain control of all data and apps on centralized Remote Desktop servers, which users connect to from their workstations in order to access these items. There are two primary means of providing this information to users. The first is through a remote session, where users log into a **Remote Desktop Session Host** (RDSH) server and end up landing inside a session hosted on the server. This session looks and feels like a regular desktop computer to the user, as they have a full desktop and Start button and are able to launch any application available to them within that session. They are also able to save documents inside their session, keeping everything centralized. This is the most common flavor of RDS that I see used in the field and is where we will focus the majority of our administrative tasks that we discuss today.

A second way to provide data to users via RDS is **RemoteApp**. This is a neat function that is able to provide only the application itself remotely to the user's computer, rather than a full desktop session. This is a nice way to further restrict the access that is being provided to the user and simplifies the steps the user must take in order to access those resources.

An RDS environment has the potential to contain many servers, enough to fill its own book. Given that, let's work together to get a simple RDS environment online that you can start testing with, and provide you with knowledge of some common administrative tasks that will be useful in an environment like this.

In this chapter, you'll be taking a look at the following recipes:

- Building a single server Remote Desktop Services environment
- Adding an additional RDSH server to your RDS environment
- Installing applications on a Remote Desktop Session Host server

- Disabling the redirection of local resources
- Shadowing another session in RDS
- Installing a printer driver to use with redirection
- Removing an RD Session Host server from use for maintenance
- Publishing WordPad with RemoteApp
- Tracking user logins with Logon/Logoff scripts

Introduction

I would like to take a minute and describe the different parts and pieces that could potentially make up your RDS environment. We won't be covering the installation or use of all components that might be involved with a full RDS deployment, but you should at least be aware of the components and their intended functions:

- **Remote Desktop Session Host**: This is the most common type of RDS server, as it is the one hosting the programs and sessions that users connect to. Depending on the size of your environment, there may be many of these servers running concurrently.
- **Remote Desktop Connection Broker**: This is like the load balancer for RDS servers. It distributes users evenly across RDSH servers, and helps users to reconnect to existing sessions rather than creating fresh ones.
- **Remote Desktop Licensing**: This is responsible for managing the licenses that are required for RDS use in a network.
- **Remote Desktop Gateway**: This is a gateway device that can bring remote users out on the Internet into an RDS environment. For example, a user at home could utilize the connection provided by an RD Gateway in order to access work information.
- **Remote Desktop Web Access**: This enables users to access desktops and applications by using the local Start menu on their Windows 7, 8, or 10 computers. Users can also utilize this to access applications via a web browser.
- **Remote Desktop Virtualization Host**: This is a role that integrates with Hyper-V in order to provide virtual desktop sessions to users. The difference here is that resources given to those users are spun up from Hyper-V, rather than shared resources such as an RDSH.

Many of these roles can be placed together on a single server, which is what we will be doing in our recipe to bring a simple RDS environment online. As your deployment grows and you continue to add users and servers, it is generally a good idea to make these roles decentralized and redundant when possible.

Building a single server Remote Desktop Services environment

If you aren't coming into an environment where RDS is already up-and-running, it will be helpful to understand where the roles come from and how they are put into place. In this recipe, we are going to combine a number of Remote Desktop roles onto a single server so that we can take a look at that installation process. When we are finished, we should have an RDS server that will allow users to connect and utilize a Remote Desktop session.

Getting ready

We will be using a Windows Server 2016 machine to install the RDS roles. This server is already joined to our domain.

How to do it...

The following steps will direct you through installing the roles necessary for starting your first simple RDS server:

1. Open up **Server Manager** and click on the **Add roles and features** link.
2. Click **Next**, which will bring you to the **Installation Type** screen. This is where we differ from normal as far as role installations go. For the majority of roles, we tend to blow right through this screen without a second thought. For Remote Desktop Services, though, we need to make a change on this screen.

3. Choose the option for **Remote Desktop Services installation**. Then click **Next**.

○ **Role-based or feature-based installation**

Configure a single server by adding roles, role services, and features.

● **Remote Desktop Services installation**

Install required role services for Virtual Desktop Infrastructure (VDI) to create a virtual machine-based or session-based desktop deployment.

---

4. Leave the default setting as **Standard deployment** and click **Next**. On this screen, we could choose the Quick Start option since we are intending to only configure a single server at this time. I am choosing not to take this shortcut route because we want a good look at the different services that are going to be installed, and want to leave our installation open to having multiple RDS servers down the road.

5. With this RDS server, we are planning to provide access to traditional desktop sessions, not integration with Hyper-V. So on the **Deployment Scenario** screen, choose **Session-based desktop deployment**.

Remote Desktop Services can be configured to allow users to connect to virtual desktops, RemoteApp programs, and session-based desktops.

○ Virtual machine-based desktop deployment

Virtual machine-based desktop deployment allows users to connect to virtual desktop collections that include published RemoteApp programs and virtual desktops.

● Session-based desktop deployment

Session-based desktop deployment allows users to connect to session collections that include published RemoteApp programs and session-based desktops.

---

6. We now see a summary of the role services required for our installation. Based on the options we have chosen, you should see **RD Connection Broker, RD Web Access,** and **RD Session Host** in this list. The next few screens will be used to define which servers are going to be used for these roles.

7. Since we are installing everything onto a single server, for now, we only have one option in the **Server Pool** list and we simply move it over to the right column. Go ahead and click the arrow to do this on the **RD Connection Broker** page.

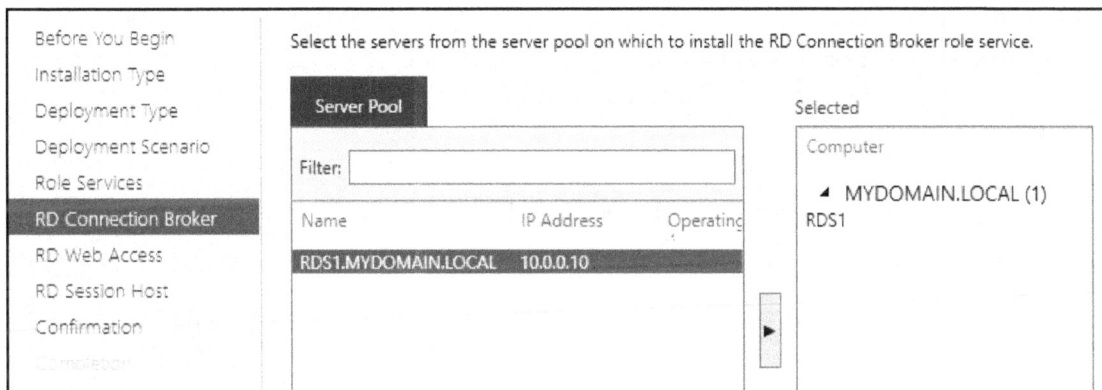

Before You Begin	Select the servers from the server pool on which to install the RD Connection Broker role service.
Installation Type	
Deployment Type	**Server Pool** Selected
Deployment Scenario	
Role Services	Filter: Computer
RD Connection Broker	◢ MYDOMAIN.LOCAL (1)
RD Web Access	Name IP Address Operating RDS1
RD Session Host	RDS1.MYDOMAIN.LOCAL 10.0.0.10
Confirmation	▶
Completion	

8. Now do the same thing on the next two screens. In our example, we are using the server named RDS1, so I am going to use it as both the RD Web Access server as well as the RD Session Host server.

9. Now you should be up to the **Confirmation** screen, which gives you a summary of the actions about to be performed. For us, all three RDS services are being installed onto the RDS1 server. We must now check the box that says **Restart the destination server automatically if required** and then press the **Deploy** button.

RD Connection Broker (1 server selected)

RDS1.MYDOMAIN.LOCAL

RD Web Access (1 server selected)

RDS1.MYDOMAIN.LOCAL

RD Session Host (1 server selected)

⚠ The following servers may restart after the role service is installed.

RDS1.MYDOMAIN.LOCAL

☑ Restart the destination server automatically if required

< Previous | Next > | Deploy | Cancel

How it works...

We can follow this recipe to get our first simple RDS environment up-and-running. Our server will now allow users to connect and access virtual sessions that are hosted right on this RDS1 server. To log in, users may either launch the Remote Desktop Connection tool on their client computer and type in the RDS1 name of our server or open up a web browser and head over to `https://rds1/rdweb`. Either way, they will land inside a desktop session that looks and feels pretty similar to a Windows 10 desktop. Inside this desktop provided by the RDS server, they are able to launch applications and save documents, having everything run and stored right on the server itself rather than their local desktop computers. From this simple, single server RDS implementation, we can build and grow out to provide additional RDS roles on more servers, or for the purposes of handling additional user loads.

Adding an additional RDSH server to your RDS environment

Most RDS implementations start out with a single server or at least a single RDSH. Once you have the roles established for successful connectivity here, it is a natural next step to add additional RDSH servers to accommodate more users. Or perhaps you want to segregate different types of users (and their applications) onto different RDSH servers. Whatever your reasoning, chances are that at some point you will want to add additional servers into your RDS environment. Let's add a second server to ours so that you can see how this process works.

Getting ready

We have a single RDS server online, running Windows Server 2016. It is named RDS1 and is already performing the roles of RD Connection Broker, RD Session Host, and RD Web Access. We will now use the management interface on RDS1 in order to add a second RDSH server to our infrastructure. The name of our new server is RDS2, and it is already joined to our domain.

How to do it...

Follow these steps to add a new RDSH server to our existing RDS environment:

1. On the existing RDS server, RDS1, open up Server Manager.

> **TIP**
>
> We have to add our new RDS2 server to the instance of Server Manager that is running on RDS1. Until we perform this step, we will be unable to make modifications to RDS2 from here.

2. Click on the **Add other servers to manage** link.

```
2   Add roles and features

3   Add other servers to manage

4   Create a server group
```

3. Type in the name of the new server that you intend to turn into an RDSH. For our example, the server name is RDS2. Then click the arrow to add this server into the **Selected** list and click on **OK**.

4. Now back on the main page of Server Manager, go ahead and click on the listing for **Remote Desktop Services** in the left window pane. This will bring us into the management interface for RDS. Take a look at the **DEPLOYMENT OVERVIEW**, which is a self-generated diagram of what your current RDS deployment looks like. Since we are only testing with our current servers and not accessing them from outside the network, we see plus symbols next to **RD Gateway** and **RD Licensing**. This simply means we have not yet configured these roles, and we could click on those pluses and follow the prompts if we intended to do so. We have no requirement for these services at the present time, so we will ignore this for now.

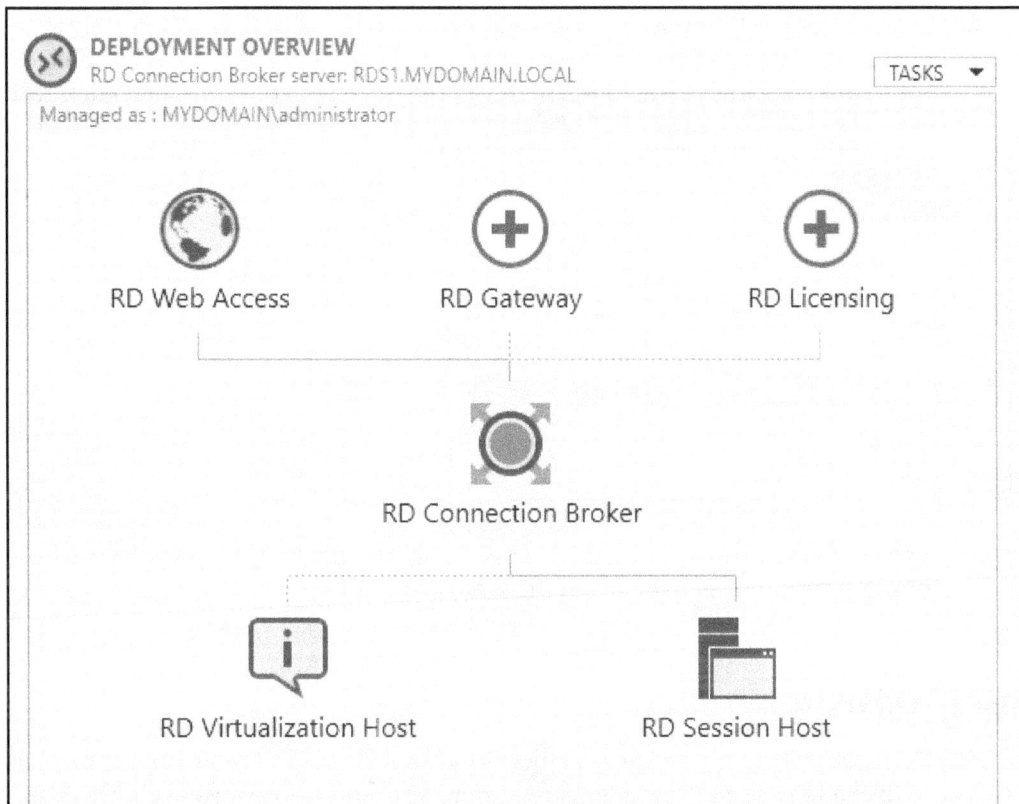

DEPLOYMENT OVERVIEW
RD Connection Broker server: RDS1.MYDOMAIN.LOCAL

Managed as : MYDOMAIN\administrator

TASKS ▼

RD Web Access

RD Gateway

RD Licensing

RD Connection Broker

RD Virtualization Host

RD Session Host

5. To add a new RDSH server, head over to the top right of this window and click on the link that says **Add RD Session Host servers**.

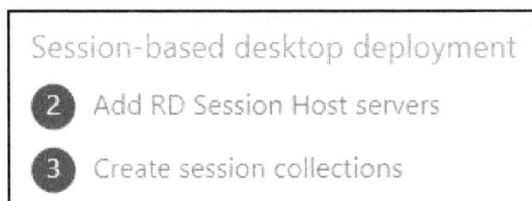

Session-based desktop deployment

2 Add RD Session Host servers

3 Create session collections

6. Since we added it into Server Manager earlier in the recipe, we should now be able to see in this list the new server available to select. Select the new RDS2 server and click the arrow to move it into the **Selected** column. Then click **Add**.

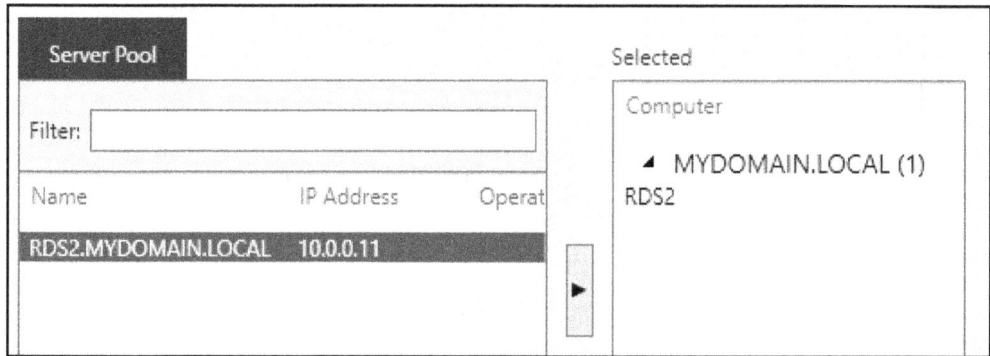

7. Click the **Next** button, and you will need to check the box that says **Restart remote computers as needed** on the **Confirmation** screen. Then click on **Add**.

How it works...

In this recipe, we used the Remote Desktop Services management console on our primary RDS server to take a new server that we had running and turn it into a **Remote Desktop Session Host (RDSH)** server. This RDSH is now part of our RDS infrastructure, and can be managed right from this centralized management platform. In an RDS environment, this is typically the way that new roles are added onto servers that are being brought into the environment. Using the centralized management console to perform many tasks in RDS makes a lot of sense, because it is easy to see the big picture of your RDS infrastructure as you make changes or updates.

Installing applications on a Remote Desktop Session Host server

As soon as you take a Windows Server and turn it into a RDSH server to be used within an RDS environment, the way that applications work on that server changes significantly. Whenever programs and apps are installed onto that RDSH, it first needs to be put into a special **Install Mode**. Placing the server into Install Mode prior to launching the program installer is important to make sure that applications are going to be installed in a way that will allow multiple users to run them simultaneously. Remember, our RDSH servers will be hosting multiple user sessions, probably dozens of them.

Using Install Mode is so important to applications working properly on an RDSH that you really should not install any programs onto the server before you turn it into an RDSH. Once that role has been established, then apps can be safely installed, as long as you are using Install Mode. Programs installed prior to converting that server into an RDSH may not work properly, and you might have to uninstall and reinstall them. There are a couple of different ways that Install Mode can be invoked during a program installation; let's take a look at both of them.

Getting ready

We need to install a program onto our RDSH server. This box is running Windows Server 2016 and is already part of our RDS environment. We will also need, of course, the application installer files that we intend to launch.

How to do it...

One way to properly install programs onto an RDSH is by using Control Panel to install the application:

1. Right-click on your **Start** flag and choose to open Control Panel.
2. Click on **Programs**.

3. Choose the button that says **Install Application on Remote Desktop...**.

Install Application on Remote Desktop...

4. Click **Next** and you will be able to specify the location of your installer file for the application.

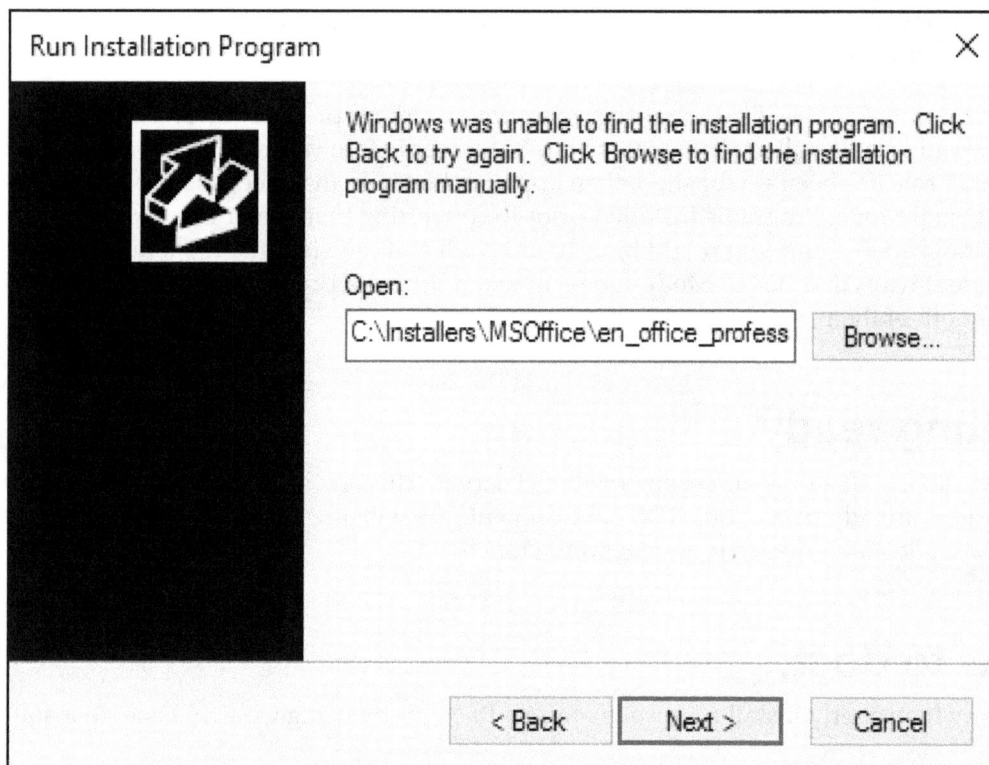

Run Installation Program	X

Windows was unable to find the installation program. Click Back to try again. Click Browse to find the installation program manually.

Open:

C:\Installers\MSOffice\en_office_profess   Browse...

< Back   Next >   Cancel

5. Click **Next**, and your program will install. When finished, make sure you click the **Finish** button on the Install Mode mini-wizard screen, so that the RDSH is placed back into Execute Mode and is ready for normal operation.

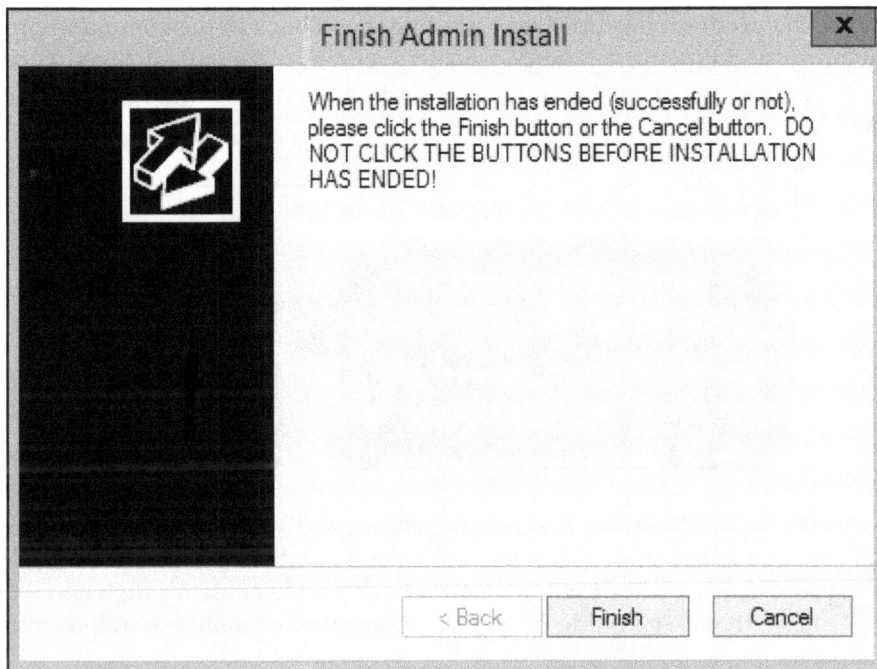

The second way to place an RDSH into Install Mode is by using the command prompt:

1. Right-click on the **Start** flag and choose to open **Command Prompt (Admin)**.
2. Type `change user /install` and press *Enter*.

3. Now find your program installer file and launch it. Walk through the installation steps in the same way you would on any regular server or computer.

4. Once the program has finished installing, head back to the command prompt window and now type `change user /execute`. Then press *Enter*. This takes the RDSH out of the special Install Mode and places it back into normal Execute Mode.

```
Administrator: Command Prompt

C:\>change user /execute
User session is ready to execute applications.

C:\>_
```

> **TIP**
>
> Restarting the server also automatically places it back into Execute Mode. So if your application installer asks you to restart as part of the installation process, your RDSH will be placed back into Execute Mode when it boots, and in that case you do not have to enter the command manually.

How it works...

When installing applications onto an RDSH, it must first be placed into a special Install Mode. Doing this re-maps certain parts of the program being installed so that it can be run and utilized by many users at the same time. Installing your applications by using one of the methods discussed in this recipe will be critical to the success of your RDS environment being able to provide applications to users.

Also keep in mind that it is recommended you have no users logged into an RDSH during the time of installation. When you are building fresh servers, this is easy as you don't typically allow anyone to connect until everything is installed and configured. But if you need to install new programs or updates to existing programs onto a production RDSH, you will want to take steps to ensure that users are not logged in to the server before you place it into Install Mode and launch those executables. If you are running a farm of RDS servers and want to remove just one or some of them for maintenance or the installation of an application, make sure to check out the *Removing an RD Session Host server from use for maintenance* recipe.

I mentioned placing the RDSH into Install Mode even when just installing updates to existing applications. This is important. However, you do not need to place a server into Install Mode in order to install regular Windows operating system updates. These are able to install correctly even when the server is in normal Execute Mode.

Disabling the redirection of local resources

One of the neat things about users connecting to virtual sessions within an RDS environment, especially when connecting remotely, is local resource redirection. This feature enables the users to have access to things that are local to where they are sitting, from inside their virtual session, such as the clipboard, so that copy and paste functions will work between local computer and RDS session and drive redirection so that you can save documents back and forth between the local hard drive and the RDS session. One of the most common uses of resource redirection is printers so that users can print from inside their RDS session, which is sitting on a server in the corporate network, directly to a printer on the local network where they are connected. An example could be someone needing to print a work document on a home printer.

This redirection technology can be very helpful but is often not desirable from a security and policies standpoint. Many organizations have a written security policy, which dictates that corporate data must remain within the corporate network and cannot move outside. Most often I see this in medical environments, where strict standards are in place to make sure data stays private and secure. This means that data cannot be copied and pasted to the local computer, documents cannot be saved outside the RDS session, and printing documents is also often not allowed.

While it may be disappointing that you cannot use these functions if your security policy dictates it, thankfully disabling redirection is an easy thing to accomplish. Follow along to learn where these settings reside.

Getting ready

We are logged into our Server 2016 RDSH server. This server is hosting some sensitive information and we want to make sure that users cannot save documents to their local computers, cannot print documents to local printers, and cannot copy/paste within the clipboard in order to move data from the RDS session to their local computers.

How to do it...

Follow along to disable these redirection features on our RDSH collection:

1. Open up **Server Manager** and click on **Remote Desktop Services** to open up the management of your RDS environment.

2. We currently only have one RDSH collection listed, which contains both of our RDSH servers. This is the collection that all of our users connect to when they have to access this sensitive information. Click on the name of that collection. For our example, this one is called **MDomain RDSH Servers**.

3. Near the top of the screen, look for the section called **Properties**. Drop down the **Tasks** box and click on **Edit Properties**.

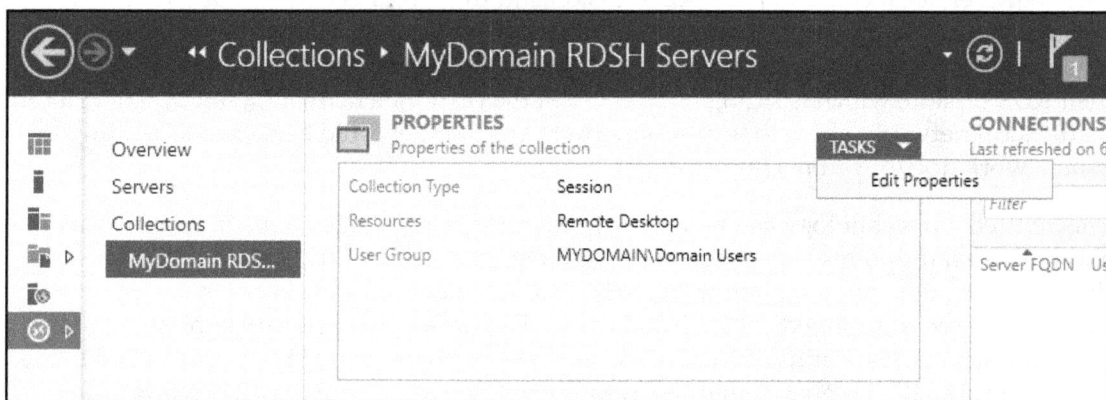

4. Click on **Client Settings**.

5. Here is your list of the items that are currently capable of being redirected. Go ahead and deselect each of the redirections that you want to disable. For our example, we are unchecking **Drives**, **Clipboard**, and **Allow client printer redirection**.

MyDomain RDSH Servers Properties   —   □   ✕

Session Collection

Show All

General	+
User Groups	+
Session	+
Security	+
Load Balancing	+
Client Settings	**−**
User Profile Disks	+

Configure client settings

You can specify devices and resources on the client device that can be accessed when a user connects to a session-based desktop.

Enable redirection for the following:

☑ Audio and video playback
☑ Audio recording
☑ Smart cards
☑ Plug and play devices
☐ Drives
☐ Clipboard

Printers

☐ Allow client printer redirection
    ☑ Use the client default printing device
    ☑ Use the Remote Desktop Easy Print print driver first

Monitors

Maximum number of redirected monitors: 16

[OK]   [Cancel]   [Apply]

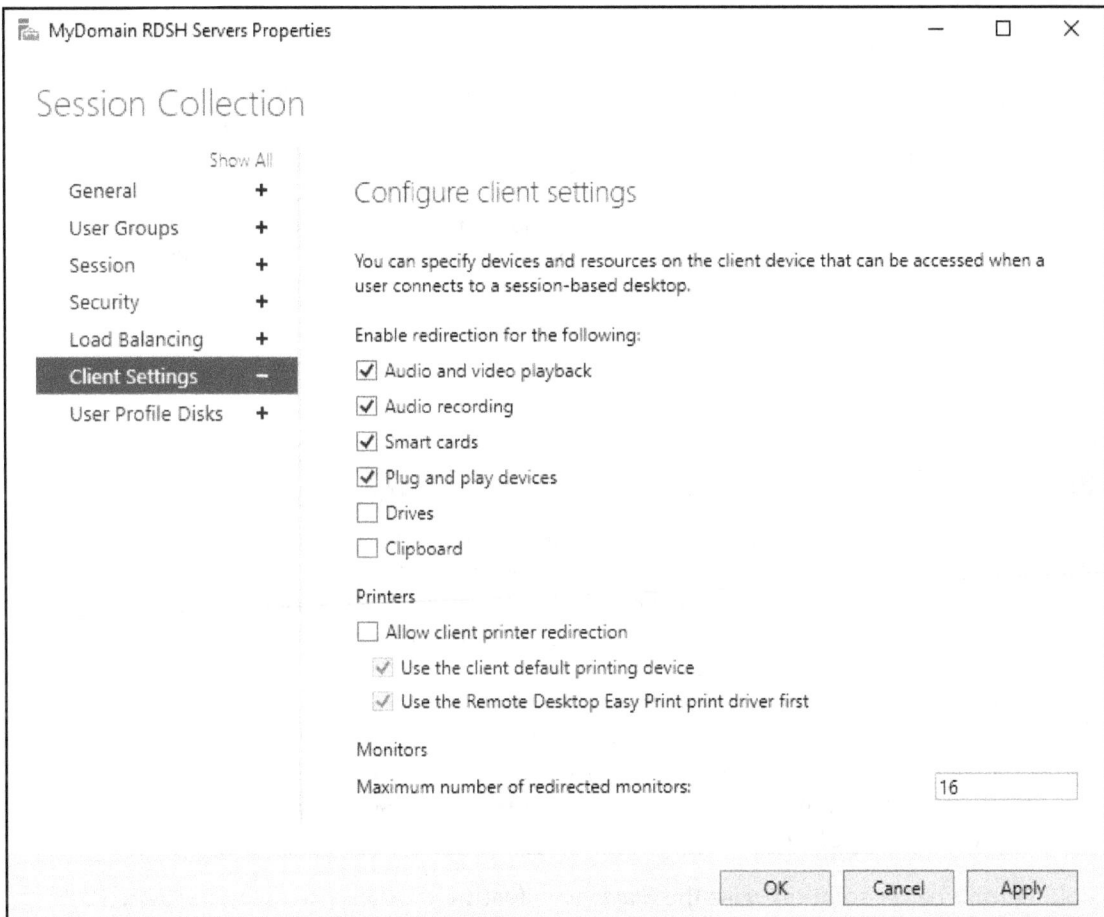

6. Click **OK** and those redirected resources are no longer available to client computers connecting to this RDSH collection.

How it works...

Providing users with the capability of moving data back and forth between their local computers and RDS sessions sounds like a great feature, but is often less than desirable. With some simple checkboxes, we can disable these capabilities wholesale so that you can adhere to security policies and make sure sensitive data remains protected. Once you are familiar with the location of these settings, the enablement or disablement of them is intuitive and easy to accomplish. What is even better is that these settings can be changed at any time; it doesn't have to be a decision made while the RDS environment is being built. If you make the decision down the road to turn some of these options on or off, you can make these changes at any time to a production RDS.

Shadowing another session in RDS

Let's say you receive a phone call from a remote user in your company; they are currently sitting in a hotel and are having trouble figuring out how to open an application. This application isn't installed on their local computer, they are an RDS user, and they connect into a virtual session on an RDSH server in your network whenever they need to access this app. You think about asking for their password, as that way you could just log into the RDSH as them and take care of the problem. But alas, asking for a password is a serious breach of company security policy. Instead, perhaps you can use some kind of online meeting software to share the screen of their laptop and try to walk them through fixing the problem. But that would mean walking them through the installation of that meeting software and hoping you could explain over the phone how to use it.

Looking for a better solution? Use the *Shadowing* feature of RDS. If you log in to the RDSH server where the user is already logged in, you can simply shadow their session in order to see what they are seeing. You can then work together to resolve the issue. You'll be able to take control and fix the problem, and maybe they can even take some notes and learn how to do it themselves next time to save the phone call.

This recipe is included here particularly because RDS Shadowing was always available in older versions of Terminal Server, but was then removed from Server 2012 RDS. Well, good news! It was brought back by popular demand in Server 2012 R2, and remains here to stay in Windows Server 2016!

Getting ready

Our remote user is logged into a virtual session on our RDSH server, which is called RDS1. This is a Server 2016 machine that is part of our RDS infrastructure.

How to do it...

Let's help out this remote user by shadowing their RD session:

1. First, we need to log into the same RDSH server that the user is logged into. On your computer, open **Remote Desktop Connection** and input the server name in order to connect.

2. Now that you are logged into the RDSH, right-click on the Taskbar and open **Task Manager**.

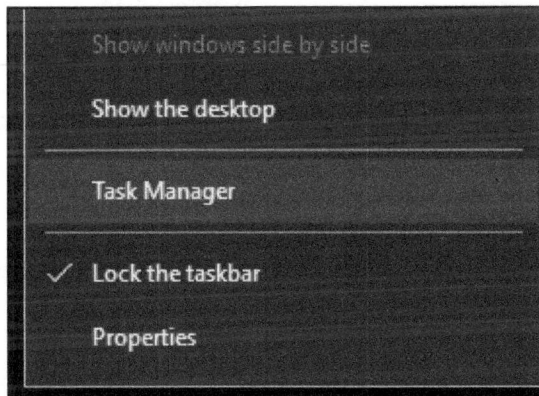

3. Click on **More details** in order to see more information about the server.

4. Navigate to the **Users** tab.

5. Right-click on one of the column headings and choose to show the **ID** column.

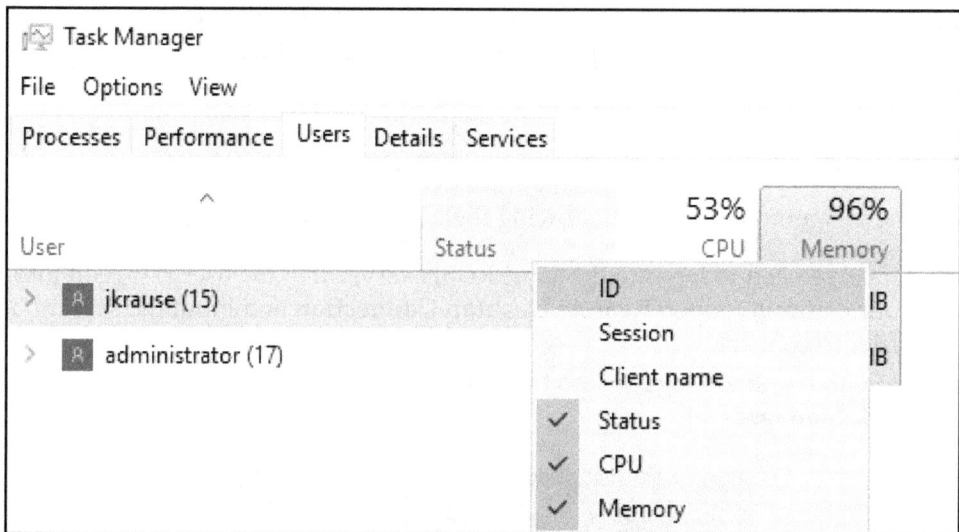

```
 Task Manager

File   Options   View

Processes   Performance   Users   Details   Services

                            ^                          53%      96%
User                                     Status        CPU      Memory
>   [R]  jkrause (15)                            ID                    IB
                                                 Session
>   [R]  administrator (17)                                            IB
                                                 Client name
                                            ✓    Status
                                            ✓    CPU
                                            ✓    Memory
```

6. Leave Task Manager open so that you can see the username that you want to connect to and their ID number.

7. Now open a Command Prompt and type the following: `mstsc /shadow:<id> /control`. So for our particular **jkrause** user, who is currently running on ID 3 as you can see inside Task Manager, we use this command: `mstsc /shadow:3 /control`.

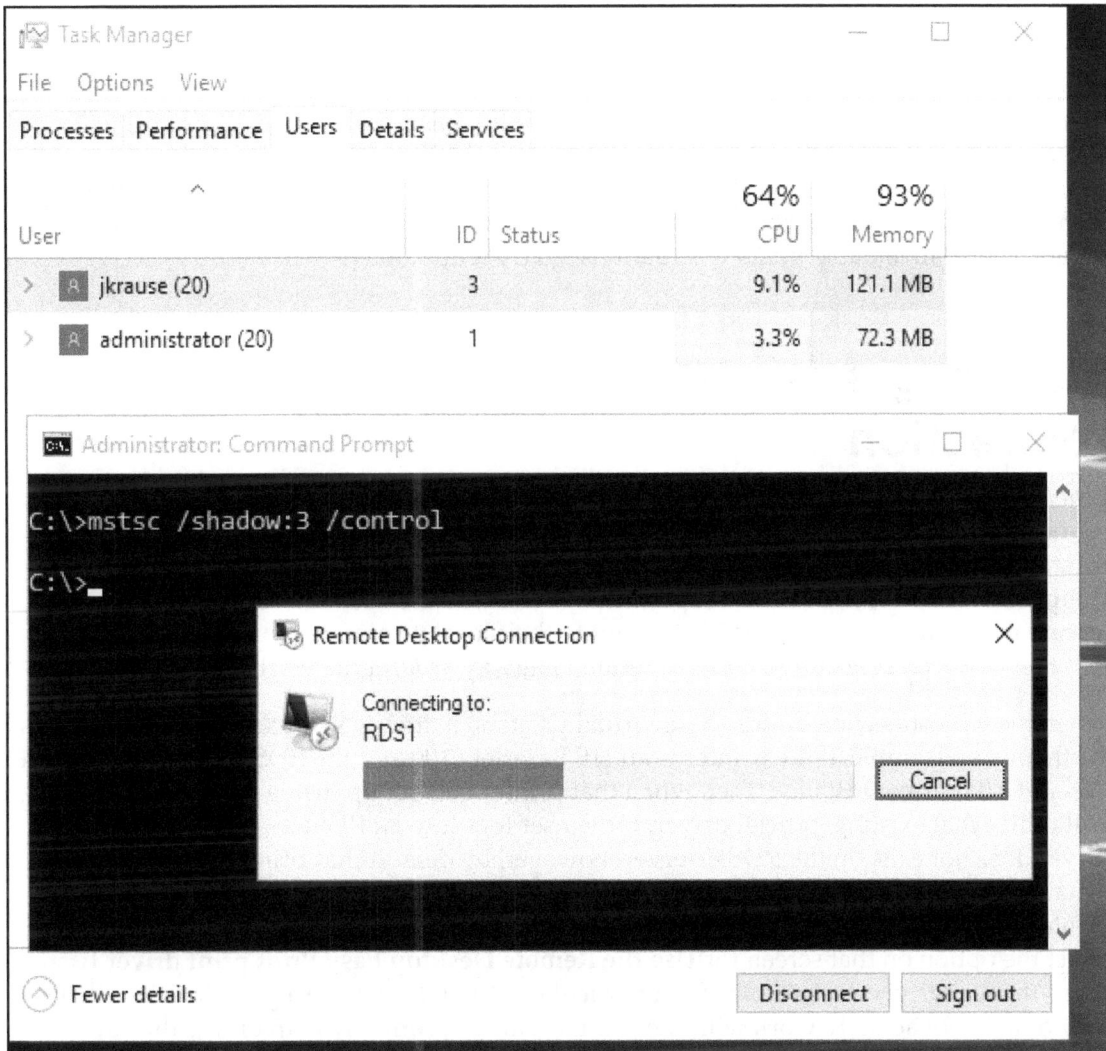

8. This command will launch a shadowing session to the RD session of the ID
   number that you used, so make sure to use the correct ID for the user you want to
   shadow. Since we used the /control switch, you should also have the capability
   of using your own mouse and keyboard inside the user's session.

How it works...

While shadowing in Server 2016 isn't quite as easy as it used to be in earlier versions of Terminal Server, it's great to know that this capability has returned after a noticeable absence in Server 2012. RDS Shadowing is a great tool to use for troubleshooting or collaboration, as it enables you to share the screen of other personnel and assist with your own keyboard and mouse control when necessary. Having two sets of eyes on the same RD session can be invaluable in many situations; go try it out today!

Installing a printer driver to use with redirection

When a user connects to an RD session, if the client and server are configured properly, that connection will attempt to set up printer redirection between the RD session and the local computer. Specifically, what happens is that every printer that is installed onto the local computer will be configured as a separate printer inside the user's RD session. This is the feature that enables users to be able to print to their local printers, even if the information that they are accessing and printing is located halfway around the world.

When the RD connection builds these virtual printers, it attempts to use real printer drivers for them. For example, if the printer is an HP LaserJet 4100 and the RDSH server has the HP LaserJet 4100 driver installed, then when that printer gets set up inside the user session, it will utilize that existing, official driver. If the user logs into an RDSH with a printer whose driver does not exist on the RDSH server, however, by default that printer will not be installed. There is a setting in the same configuration page where we enable or disable printer redirection on the RDSH server collection that can partially help with this. If you select the option on that screen for **Use the Remote Desktop Easy Print print driver first**, when the real driver doesn't exist for a particular printer, it will use a generic driver that may or may not actually work with the printer. This can certainly help bridge the gap when it comes to missing printer drivers but doesn't always solve the problem.

The best way to make sure your users are going to be able to print properly is to install the real driver onto the RDSH. So what's the point of this recipe? Who doesn't know how to install a printer driver, right? I write this because most printer driver software packages are now full-blown applications, and we don't need a quarter of what comes with them. Driver install packages consume much more space than necessary for use with RDS, and we have to take into consideration that we are installing actual applications, which could potentially show up inside user sessions and cause confusion. So what is the answer? Extract the simple driver files from those driver packages and use just the files themselves in order to install the driver into Windows. Let's do one together so you can see what I'm talking about.

Getting ready

We will be installing this printer driver onto our RDSH server running Windows Server 2016. For our example, we will be using a Brother MFC-J625DW printer, since that is one I installed for a customer just recently. Brother is usually good about providing a simple, small driver download that contains only the files we need for the driver itself.

How to do it...

Let's work together to download and install this printer driver onto our RDSH so that it can be used for printer redirection:

1. First, download the driver files onto your RDSH server. Make sure to choose the driver for the server's operating system, not the client. So when possible, I am going to choose Windows Server 2016. You can see in the following list that Windows Server 2016 is not an option available to me with this particular model of printer, and that is okay. In the event that the actual operating system driver is not available, you can often use one from a recent version of Windows and make it work. I will attempt to download the Windows 10 64-bit driver and see if it will install onto my Windows Server 2016. Alternatively, I could probably also get the Windows Server 2012 R2 64-bit driver to install as well.

Support & Downloads	MFC-J625DW
MFC-J625DW	**Downloads**

Select Your Operating System (OS)

STEP 1: Select OS Family

◉ Windows ○ Mac ○ Linux ○ Mobile

STEP 2: Select OS Version

○ Windows® 10 (32-bit)	○ Windows Vista® (64-bit)
◉ Windows® 10 (64-bit)	○ Windows® XP (32-bit)
○ Windows® 8.1 (32-bit)	○ Windows® XP (64-bit)
○ Windows® 8.1 (64-bit)	○ Windows Server® 2012 R2 (64-bit)
○ Windows® 8 (32-bit)	○ Windows Server® 2012 (64-bit)
○ Windows® 8 (64-bit)	○ Windows Server® 2008 R2 (64-bit)
○ Windows® RT	○ Windows Server® 2008 (32-bit)
○ Windows® 7 (32-bit)	○ Windows Server® 2008 (64-bit)
○ Windows® 7 (64-bit)	○ Windows Server® 2003 (32-bit)
○ Windows Vista® (32-bit)	○ Windows Server® 2003 (64-bit)

How to identify your Operating System (OS)

Search

▸ Not your product?

Downloads

FAQs & Troubleshooting

Manuals

Consumables & Accessories

Supported OS

Specification

United States(English)

▸ Change Country (Language)

2. We can see that there are a few different options available for downloading the driver. The first that is presented is the full software package, but that is 134 MB and remember we said earlier that the full software package is totally unnecessary on an RDS server. We only need the driver. A little further down the page, there is an option for **Add Printer Wizard Driver**. This is exactly what we need, and what do you know, it's only 23 MB!

Drivers			
Title	Description	Release Date (Version)	Size
Printer Driver & Scanner Driver for Local Connection	This download only includes the printer and scanner (WIA and/or TWAIN) drivers. ...more	11/28/2012 (D1)	23.04 MB
Add Printer Wizard Driver	This download only includes the printer drivers and is for users who are familiar with ...more	11/28/2012 (1.11)	23.04 MB

> **TIP**
>
> With most driver downloads, you will also have to double-click on it once downloaded in order to extract the files.

3. Right-click on your **Start** flag and choose **Control Panel**.
4. Navigate to **Hardware | View devices and printers**.
5. Click on any existing printer in the list and then click on the button in the top Taskbar that says **Print server properties**.

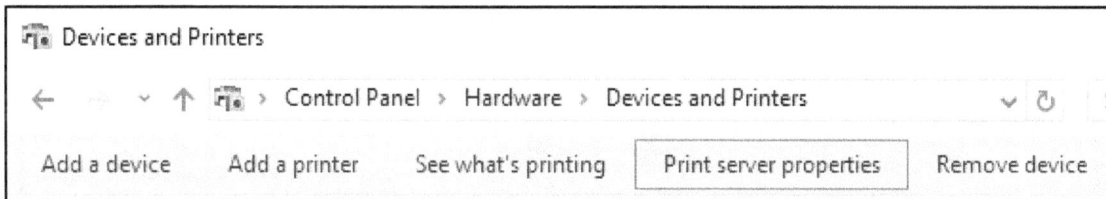

Devices and Printers
← ∨ ↑ 🖶 › Control Panel › Hardware › Devices and Printers ∨ ↻
Add a device   Add a printer   See what's printing   [Print server properties]   Remove device

6. Browse to the **Drivers** tab. This displays a list of currently installed printer drivers on this server. Then click the **Add...** button.
7. Click **Next** twice. We can leave the **Processor Selection** screen marked as only **x64**, since Windows Server 2016 only comes in 64-bit.

8. Now click on **Have Disk...** and browse to the location of the driver files that you downloaded. You are looking for an INF file that typically sits in the root of that driver folder. Sometimes you will have to poke around a little until you find it, but the file is always an INF file.

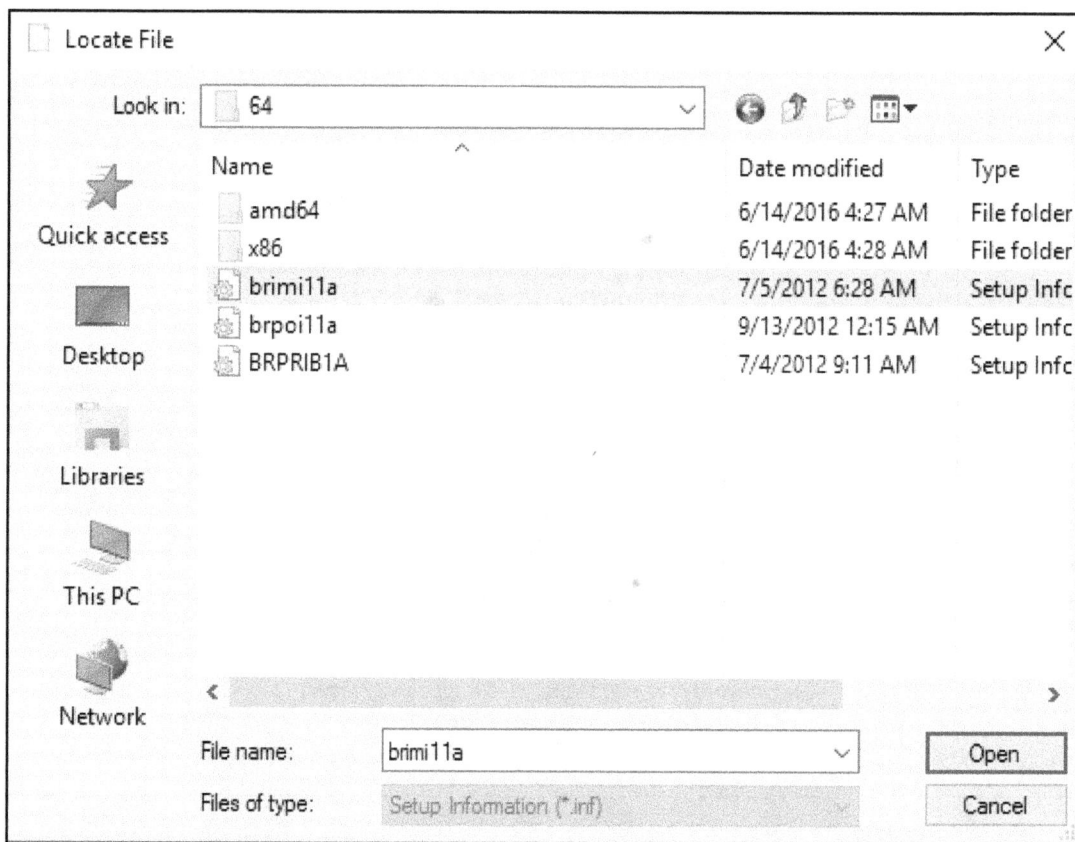

9. Once you have selected the INF file, the **Add Printer Driver Wizard** will now display a list of the drivers that are contained within that INF file. Choose the specific printer driver that you want to install and click **Next**.

Printers ∧

🖳 Brother DCP-J540N Printer

🖳 Brother DCP-J725DW Printer

🖳 Brother DCP-J725N Printer

🖳 Brother DCP-J740N Printer

🖳 ~~Brother DCP-J925DW Printer~~ ∨

🖳 This driver is digitally signed. | Windows Update | Have Disk...

Tell me why driver signing is important

< Back | Next > | Cancel

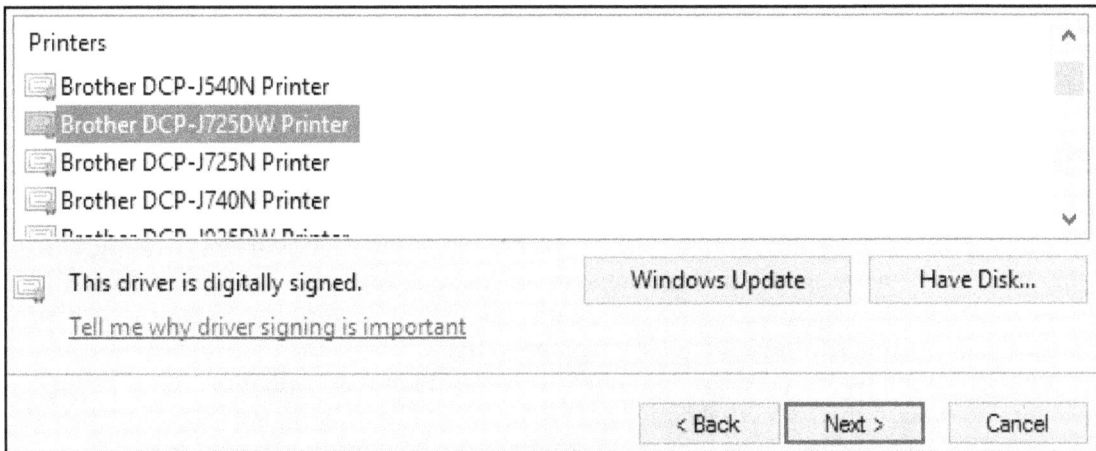

10. Click **Finish** and the driver will install. You should now see it in the list of printer drivers that are installed on this server.

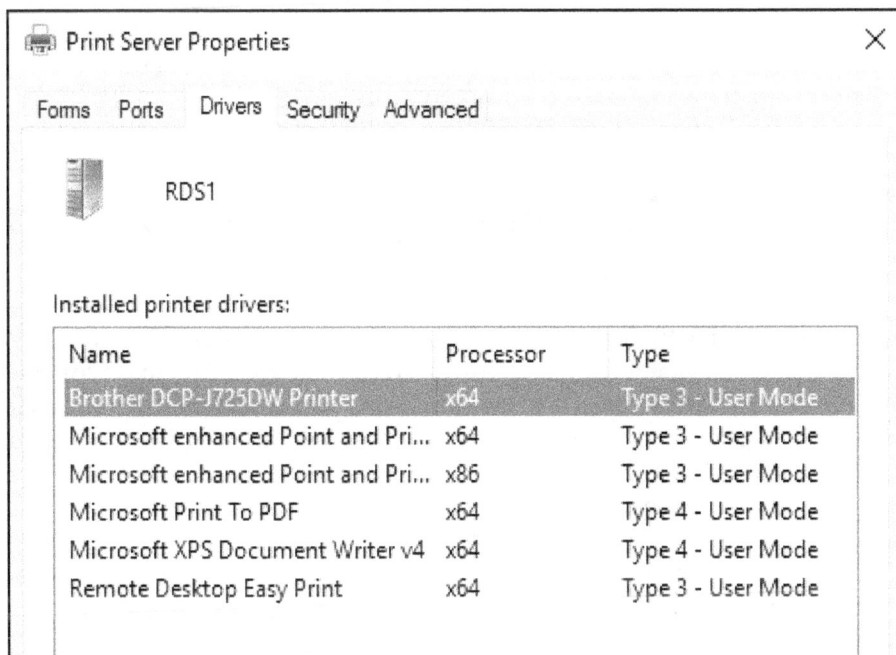

🖨 Print Server Properties ✕

Forms   Ports   Drivers   Security   Advanced

▮ RDS1

Installed printer drivers:

Name	Processor	Type
Brother DCP-J725DW Printer	x64	Type 3 - User Mode
Microsoft enhanced Point and Pri...	x64	Type 3 - User Mode
Microsoft enhanced Point and Pri...	x86	Type 3 - User Mode
Microsoft Print To PDF	x64	Type 4 - User Mode
Microsoft XPS Document Writer v4	x64	Type 4 - User Mode
Remote Desktop Easy Print	x64	Type 3 - User Mode

How it works...

Installing printer drivers onto RDSH servers is a pretty common administrative task in environments where printer redirection is allowed. We walked through one of the nice, simple installers that was easy to extract and contained only the actual driver files that we needed. These kinds of driver downloads are perfect for our purposes here.

As you experience more and more of these driver installations, you will start to learn which manufacturers provide simple driver packages for this purpose and which ones do not. Ultimately, though, the software always contains the simple driver files; sometimes it's just a matter of launching the huge installer program so that it places the files somewhere in a temporary location on the hard drive. What I normally do in these situations is launch the installer and walk it through whatever steps are necessary in order to see that it is unpacking/extracting files. Once it has done that, you don't have to run any more of the wizard to install the software applications because you know that the driver files you need are sitting on the hard drive of the server somewhere. We just need to find them. Using a utility such as FileMon can help identify file locations that have been recently modified, and is a pretty quick way to track down those driver files that are usually hidden away in a `temp` folder. Once you find the files, you can copy and paste them into a more permanent folder for driver installation purposes, cancel out of the install wizard, and walk through the steps in this recipe to install that driver manually instead.

Removing an RD Session Host server from use for maintenance

Occasionally, you will have to perform some maintenance on your RDSH servers. Whether it is for installing updates, installing new applications, or taking them down for some physical maintenance, it will happen sooner or later. If you have multiple RDSH servers in a collection and simply take one offline, user loads will eventually sort themselves out as the RD broker will send new connections to the RDSH servers that are still online, but you will have caused frustration and headaches for any users who were logged in when you shut it down. It is much more user-friendly to flag an RDSH to make it unable to accept new user connections and let the existing ones dissolve naturally over a period of time. This is kind of like a *drain stop* in the NLB world.

Let's take a look at the setting included in RDS that allows us to flag an RDSH as unusable and force the broker to keep new connections from coming through to it. We'll also reverse that change to make sure it starts accepting user connections again after our maintenance is complete.

Getting ready

We have an RDS environment configured with two RDSH servers. These are called RDS1 and RDS2, and we are required to do some maintenance on RDS2. All of our work will be accomplished from inside the Remote Desktop management console on RDS1.

How to do it...

To stop new user connections from flowing to RDS2:

1. Open **Server Manager** and click on **Remote Desktop Services** in the left window pane.
2. Navigate to **Collections | MyDomain RDSH Servers**. This is the name of the collection in my environment; you will need to click on whatever the name of your collection is.
3. Scroll down to the bottom, where you can see the **Host Servers** section. This is a list of the RDSH servers that are part of your collection.
4. Right-click on the RDSH server that we need to perform some maintenance on. In our case, it is **RDS2**.
5. Click on **Do not allow new connections**.

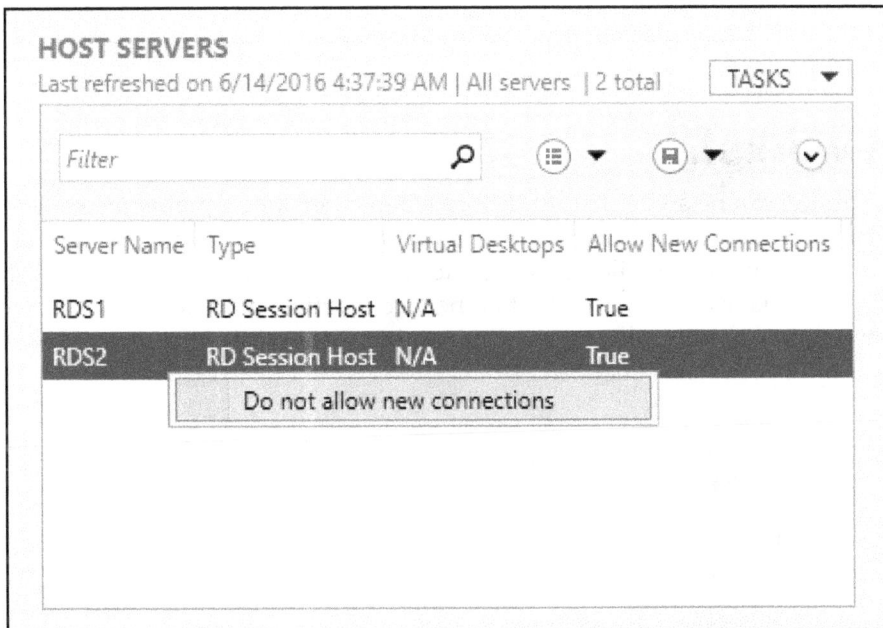

HOST SERVERS

Last refreshed on 6/14/2016 4:37:39 AM | All servers | 2 total   TASKS ▼

Server Name	Type	Virtual Desktops	Allow New Connections
RDS1	RD Session Host	N/A	True
RDS2	RD Session Host	N/A	True

Do not allow new connections

6. This will cause any new connections to be sent over to RDS1 or whatever other RDSH servers you have in your collection. Then, once your maintenance is complete and you are ready to reintroduce RDS2 back into the collection, simply right-click on its name here again and this time choose **Allow new connections**.

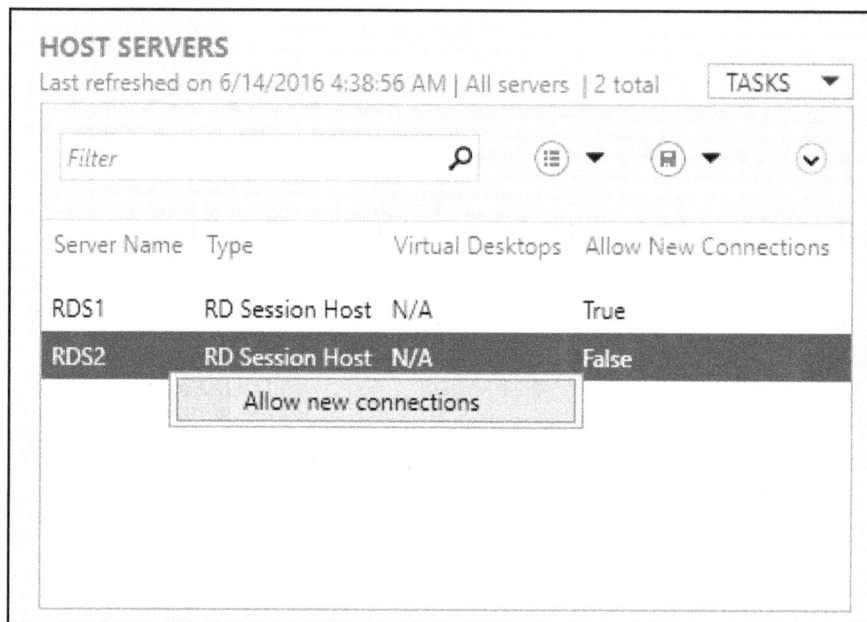

How it works...

This simple option can be a very helpful utility when considering maintenance within your RDS infrastructure. Remember, disallowing new connections to a particular RDSH does not mean that it is immediately available for maintenance because existing users will still be logged in to it. We have only set it so that no new connections will flow there. You can give it some planned time to naturally drop the remaining connections that do exist on the server before performing your maintenance.

Publishing WordPad with RemoteApp

Most of the recipes in this chapter are focused on full desktop sessions provided by RDSH servers because this is the most common scenario that I find RDS used for in the field. One additional piece I would like to take a quick look into is RemoteApp publishing. This is the ability to publish individual applications out to remote users from an RDSH server, rather than a full desktop session. It provides a seamless window for the application, allowing the RemoteApp to look and feel like any other program on the user's computer. Let's set up a sample application and test using it from a client computer. For the sake of simplicity in demonstrating this capability, we will use WordPad as our application to publish and launch.

Getting ready

Our work to publish WordPad as a RemoteApp will be performed from our Server 2016 RDSH called RDS1. We will also use a client computer in order to test accessing this application once we are finished publishing it.

How to do it...

To publish WordPad as a RemoteApp, follow these steps:

1. On RDS1, launch **Server Manager** and click on **Remote Desktop Services** from the left window pane.
2. Browse to the collection of RDSH servers where you want to publish this new application. For our example, I am browsing to **Collections** | **MyDomain RDSH Servers**.

3. Near the middle of this window, you will see a section called **REMOTEAPP PROGRAMS**. Click on the link in the middle of this window that says **Publish RemoteApp programs**.

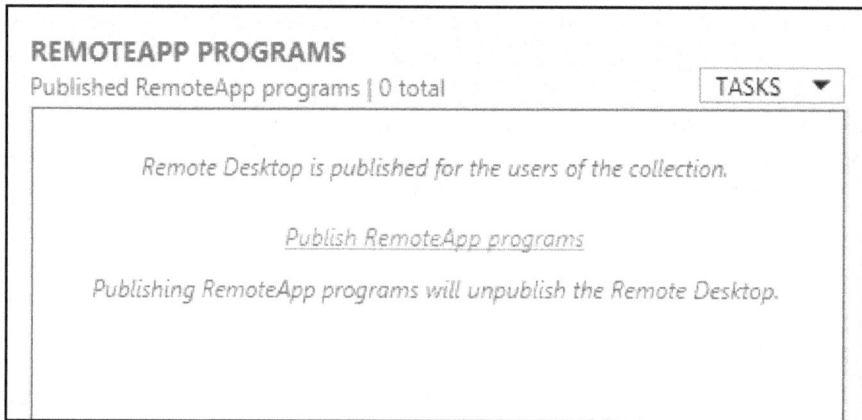

REMOTEAPP PROGRAMS
Published RemoteApp programs | 0 total   TASKS ▼

Remote Desktop is published for the users of the collection.

Publish RemoteApp programs

Publishing RemoteApp programs will unpublish the Remote Desktop.

4. The wizard will now poll the server for a list of available applications. Look through the list until you see **WordPad**; it is most likely on the bottom. Choose it and click **Next**.

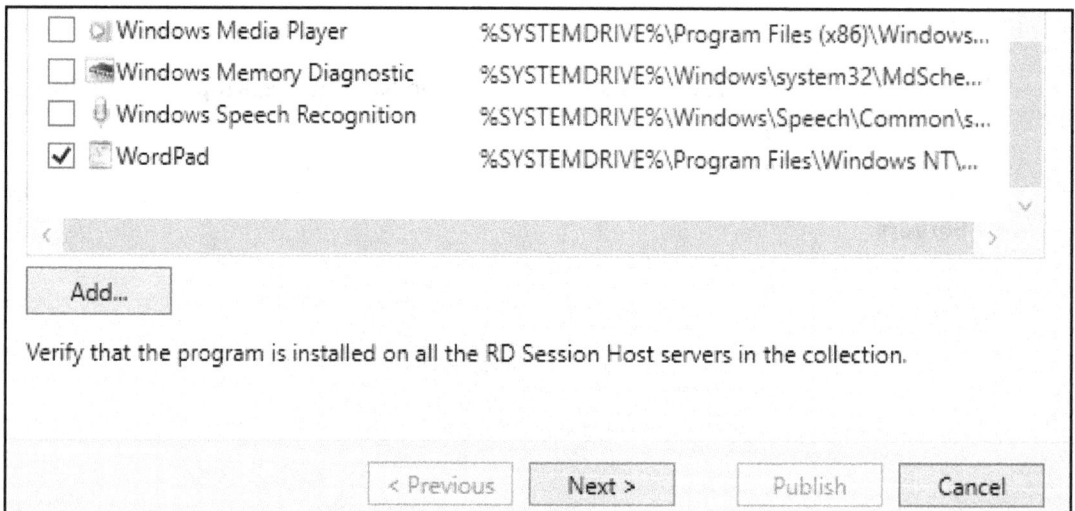

☐	Windows Media Player	%SYSTEMDRIVE%\Program Files (x86)\Windows...
☐	Windows Memory Diagnostic	%SYSTEMDRIVE%\Windows\system32\MdSche...
☐	Windows Speech Recognition	%SYSTEMDRIVE%\Windows\Speech\Common\s...
☑	WordPad	%SYSTEMDRIVE%\Program Files\Windows NT\...

Add...

Verify that the program is installed on all the RD Session Host servers in the collection.

< Previous   Next >   Publish   Cancel

5. On the **Confirmation** screen, click **Publish**.

6. Now that we have the WordPad application published, log in to a client computer so that we can test accessing it.

7. On the client computer, open up a web browser and navigate to `https://RDS1/RDweb`.

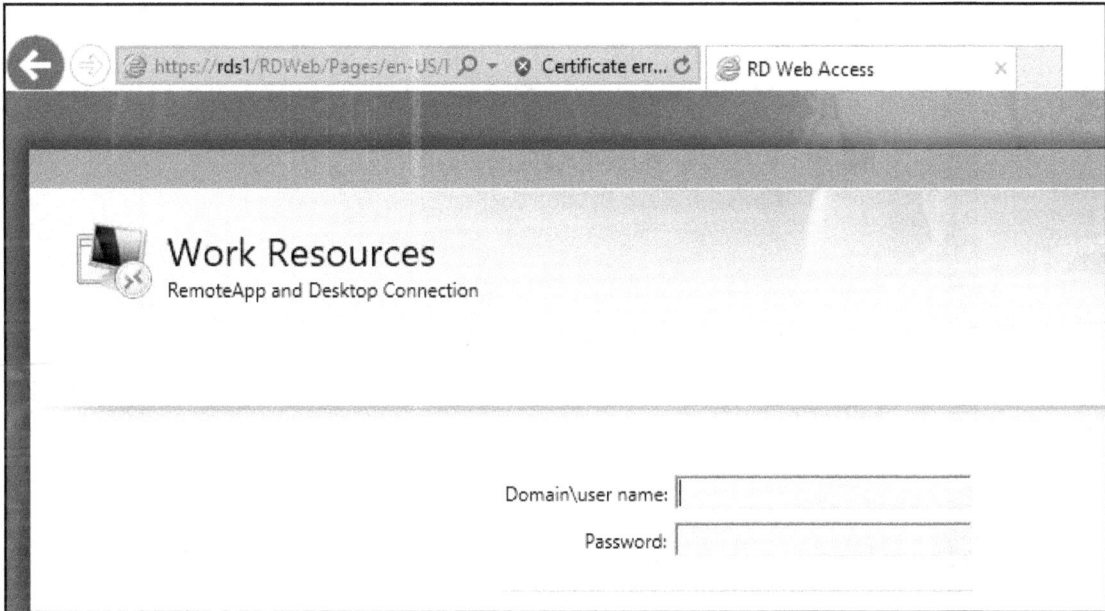

8. Input your credentials, and you should see our published resources that are available in the RDS environment. As expected, WordPad is now visible here.

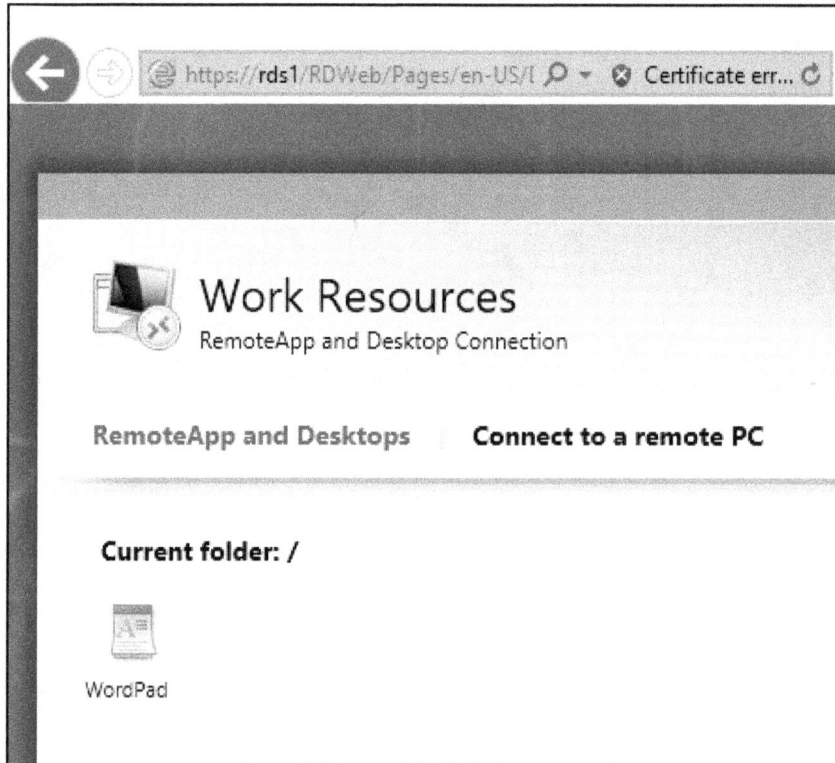

9. Click on the **WordPad** icon and it opens on your computer.

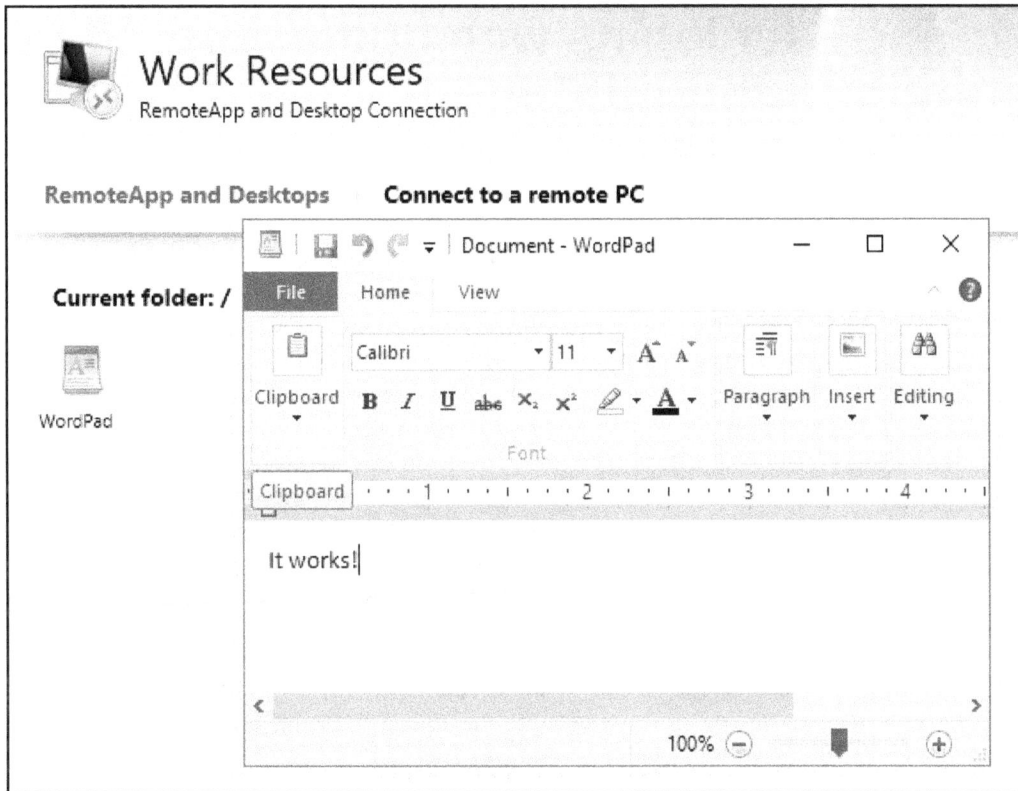

Work Resources
RemoteApp and Desktop Connection

RemoteApp and Desktops   **Connect to a remote PC**

Current folder: /

WordPad

Document - WordPad   — □ ✕

File   Home   View

Clipboard

Calibri   ▼ 11 ▼ A A

Clipboard **B** *I* U abc x₂ x² ✎ ▾ **A** ▾   Paragraph Insert Editing

Font

Clipboard · · · 1 · · · I · · · 2 · · · I · · · 3 · · · I · · · 4 · · · I

It works!|

‹   ›

100% ⊖   ⬇   ⊕

How it works...

If you do not have a need for users to receive access to a full desktop when they log in to the RDS environment, you have the option of publishing individual applications instead. This can be useful for restricting the resources that employees have access to, or perhaps for someone such as a vendor or a temporary assignment that only needs access to certain programs and data. While this was a very simple demonstration using the WordPad program baked into Windows, you can use this same process with other applications you have installed onto your RDSH servers yourself.

> **TIP**
> Make sure you install the applications onto all of the RDSH servers in your collection.

Tracking user logins with Logon/Logoff scripts

I have been working with RDS since before it was called RDS, and something that absolutely every single customer asks for is the ability to report on which users are connecting to which RDSH servers. Ideally, they would like to be able to see, historically, a list of people logging in, and sometimes even some data about when the user logged off the server as well. The only information I have ever found natively inside Windows that can help with this information gathering is the Windows Security Event Logs, but those are extremely messy to try and weed through to find what you are looking for. It's definitely not worth the hassle. So what's the solution here? The easiest way I have found to record login and logout information is to build and utilize some scripts that will run during every user logon and logoff. This is quite simple to do on each of your RDSH servers; let's give it a try together so you can have an idea of what I typically do, and then you can adjust from there based on your specific needs.

Getting ready

Here, we are going to build a couple of scripts on our RDS1 server, which is a Remote Desktop Session Host. Everything we will do is right on this Windows Server 2016 box.

How to do it...

Follow these steps to start recording information about user logins on your RDSH servers:

1. Log into RDS1 and create a new batch file. We are going to utilize good old batch file scripts, but you could also create something with PowerShell to accomplish the same function. I find, however, that a single line of code inside a batch file does the trick quite well. I have created the following script on mine:
   `C:\Reporting\Logon.bat`

2. Now right-click on that script, and choose **Edit** in order to open it up in Notepad.

3. Input the following text:

   ```
   Echo %date%,%time%,%username%,%computername% >>
   C:\Reporting\Logons.txt
   ```

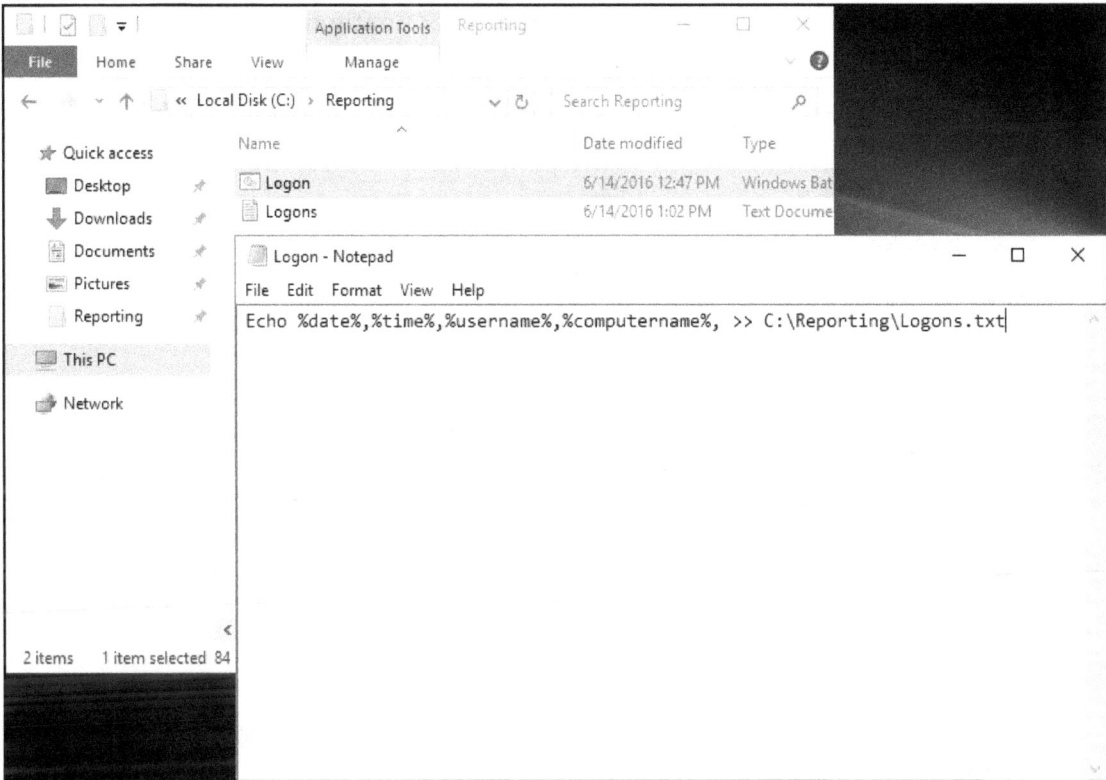

```
Echo %date%,%time%,%username%,%computername%, >> C:\Reporting\Logons.txt
```

4. Now you need to copy your logon script and place it inside the following folder: `C:\Windows\System32\grouppolicy\user\scripts\logon`.

> **TIP**
>
> You may have to create this folder structure if it doesn't already exist.

5. Now open up **gpedit.msc** and navigate to **User Configuration | Windows Settings | Scripts (Logon/Logoff).** Go ahead and specify your **Logon** script here.

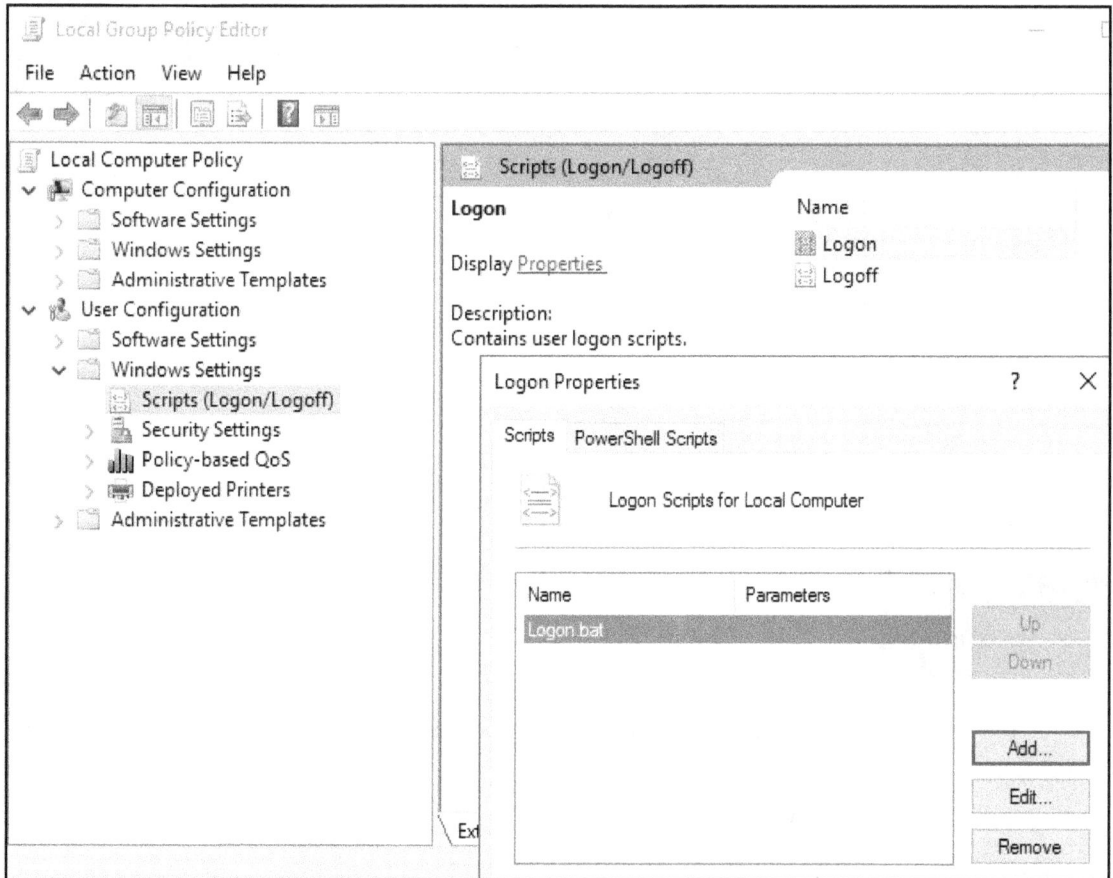

6. With this single command, we are logging quite a bit of data into the Logons.txt file: the current date, time, user's login name, and the RDSH server name they are logging into. Go ahead and log in to RDS1 a few times with different user accounts, and then open up this text file. You can see some information now being logged.

```
Logons - Notepad
File   Edit   Format   View   Help
Tue 06/14/2016,12:54:37.46,administrator,RDS1
Tue 06/14/2016,12:55:00.79,jkrause,RDS1
Tue 06/14/2016,12:57:50.45,administrator,RDS1
Tue 06/14/2016,12:57:54.31,jkrause,RDS1
```

> **TIP**
> I typically use commas to separate the pieces of data so that this text file can be imported into Excel later to be further manipulated and categorized.

Alternatively, you could utilize two separate batch files, one for logons, and one for logoffs. I like this method because we can also split up the logging into multiple smaller text files, one for each username. Then we can see very quickly all the times that each username logged in and logged out. Here is an example of how to accomplish that:

1. Logon script: `Echo LOGON,%date%,%time%,%username%,%computername% >> "C:\Reporting\%username%.log"`.
2. Logoff script: `Echo LOGOFF,%date%,%time%,%username%,%computername% >> "C:\Reporting\%username%.log"`.
3. Place your new Logon script inside `C:\Windows\System32\grouppolicy\user\scripts\logon`.
4. Place your new Logoff script inside `C:\Windows\System32\grouppolicy\user\scripts\logoff`.
5. Inside **gpedit.msc,** make sure that you incorporate both the **Logon** and **Logoff** scripts. These are in the same location we visited before.

6. Once your logon and logoff scripts are copied into the right places and specified inside **gpedit**, you can start logging in and out of your RDS1 server. After a few attempts, take a look inside the `C:\Reporting` folder. Now we have multiple text files listed here, one for each username. Inside each text file we can see timestamps for both logons and logoffs that were performed by that user. It's pretty neat data collection for how simple those scripts are!

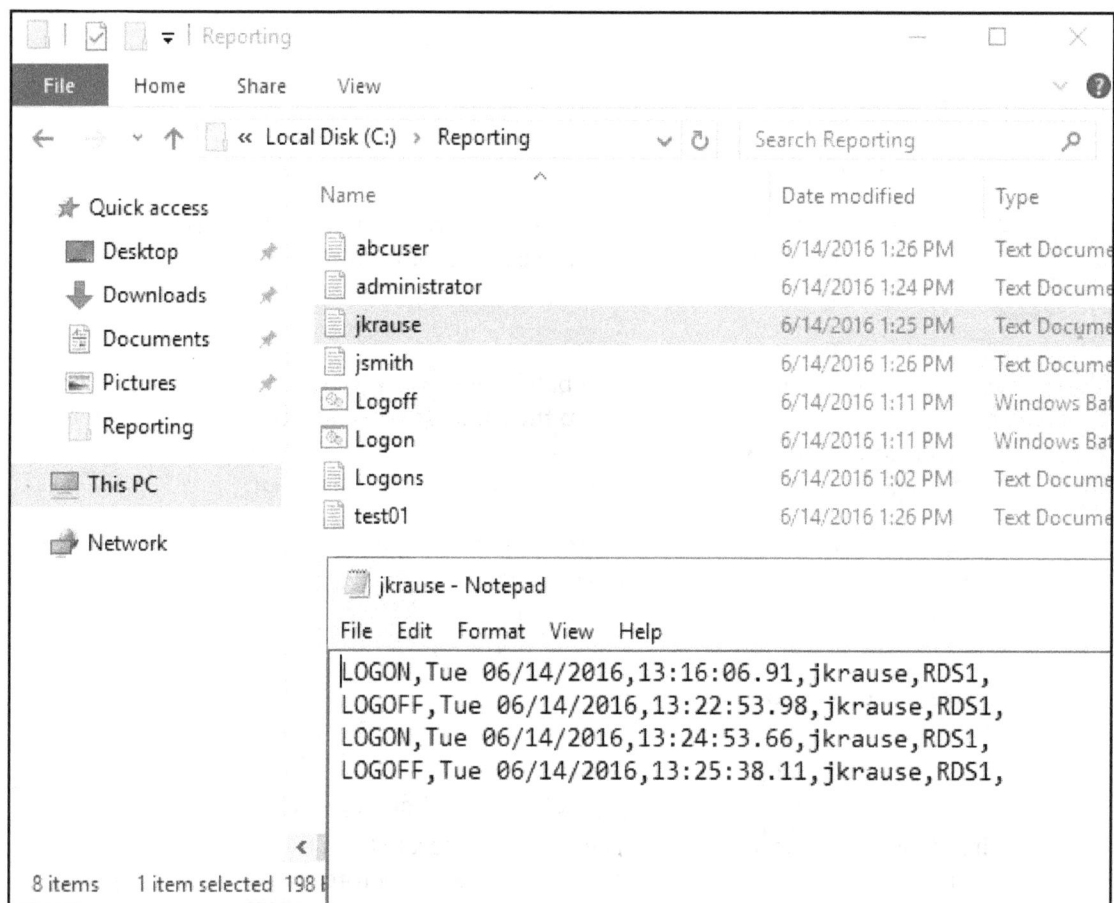

How it works...

We can utilize some very simple logon and logoff scripts on RDSH servers in order to generate reporting information about who is logging in, where they are logging in, and at what times they are coming and leaving. Incorporating these reporting scripts onto each of your RDSH servers and then having them all report to a central location can greatly improve your ability to generate user accounting information. This is a common question among those utilizing RDS, and hopefully you can take this information and build on top of it further to gather whatever info is important to your organization.

8
Monitoring and Backup

Monitoring and backing up servers are usually mundane tasks that are easily overlooked or forgotten. When everything is running smoothly, you may not even think about whether or not your servers have backed up properly, maybe for weeks at a time. Except in the largest of companies, there usually aren't dedicated backup admins or performance monitoring gurus. In IT, we all wear many different hats, and they don't always fit on top of each other.

The key phrase above is *when everything is running smoothly*. Unfortunately, this state of bliss cannot continue indefinitely. Hardware fails, malware happens, files are accidentally deleted. Suddenly, those dull chores of due diligence, such as monitoring the health of your servers and making sure you have solid backups, jumps from backburner to mission-critical on the importance scale.

The good news is that monitoring and backups have never been easier than they are in Windows Server 2016. Let's explore together some of the tools that exist to make these areas of your infrastructure efficient and automatic:

- Using Server Manager as a quick monitoring tool
- Using the new Task Manager to its full potential
- Evaluating system performance with Windows Performance Monitor
- Using Format-List to modify PowerShell data output
- Configuring a full system backup using Windows Server Backup
- Recovering data from a Windows backup file
- Using IP Address Management to keep track of your used IP addresses
- Checking for viruses in Windows Server 2016

Introduction

There are many third-party tools available for performing functions such as data backups and performance monitoring, and because these tools exist, it is easy to automatically assume that they will do a better job than anything that comes with the operating system. Given that, we often categorize backups and monitoring into areas where we will have to spend extra money. I'm not trying to argue that every add-on tool for these functions is unnecessary because they do certainly benefit the right kinds of company. But anyone willing to dig into Server 2016 and discover what it can accomplish on its own accord, without extra add-ons, I think you will find that it meets the needs of many businesses.

Using Server Manager as a quick monitoring tool

Sometimes change is difficult for us old-school IT guys. You know, the ones who prefer keyboards over mice and command lines over graphical interfaces. Starting in Server 2012, Server Manager changed a lot. I find that many admins automatically dislike it, even before they have started using it. It looks *cloudy*, full of links to click on rather than applications. It's certainly more of a web app interface than the Server Manager we are used to.

Let's use this recipe to point out some of the important data that exists in Server Manager, and discover for ourselves that Microsoft may actually have a valid point in causing it to open automatically every time that you log in to a server. No, it's not just there to annoy you.

Getting ready

All we need is Windows Server 2016 in order to poke around in Server Manager. The server we are using is domain joined with a few roles installed so that we can get a better feel for the layout of data on a production system.

How to do it...

Follow these steps to discover some of the functions that Server Manager can perform:

1. Open up **Server Manager**. If you just logged into your server, it is probably opening automatically. Otherwise, click on the **Server Manager** button inside your Start menu.

2. Normally, at the top of Server Manager is the section entitled **Welcome to Server Manager**. In the lower right corner of that section is a button that says **Hide**. Go ahead and click on that button to hide this section of the screen.

3. Now take a look at the information on your screen. These normally green bars listed under each service that you have installed are your first indication as to whether or not everything is running smoothly. Everything is green on mine, which indicates that everything is working properly.

ROLES AND SERVER GROUPS
Roles: 4 | Server groups: 1 | Servers total: 1

AD DS 1	DHCP 1	DNS 1
Manageability	Manageability	Manageability
Events	Events	Events
Services	Services	Services
Performance	Performance	Performance
BPA results	BPA results	BPA results

File and Storage Services 1	Local Server 1	All Servers 1
Manageability	Manageability	Manageability
Events	Events	Events
Services	Services	Services
Performance	Performance	Performance
BPA results	BPA results	BPA results

---

4. Now I'm going to break my AD DS service purposefully to demonstrate what it looks like when things aren't running smoothly. You may or may not want to do this depending on whether or not you are looking at this on a production server. I have stopped my DFSR service on this box, and now see the following in Server Manager.

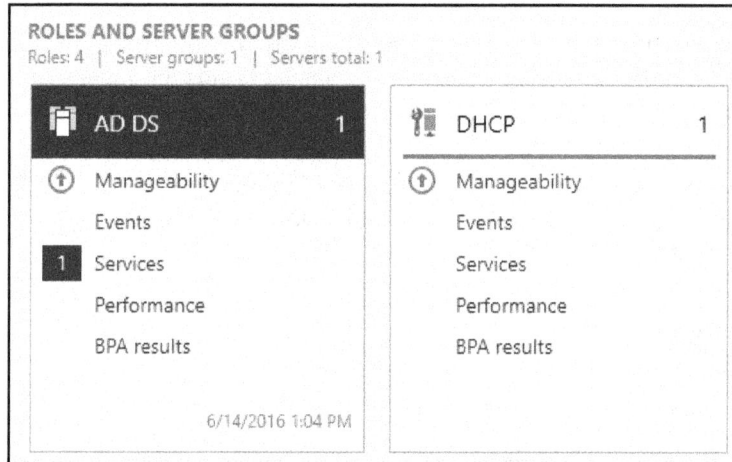

ROLES AND SERVER GROUPS
Roles: 4 | Server groups: 1 | Servers total: 1

⊞ AD DS	1	▮ DHCP	1
⊕ Manageability		⊕ Manageability	
Events		Events	
1 Services		Services	
Performance		Performance	
BPA results		BPA results	
	6/14/2016 1:04 PM		

5. If I click on the **Services** button, where it is indicating that I have one notification, I can see the details of what is going on. Right from here I have the ability to right-click on the warning message and choose a repair method of **Start Services**.

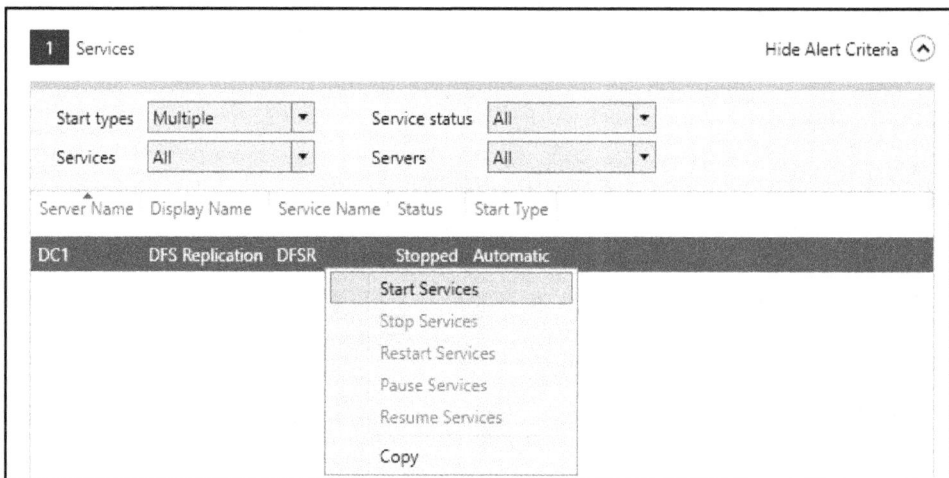

1 Services					Hide Alert Criteria ⌃

Start types	Multiple ▼		Service status	All ▼
Services	All ▼		Servers	All ▼

Server Name	Display Name	Service Name	Status	Start Type
DC1	DFS Replication	DFSR	Stopped	Automatic

Start Services
Stop Services
Restart Services
Pause Services
Resume Services

Copy

6. There is a button near the bottom of this screen that says **Go To AD DS**. Go ahead and click on that button and you will see that it brings us to the same screen as if we had clicked on **AD DS** in the left window pane in Server Manager. On this screen, we can see even more information about our AD DS role and any trouble that it may be having.

For any role that you have installed on your server, there is a quick link to that role's section of Server Manager in the left window pane. Click on each role to view events and information specific to that role.

7. Now click on **Local Server** from the left window pane. Here we see a number of items listed that are helpful for troubleshooting any facet of the operating system, and for reviewing the general status and health of the server. Scroll down near the bottom of this page for a list of events that are happening on this server, without having to open a separate Event Viewer window.

8. Many of the items listed inside this **Local Server** screen are links to open additional configuration windows. For example, where it tells us that **the IE Enhanced Security Configuration** is currently **On**, if we click on **On**, we get the properties page for configuring the IE Enhanced Security Configuration settings on this server.

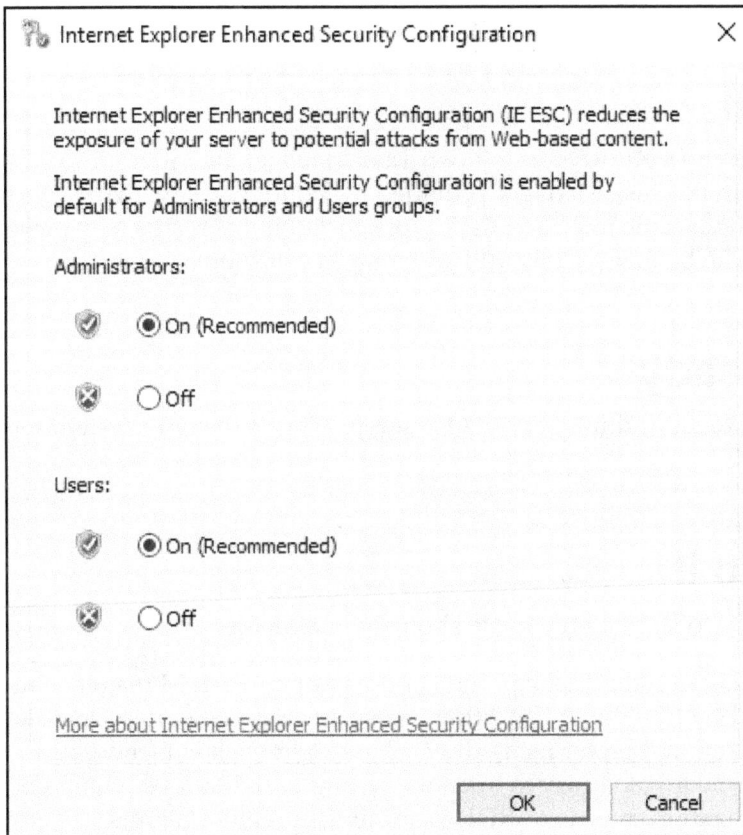

How it works...

Server Manager is full of opportunities to quickly find information that will help monitor your servers. This recipe is just a sample of the data that you can pull into Server Manager, so I suggest you continue navigating around in there to make it look and feel the best that it can for your environment. Another extremely helpful option here is to add multiple servers into your Server Manager for monitoring purposes. If you use the **Manage** menu near the top and the **Add Servers** function in that menu, you can add additional systems into your Server Manager window pane. Doing this causes Server Manager to pull information not only about the local server that you are logged in to, but also about these remote servers, all into one pane of glass. This way you can use Server Manager on one server in order to monitor and maintain your entire server infrastructure, if you choose to do so.

Using the new Task Manager to its full potential

We have all used *Ctrl + Alt + Delete* to open Task Manager and attempt to close problematic applications. With the Task Manager provided by Windows Server 2016, we can do much more right from that same interface. Let's work through this recipe to explore some of the new things that can be done to take full advantage of this tool.

Getting ready

We are logged into a Windows Server 2016 server. This is the only system required for our recipe.

How to do it...

Follow these steps to learn a little more about Task Manager:

1. Right-click on the Taskbar and choose to open **Task Manager**. This is an alternate way to get into the utility, other than using the *Ctrl + Alt + Delete* key combination. I prefer using the Taskbar right-click in fact because, when using the keyboard, it is easy to open the wrong Task Manager when you are using a virtualization console or RDP to administer remote servers.

2. You are now looking at the simple version of Task Manager, where you can choose an application and click **End task** in order to forcibly close that application. To dig a little deeper, click on the **More details** link near the bottom.

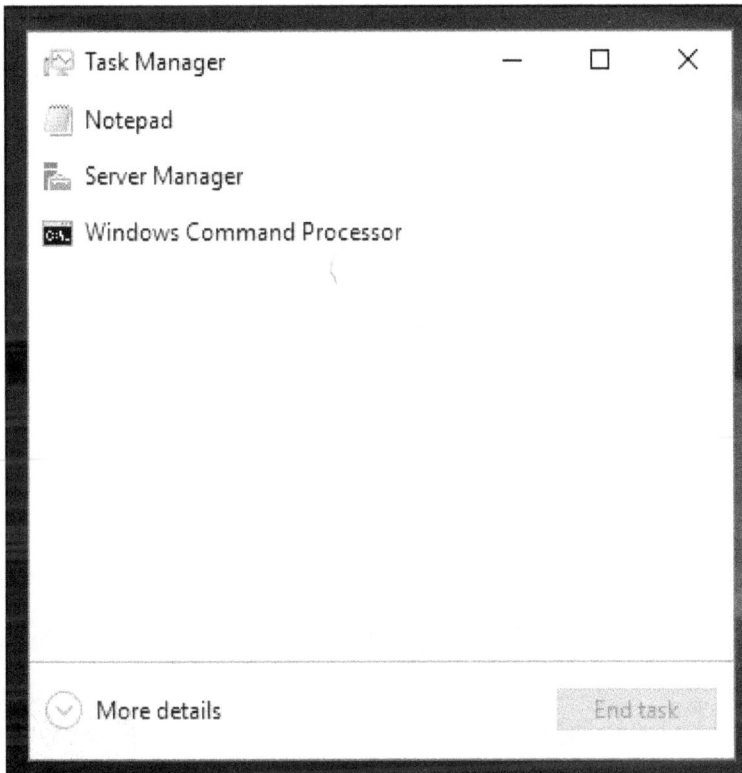

3. Now this is more like it! We can see all open applications at a quick glance, including how many resources each one is consuming. This makes it pretty easy to identify applications that might be stuck and consuming large amounts of CPU or memory. It also lists **Background processes** separately, which can be hugely helpful for finding malware or rogue processes.

Task Manager		
File Options View		
Processes Performance Users Details Services		
Name ∧	**7%** CPU	**71%** Memory
Apps (4)		
> 📝 Notepad	0%	1.4 MB
> 📇 Server Manager	0%	100.7 MB
> 📋 Task Manager	0%	7.9 MB
> ⬛ Windows Command Processor	0%	0.4 MB
Background processes (18)		
> 🗐 Distributed File System Replicati...	0%	9.3 MB
> 🗐 Domain Name System (DNS) Se...	0%	12.1 MB
🗐 Host Process for Windows Tasks	0%	1.1 MB
🗐 Host Process for Windows Tasks	0%	2.1 MB
🗐 Host process for WinRM plug-ins	0%	55.4 MB
> 🔗 Microsoft Distributed Transacti...	0%	1.4 MB
> 🗐 Microsoft.ActiveDirectory.WebS...	0%	9.3 MB
> 🗐 Microsoft® Volume Shadow Co...	0%	1.8 MB

4. The **Details** and **Services** tabs are pretty self-explanatory. **Details** will show even more information about the individual processes that are running and consuming resources on your server. The **Services** tab shows a list of services installed on your server and their current statuses.

5. Click on the **Users** tab and then click the arrow listed under your username to see the expanded view. Listed under each username are the applications that they have open. This sorted list of running programs is especially nice when logged into a server hosting many user connections at once, such as a Remote Desktop Session Host.

User	Status	3% CPU	69% Memory
∨ 🅰 Administrator (17)		2.8%	207.4 MB
Client Server Runtime Proc...		0%	0.9 MB
Console Window Host		0%	4.7 MB
Desktop Window Manager		0%	19.3 MB
Host Process for Windows ...		0%	1.1 MB
Host Process for Windows ...		0%	2.1 MB
Host process for WinRM pl...		0%	55.3 MB
Notepad		0%	1.1 MB
Runtime Broker		0%	2.2 MB
Search		0%	0.1 MB
Server Manager		0%	100.7 MB
Service Host: Unistack Serv...		0%	1.6 MB
Shell Infrastructure Host		0%	2.7 MB
Task Manager		2.8%	7.6 MB
Windows Command Proce...		0%	0.3 MB

6. Now browse over to the**Performance** tab. You will find that this screen looks much nicer than in previous versions. You can click between the different performance counters on the left to see the different details. If you right-click on the graph itself, you will notice there are some additional options. You can click on **Graph summary view** in order to change the Task Manager window into a smaller, graph-only mode that you can leave running in the corner of the screen. You can also choose to copy the screen, which can be helpful for grabbing a quick copy of this data and sending it on for troubleshooting or monitoring purposes.

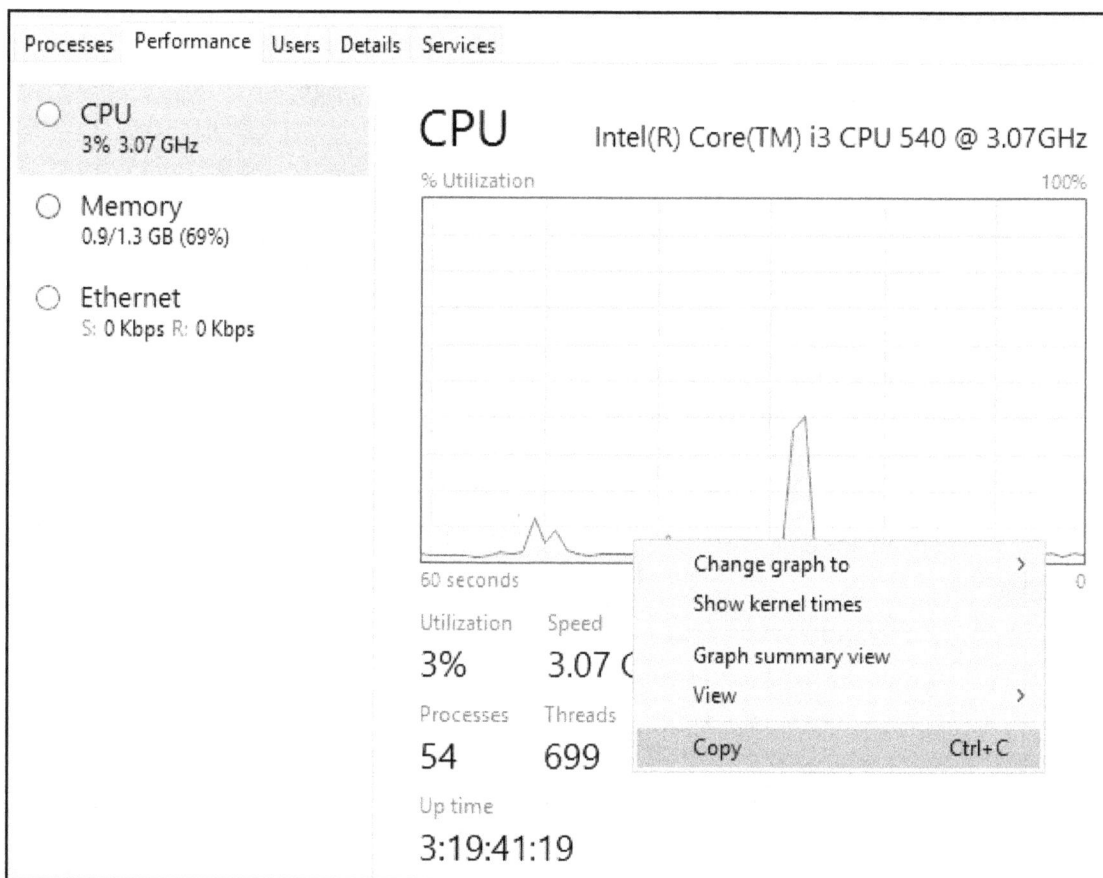

Processes	Performance	Users	Details	Services

CPU
3% 3.07 GHz

Memory
0.9/1.3 GB (69%)

Ethernet
S: 0 Kbps R: 0 Kbps

CPU   Intel(R) Core(TM) i3 CPU 540 @ 3.07GHz

% Utilization   100%

60 seconds

Change graph to >

Show kernel times

Graph summary view

View >

Copy   Ctrl+C

Utilization   Speed

3%   3.07 G

Processes   Threads

54   699

Up time

3:19:41:19

7. At the bottom of your Task Manager screen, click on **Open Resource Monitor**. This runs the new Resource Monitor, which is an even more extensive tool for monitoring hardware resources and utilization. This is very helpful for monitoring hardware in real time.

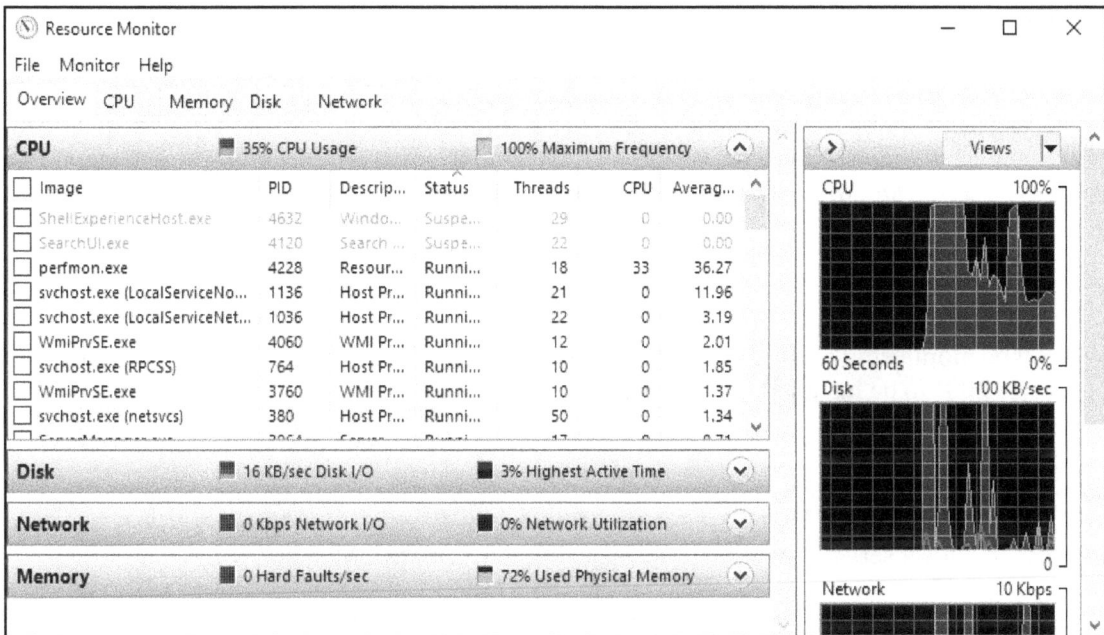

How it works...

The new Task Manager provided with Server 2016 contains many additional pieces of information that are helpful for monitoring system performance in real time. As you start to administer your new Server 2016 machines, make sure you spend some time in this interface so that you are familiar with the new layout when you need to access information quickly.

Evaluating system performance with Windows Performance Monitor

While good old Task Manager and the new Resource Monitor are great utilities for monitoring system performance in real time, for any more extensive monitoring needs I tend to prefer Performance Monitor. `Perfmon`, as it is often nicknamed, is an excellent tool that can be used for collecting specific data over a predefined period of time.

We have all had cases where a report comes across our desk that a certain server is misbehaving or running slowly. By the time we get logged in, everything looks normal. Other than Event Viewer, we don't have a whole lot of options for investigating what was happening during the time of the problem. But it might happen again, and if we plan ahead with the Performance Monitor tool, we might be able to catch the server in the act, even if we don't see the data until after the event has finished.

Getting ready

We will be monitoring a Windows Server 2016 server in our environment for this recipe. Nothing needs to be installed, as Performance Monitor is part of Windows by default.

How to do it...

In order to collect server performance data using Performance Monitor, follow these steps:

1. Open up a command prompt or your **Run** box and type `perfmon`. This will launch the Performance Monitor tool.

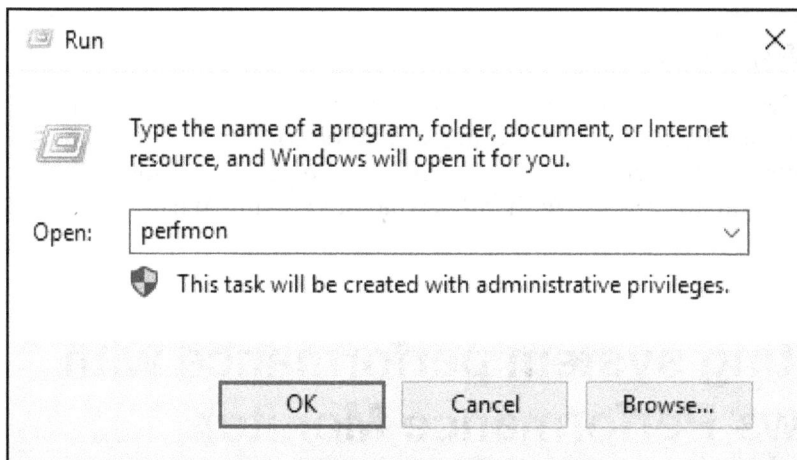

2. From the left window pane, navigate to **Monitoring Tools** | **Performance Monitor**. You can see that it shows some real-time data about the processor by default.

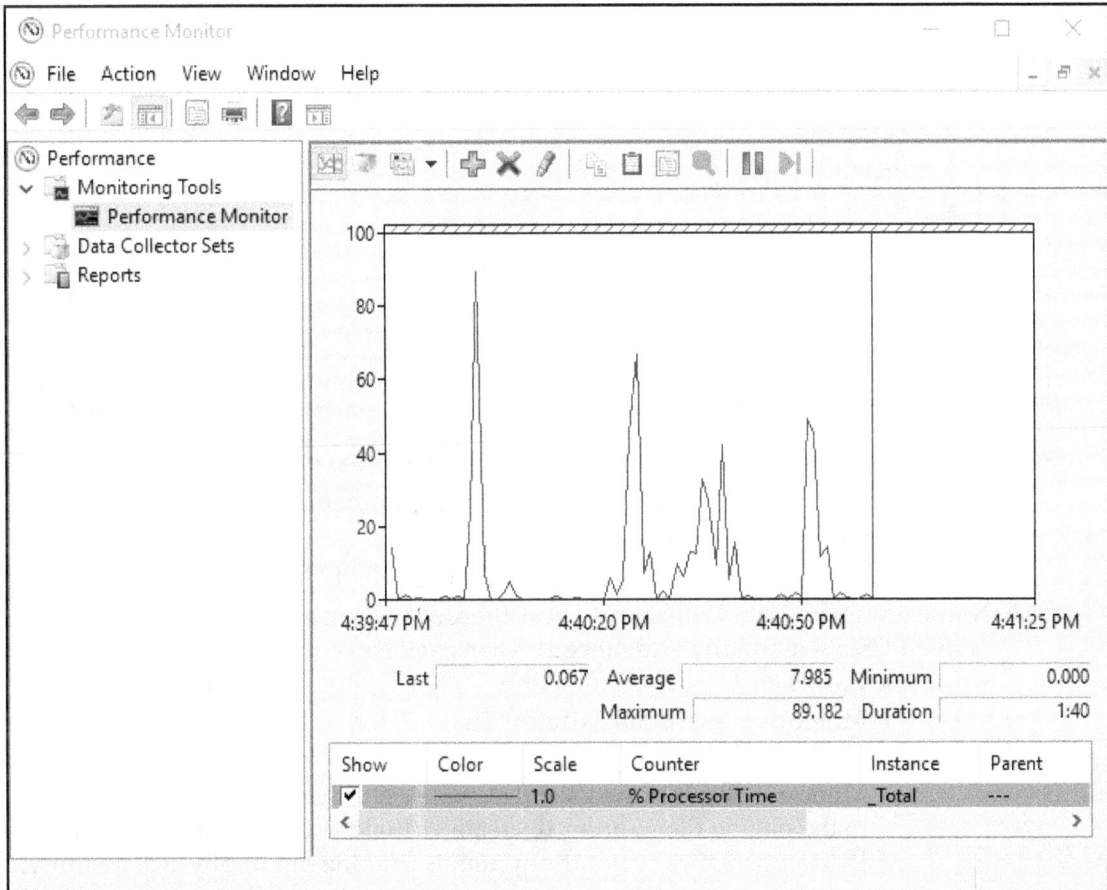

3. Browse to **Data Collector Sets** | **User Defined**. Right-click on this folder and choose **New** | **Data Collector Set**.

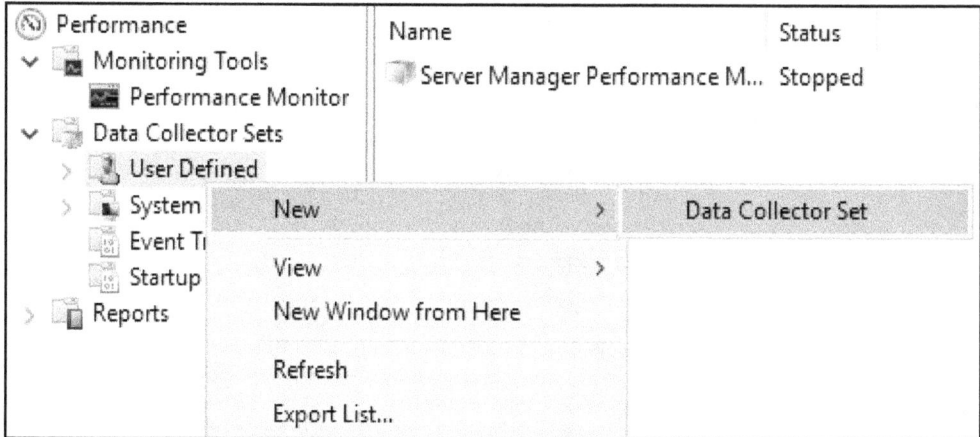

4. For my evaluation on this server, I am going to add the following counters:
5. Click the **Add...** button in order to add some performance counters that we want to keep track of on this server.
6. Check the box for **Performance counter** and click **Next**.
7. Name your new Data Collector Set and choose the bottom radio button entitled **Create manually (Advanced)**. Then click **Next**.
    - **Processor** | **% Processor Time**: This will tell us how busy the CPU is.
    - **Memory** | **Available MBytes**: This will tell us how much RAM is available.
    - **Memory** | **Page Writes/sec**: This will tell us how often Windows looks to the paging file in order to create virtual memory, which helps to indicate whether or not the system is running out of physical memory.

8. As you can see, there are so many different counters that you can add. We are only interested in these three, and so we can click on the **OK** button.

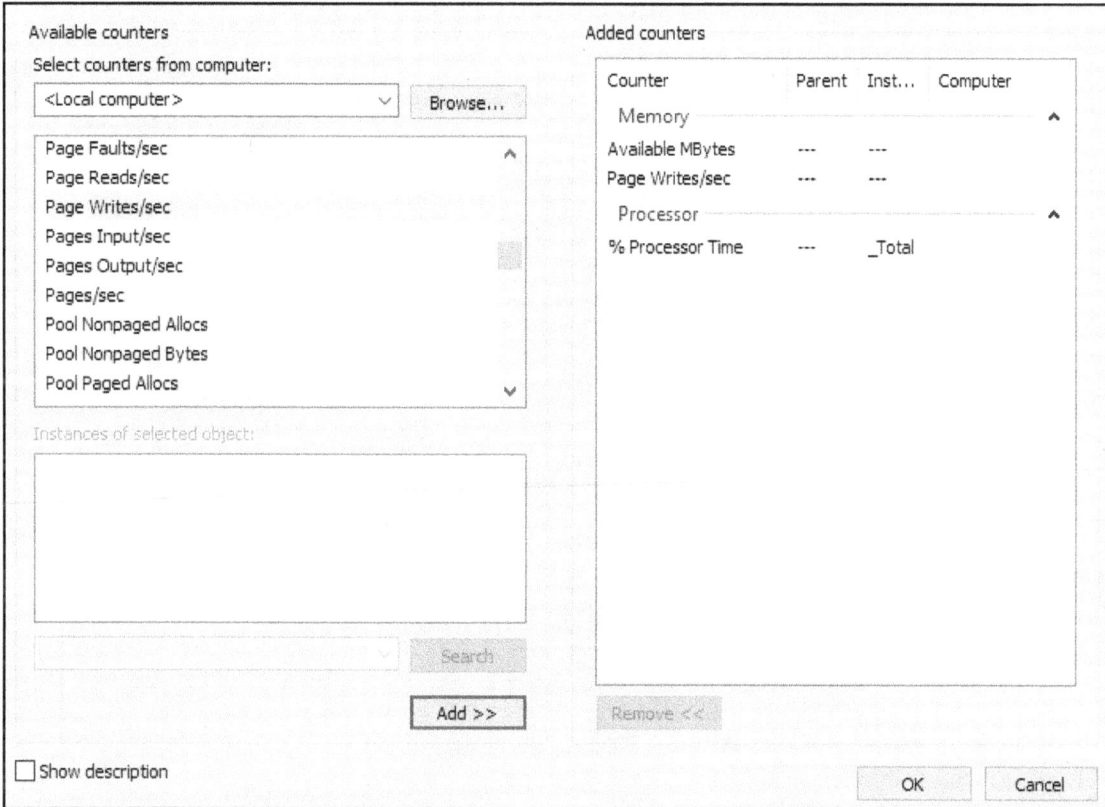

Available counters			Added counters			
Select counters from computer:			Counter	Parent	Inst...	Computer
<Local computer> ▽	Browse...		Memory			⌃
Page Faults/sec		⌃	Available MBytes	---	---	
Page Reads/sec			Page Writes/sec	---	---	
Page Writes/sec			Processor			⌃
Pages Input/sec			% Processor Time	---	_Total	
Pages Output/sec						
Pages/sec						
Pool Nonpaged Allocs						
Pool Nonpaged Bytes						
Pool Paged Allocs		⌄				
Instances of selected object:						
▽	Search					
	Add >>		Remove <<			
☐ Show description					OK	Cancel

9. Back in our wizard for setting up the new Data Collector set, we should see our three counters now listed. Go ahead and click **Next**.

10. Change where you would like the data saved, if necessary. Then click **Next**.

11. On the last screen of the wizard, choose the radio button for **Open properties for this data collector set**. Then click the **Finish** button.

12. Navigate over to the **Schedule** tab and click the **Add** button to set your preferred time in the **Start time** field for these performance counters to be collected.

13. Once you have set a start time, you can either plan to stop the data collection manually, or you can use the **Stop Condition** tab in order to stop the collection after a predetermined amount of time. Using a combination of the **Schedule** and **Stop Condition** tabs is a great way to collect data for a specific time range, such as one day.

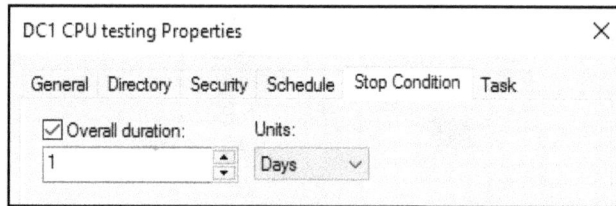

14. Now that we have some data that has been collected, head down to **Reports | User Defined** in order to see the data that was stored during the time period that we specified.

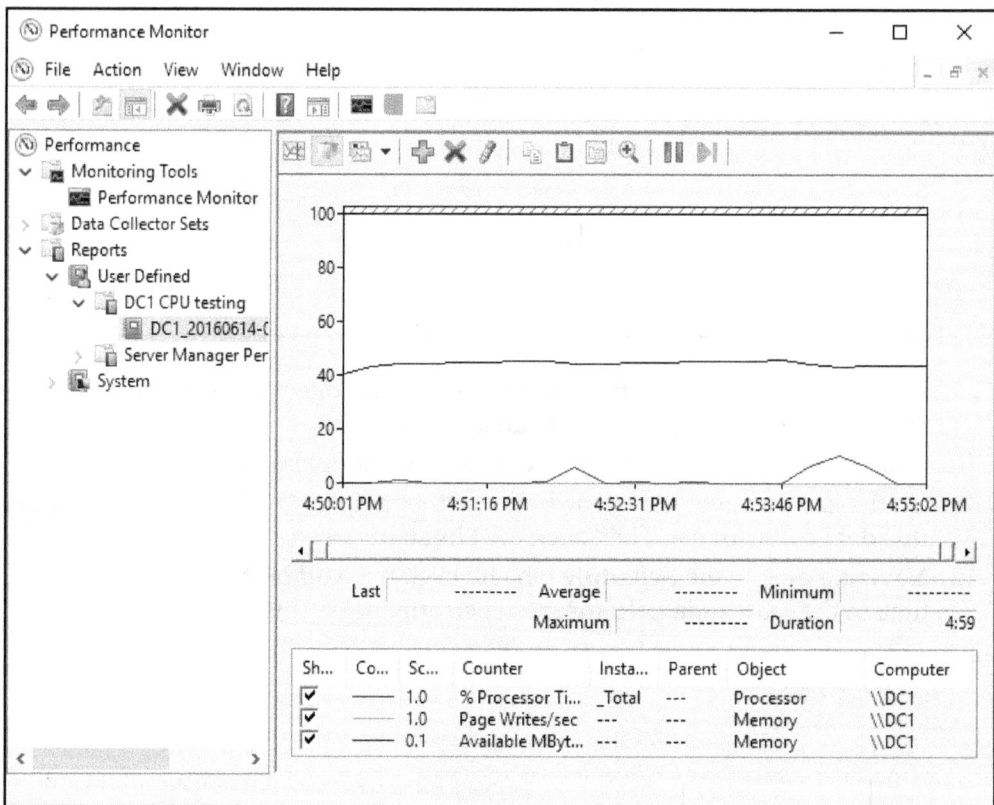

How it works...

Performance Monitor is a great tool for collecting hardware and server performance data. The ability to be very granular in identifying which resources you want to monitor is extremely helpful. Combine that with scheduling capabilities for collection times and you have a recipe for successful server monitoring. It can also be useful to run a Performance Monitor data set as a baseline after installing a new server. This way you can hold onto that report and compare it against later similar reports when the user load increases, to look back and find out what kind of an impact certain services or users have on a system.

Using Format-List to modify PowerShell data output

There is a special parameter that can be used with just about any PowerShell command or cmdlet in order to display different, and usually more, data from that particular command. This parameter is called **Format-List**, and if you are a fan of finding as much information as possible about the tools you are working with, this is something you will definitely want to become familiar with. PowerShell is often used to monitor many different facets of Windows Server, and getting to know the intricacies of Format-List will certainly help you to sculpt the output information that you are looking for when performing monitoring functions from the PowerShell command line.

We all know that a `dir` command will display a list of files and folders that are within our current directory; this works in either Command Prompt or in PowerShell. Let's start learning how to make use of Format-List by using it to modify the output of our `dir` information.

Getting ready

We will be running these commands from a PowerShell prompt on one of our Windows Server 2016 machines.

How to do it...

Let's use Format-List to modify our information output on a couple of different PowerShell cmdlets:

1. Open up PowerShell with administrative rights.
2. Browse to a location that contains some files. I have a few saved in my `documents` folder, so I will input `cd documents` in order to navigate into my `documents` folder.
3. Type `dir`. Then press *Enter*. You see the normal output of the `dir` command, a simple list of files, and a little bit of information about each of them.

```
Administrator: Windows PowerShell

Windows PowerShell
Copyright (C) 2016 Microsoft Corporation. All rights reserved.

PS C:\Users\administrator.MYDOMAIN> cd documents
PS C:\Users\administrator.MYDOMAIN\documents> dir


    Directory: C:\Users\administrator.MYDOMAIN\documents


Mode                LastWriteTime         Length Name
----                -------------         ------ ----
-a----        6/15/2016     3:44 AM              0 Doc1.txt
-a----        6/15/2016     3:44 AM              0 Doc2.txt
-a----        6/15/2016     3:44 AM              0 Doc3.txt
-a----        6/15/2016     3:44 AM              0 Doc4.txt
-a----        6/15/2016     3:44 AM              0 Doc5.txt


PS C:\Users\administrator.MYDOMAIN\documents>
```

4. Now instead of using a simple `dir`, give this command a try: `Dir | Format-List`.
5. That is a lot more data! As you can see, by simply adding a pipe with Format-List following it, we have enhanced the `dir` command to give us more information about these files.

```
Name          : Doc5.txt
Length        : 0
CreationTime  : 6/15/2016 3:44:06 AM
LastWriteTime : 6/15/2016 3:44:31 AM
LastAccessTime : 6/15/2016 3:44:31 AM
Mode          : -a----
LinkType      :
Target        : {}
VersionInfo   : File:             C:\Users\administrator.MYDOMAIN\documents\Doc5.txt
                InternalName:
                OriginalFilename:
                FileVersion:
                FileDescription:
                Product:
                ProductVersion:
                Debug:            False
                Patched:          False
                PreRelease:       False
                PrivateBuild:     False
                SpecialBuild:     False
                Language:
```

6. Using Format-List by itself will adjust the data output to another default format, but one that contains more information. In order to see everything there is to see in the output of a particular command, you can also add a * to the end of the command. Let's give that a try.

7. Type this command: Dir | Format-List *.

8. Now we have yet another different output of information for these files.

```
Administrator: Windows PowerShell                                         —   □   ✕

BaseName         : Doc5
Target           : {}
LinkType         :
Name             : Doc5.txt
Length           : 0
DirectoryName    : C:\Users\administrator.MYDOMAIN\documents
Directory        : C:\Users\administrator.MYDOMAIN\documents
IsReadOnly       : False
Exists           : True
FullName         : C:\Users\administrator.MYDOMAIN\documents\Doc5.txt
Extension        : .txt
CreationTime     : 6/15/2016 3:44:06 AM
CreationTimeUtc  : 6/15/2016 10:44:06 AM
LastAccessTime   : 6/15/2016 3:44:31 AM
LastAccessTimeUtc : 6/15/2016 10:44:31 AM
LastWriteTime    : 6/15/2016 3:44:31 AM
LastWriteTimeUtc : 6/15/2016 10:44:31 AM
Attributes       : Archive


PS C:\Users\administrator.MYDOMAIN\documents> _
```

9. Before we lay this one to rest, let's test Format-List with another cmdlet just to make sure this isn't something that only works with file information.

10. Use the `Get-Date` cmdlet to see the current date and time. Pretty simple, right?

```
Administrator: Windows PowerShell                        —    □    ×
PS C:\> Get-Date

Sunday, October 16, 2016 1:31:06 PM


PS C:\>
```

11. Now try this: `Get-Date | Format-List`.

```
Administrator: Windows PowerShell                        —    □    ×
PS C:\> Get-Date | Format-List

DisplayHint : DateTime
Date        : 10/16/2016 12:00:00 AM
Day         : 16
DayOfWeek   : Sunday
DayOfYear   : 290
Hour        : 13
Kind        : Local
Millisecond : 261
Minute      : 32
Month       : 10
Second      : 34
Ticks       : 636122215542614223
TimeOfDay   : 13:32:34.2614223
Year        : 2016
DateTime    : Sunday, October 16, 2016 1:32:34 PM
```

How it works...

As we have shown in this recipe, using the Format-List parameter on the end of any command or cmdlet is a good practice to get into because it can help display much more information than would normally be available with the original command, from system timestamps and file information up to very specific information about NIC settings and system components; making Format-List part of your regular arsenal will therefore help to get you a greater quantity of information that you can use to do your job.

Configuring a full system backup using Windows Server Backup

Maintaining a good backup solution is so critical to administering a corporate server environment in today's IT world. There are limitless potential options for designing your particular backup plan, all the way from file copy backups to redundant servers sitting in hot standby mode.

While many third-party tools and technologies provide the capability to back up all of your servers simultaneously while retaining multiple previous versions of each, those tools are not always on the table because of cost and implementation complexity. Let's take a few minutes and familiarize ourselves with the built-in backup solution that Microsoft provides free of charge, right in the Server 2016 operating system.

Getting ready

We are logged in to our Server 2016 web server. We will be using the built-in Windows Server Backup tool in order to create a full image of this server.

How to do it...

Follow these steps to back up your Server 2016 using the built-in Windows Server Backup:

1. Open **Server Manager** and click **Add roles and features**. Go through this wizard, following the steps in order to install the feature called **Windows Server Backup**. Remember that this is a Feature, not a Role, so look for it on the second screen.

2. Launch **Windows Server Backup** from your**Start** menu, or from the **Tools** menu inside Server Manager.

3. In the left window pane, choose **Local Backup**.

4. Then, toward the right of your screen, click on the **Backup Schedule…** action and click on **Next**.

5. On the **Select Backup Configuration** screen, I am going to choose **Full server**. If you have only specific items you would like to back up, you can use the **Custom** option for that purpose.

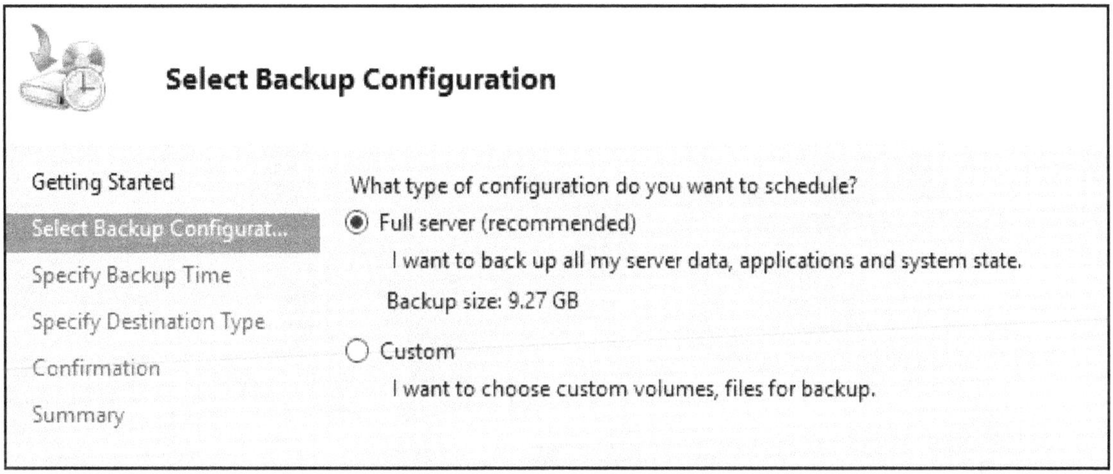

Select Backup Configuration

Getting Started

Select Backup Configurat...

Specify Backup Time

Specify Destination Type

Confirmation

Summary

What type of configuration do you want to schedule?

⦿ Full server (recommended)

   I want to back up all my server data, applications and system state.

   Backup size: 9.27 GB

○ Custom

   I want to choose custom volumes, files for backup.

6. Specify the schedule for how often you would like these backups to run. I'm going to have mine run every morning at **2:00 AM**.

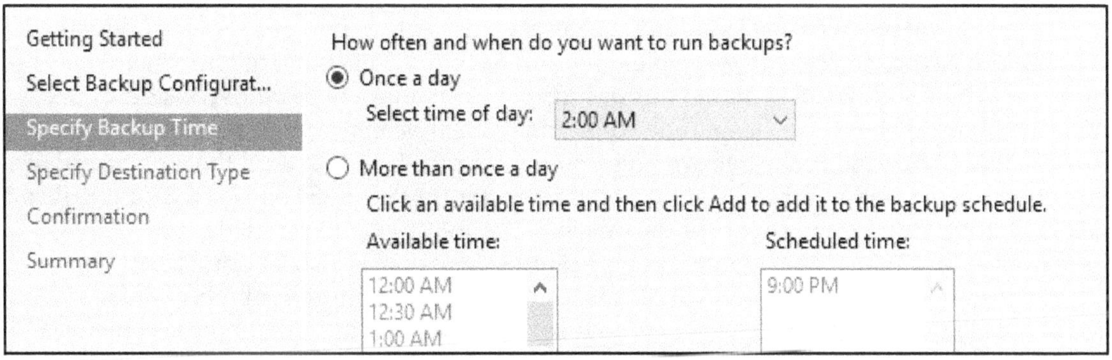

Getting Started

Select Backup Configurat...

Specify Backup Time

Specify Destination Type

Confirmation

Summary

How often and when do you want to run backups?

⦿ Once a day

   Select time of day: | 2:00 AM | ⌄

○ More than once a day

   Click an available time and then click Add to add it to the backup schedule.

   Available time: Scheduled time:

12:00 AM	^		9:00 PM	^
12:30 AM				
1:00 AM				

7. As you can see in the text, the best way to store backups is to have a dedicated hard disk plugged into your server. However, I don't have an extra drive installed here, so I am going to choose **Back up to a volume** and specify my D drive, a separate partition that has no data on it currently, as my storage container for backups.

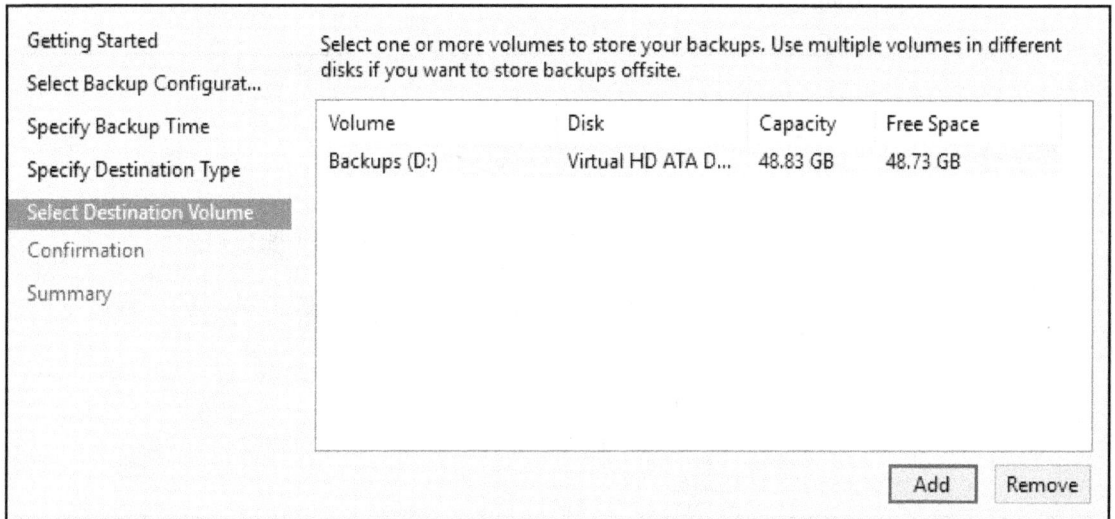

Getting Started	Select one or more volumes to store your backups. Use multiple volumes in different disks if you want to store backups offsite.			
Select Backup Configurat...				
Specify Backup Time	Volume	Disk	Capacity	Free Space
Specify Destination Type	Backups (D:)	Virtual HD ATA D...	48.83 GB	48.73 GB
Select Destination Volume				
Confirmation				
Summary				

Add   Remove

How it works...

In this recipe, we installed the Windows Server Backup feature into our server and walked through the wizard in order to schedule daily full backups. This is a straightforward process, but the storage location of your backup files can take a little bit of consideration. A dedicated hard disk is the best solution for storing backups; that way, if your drive goes down you will have all of the backup files on another physical disk. And then, of course, if you configure an option for replicating that data to another physical site, or rotating drives on a schedule, that will protect your data even better in the event of a site failure or catastrophe. Storing onto a separate volume on the same disk is also an option, but then you are in a situation where that physical disk is a single point of failure for both your live operating system and the backup files. The third option is storing backup files on the network. This is something that I expect a lot of admins will choose, but you have to keep in mind that, when making this configuration, you will only be able to have one backup file stored in that network location at a time from your server, as they will be overwritten with each new backup process.

There is a second action available from inside the backup console that we didn't touch on. In order to accomplish ad hoc backups, or backups that you intend to create manually on an as-needed basis, you could launch an action called **Backup Once...** Use this to create a manual backup copy at any time.

Recovering data from a Windows backup file

Creating a backup or even a backup schedule is easy enough, but what is the process for restoring information from one of those backup files that we have sitting around? This is where the rubber really meets the road, as they say. Let's run through the process of restoring some data from a backup file that was taken yesterday. Perhaps some data was corrupted or accidentally deleted. Whatever the reason for our recovery needs, we will work together to restore some data from a backup file and get comfortable with that interface.

Getting ready

We are still working on our Server 2016 web server. This server was previously configured for Windows Server Backup, so it already has that feature installed. Yesterday we created a full backup of our server, and today we need to recover some of the data from that backup file.

How to do it...

Follow these steps in order to restore the server using the Windows Server Backup utility:

1. Open up the Windows Server Backup management interface. You can launch this from either the Start menu or from the **Tools** menu of Server Manager.
2. Choose **Local Backup** from the left window pane.
3. Near the right side of your screen, click on the **Recover...** action.

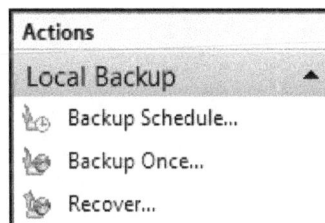

Actions	
Local Backup	▲
🔧 Backup Schedule...	
🔧 Backup Once...	
🔧 Recover...	

4. Since our backup file is stored right here on one of the server's volumes, we choose **This server** and click **Next**.

5. Now you will see a calendar with bold dates indicating which days have valid backup files that you can restore back to. We are selecting the backup that ran yesterday and clicking **Next**.

Oldest available backup:	6/15/2016 5:38 AM
Newest available backup:	6/15/2016 5:38 AM

Available backups

Select the date of a backup to use for recovery. Backups are available for dates shown in bold.

June 2016								Backup date:	6/15/2016
Sun	Mon	Tue	Wed	Thu	Fri	Sat		Time:	5:38 AM
			1	2	3	4		Location:	Backups (D:)
5	6	7	8	9	10	11		Status:	Available online
12	13	14	**15**	16	17	18		Recoverable items:	Bare metal recover...
19	20	21	22	23	24	25			
26	27	28	29	30					

6. Now in the **Select Recovery Type** screen, we are going to choose **Files and folders** and click **Next**.

> **TIP**
>
> You will notice a grayed out option here for Hyper-V. If you use Windows Server Backup on a Hyper-V server, you have options for backing up and restoring individual virtual machines on that host. This is a great feature enhancement and a good reason to start using Windows Server Backup on your Hyper-V servers.

7. We are now looking at the **Select Items to Recover** screen. Simply choose the files and folders that you want to restore from yesterday's backup. For our web server, which is the DirectAccess NLS server we set up a couple of chapters ago, it was the website itself that was compromised and we want to roll back to the website files that were running yesterday. So I am going to choose to restore the `C:\NLS` folder.

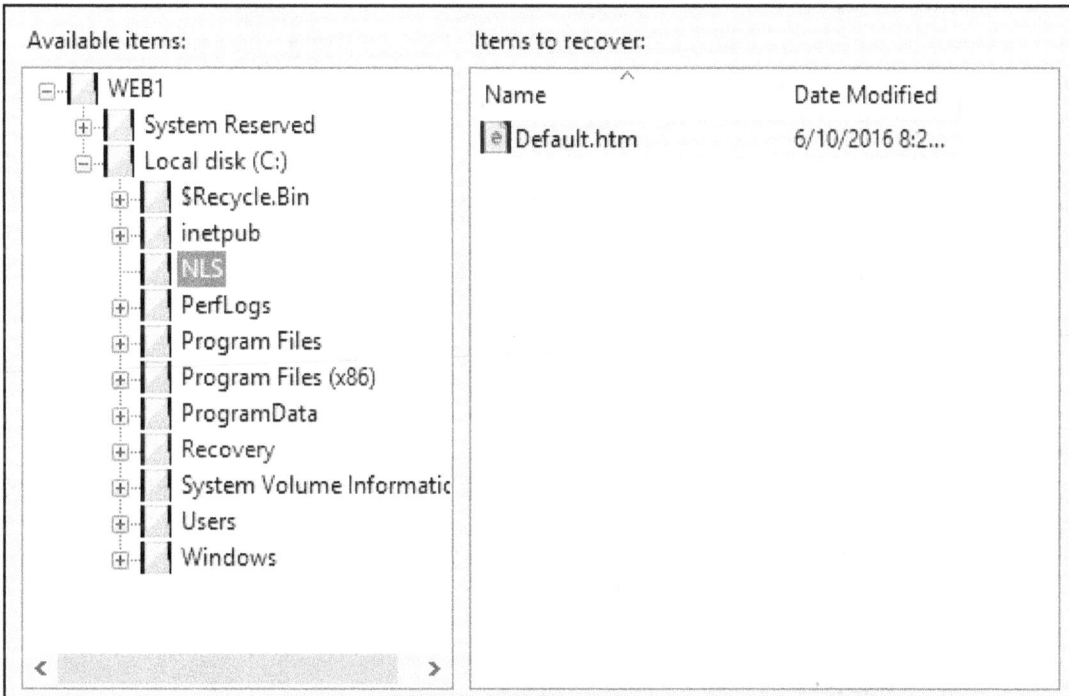

8. Choose the option to recover files to **Original location** and click **Overwrite the existing versions with the recovered versions**. This will ensure that the files from yesterday's backup get placed on top of the files that still exist on our server today.

9. On the **Confirmation** screen, you will see a summary of the items that are going to be recovered. If everything looks good, click on the **Recover** button.

How it works...

This recovery recipe is a good baseline for getting familiar with the options that are available to you for restoring from Windows backup files. Here we restored some simple files that had been compromised on our web server. In the event of a more serious system failure, where you might need to take a full disk backup and recover the whole thing onto a new server, that process is slightly more complicated. To accomplish a full system recovery of that magnitude, you would boot the server into your Windows setup disk and choose to run Windows Recovery Environment. Through this tool, you could make use of your Windows backup file and restore the server.

Using IP Address Management to keep track of your used IP addresses

The **IP Address Management (IPAM)** tool is a little-known utility built into Windows Server 2016. IPAM is a way that you can centrally monitor and manage some of the common infrastructure roles spread out around your network. Specifically for this recipe, we will be taking a look at IP addressing by using IPAM. Particularly in environments where there may be many different DHCP servers hosting different scopes spread out around your network, IPAM can be extremely useful for pulling all of that information into one management interface. This saves a lot of time and effort as opposed to launching the DHCP Manager console on each of your DHCP environments separately and trying to monitor them individually.

Getting ready

We have a domain network running that consists of all Server 2016 servers. Included in our network is a domain controller that is also serving as a DHCP server. We are adding a new server to this mix called IPAM1. This new server will be our IPAM management server, as the IPAM feature should not co-exist with either the AD DS Role or with the DHCP Role.

How to do it...

Let's take a look at our IP address utilization with the IPAM feature:

1. While logged in to the new server that you intend to use for IPAM, click the **Add roles and features** link from inside Server Manager.

2. Walk through this wizard, choosing the option to add the feature called **IP Address Management (IPAM) Server**.

3. Once the feature has been installed, you should see a new listing for IPAM in the left window pane of Server Manager. Go ahead and click there.

4. You will see that step 1 is already accomplished; the IPAM console is successfully connected to the local server. Go ahead and click on step 2 in order to provision the IPAM server.

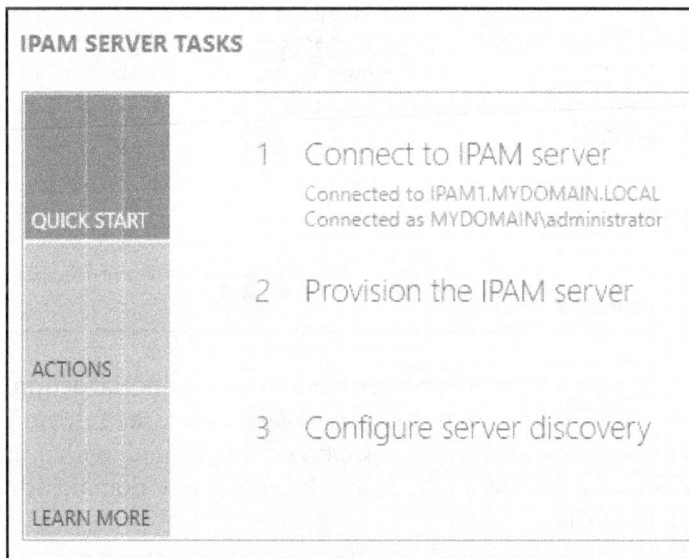

5. Click **Next**, after reading the information listed on that screen. As you can see, the best way to set up the interaction between the IPAM server and the infrastructure servers is to utilize Group Policy. We will define the settings for that on an upcoming screen in this wizard.

6. You should now be on the **Configure database** screen and we will leave the default option selected to utilize **Windows Internal Database (WID)**.

7. Now we get to select our provisioning method, which is where we are going to tell IPAM to use Group Policy in order to distribute the settings that it needs in order to manage and grab data from our infrastructure servers. Define a GPO prefix that is specific to this IPAM server.

Select a provisioning method for managed servers:

○ Manual

The manual provisioning method requires that you configure the required network shares, security groups, and firewall rules manually on each managed server.

◉ Group Policy Based

The Group Policy based provisioning method requires Group Policy Objects (GPO) to be created in each domain that you manage with this IPAM server. IPAM will automatically configure settings on managed servers by adding the server to appropriate GPO. This can be especially useful in a large network with many managed servers. GPOs that you create must follow naming conventions used by IPAM, however you can customize the GPO name with a prefix of your choice. The GPO name prefix you specify should be unique for each IPAM server in the Active Directory forest.

˅ GPO name prefix: IPAM1

🛈 You can create GPOs in each IPAM managed domain using the Invoke-IpamGpoProvisiong IPAM Windows PowerShell cmdlet.

---

8. Before we complete this wizard, we need to take a special action in order to provision these GPOs so that the wizard can make use of them. To do this, we are going to use a PowerShell cmdlet. Open up PowerShell with administrative rights. Make sure you are logged into the server as a domain admin before running this cmdlet.

9. Type the following command into PowerShell: `Invoke-IpamGpoProvisioning`.

10. It will ask you to key in the name of your domain, as well as the GpoPrefixName. This is the same prefix that you just typed into the IPAM Wizard, so make sure you enter it exactly the same.

```
Administrator: Windows PowerShell                           —    □    ×
PS C:\> Invoke-IpamGpoProvisioning

cmdlet Invoke-IpamGpoProvisioning at command pipeline position 1
Supply values for the following parameters:
Domain: MYDOMAIN.LOCAL
GpoPrefixName: IPAM1

Confirm
The Invoke-IpamGpoProvisioning cmdlet creates and links three Group
Policy Objects in the domain indicated by Domain parameter, for
provisioning IPAM access settings on the servers that are managed by
IPAM. The cmdlet also modifies the domain wide DNS ACL to enable read
access for IPAM. The value of GpoPrefixName must be the same as the one
provided in the IPAM provisioning wizard when selecting the option of
Group Policy Based provisioning.

You have not specified the optional parameters DelegatedGpoUser or
DelegatedGpoGroup. The delegation parameters can be used to enable IPAM
GPO edit privileges for users or groups who do not have domain or
enterprise administrator privileges, but need to mark servers as managed
or unmanaged in IPAM. Do you want to perform this action?
[Y] Yes  [N] No  [S] Suspend  [?] Help (default is "Y"): y
PS C:\>
```

11. Now that our GPOs have been created, head back over to the IPAM Wizard and click the **Apply** button to finish it.
12. Now back at the IPAM section of Server Manager, click on step 3-**Configure server discovery**.

13. Use the **Add** button in order to query your domain for infrastructure services that can be monitored by IPAM. Select the roles you would like to pull data from (I am going to leave all three checked) and click the **OK** button.

Select the forest:

MYDOMAIN.LOCAL	✓	Get forests

Select domains to discover:

	✓	Add

Select the server roles to discover:

Domain	Domain controller	DHCP server	DNS server
(root domain) mydomain.local	✓	✓	✓

14. Click on step 4-**Start server discovery**. Wait for discovery to complete.
15. Click on step 5-**Select or add servers to manage and verify IPAM access**.

16. Right-click on the server that you want to collect data from and choose **Edit Server...**.

Recommended Action	Manageability Status	IPAM Access Status	Server Name	DNS Suffix	Domain Name	Forest Na
⚠ Set Manageability Status	Unspecified	Blocked	DC1	MYDOMAIN.LOCAL	mydomain.local	MYDOMA

Edit Server...

Retrieve All Server Data

Refresh Server Access Status

Delete

17. Change the server's **Manageability status** field to **Managed**.
18. Now head back to the main IPAM window in Server Manager and click on step 6-**Retrieve data from managed servers**.

You may have to wait for a little while to allow Group Policy to do its job in rolling out the settings.

19. Once data collection completes, you now have the ability to browse around inside the IPAM management console and view data about your DNS and DHCP infrastructure. For example, click on **IP Address Range Groups** to see a list of the DHCP scopes that are present on the DHCP servers that you are currently managing.

How it works...

The **IP Address Management (IPAM)** tool takes a little bit of work to configure initially but can be very beneficial later. Once configured to pull in data from your Domain Controllers, DNS servers, and DHCP servers, IPAM can be your one-stop-shop for monitoring and managing data related to these infrastructure roles. This is particularly helpful where you have many servers providing these roles, such as the case of multiple DHCP servers that each contain different scope definitions. In the past, you would have had to log in to each DHCP server or at least do remote management of them via Server Manager or some other tool, but ultimately you would still be viewing and managing the DHCP scopes individually. With IPAM, it brings all of this information into one place so that you can make decisions and configuration changes within your network while looking at the overall bigger picture.

Checking for viruses in Windows Server 2016

Monitoring and scanning for viruses on a Windows Server historically isn't a task that would have shown up in a book about the operating system, because in the past this functionality was always provided by third-party software. Starting with Windows 8, we got something called Windows Defender built into the operating system; this provided some semblance of free, built-in antivirus protection. Well, I'm excited to say that Windows Defender has continually improved over the past few years, and starting with Windows Server 2016, we finally have it available to us inside a Microsoft Server operating system! Installing third-party antivirus programs on servers has always been dangerous territory because they love to consume memory and cause random reboots. I've dealt with many different kinds of issues with antivirus programs on Windows Servers. Thankfully, Defender is baked right into the operating system, so we should never have to worry about those kinds of problems. Let's take a look at Windows Defender, which now comes standard as part of the Windows Server 2016 operating system.

Getting ready

Any Windows Server 2016 will do for this task, as Windows Defender exists on them by default. Today I happen to be using my WEB1 web server, and I want to make sure that Defender is turned on and protecting this system.

How to do it...

Follow these steps to look into the Windows Defender settings on your server:

1. From the **Start** menu, navigate to **Windows System** | **Windows Defender**.

2. Nice, this looks just like the Windows Defender that is provided inside my Windows 10 laptop, so it's familiar territory. From the Defender application you can see that I can update definition files, and run antivirus scans. You can also see that my definitions are currently out of date, oops! That is because my WEB1 server is inside an isolated test lab, and does not have access to the Internet.

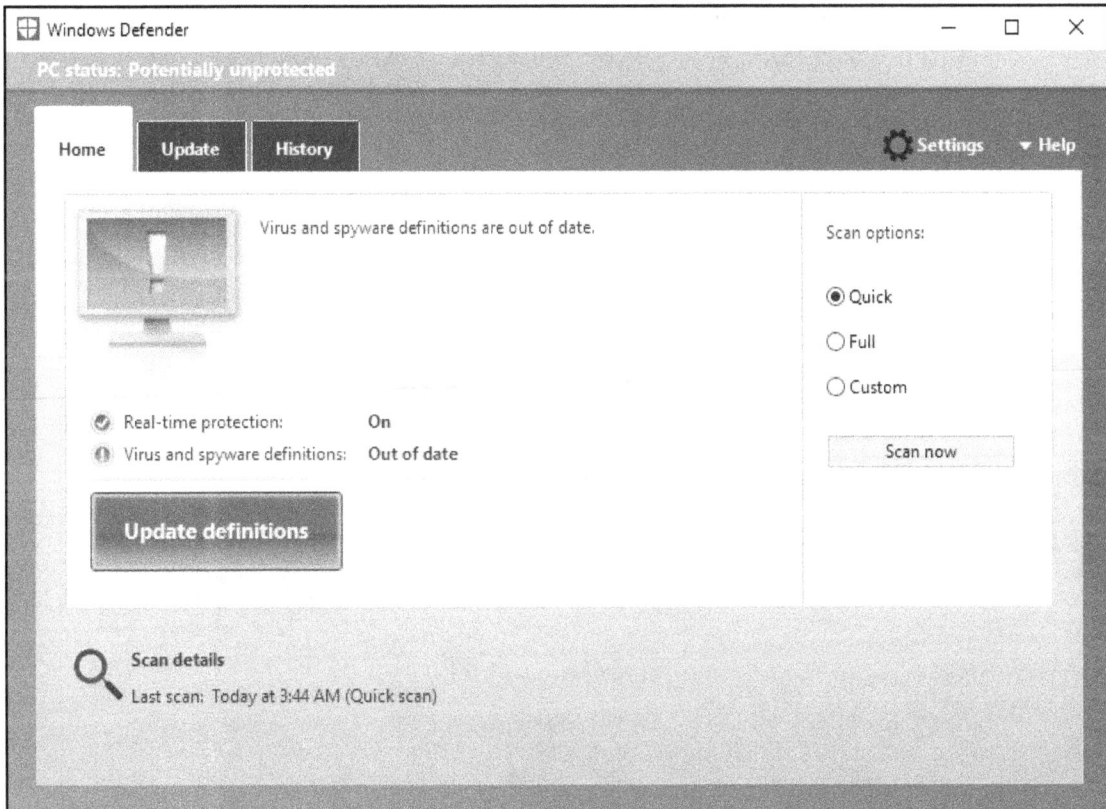

3. If you are paying attention, you will notice that there really aren't any settings in here about how Defender interacts with the operating system. In fact, there's not even a way to turn it off. To get into those settings, you need to open the Windows Defender section, available inside the Windows **Settings** menu itself. To get there, you can either click on **Settings** near the top-right corner of Windows Defender, or you can launch **Settings** from the Start menu. Let's take the Start menu approach.

4. Open the Start Menu and click on **Settings**.

5. Once inside **Settings**, click on **Update & security**.

6. Now choose **Windows Defender**.

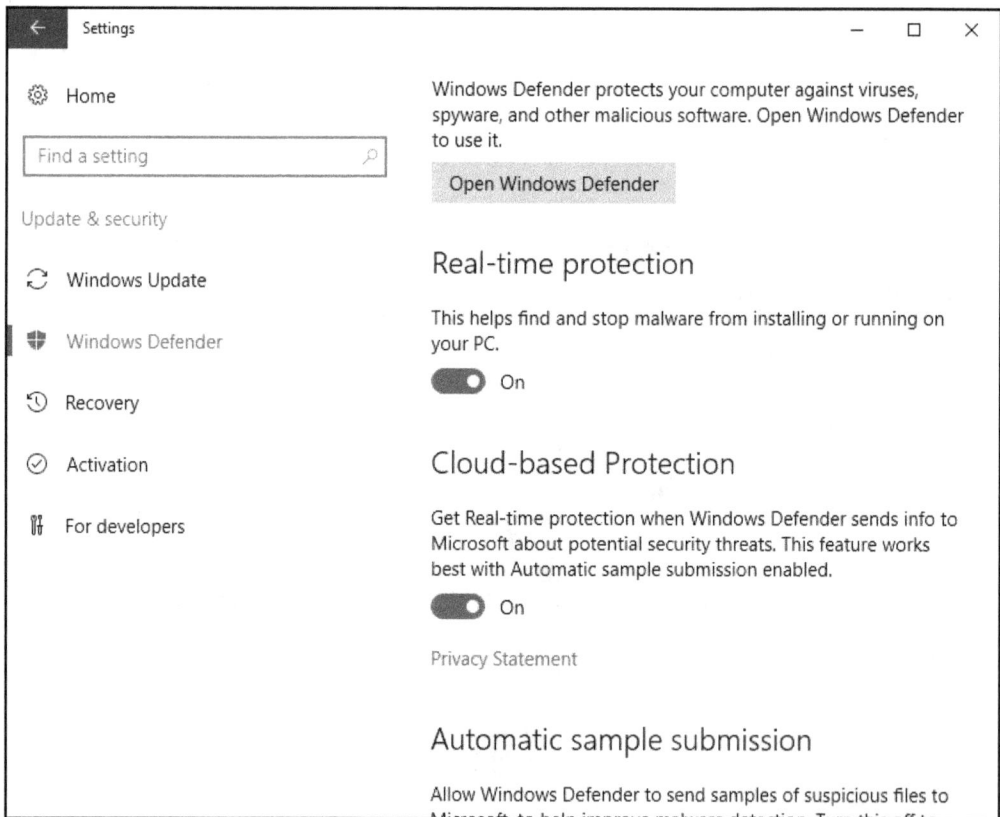

How it works...

I believe that having Windows Defender built into the Windows Server 2016 operating system is going to be a game-changer. The process of installing third-party antivirus software onto your servers is one of those things that always make admins cringe. You never really know whether or not it's going to play well with the server you have built. Now, I'm sure that many of you are not going to automatically trust Defender as an enterprise-ready and capable antivirus solution, but I believe that too will change over time. If it wasn't doing a good job, wouldn't Microsoft have thrown it away at this point, rather than continue to improve it and now trust it enough to exist inside a server operating system?

As you can see in the last screenshot, it is easy to disable Windows Defender if you want to continue using an antivirus that you have to pay extra money for. Fine, that is your prerogative. However, I think that, particularly in the small and medium businesses, this new inclusion is going to be incredibly useful from a safety and security standpoint.

9
Group Policy

In this book, we have already discussed a few recipes that call for the modification of **Group Policy Objects** (**GPOs**), but we have not taken the time to discuss why Group Policy is important in the first place. To those who have worked within Active Directory for a while, Group Policy may be familiar territory. I still find, though, that many IT folks working in the Server Administrator role are not overly familiar with Group Policy and how it can benefit them. Particularly in smaller companies, this incredibly powerful feature of Windows tends to be overlooked. It is easy to think of Active Directory as the storage container for your user and computer accounts, because those are the core necessary tasks that it accomplishes. But as soon as you install the Domain Services role to configure your first Domain Controller, you have automatically included Group Policy capabilities into that domain.

Let's walk through some recipes together to make sure you are able to interact with Group Policy comfortably and begin to explore its underlying capabilities:

- Creating and assigning a new Group Policy Object
- Mapping network drives with Group Policy
- Redirecting the My Documents folder to a network share
- Creating a VPN connection with Group Policy
- Creating a printer connection with Group Policy
- Using Group Policy to enforce an Internet proxy server
- Viewing the settings currently enabled inside a GPO
- Viewing the GPOs currently assigned to a computer
- Backing up and restoring GPOs
- Plugging in ADMX and ADML templates

Introduction

Group Policy is a centralized administration tool for your domain joined systems. To summarize its capabilities, you can create policies in Active Directory, assign those policies to particular users or computers, and within those policies change any number of settings or configurations that are within the Windows operating system. The item inside Active Directory that contains these settings is called a **Group Policy Object** (**GPO**), so we will be focusing on the creation and manipulation of these in order to make some centralized management decisions that will affect large numbers of computers in our environment. GPOs can be utilized for user accounts, client computer settings, or for putting configurations onto your servers. Any domain joined system can be manipulated by a GPO, and typically settings put into place by GPOs cannot be overridden by users, making them a very integral part of security for companies familiar with making use of Group Policy regularly.

We will place a number of different configuration settings inside the GPOs that we create throughout this chapter, but we will not come close to covering even a fraction of the available settings that could be manipulated. For full coverage Group Policy settings that are available, please check out the following link:

`http://www.microsoft.com/en-us/download/details.aspx?id=25250`.

Creating and assigning a new Group Policy Object

In order to start using Group Policy, we first need to create a Group Policy Object. Most commonly referred to as a GPO, this object contains the settings that we want to deploy. It also contains the information necessary for domain joined systems to know which machines and users get these settings and which ones do not. It is critical that you plan GPO assignment carefully. It is easy to create a policy that applies to every domain-joined system in your entire network but, depending on what settings you configure in that policy, this can be detrimental to some of your servers. Often I find that admins who are only somewhat familiar with Group Policy are making use of a built-in GPO called Default Domain Policy. This, by default, applies to everything in your network. Sometimes this is actually what you want to accomplish. Most of the time, it is not!

We are going to use this section to detail the process of creating a new GPO, and use some assignment sections called **Links** and **Security Filters**, which will give us complete control over which systems receive these systems, and more importantly, which do not.

Getting ready

Our work today will be accomplished from a Server 2016 domain controller server. If you are running the Domain Services role, you already have the items installed that are necessary to manage Group Policy.

How to do it...

Follow these steps to create and assign a new GPO:

1. Open **Server Manager**, click on the **Tools** menu, and choose to open the **Group Policy Management** Console.
2. Expand your domain name and click on the folder called **Group Policy Objects**. This shows you a list of your current GPOs.
3. Right-click on the **Group Policy Objects** folder and click on **New**.
4. Insert a name for your new GPO. I am going to call mine `Map Network Drives`. We will end up using this GPO in a later recipe.

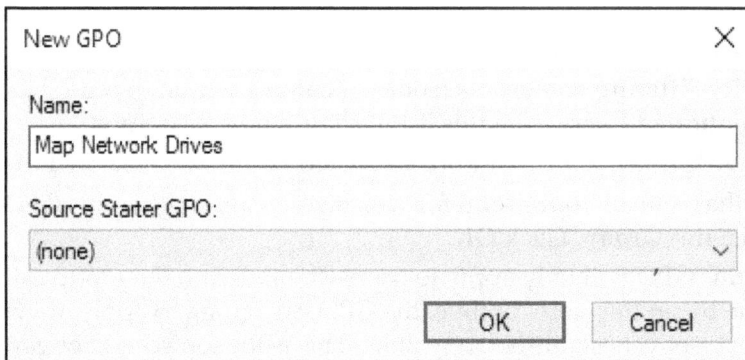

5. Click **OK**, and then expand your **Group Policy Objects** folder if it isn't already. You should see the new GPO in this list. Go ahead and click on the new GPO in order to see its settings.

6. We want this new GPO to apply only to a specific group of users that we have established. This assignment of the GPO is handled at the lowest level by the **Security Filtering** section, which you see on the following screen. You can see that, by default, **Authenticated Users** is in the list. This means that, if we created a link between this GPO and an **Organizational Unit** (**OU**) in the domain, the policy settings would immediately start applying to any user account.

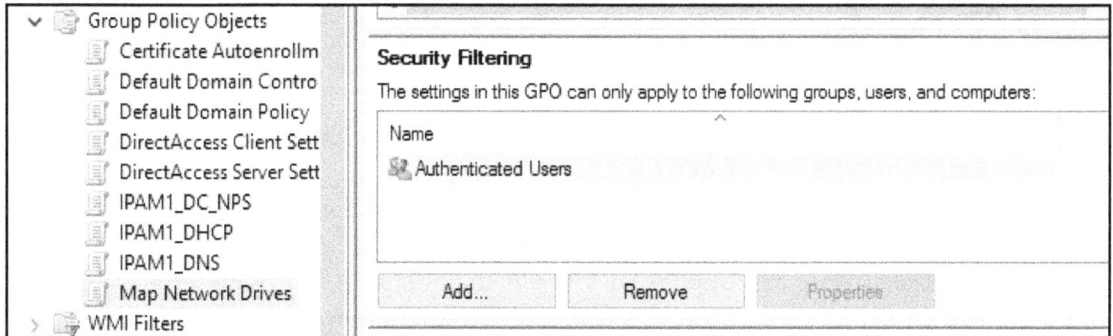

7. Since we want to make absolutely sure that only specific user accounts get these drive mappings, we are going to modify the **Security Filtering** section and list only the user group that we have created to house these user accounts. Under the **Security Filtering** section, click on the **Remove** button in order to remove **Authenticated Users** from this list. It should now be empty.
8. Now click on the **Add...** button, also listed under the **Security Filtering** section.
9. Type the name of your group for which you want to filter this GPO. My group is called **Sales Group**. Click **OK**.
10. Now this GPO will only apply to users we place into the group called **Sales Group**, but at this point in time, the GPO isn't going to apply anywhere because we have not yet established any links. This is the top section of your **Scope** tab, which is currently blank.

Map Network Drives

Scope Details Settings Delegation Status

Links

Display links in this location: MYDOMAIN.LOCAL

The following sites, domains, and OUs are linked to this GPO:

Location	Enforced	Link Enabled	Path

Security Filtering

The settings in this GPO can only apply to the following groups, users, and computers:

Name
Sales Group (MYDOMAIN\Sales Group)

Add...	Remove	Properties

11. We need to link this GPO to some place in our domain structure. This is essentially telling it, *apply this policy from here down* in our OU structure. By creating a link with no security filtering, the GPO will apply to everything under that link. However, since we do have security filtering enabled and specified down to a particular group, the security filtering will be the final authority in saying that these GPO settings will only apply to members of our Sales group. For this Map Network Drives policy, we want it to apply to the OU called **US Laptops**.

12. Right-click on the OU called **US Laptops** and then click on the option for **Link an Existing GPO…**.

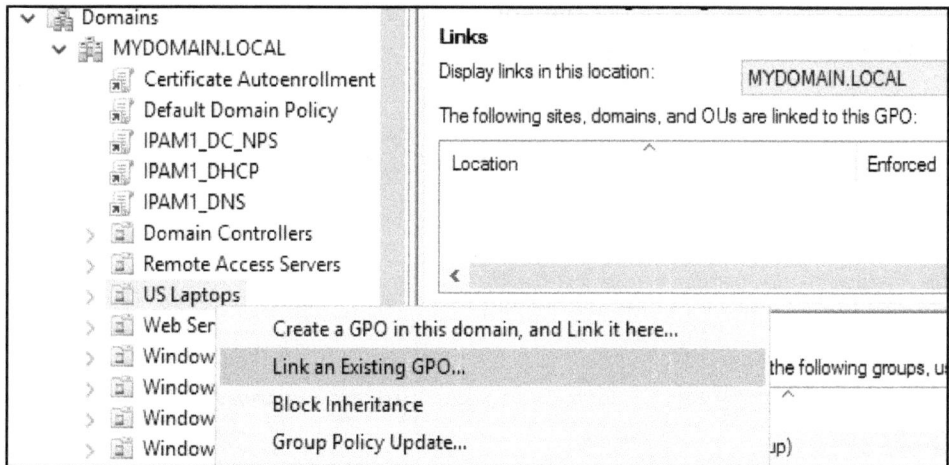

```
∨ 📇 Domains                                    Links
  ∨ 📇 MYDOMAIN.LOCAL                           Display links in this location:        MYDOMAIN.LOCAL
      📑 Certificate Autoenrollment           The following sites, domains, and OUs are linked to this GPO:
      📑 Default Domain Policy
      📑 IPAM1_DC_NPS                          Location                                        Enforced
      📑 IPAM1_DHCP
      📑 IPAM1_DNS
    > 📑 Domain Controllers
    > 📑 Remote Access Servers                 ‹
    > 📑 US Laptops
    > 📑 Web Ser    Create a GPO in this domain, and Link it here...
    > 📑 Window     Link an Existing GPO...                           the following groups, u
    > 📑 Window
    > 📑 Window     Block Inheritance
    > 📑 Window     Group Policy Update...                            ip)
```

13. Choose the name of our new GPO, **Map Network Drives**, and click **OK**.

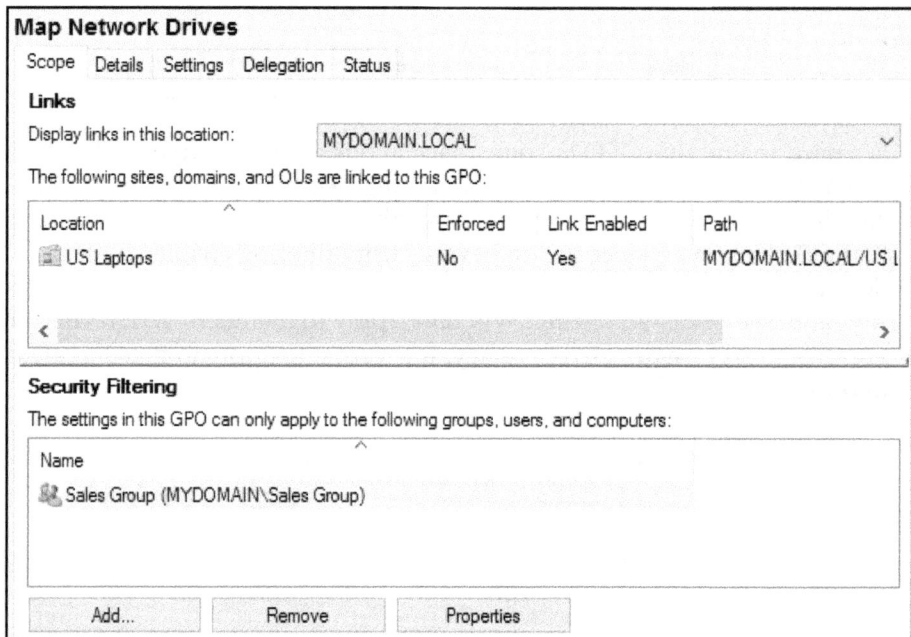

Map Network Drives

Scope Details Settings Delegation Status

Links

Display links in this location: MYDOMAIN.LOCAL   ∨

The following sites, domains, and OUs are linked to this GPO:

Location	Enforced	Link Enabled	Path
📑 US Laptops	No	Yes	MYDOMAIN.LOCAL/US L

Security Filtering

The settings in this GPO can only apply to the following groups, users, and computers:

Name
🧑 Sales Group (MYDOMAIN\Sales Group)

| Add... | Remove | Properties |

Our new GPO is now linked to the **US Laptops** OU, so at this level, any system placed inside that OU would get the settings if we hadn't paired it down a step further with the Security Filtering section. Since we populated this with only the name of our specific **Sales Group**, this means that this new drive mapping policy will only apply to those users added into this group.

How it works...

In our example recipe, we created a new Group Policy Object and took the necessary steps in order to restrict this GPO to the computers and users that we deemed necessary inside our domain. Each network is different, and you may find yourself relying only on the Links to keep GPOs sorted according to your needs, or you may need to enforce some combination of both Links and Security Filtering. In any case, whichever works best for you, make sure that you are confident in the configuration of these fields so that you can know beyond a shadow of a doubt where your GPO is being applied. You may have noticed that, in our recipe here, we didn't actually configure any settings inside the GPO, so at this point it still isn't doing anything to those in the Sales Group. Continue reading to navigate the actual settings portion of Group Policy.

Mapping network drives with Group Policy

Almost everyone uses mapped drives of some flavor in their environments. Creating drive mappings manually as part of a new user start-up process is cumbersome and unnecessary. It is also work that will probably need to be duplicated as users move from one computer to another in the future. If we utilize Group Policy to centralize the creation of these drive mappings, we can ensure that the same users get the same drive mappings wherever they log into the network. Planned correctly, you can enable these mappings to appear on any domain-joined system across the network by the user simply logging in to the computer like they always do. This is a good, simple first task to accomplish within Group Policy to get our feet wet and to learn something that could turn out to be useful in your organization.

Getting ready

We are using a Server 2016 domain controller in our environment in order to create and configure this Group Policy Object. We will assume that you have already created a new GPO for this task that has been configured for Links and Security Filtering.

How to do it...

To create a drive mapping in Group Policy:

1. Open the **Group Policy Management** Console from the **Tools** menu of Server Manager.
2. Expand the name of your domain and then expand the **Group Policy Objects** folder. There we see our new GPO called **Map Network Drives**.
3. Right-click on the **Map Network Drives** GPO and click on **Edit...**.

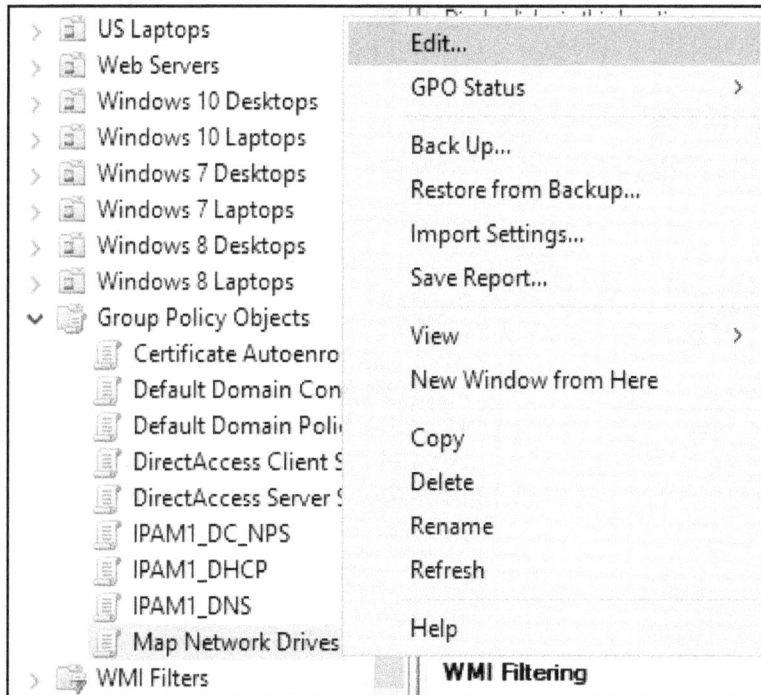

4. Navigate to **User Configuration** | **Preferences** | **Windows Settings** | **Drive Maps**.

5. Right-click on **Drive Maps** and choose **New | Mapped Drive**.

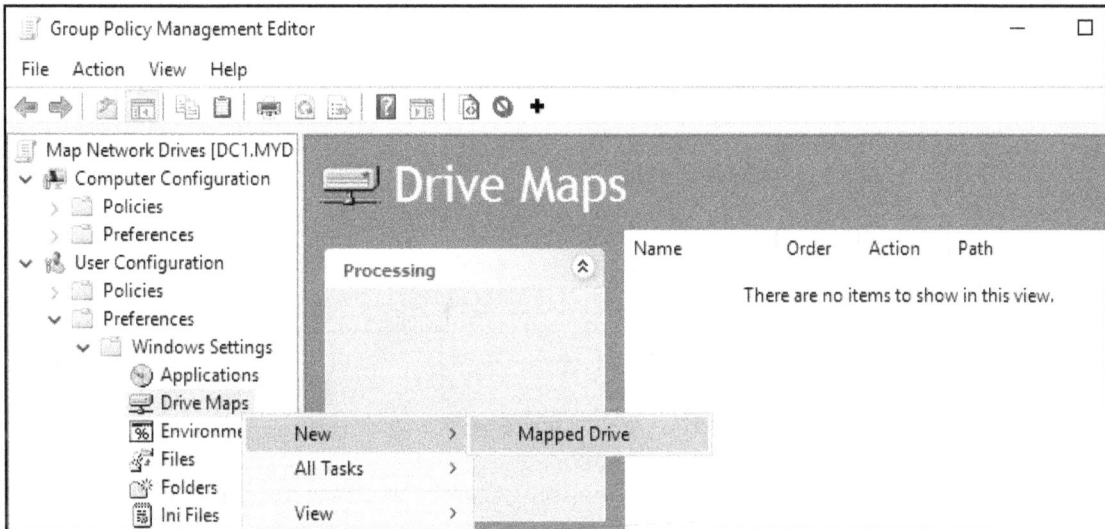

6. Set **Location** as the destination URL of the drive mapping, and use the **Label as** field if you want a more descriptive name to be visible to users.

7. Choose a **Drive Letter** to be used for this new mapping from the drop-down menu listed on this screen.

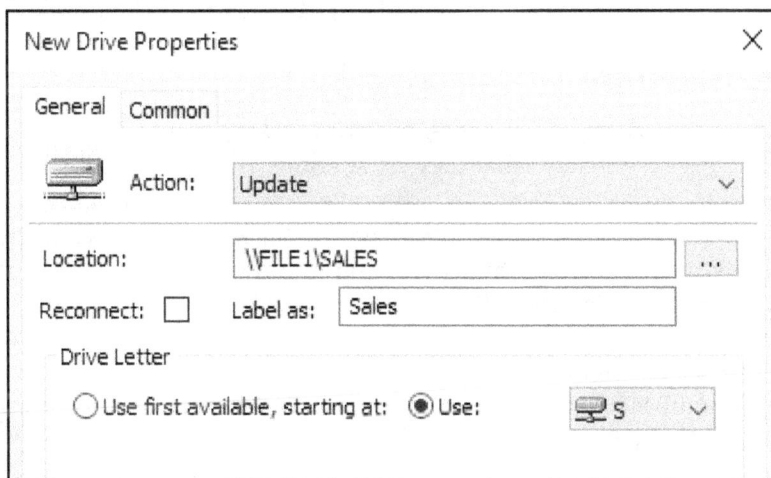

8. Click **OK**.

9. We are assuming you have already created the Links and Security Filtering appropriate to where you want this GPO to apply. If so, you may now log in to a computer on your domain as a user account to which this policy will apply. Once logged into the computer, open up File Explorer and you should see the new network drive mapped automatically during the login process.

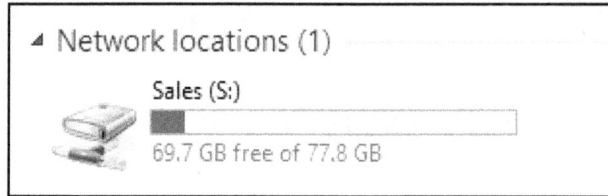

How it works...

There are a few different ways that drive mappings can be automated within a Windows environment, and our recipe today outlines one of the quickest ways to accomplish this task. By using Group Policy to automate the creation of our network drive mappings, we can centralize the administration of this task and remove the drive mapping creation load from our helpdesk processes.

Redirecting the My Documents folder to a network share

Users are accustomed to saving documents, pictures, and more into their Documents or My Documents folder, because that is what they do at home. When working on an office computer at their job, the natural tendency is to save right into the local Documents folder as well. This is generally not desired behavior because backing up everyone's documents folders individually would be an administrative nightmare. So the common resolution to this problem is to provide everyone with mapped network drives and train users to save documents into these mapped drives. This is good in theory, but difficult to execute in practice. As long as users still have the capability to save documents into their local My Documents folder, there is a good chance that they will save at least some things in there, probably without realizing it.

This recipe is a quick Group Policy change that can be made so that the My Documents folders on your domain joined computers get redirected onto a network share. This way, if users do save a document into My Documents, that document gets written over to the file server where you have directed them.

Getting ready

We will set up our new GPO on a Server 2016 domain controller.

How to do it...

To redirect the My Documents folders via Group Policy, follow these steps:

1. Launch the **Group Policy Management** Console from the **Tools** menu of Server Manager.
2. Right-click on the name of your domain and choose **Create a GPO in this domain, and Link it here....**

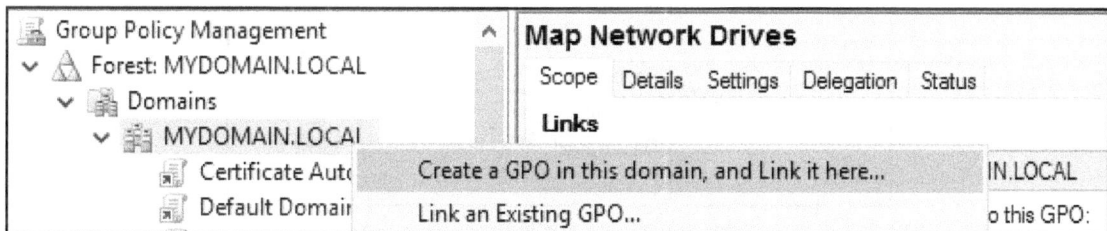

3. Input something in the **Name** field for your new GPO. I am going to call mine **Redirect My Documents**. Then click **OK**.
4. Browse to the **Group Policy Objects** folder that is listed under your domain name.
5. Right-click on the name of our new redirection GPO and click **Edit....**
6. Navigate to **User Configuration** | **Policies** | **Windows Settings** | **Folder Redirection** | **Documents**.

7. Right-click on **Documents** and go into **Properties**.

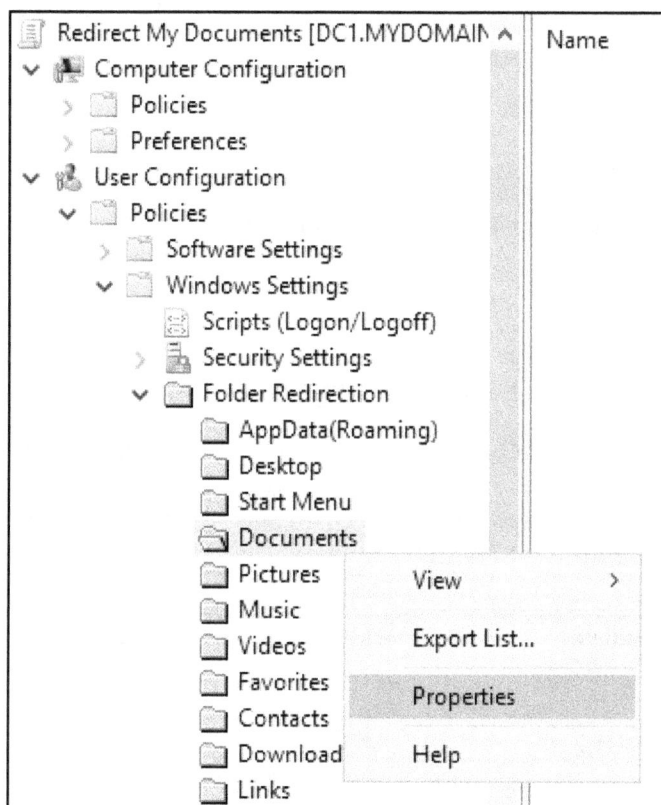

8. Drop down the **Setting** menu and choose **Basic – Redirect everyone's folder to the same location**.
9. Type in the **Root Path** field where you want everyone's Documents folder to be directed to. I am going to use a share that I have created on our file server. Mine will look like this: \\file1\users\.

Documents Properties   ?   X

Target   Settings

You can specify the location of the Documents folder.

Setting: | Basic - Redirect everyone's folder to the same location   ▼ |

This folder will be redirected to the specified location.

Target folder location

| Create a folder for each user under the root path   ▼ |

Root Path:

| \\file1\users |

          Browse...

For user Clair, this folder will be redirected to:

\\file1\users\Clair\Documents

OK   Cancel   Apply

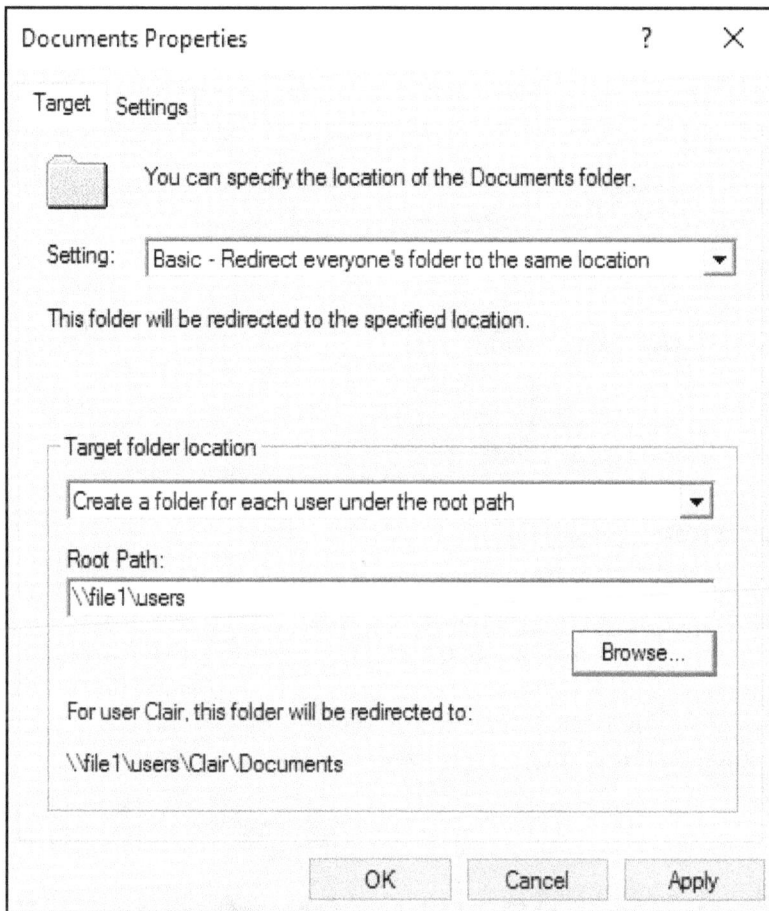

10. Click **OK**.
11. Your setting should be put immediately into place within the GPO. Now go ahead and log in to a test client machine and open up the Documents folder.
12. Create a new text document inside the local Documents folder. We are just creating something here in local Documents so that we can see where it is actually being stored.

13. Now log in to your file server and check inside the `Users` directory that we specified. We now have a folder in there with my username, and inside that folder is a `Documents` folder that contains the new text document that I just created and stored inside the local `My Documents` on my client computer!

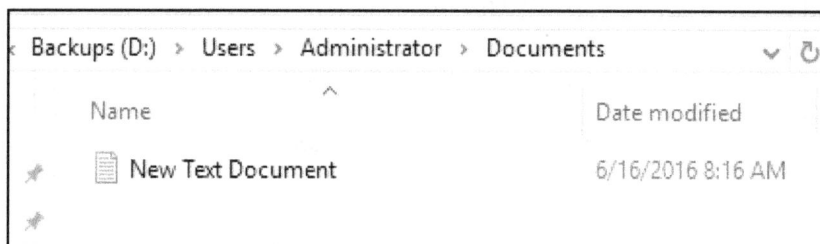

‹ Backups (D:) › Users › Administrator › Documents		⌄ ↻
Name		Date modified
📄 New Text Document		6/16/2016 8:16 AM

How it works...

Redirecting everyone's `My Documents` to be automatically stored on a centralized file server is an easy change with Group Policy. You could even combine this configuration with another that maps a network drive, then simply specify the drive letter in under your Document Redirection setting rather than typing out a UNC that could potentially change in the future. However you decide to configure it in your environment, I guarantee that using this setting will result in more centralized administration of your data and fewer lost files for your users.

Creating a VPN connection with Group Policy

If you have administered or helped support a VPN connectivity solution in the past, you are probably more than familiar with setting up VPN connection profiles on client computers. In an environment where VPN is utilized as the remote access solution, what I commonly observe is that the VPN profile creation process is usually a manual step that needs to be taken by human hands, following the user's first login to the computer. This is inefficient and easily forgotten. With tools existing in your Windows Server 2016, you can automate the creation of these VPN connections on the client computers. Let's use Group Policy to create these profiles for us during user login.

Getting ready

We will use a Server 2016 domain controller in order to configure our new Group Policy Object. Once finished, we will also use a Windows 10 client computer to log in and make sure that our VPN profile was successfully created. For this recipe, we are going to assume that you created the GPO and setup links, and filtered them according to your needs before getting started with the actual configuration of this GPO.

How to do it...

Follow these steps to configure a GPO that will automatically create a VPN connection profile on your remote client computers:

1. Inside the **Group Policy Management** Console, right-click on your new GPO that will be used for this task and click on **Edit...**.
2. Navigate to **User Configuration** | **Preferences** | **Control Panel Settings**.
3. Right-click on **Network Options** and choose **New** | **VPN Connection**.

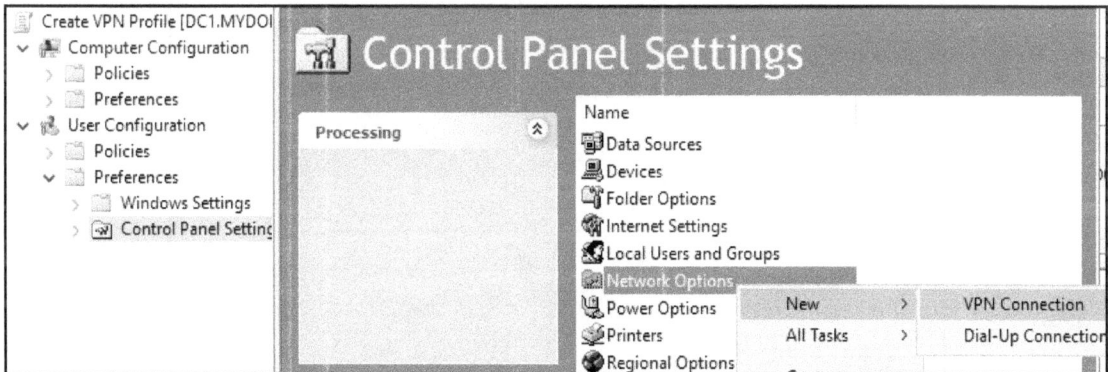

4. Input something in the **Connection name** field for this new VPN connection; this name will be displayed on client computers and the public **IP address** field that client computers will need to connect to while working remotely. Depending on the needs for your particular VPN connection, you may also have to visit the additional tabs available on this screen to finish your specific configurations. Then click **OK**.

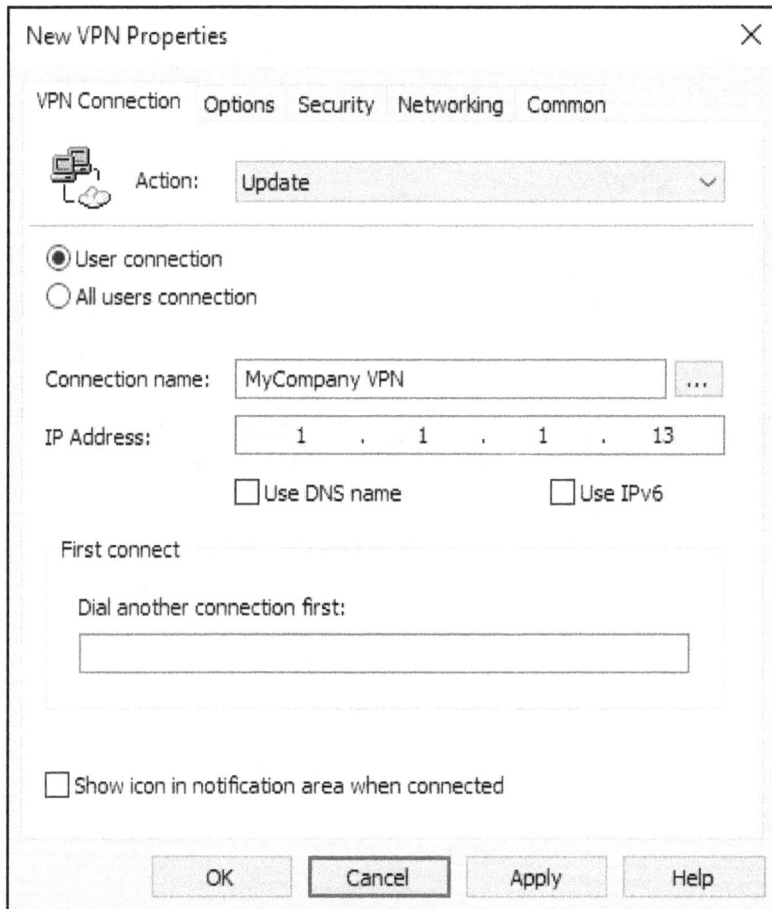

New VPN Properties   ✕

| VPN Connection | Options | Security | Networking | Common |

Action: Update   ⌄

◉ User connection
◯ All users connection

Connection name: MyCompany VPN   ...

IP Address: 1 . 1 . 1 . 13

☐ Use DNS name   ☐ Use IPv6

First connect

Dial another connection first:

☐ Show icon in notification area when connected

| OK | Cancel | Apply | Help |

5. Now log in to your client computer and click on the Network icon in the systray, the same place where you would click in order to connect to a wireless network. You can see that, during our login to this computer, a new VPN connection called **MyCompany VPN** has been added and is now available to click on.

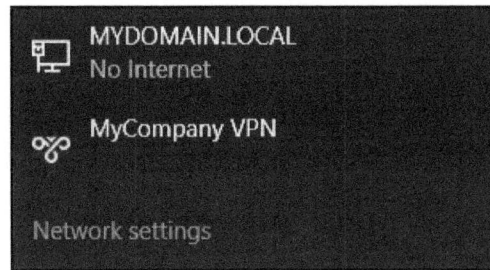

MYDOMAIN.LOCAL
No Internet

MyCompany VPN

Network settings

How it works...

In this recipe, we used Group Policy to automate the creation of a new VPN connection for our remote laptops. Using a GPO for something like this saves time and effort, since you are no longer setting up these connections by hand during a new PC build. You can also use this function to update settings on an existing VPN connection in the future, if you need to change IP addresses or something like that. As you are starting to see throughout these recipes, there are all kinds of different things that Group Policy can be used to accomplish.

Creating a printer connection with Group Policy

Let's say you just installed a new network printer in the office. You have installed it on a few computers to make sure it works properly, but now you are staring down the rows and rows of computers that would like to print to this printer occasionally. The prospect of logging in to every computer in order to launch and walk through the printer creation wizard isn't sounding like the way you would like to spend your Friday night. Let's see if we can once again make use of Group Policy to save the day. We will utilize a new GPO that will be configured to automatically install this new printer on the client desktops.

Getting ready

We are assuming you have already created the new GPO and have linked it accordingly so that only computers that need this new printer are going to receive these GPO settings. Now we are going to use Group Policy Management Console on our primary domain controller, which is running Windows Server 2016.

How to do it…

To configure your new GPO for a new printer creation, follow these steps:

1. Open **Group Policy Management** Console from the **Tools** menu of Server Manager.
2. Right-click on the new GPO that is going to be used for printer creation and click **Edit…**.
3. Navigate to **User Configuration** | **Preferences** | **Control Panel Settings**.
4. Right-click on **Printers** and choose **New** | **TCP/IP Printer**.

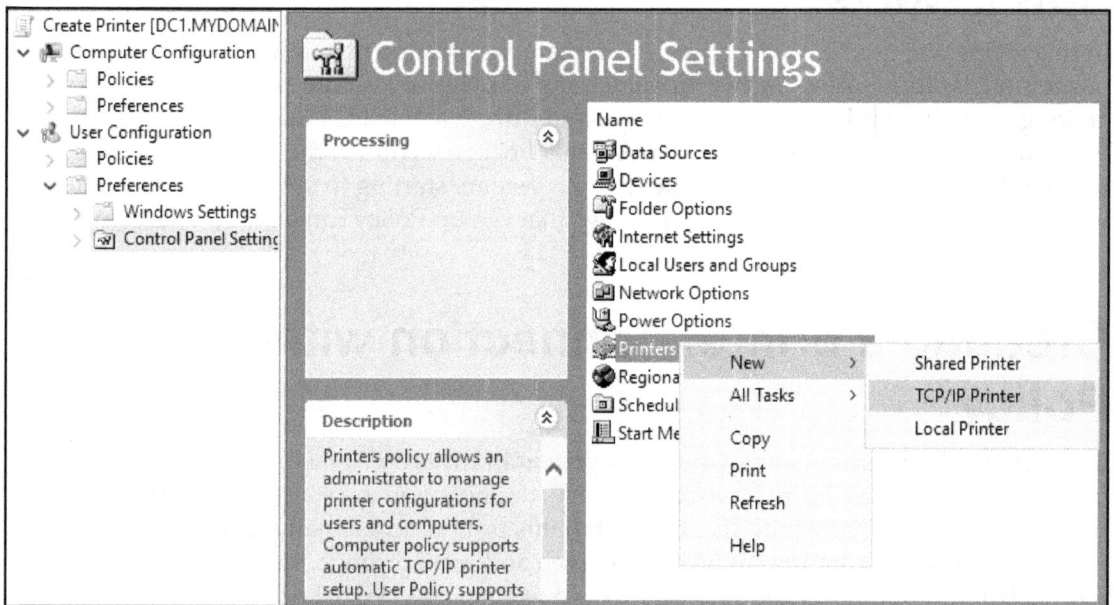

5. Input the information that is necessary for the printer connection. Since we chose to set up a new TCP/IP Printer, we need to input something in the **IP Address** and **Local Name** fields for users to be able to see this new printer in their list. I am also going to choose **Set this printer as the default printer…only if a local printer is not present**.

New TCP/IP Printer Properties   ✕

General   Port Settings   Common

Action: | Update   ⌄ |

☐ Delete all IP printer connections

IP Address: | 10 . 0 . 0 . 200 |
                  ☐ Use DNS name   ☐ Use an IPv6 addres

Local Name: | Sales Group Network Printer |

Printer path: | | [...]

☑ Set this printer as the default printer...
   ☑ ...only if a local printer is not present

Location: | |

Comment: | |

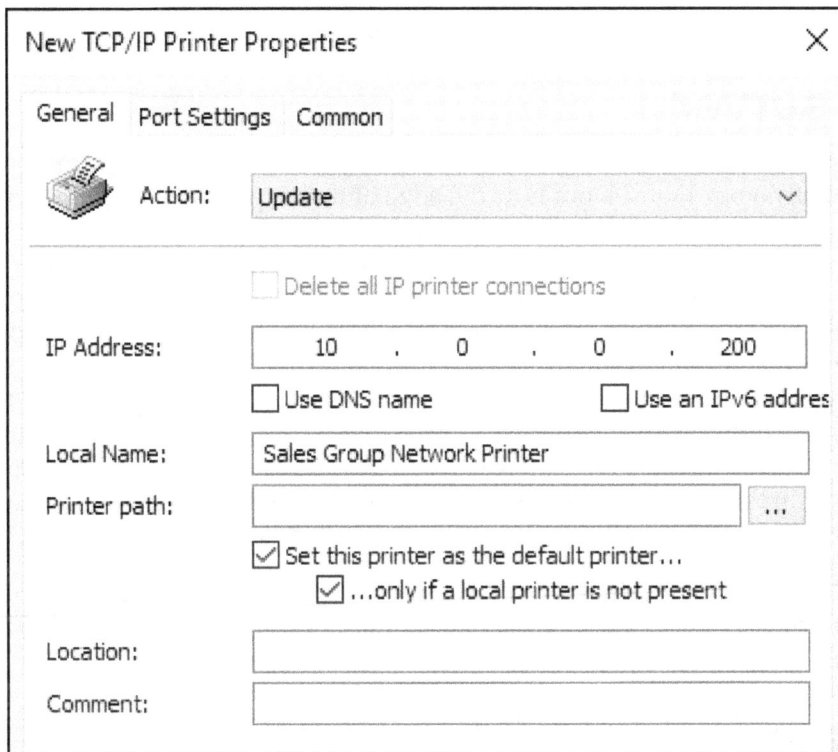

6. Click **OK**, and this printer will be distributed to those users you filtered the GPO to.

How it works...

Using Group Policy to automate regular IT tasks makes a lot of sense for all kinds of technologies. In this recipe, we built a simple printer connection so that we didn't have to do it by hand on our dozens of computers that needed the ability to be able to print here.

Using Group Policy to enforce an Internet proxy server

Most networks of significant size use a forward proxy server to filter their Internet traffic. This is essentially a box that sits out near the edge of the corporate network; whenever client computers in the network try to access the Internet, their requests are sent out through this server. Doing this enables companies to monitor Internet use, restrict browsing permissions, and keep many forms of malware at bay. When implementing a proxy server, one of the big questions is always "How do we enforce the use of this proxy?". Some solutions do a default route through the proxy server so that all traffic flows outbound that way at a network level. More often, though, it is desirable for the proxy server settings to be configured at the browser level because it is probably unnecessary for all traffic to flow through this proxy; only the browser's web traffic should do so. In these cases, you could certainly open up the Internet Explorer options on everyone's computers and enter the proxy server information, but that is a huge task to undertake, and it gives users the ability to remove those settings if they choose to.

By using Group Policy to set the Internet Explorer proxy configuration, this task will be automated and hands-off. This also ensures that users are not able to manipulate these fields in the future, and you can be assured that your web traffic is flowing through the proxy server as you have defined it.

Getting ready

Our GPO has already been created; now we are using the Group Policy Management Console on our Server 2016 domain controller to configure settings within the GPO. A Windows 10 client computer is also sitting waiting for use as we will want to test this GPO after we finish the configuration.

How to do it...

Follow these steps to set everyone's Internet proxy settings via Group Policy:

1. Open the **Group Policy Management** Console from the **Tools** menu of Server Manager.
2. Find the new GPO that you have created for this task, right-click on it, and choose **Edit...**.

3. Navigate to **User Configuration** | **Preferences** | **Control Panel Settings** | **Internet Settings**.
4. Right-click on **Internet Settings** and choose **New** | **Internet Explorer 10**.

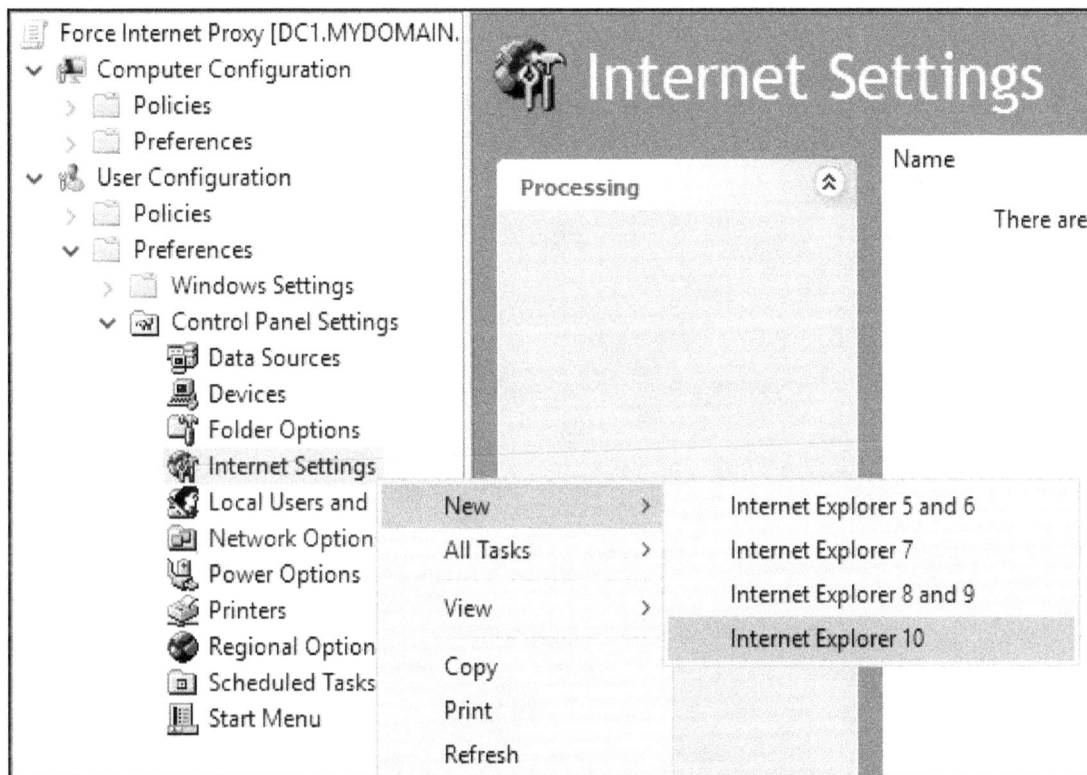

You may have to create multiple policies here if you are using multiple versions of Internet Explorer on your workstations.

5. You will see a dialog box that looks just like the regular Internet options available in IE. You have the ability to change many things here, but for our purposes today, we are heading over to the **Connections** tab.
6. Click on the **LAN settings** button.

7. Check the box for **Proxy server**. Then input the **Address** and **Port** fields for your particular proxy server.

```
┌──────────────────────────────────────────────────────────────────┐
│ Local Area Network (LAN) Settings                              ✕   │
│                                                                    │
│  Automatic configuration                                           │
│  Automatic configuration may override manual settings.  To ensure  │
│  the use of manual settings, disable automatic configuration.      │
│                                                                    │
│     ☐ Automatically detect settings                                │
│     ☐ Use automatic configuration script                           │
│                                                                    │
│   Address:   [_____]                    │
│                                                                    │
│                                                                    │
│  Proxy server                                                      │
│     ☑ Use a proxy server for your LAN (These settings will not     │
│        apply to dial-up or VPN connections).                       │
│                                                                    │
│   Address: [ WebProxy1    ]   Port: [ 8080    ]   [ Advanced... ]   │
│                                                                    │
│          ☐ Bypass proxy server for local addresses                 │
│                                                                    │
│                              [      OK      ]      [   Cancel   ]   │
│                                                                    │
└──────────────────────────────────────────────────────────────────┘
```

8. Click **OK**, and your setting will be put into place.
9. Now log in to the client computer, and let's see whether this proxy server information was successfully implemented. Launch Internet Explorer and open **Internet options**.
10. Browse to the **Connections** tab and click on the **LAN settings** button to ensure your proxy server settings have been properly plugged in. Also notice that they are now grayed out, showing you that they have been configured by Group Policy, and cannot be manipulated manually.

How it works...

Using Group Policy to assign Internet proxy server settings to all of your client computers with one simple GPO creation is another example of the power behind Group Policy. The possibilities for the centralized administration of your domain joined machines are almost endless; you just need to do a little digging and find the right place inside the GPOs for changing your settings. Maybe you don't have a proxy server in your network and don't need this recipe. But I still encourage you to take the steps listed here and apply them to some piece of technology that you do utilize. I guarantee anyone working in IT will find some setting inside Group Policy that will benefit them! Go out and find some that will help save you time and money.

Viewing the settings currently enabled inside a GPO

So far we have been creating GPOs and putting settings into them, so we are well aware of what is happening with each of our policies. Many times, though, you enter a new environment that contains a lot of existing policies, and you may need to figure out what is happening in those policies. I have had many cases where I install a new server, join it to the domain, and it breaks. It doesn't necessarily nose dive, but some component won't work properly or I can't flow network traffic to it for some reason. Something like that can be hard to track down. Since the issue seemed to happen during the domain join process, I suspect that some kind of policy from an existing GPO has been applied to my new server and is having a negative effect on it. Let's take a look inside Group Policy at the easiest way to display the settings that are contained within each GPO.

Getting ready

For this recipe, we only need access to the Group Policy Management Console, which I am going to run from my Server 2016 domain controller server.

How to do it...

To quickly view the settings contained within a GPO, follow these steps:

1. In the Domain Controller, open up Server Manager and launch the **Group Policy Management** Console from inside the **Tools** menu.

2. Expand the name of your domain, then expand the **Group Policy Objects** folder. This displays all of the GPOs currently configured in your domain.

3. Click on one of the GPOs so that you see the **Links** and **Security Filtering** sections in the right window pane.

4. Now click on the **Settings** tab near the top.

5. Once you have **Settings** tab open, click on the **show all** link near the top right. This will display all of the settings that are currently configured inside that GPO.

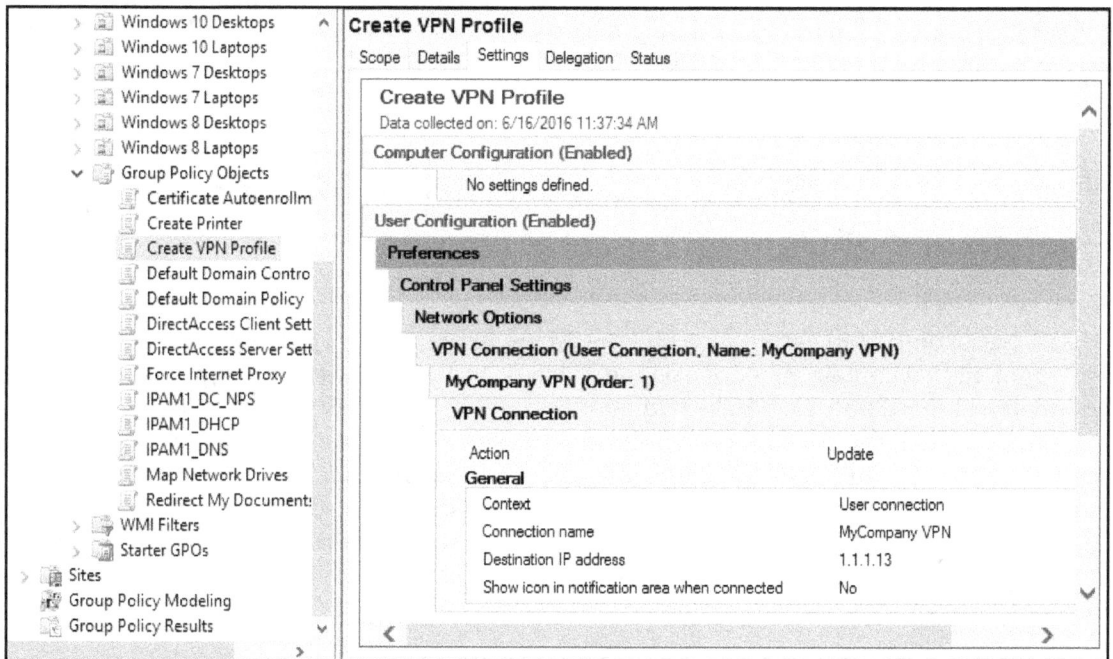

How it works...

In this very simple recipe, we use the Group Policy Management Console in order to view the currently configured settings inside our GPOs. This can be very useful for checking over existing settings and for comparing them against what is actually being configured on the client computers. Taking a look through this information can also help you to spot potential problems, such as duplicate settings spread across multiple GPOs.

See also

Viewing the settings included in a GPO can be helpful during troubleshooting, but there are many other tools that can be additionally used in order to troubleshoot Group Policy. Here are a couple of links to help you understand the recommended procedures for troubleshooting Group Policy:

- http://technet.microsoft.com/en-us/library/jj134223.aspx
- http://technet.microsoft.com/en-us/library/cc749336%28v=ws.10%29.asp x

Viewing the GPOs currently assigned to a computer

Once you start using Group Policy to distribute settings around to many client computers, it will quickly become important to be able to view the settings and policies that have or have not been applied to specific computers. Thankfully, there is a command built right into the Windows operating system to display this information. There are a number of different switches that can be used with this command, so let's explore some of the most common ones that I see used by server administrators.

Getting ready

We have a number of GPOs in our domain now; some are applied at the top level of the domain and some are only applied to specific OUs. We are going to run some commands on our Server 2016 web server in order to find out which GPOs have been applied to it and which have not.

How to do it...

Let's use the `gpresult` command to gather some information on policies applied to our server:

1. Log in to the web server, or whatever client computer you want to see these results on, and open up an administrative Command Prompt.

2. Type `gpresult /r` and press *Enter*. This displays all of the resultant data on which policies are applied, and are not applied, to our system. You can scroll through this information to get the data that you need.

```
Administrator: Command Prompt                                    —    □    ×
COMPUTER SETTINGS
-------------------
    CN=WEB1,CN=Computers,DC=MYDOMAIN,DC=LOCAL
    Last time Group Policy was applied: 6/16/2016 at 11:28:06 AM
    Group Policy was applied from:      DC1.MYDOMAIN.LOCAL
    Group Policy slow link threshold:   500 kbps
    Domain Name:                        MYDOMAIN
    Domain Type:                        Windows 2008 or later

    Applied Group Policy Objects
    -----------------------------------
        Default Domain Policy
        Certificate Autoenrollment Policy

    The following GPOs were not applied because they were filtered out
    -------------------------------------------------------------------
        Local Group Policy
            Filtering:  Not Applied (Empty)

    The computer is a part of the following security groups
    -------------------------------------------------------------
        BUILTIN\Administrators
        Everyone
        BUILTIN\Users
```

3. Now let's clean that data up a little bit. For instance, the general output we just received had information about both computer policies and user policies. Now we want to display only policies that have applied at the User level. Go ahead and use this command: `gpresult /r /scope:user`.

```
Administrator: Command Prompt                              —    □    ✕
USER SETTINGS
-------------
    CN=Administrator,CN=Users,DC=MYDOMAIN,DC=LOCAL
    Last time Group Policy was applied: 6/16/2016 at 10:39:31 AM
    Group Policy was applied from:      DC1.MYDOMAIN.LOCAL
    Group Policy slow link threshold:   500 kbps
    Domain Name:                        MYDOMAIN
    Domain Type:                        Windows 2008 or later

    Applied Group Policy Objects
    ----------------------------------
        Redirect My Documents
        Create VPN Profile

    The following GPOs were not applied because they were filtered out
    ------------------------------------------------------------------
        Local Group Policy
            Filtering:  Not Applied (Empty)

    The user is a part of the following security groups
    ---------------------------------------------------
        Domain Users
        Everyone
        BUILTIN\Users
```

You can use either the `/SCOPE:USER` switch or the `/SCOPE:COMPUTER` switch in order to view specifically the user or computer policies applied to the system.

4. And if you aren't a huge fan of looking at this data via a command prompt, never fear! There is another switch that can be used to export this data to HTML format. Try the following command: `gpresult /h c:\gpresult.html`.

5. After running that command, browse to your `C:` drive and you should have a file sitting there called `gpresult.html`. Go ahead and open that file to see your gpresult data in a web browser with a nicer look and feel.

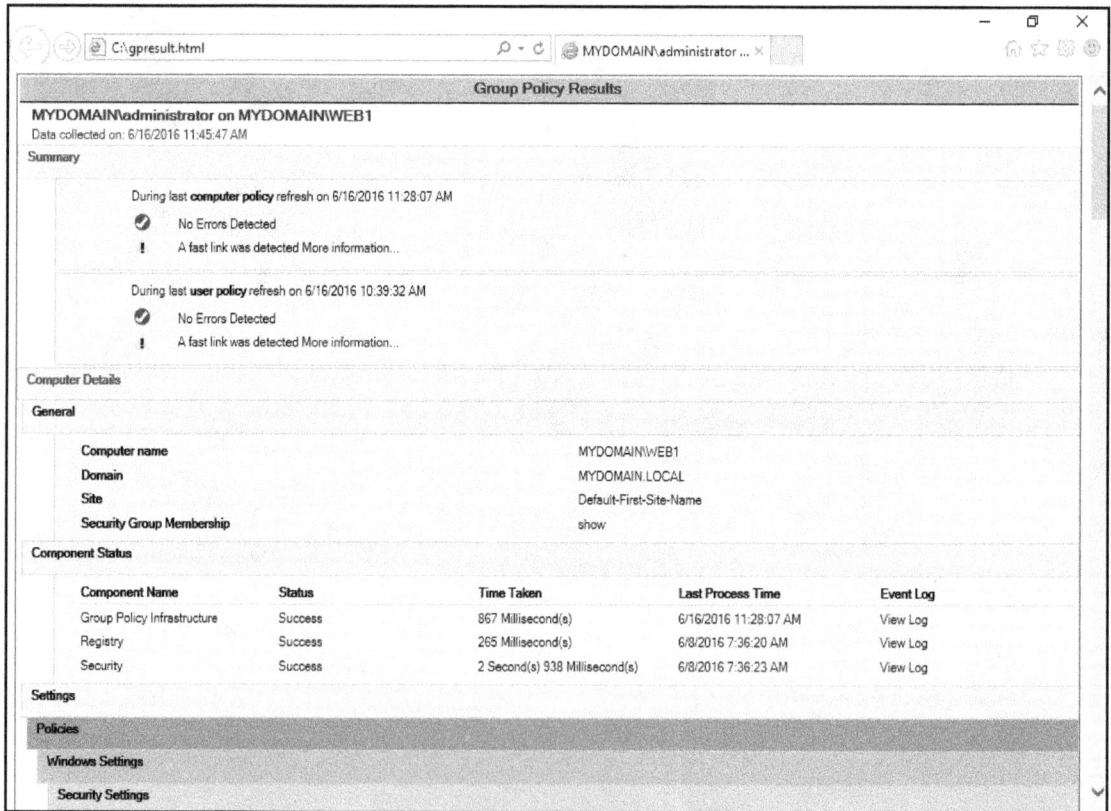

How it works...

The `gpresult` command can be used in a variety of ways to display information about which Group Policy Objects and settings have been applied to your client computer or server. This can be especially useful when trying to determine what policies are being applied, and maybe even more helpful when trying to figure out why a particular policy hasn't been applied. If a policy is denied because of rights or permissions, you will see it in this output. This likely indicates that you have something to adjust in your Links or Security Filtering in order to get the policy applied successfully to your machine. However you decide to make use of the data for yourself, make sure to play around with the `gpresult` command and get familiar with its results if you intend to administer your environment using Group Policy.

One additional note about another command that is very commonly used in the field. Windows domain joined machines only process Group Policy settings every once in a while; by default they will refresh their settings and look for new policy changes every 90 minutes. If you are creating or changing policies and notice that they have not yet been applied to your endpoint computers, you could hang out for a couple of hours and wait for those changes to be applied. If you want to speed up that process a little, you can log in to the endpoint client computer, server, or whatever it is that should receive the settings, and use the `gpupdate /force` command. This will force that computer to revisit Group Policy and apply any settings that have been configured for it. When we make changes in the field and don't want to spend a lot of time waiting around for replication to happen naturally, we often use `gpupdate /force` numerous times as we make changes and progress through testing.

See also

I tend to prefer `gpresult` to view the policies that are currently applied to a computer that I am working on, but it's not the only way. You may also want to check out `RSOP.MSC`. This is a tool that can be launched in order to see a more visually stimulating version of the policies and settings that are currently applied to your computer. Check out the details here:

- http://technet.microsoft.com/en-us/library/cc772175.aspx

Backing up and restoring GPOs

As with any piece of data in your organization, it is a good idea to keep backups of your GPOs. Keeping these backups separately from a full Domain Controller or full Active Directory backup can be advantageous, as it enables a quicker restore of individual GPOs in the event of an accidental deletion. Or perhaps you updated a GPO, but the change you made is now causing problems and you want to roll that policy back to make sure it is configured the way that it was yesterday. Whatever your reason for backing up and restoring GPOs, let's take a look at a couple of ways to accomplish each task. We will use the Group Policy Management Console to perform these functions, and will also figure out how to do the same backup and restores via PowerShell.

Getting ready

We are going to perform these tasks from a Windows Server 2016 domain controller in our environment. We will utilize both the Group Policy Management Console and the PowerShell command line.

How to do it…

There is a GPO in our domain called **Map Network Drives**. First, we will use Group Policy Management Console to back up and restore this GPO:

1. From the **Tools** menu of Server Manager, open up the **Group Policy Management** Console.
2. Navigate to **Forest** | **Domains** | **Your Domain Name** | **Group Policy Objects**.
3. If you want to back up a single GPO, you simply right-click on the specific GPO and choose **Back Up…**. Otherwise, it is probably more useful for us to back up the whole set of GPOs. To accomplish that, right-click on the **Group Policy Objects** folder and then choose **Back Up All…**.

	Windows 7 Laptops		
Windows 8 Desktops		
Windows 8 Laptops		
Group Policy Objects		

Create VPN Profile

Data collected on: 6/16/2016 11:37:34 AM

Computer Configuration (Enabled)

Certificate Auto	New	d.
Create Printer	Back Up All...	d)
Create VPN Prof	Manage Backups...	
Default Domain	Open Migration Table Editor	
Default Domain		
DirectAccess Cli	New Window from Here	
DirectAccess Se		ser Connection, Name: MyCompany VPN)
Force Internet P	Refresh	(Order: 1)
IPAM1_DC_NPS	Help	
IPAM1_DHCP		

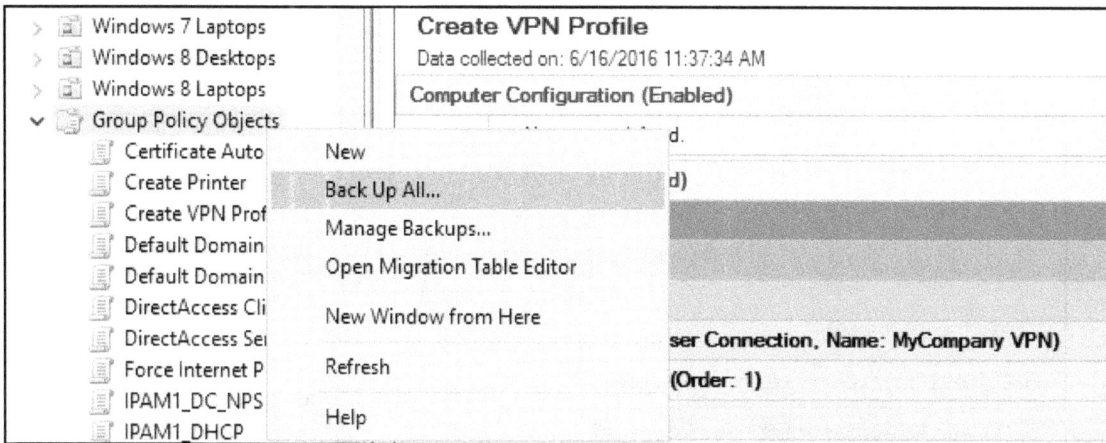

4. Specify a location where you want the backups to be saved and a description for the backup set. Then click **Back Up**.

Back Up Group Policy Object   ✕

Enter the name of the folder in which you want to store backed up versions of this Group Policy Object (GPO). You can back up multiple GPOs to the same folder.

Note: Settings that are external to the GPO, such as WMI filters and IPsec policies, are independent objects in Active Directory and will not be backed up.

To prevent tampering of backed up GPOs, be sure to secure this folder so that only authorized administrators have write access to this location.

Location:

C:\GPO_Backups   ⌄

                                                          Browse...

Description:

Full_GPO_Backup

                                        Back Up   Cancel

5. Once the backup process is complete, you should see the status of how many GPOs were successfully backed up.

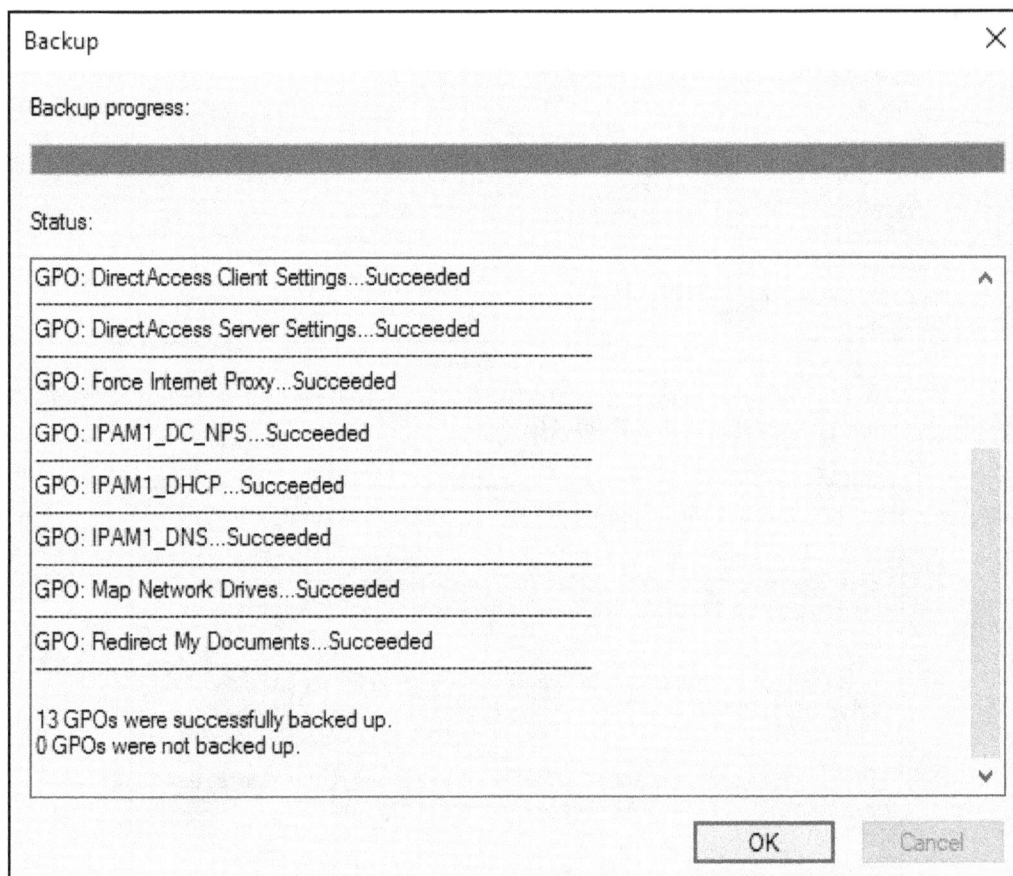

```
Backup                                                                    ✕

Backup progress:

▓▓▓▓▓▓▓▓▓▓▓▓▓▓▓▓▓▓▓▓▓▓▓▓▓▓▓▓▓▓▓▓▓▓▓▓▓▓▓▓▓▓▓▓▓▓▓▓▓▓▓▓▓▓▓

Status:
┌──────────────────────────────────────────────────────────────────┐
│ GPO: DirectAccess Client Settings...Succeeded                    ∧ │
│ ------------------------------------------------------------------ │
│ GPO: DirectAccess Server Settings...Succeeded                      │
│ ------------------------------------------------------------------ │
│ GPO: Force Internet Proxy...Succeeded                              │
│ ------------------------------------------------------------------ │
│ GPO: IPAM1_DC_NPS...Succeeded                                      │
│ ------------------------------------------------------------------ │
│ GPO: IPAM1_DHCP...Succeeded                                        │
│ ------------------------------------------------------------------ │
│ GPO: IPAM1_DNS...Succeeded                                         │
│ ------------------------------------------------------------------ │
│ GPO: Map Network Drives...Succeeded                                │
│ ------------------------------------------------------------------ │
│ GPO: Redirect My Documents...Succeeded                             │
│ ------------------------------------------------------------------ │
│                                                                    │
│ 13 GPOs were successfully backed up.                               │
│ 0 GPOs were not backed up.                                       ∨ │
└──────────────────────────────────────────────────────────────────┘

                                              [   OK   ]   [ Cancel ]
```

Now let's try accomplishing the same full GPO backup, but this time using PowerShell:

1. Open an administrative PowerShell prompt.
2. Use the following command:

```
Backup-GPO -Path C:\GPO_Backups_PowerShell -All
```

```
Administrator: Windows PowerShell                                    —    □    ×

PS C:\> Backup-GPO -Path C:\GPO_Backups_PowerShell -All


DisplayName        : Default Domain Policy
GpoId              : 31b2f340-016d-11d2-945f-00c04fb984f9
Id                 : 31d0c7e9-137c-477e-a38f-5cbe3efa6031
BackupDirectory    : C:\GPO_Backups_PowerShell
CreationTime       : 6/16/2016 11:54:45 AM
DomainName         : MYDOMAIN.LOCAL
Comment            :

DisplayName        : Force Internet Proxy
GpoId              : 5a88504a-9610-4fe3-aed2-fc039d1db9c5
Id                 : 3b1ae8e6-568e-4b9d-b449-9514c9032412
BackupDirectory    : C:\GPO_Backups_PowerShell
CreationTime       : 6/16/2016 11:54:46 AM
DomainName         : MYDOMAIN.LOCAL
Comment            :

DisplayName        : Default Domain Controllers Policy
GpoId              : 6ac1786c-016f-11d2-945f-00c04fb984f9
Id                 : da05461a-f7a0-41d1-81ba-6cf42bc4cd62
BackupDirectory    : C:\GPO_Backups_PowerShell
CreationTime       : 6/16/2016 11:54:47 AM
DomainName         : MYDOMAIN.LOCAL
```

Now that we have two full backup sets of the GPOs, let's try to restore the GPO called **Map Network Drives**.

1. Navigate back inside the **Group Policy Management** Console and find the **Group Policy Objects** folder. The same location that we used to back up a minute ago.

2. Right-click on the **Map Network Drives** GPO and choose **Restore from Backup...**.

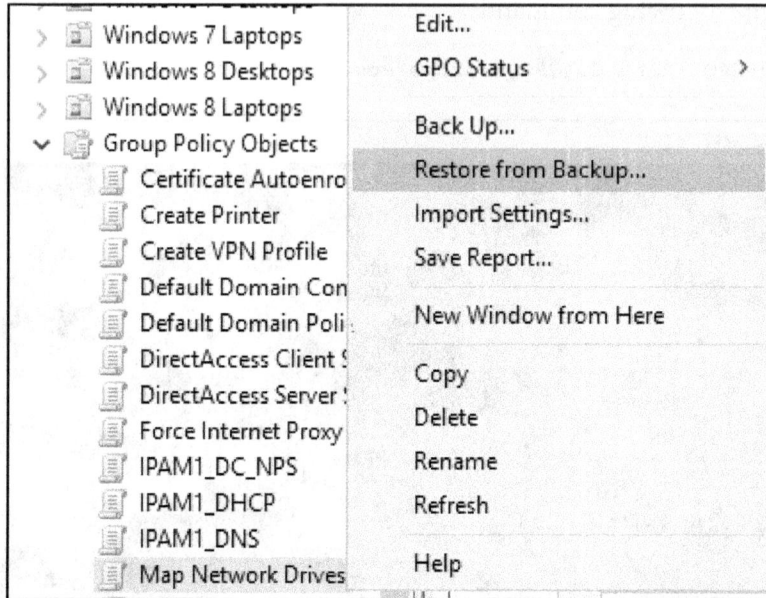

3. Click **Next** and specify the folder where your backup files are stored. Then click **Next** again.

4. As long as a backup copy of the **Map Network Drives** GPO exists in that folder, you will see it in the wizard. Select that GPO and click **Next**.

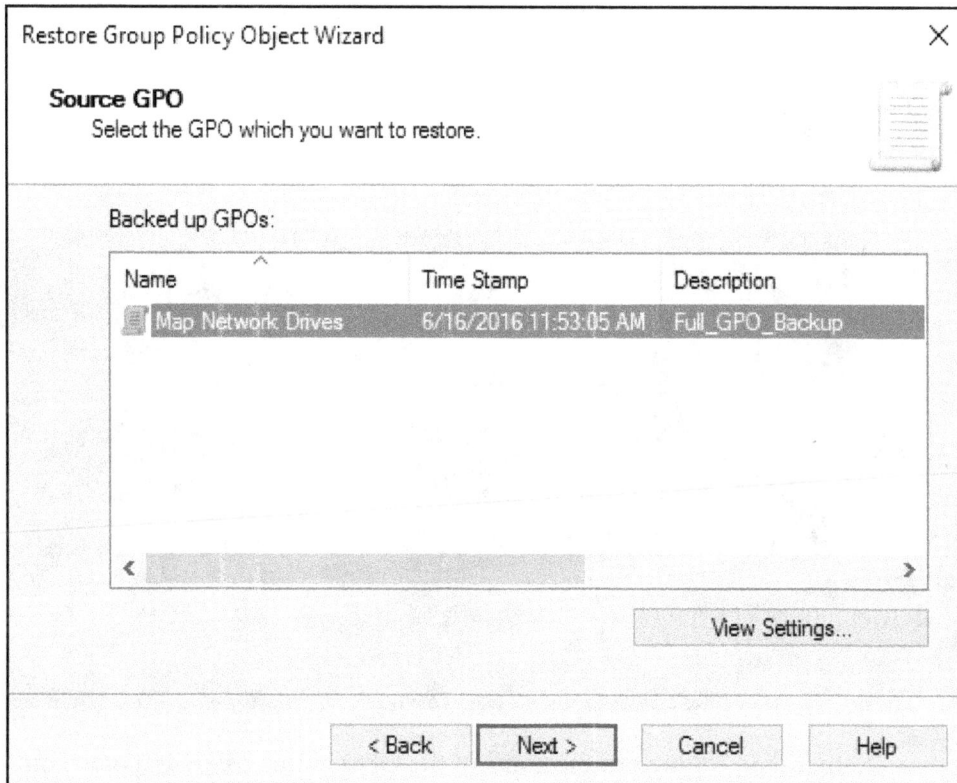

5. Click **Finish** and the GPO will be restored to its previous state.

Now we will restore the same Map Network Drives GPO, but using PowerShell as follows:

1. Head back to your administrative PowerShell prompt.
2. Use the following command to restore the previous version of this GPO from the backup we created earlier:

```
Restore-GPO -Name "Map Network Drives" -Path
C:\GPO_Backups_PowerShell
```

```
Administrator: Windows PowerShell                                    —    □    ×
PS C:\> Restore-GPO -Name "Map Network Drives" -Path C:\GPO_Backups_PowerShell

DisplayName        : Map Network Drives
DomainName         : MYDOMAIN.LOCAL
Owner              : MYDOMAIN\Domain Admins
Id                 : 77eed750-de8e-44e9-9649-96cab2f2abdc
GpoStatus          : AllSettingsEnabled
Description        :
CreationTime       : 6/16/2016 7:10:32 AM
ModificationTime   : 6/16/2016 11:58:58 AM
UserVersion        : AD Version: 2, SysVol Version: 2
ComputerVersion    : AD Version: 2, SysVol Version: 2
WmiFilter          :


PS C:\> _
```

> **TIP**
>
> Rather than typing out the name of the GPO in this command, you could instead specify the GUID of the policy. This number is generally a lot longer than the name, however, and so I tend to see admins preferring to utilize the name of the policy. For example, the GUID of our Map Network Drives GPO is 77eed750-de8e-44e9-9649-96cab2f2abdc.

How it works...

Backing up and restoring GPOs is going to be a regular task for anybody administering Active Directory and Group Policy. In this recipe, we walked through each process, using a couple of different tools for each procedure. Group Policy Management Console is nice because it is graphically interfaced, and it is easy to look at the options available to you. PowerShell is often preferred, however, because it can be automated (think scheduled backups). It also facilitates remote execution of these commands from another machine inside the network.

See also

Here are some links for more extensive information about the PowerShell cmdlets we used today:

- http://technet.microsoft.com/en-us/library/hh967480.aspx
- http://technet.microsoft.com/en-us/library/ee461030.aspx

Plugging in ADMX and ADML templates

Some day you may find yourself in a position where you are following a setup guide or some article, which instructs you to configure certain options inside a GPO. However, when you go to look for those options, they do not exist. How is that possible, if the documentation clearly shows the options existing inside Group Policy? This is the magic of ADMX and ADML files. Many configurations and settings exist inside Group Policy right out of the box, but some technologies build on additional settings or fields inside GPOs that do not exist by default. When this happens, those technologies will include files that can be placed onto your Domain Controller. These files are then imported automatically by Group Policy, and the settings will then appear in the normal GPO editing tools. The trickiest part about doing this is figuring out where the ADMX and ADML files need to reside in order for them to be seen and imported by Group Policy. Let's figure it out together.

Getting ready

I run across this one regularly when setting up DirectAccess. There is a special tool that you can install onto your Windows 7 computers that tells you some information about the DirectAccess connection, but this tool needs to be configured by a GPO. The problem is that the settings for the tool don't exist inside Group Policy by default. So Microsoft includes in the tool's download files an ADMX and an ADML file, both of which need to be plugged into Group Policy. We have downloaded this tool, called the DirectAccess Connectivity Assistant, and I have the ADMX and ADML files now sitting on the hard drive of my domain controller. The work we need to accomplish will be right from this DC1 domain controller.

How to do it...

In order to pull settings from an ADMX and ADML file into Group Policy, follow these steps:

1. Copy the **ADMX** file into `C:\Windows\PolicyDefinitions` on your domain controller. In my case, the filename is `DirectAccess_Connectivity_Assistant_2_0_GP.admx`.

2. Copy the **ADML** file into `C:\Windows\PolicyDefinitions\en-US` on your domain controller. In my case, the filename is `DirectAccess_Connectivity_Assistant_2_0_GP.adml`.

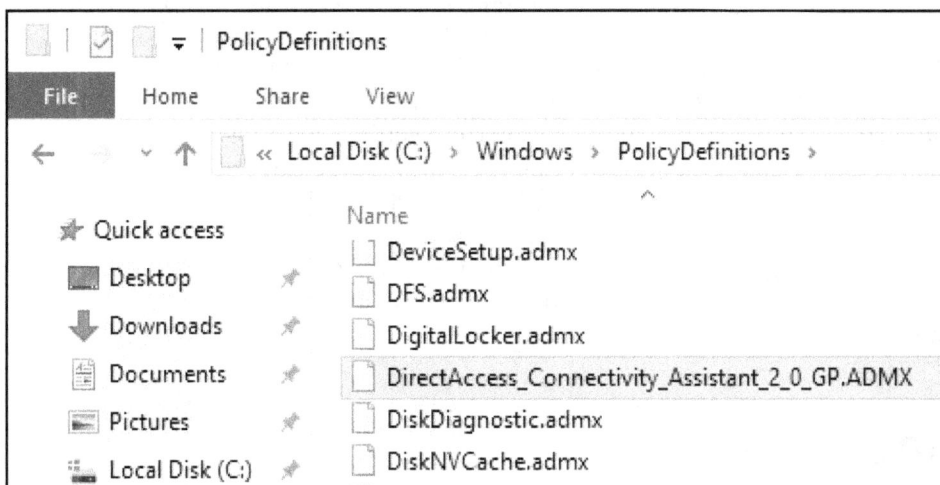

3. Now simply open your **Group Policy Management Console** from inside Server Manager.

4. Edit the GPO that you want to use with these new settings, and you can see that we have some brand new settings available to us inside here that did not exist five minutes ago! These new settings show up inside **Computer Configuration |
Policies | Administrative Templates**.

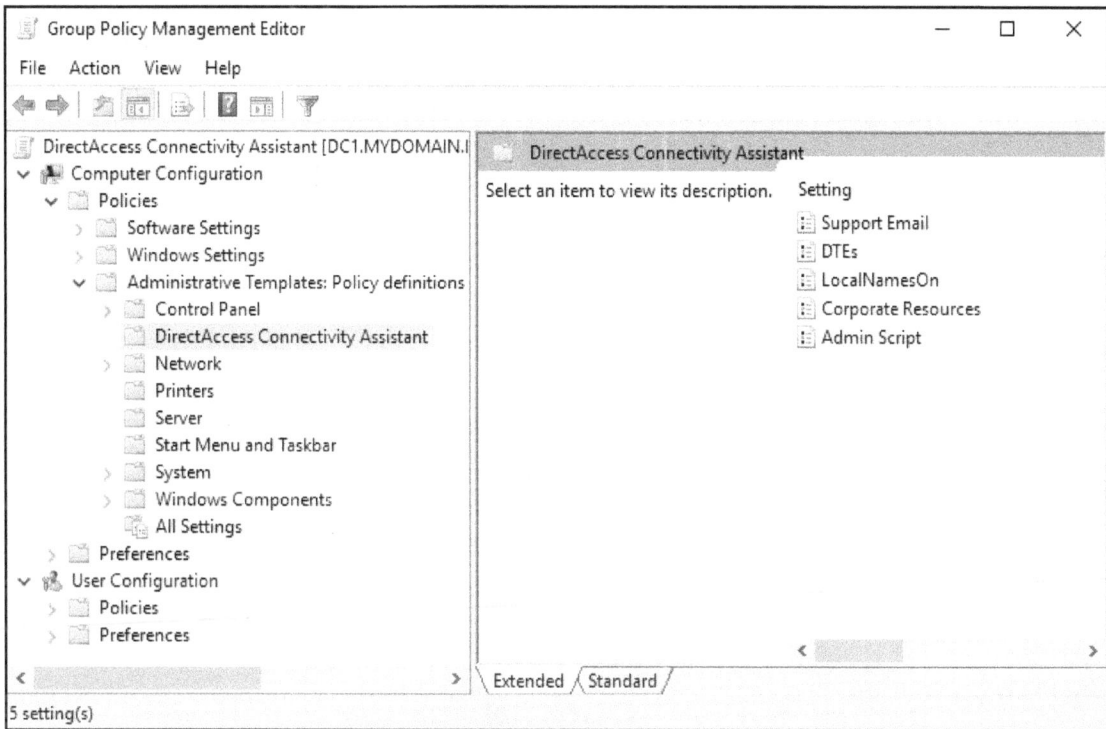

How it works...

You can import new settings and configuration options into Group Policy by taking ADMX and ADML files and putting them into the proper folders on your domain controller server. What we walked through today is an example of how to accomplish this task on a single domain controller, but what happens if your environment has multiple domain controllers? Do you have to copy the files onto each server? No, that is not the proper way to go about it. In an environment where you have multiple domain controllers, the ADMX and ADML files instead need to go inside something called the Active Directory Central Store. Instead of copying the ADMX and ADML files into their locations on the C drive, open up File Explorer and browse to
`\\<DOMAIN_NAME>\SYSVOL\<DOMAIN_NAME>\Policies\PolicyDefinitions`. This Central Store location will replicate to all of your domain controllers. Simply place the files here instead of on the local hard disk, and your new settings will then be available within the Group Policy console from any of your domain controllers.

10
File Services and Data Control

File storage needs exist for any organization of any size. Whether we are talking about simple document storage for your team of users to utilize or something like block storage accessed over a network by a high performance computing environment, you are going to have servers in your network that are responsible for storing data safely and securely. The File Services role has grown significantly over the years as our storage needs have changed and evolved. Many of us can no longer satisfy the data needs for our environments with simple file shares and physical disks. Let's use this chapter to explore some of the more interesting ways that data can be managed in a Windows Server 2016 environment:

- Enabling Distributed File System and creating a Namespace
- Configuring Distributed File System Replication
- Creating an iSCSI target on your server
- Configuring an iSCSI initiator connection
- Configuring Storage Spaces
- Turning on data deduplication
- Setting up Windows Server 2016 work folders

Introduction

I read last year that the Internet carries more than 1,800 petabytes of information every day. That is an incredible number! As all of that data comes and goes, it is easy in this day and age to think of this information as being stored in *the cloud*, a magic box in the sky. All of that data is sitting somewhere though. On hard drives, installed inside servers, sitting inside datacenters. All this talk about the cloud has really morphed for companies into talk about private clouds, and when you break it down, what they are really talking about is different ways to provide a centralized group of information to users that may be accessing it from various places. There are numerous technologies baked into Server 2016 that can assist with the centralization and securing of your data, so let's explore a few of them together.

Enabling Distributed File System and creating a Namespace

Distributed File System (DFS) is a technology included with Windows Server 2016 that enables multiple file servers to share a single Namespace, enabling end users to access files and folders from a single network name. Those accessing the files don't have to worry about which physical server they are currently in contact with; they simply utilize the namespace of the DFS environment and let the servers do all the grunt work in making sure that all files and folders are available to the users, no matter where those files happen to be physically sitting. Another way to think of it as a collection of network shares, all stuck together under the same umbrella that is the **DFS Namespace**. Users access folders and files via the Namespace, and have access to everything in one place. It helps to think of DFS Namespaces sort of like CNAME records in DNS. They essentially allow us to virtualize the file resources.

Let's work together to get a basic DFS environment up-and-running, with a single Namespace created so that we can test browsing to it without having to specify the name of our file server. We will also be taking steps during this recipe to prep our DFS server for replication, synchronizing files between two file servers. The actual configuration of replication (DFSR) will be accomplished in our next recipe, but when we build out the FILE1 server, we are prepping it for that role as well.

Getting ready

We are working inside a domain environment, and the actual work today will be accomplished from our new file server. This is called FILE1, and is running Windows Server 2016. It has been joined to the domain, but nothing else has yet been configured.

How to do it...

Follow these steps to configure this new file server for DFS:

1. Log in to FILE1 and launch Server Manager. Click on the **Add roles and features** link.
2. Click **Next** a few times until you reach the **Select server roles** screen.
3. Navigate to **File and Storage Services** | **File and iSCSI Services**.
4. Check the box for **DFS Namespaces**. When prompted to install additional required features, click **Add Features**.
5. Also check the box for **DFS Replication**. You should now have **File Server**, **DFS Namespaces**, and **DFS Replication** checked on your **Roles** screen:

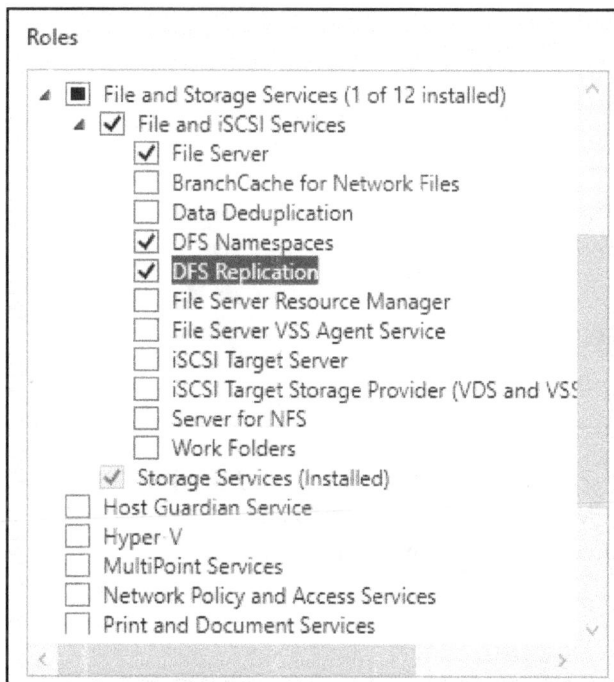

6. Click **Next**, **Next**, then **Install**. This will place the necessary roles onto FILE1.

7. Now open Server Manager's **Tools** menu and launch **DFS Management**:

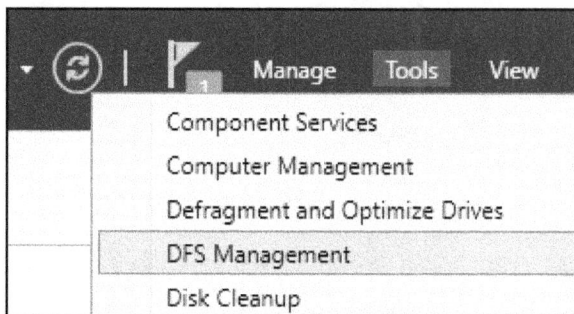

8. First we are going to create a Namespace that will be published in our domain. Right-click on **Namespaces** and choose **New Namespace...**.

9. Enter the name of the server that is going to be your **Namespace server**. We are going to use the primary file server, FILE1:

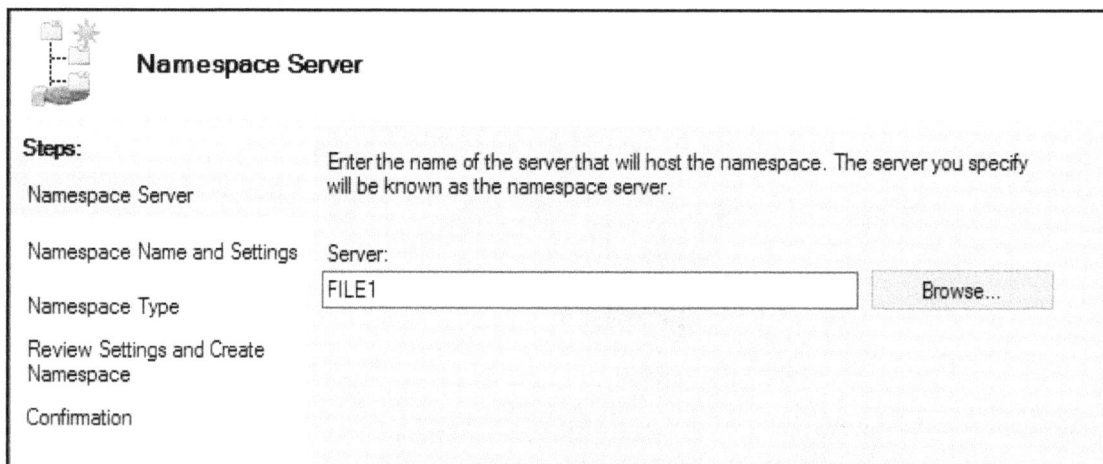

Namespace Server

Steps:

Namespace Server

Namespace Name and Settings

Namespace Type

Review Settings and Create Namespace

Confirmation

Enter the name of the server that will host the namespace. The server you specify will be known as the namespace server.

Server:

FILE1   Browse...

10. On the next screen, **Namespace Name and Settings**, input a name for this new Namespace. My first share is going to be for IT purposes, so I'm calling mine IT. Then click on the **Edit Settings...** button.

11. The wizard is going to create a new share for my Namespace storage location. If you would like this share to be created in a particular place on the hard drive, specify it here. I am also going to choose the option for **Administrators have full access; other users have read and write permissions** so that users without administrative rights can still save into this Namespace:

Edit Settings	✕

Namespace server:

```
FILE1
```

Shared folder:

```
IT
```

Local path of shared folder:

```
C:\DFSRoots\IT
```
Browse...

Shared folder permissions:

◯ All users have read-only permissions

◯ All users have read and write permissions

◯ Administrators have full access; other users have read-only permissions

◉ Administrators have full access; other users have read and write permissions

◯ Use custom permissions: Customize...

OK   Cancel

12. Click **OK**, then click **Next**.

13. Typically, you want to choose the default options on the **Namespace Type** screen. It should be pre-selected as **Domain-based namespace**, which is great, together with **Enable Windows Server 2008 mode**. You can also see here a preview of the final Namespace name listed for your review. Just go ahead and click **Next** on this screen:

Select the type of namespace to create.

⦿ Domain-based namespace

A domain-based namespace is stored on one or more namespace servers and in Active Directory Domain Services. You can increase the availability of a domain-based namespace by using multiple servers. When created in Windows Server 2008 mode, the namespace supports increased scalability and access-based enumeration.

☑ Enable Windows Server 2008 mode

Preview of domain-based namespace:

\\MYDOMAIN.LOCAL\IT

14. Review the settings you have chosen on the final screen and then click the **Create** button in order to create your Namespace.

15. Your new Namespace is now visible in the left window pane of **DFS Management**. Let's go ahead and create a folder inside this Namespace. Right-click on the new Namespace and choose **New Folder...**:

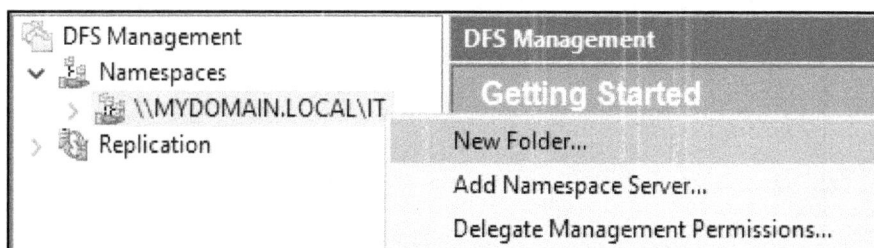

DFS Management
∨ Namespaces
  › \\MYDOMAIN.LOCAL\IT
› Replication

DFS Management
Getting Started
New Folder...
Add Namespace Server...
Delegate Management Permissions...

16. Input a name for your new folder in the Name field; this is the name that will be displayed inside the DFS Namespace when users access it. Then click the **Add...** button to specify a share that this new folder is going to link to. I am specifying a folder that happens to be sitting here on FILE1, but you could even specify a network share that is on another server:

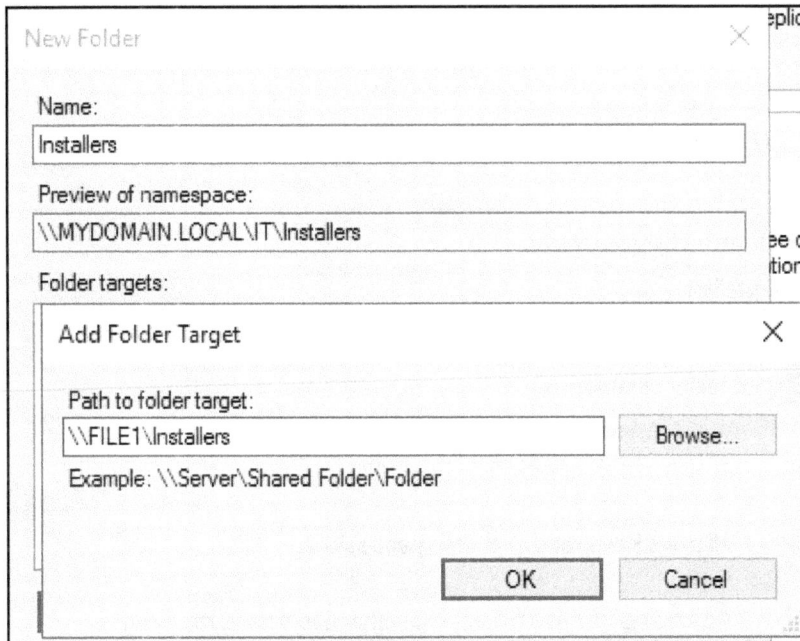

17. When you click **OK**, if the share that you entered doesn't already exist, you will be asked whether or not you want the wizard to create it for you. I chose **Yes**, so that it could create this new share for me.

18. After choosing **Yes** in order to create the new shared folder, I have another screen that allows me to specify permissions on this new folder. Go ahead and choose the permission setting that is appropriate for the kind of information you are planning to place in this folder. You must also now specify the physical location of this share on the hard drive:

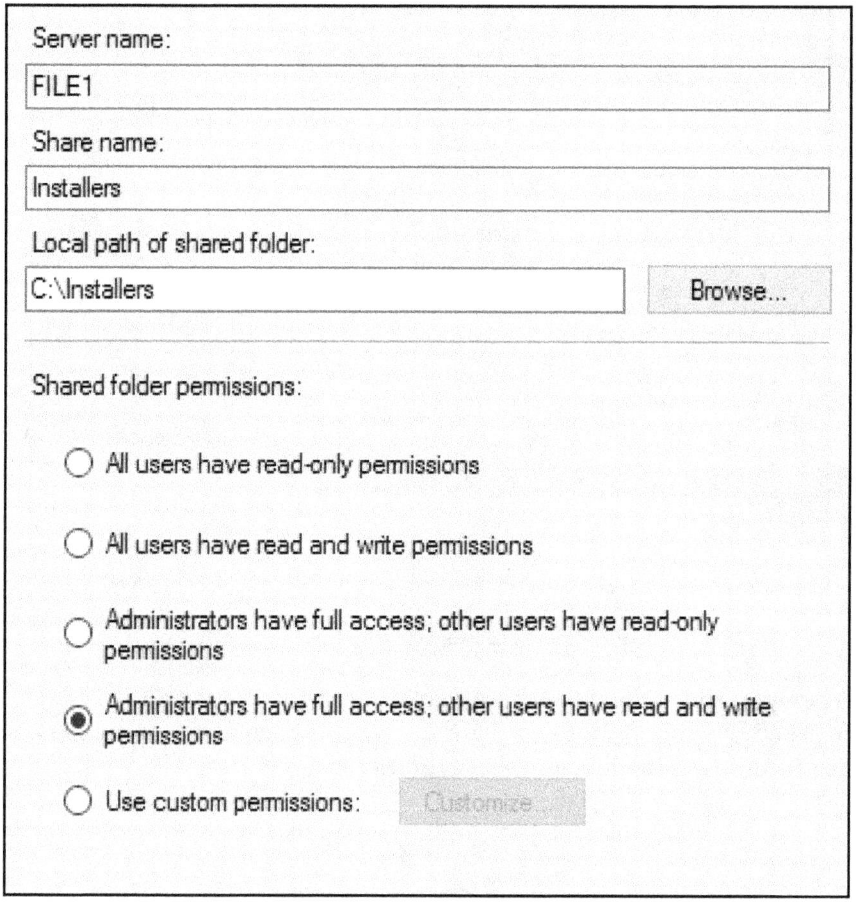

Server name:

FILE1

Share name:

Installers

Local path of shared folder:

C:\Installers   Browse...

Shared folder permissions:

○ All users have read-only permissions

○ All users have read and write permissions

○ Administrators have full access; other users have read-only permissions

◉ Administrators have full access; other users have read and write permissions

○ Use custom permissions: Customize...

19. Now that we have a DFS Namespace created and a folder within that Namespace, let's test this out! Log in to a client computer and try browsing to `\\mydomain\it`:

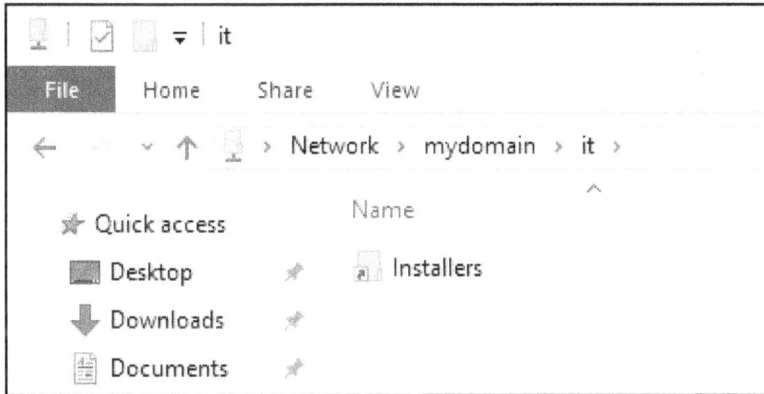

How it works...

In this recipe, we took a new file server and turned it into our first DFS box. The new Namespace that we created now contains a folder where users are able to store documents, and is published on the domain so that these files and folders can be accessed via the DFS Namespace name, rather than needing to know the name of our specific file server. DFS is a great tool for centralizing data and creating ease-of-use for employees in your company when they need to access their data. It is also a great tool for redundancy via replication, and we'll discuss that in more depth in just a minute.

Configuring Distributed File System Replication

Distributed File System Replication (**DFSR**) is a piece of DFS that enables automatic file replication between multiple servers. In the first recipe of this chapter, we added the roles and created a DFS Namespace, so we have access to files and folders that are sitting within our DFS environment. So far, though, it is all sitting on a single file server. Follow along to enable the *R* part of DFSR, Replication. We will set up DFSR between the two file servers in our environment, FILE1 and FILE2, and test it to make sure that data is being synchronized between the two.

Getting ready

We already have a DFS server online, FILE1. It is hosting a DFS Namespace with a folder inside. A new file server, FILE2, is online and joined to the domain. This recipe expects that you have already installed the necessary roles for using this server with DFS. The procedure for installing these roles is outlined in our previous recipe, *Enabling Distributed File System and creating a Namespace*. Add the roles to the new FILE2 exactly the same way that you did for FILE1, and then continue on with this recipe to configure the replication.

How to do it...

To set up DFSR between the two file servers in our environment, follow these steps:

1. On FILE1, our primary file server, launch Server Manager and then open the **DFS Management** Console from inside the **Tools** menu.

2. In the left window pane, right-click on **Replication** and choose **New Replication Group...**:

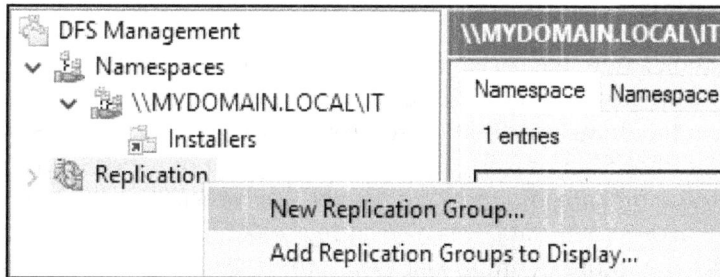

3. Choose **Multipurpose replication group** and click **Next**.

4. Enter a name for your new replication group. Then click **Next**.

5. On the **Replication Group Members** screen, click the **Add...** button and choose both of your file servers that you want to be part of this group:

Replication Group Members

Steps:

Replication Group Type

Name and Domain

Replication Group Members

Topology Selection

Hub Members

Hub and Spoke Connections

Click Add and then select two or more servers that will become members of the replication group.

Members:

Server	Domain
FILE1	MYDOMAIN.LOCAL
FILE2	MYDOMAIN.LOCAL

6. Leave the topology set to **Full mesh** and click **Next**.

7. Use the **Bandwidth** screen to throttle the connection if you need to; otherwise just click **Next** again.

8. Choose the **Primary member** from the list. For our example, it is **FILE1**:

Select the server that contains the content you want to replicate to other members. This server is known as the primary member.

Primary member:

FILE1

ⓘ If the folders to be replicated already exist on multiple servers, the folders and files on the primary member will be authoritative during initial replication.

9. Now on the **Folders to** Replicate screen, use the **Add...** button in order to add all folders that you want to replicate. For our example, I'm going to replicate the new `Installers` folder, which we configured inside our DFS Namespace:

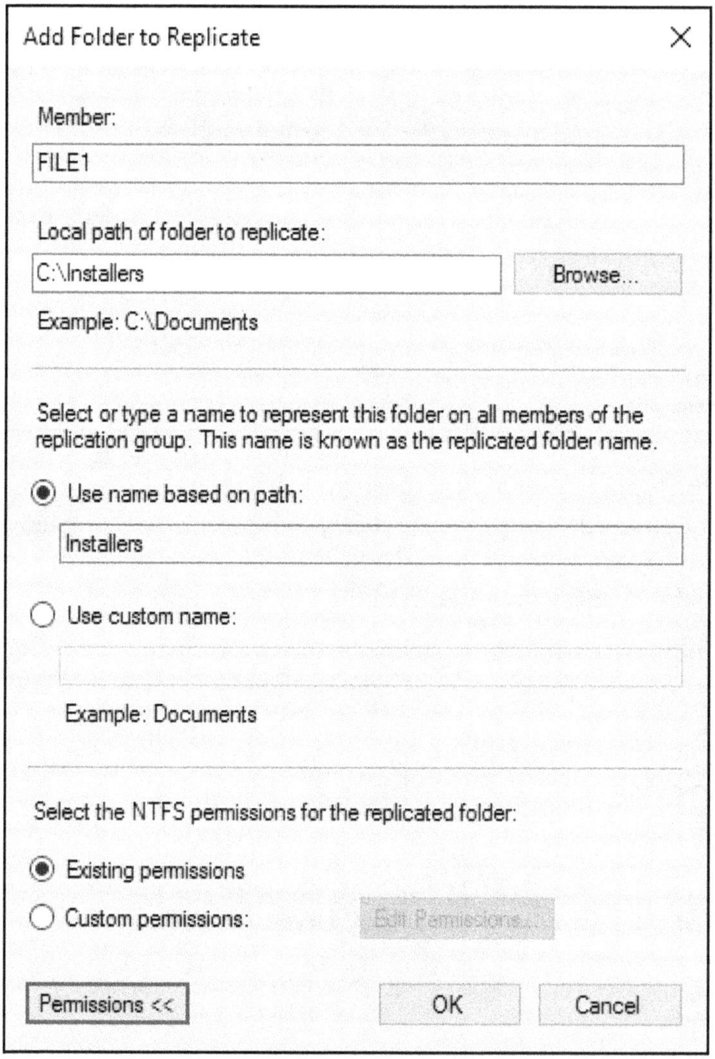

Add Folder to Replicate   ✕

Member:

FILE1

Local path of folder to replicate:

C:\Installers   Browse...

Example: C:\Documents

Select or type a name to represent this folder on all members of the replication group. This name is known as the replicated folder name.

◉ Use name based on path:

Installers

○ Use custom name:

Example: Documents

Select the NTFS permissions for the replicated folder:

◉ Existing permissions
○ Custom permissions: Edit Permissions...

Permissions <<   OK   Cancel

---

10. You now have to specify the local path for the `Installers` folder to exist on the other member server, **FILE2**. Click on the **Edit...** button and configure it as follows:

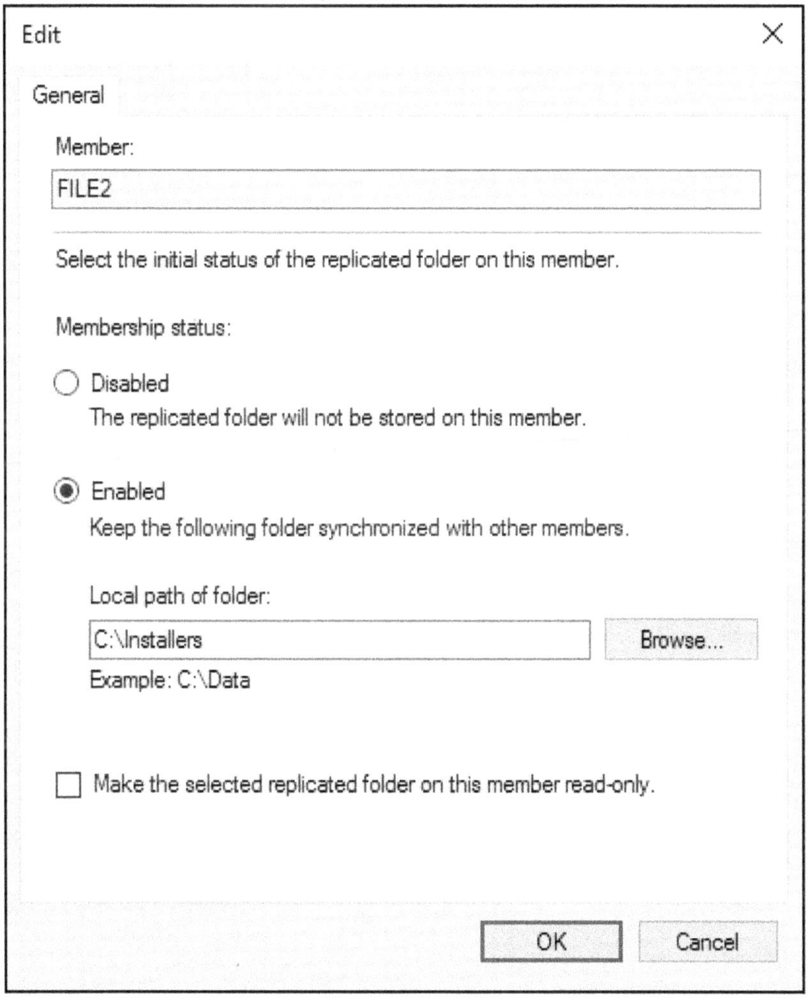

```
Edit                                                          ×

  General

    Member:

    FILE2

    Select the initial status of the replicated folder on this member.

    Membership status:

    ○ Disabled
       The replicated folder will not be stored on this member.

    ● Enabled
       Keep the following folder synchronized with other members.

       Local path of folder:
       C:\Installers                                Browse...
       Example: C:\Data

    ☐ Make the selected replicated folder on this member read-only.


                                          OK           Cancel
```

11. Take a look at the summary of settings that are about to be put into place, and once satisfied go ahead and click on the **Create** button.

12. Now back at the main **DFS** Management screen, click on the name of your new replication group listed in the left tree. You should see both member servers listed here, indicating that replication is configured!

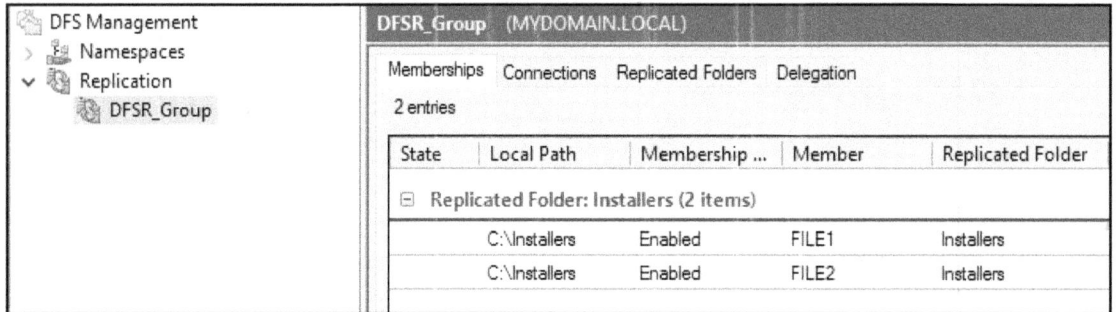

State	Local Path	Membership ...	Member	Replicated Folder
⊟ Replicated Folder: Installers (2 items)				
	C:\Installers	Enabled	FILE1	Installers
	C:\Installers	Enabled	FILE2	Installers

DFS Management
> Namespaces
∨ Replication
  DFSR_Group

DFSR_Group (MYDOMAIN.LOCAL)

Memberships Connections Replicated Folders Delegation

2 entries

13. Now let's test this thing out. From a client computer, open up File Explorer and navigate to \\mydomain\it\installers.
14. Create a few test files in this folder.
15. Give it a little bit of time for replication to happen, then check inside the C:\Installers folder on each file server. You should see that there are copies of your new files now located on both servers' hard drives!

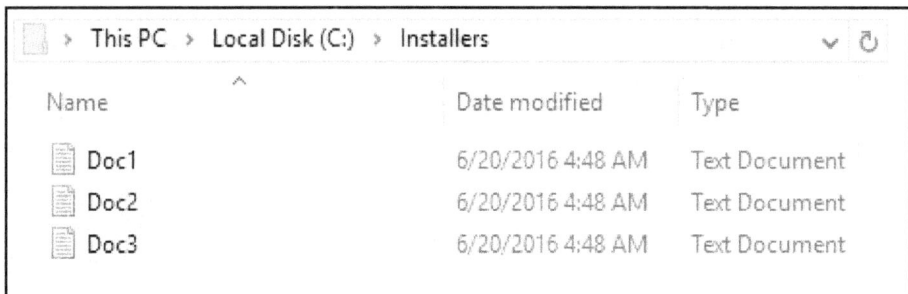

Name	Date modified	Type
Doc1	6/20/2016 4:48 AM	Text Document
Doc2	6/20/2016 4:48 AM	Text Document
Doc3	6/20/2016 4:48 AM	Text Document

This PC > Local Disk (C:) > Installers

How it works...

In this recipe, we took our DFS environment and expanded its capabilities a little by adding in replication. DFSR is a great tool to use for distributing files around to your branch offices, while keeping the user experience and drive mappings similar no matter where everyone happens to be accessing the files from. Historically speaking, Microsoft's Distributed File System has a bad reputation, because of some issues in older Windows Server operating systems. Those days are gone, and if you haven't tried out this technology in your own environment yet, you've got no reason to wait!

Creating an iSCSI target on your server

iSCSI is another way to share storage across a network. Well, the term iSCSI itself has more to do with the actual protocol level and the way that the data is transported across the LAN or WAN, but what it looks like as a consumer of iSCSI is that a machine has a drive letter for a disk, but that *disk* is not physically connected to the server. For example, you might log in to a server and see an M drive. This drive looks just like a local volume, but it is actually a network connection to storage that might be sitting on the other side of the datacenter. Sounds like a mapped network drive, right? Yes, but it works on a lower level. iSCSI virtual disks, as they are called, work with the server as if they are local disks. This gives servers the ability to interface with this data at a system level, and does not require a user context in order to work, like mapped network drives do. This is commonly referred to as **block storage**.

One good example that I worked with was a database application that a customer was installing onto a new server. The requirements for installing this software were that a drive was to be dedicated for storage, it had to be a full drive letter on the system, and it could not be a mapped drive or a UNC mapping. We were not able to add another hard drive to the physical server, and that wasn't really desirable anyway. We utilized iSCSI to create an iSCSI target on their main storage server, and then connected to that block of storage with an iSCSI initiator on the application server where we were installing the software.

I haven't seen a lot of places utilize iSCSI, which is exactly why I thought we should test the waters with it here. We now have the option in Server 2016 to create our own iSCSI targets right on the server, so let's work on creating one of these targets together.

Getting ready

We have a Windows Server 2016 running, which we are going to prep to be our iSCSI target server.

How to do it...

To create an iSCSI target on your server, go through the following steps:

1. Open **Server Manager** and click on the **Add roles and features** link.
2. Click **Next** until you come to the **Select server roles** screen.
3. Navigate to **File and Storage Services | File and iSCSI Services,** and check the box next to **iSCSI Target Server:**

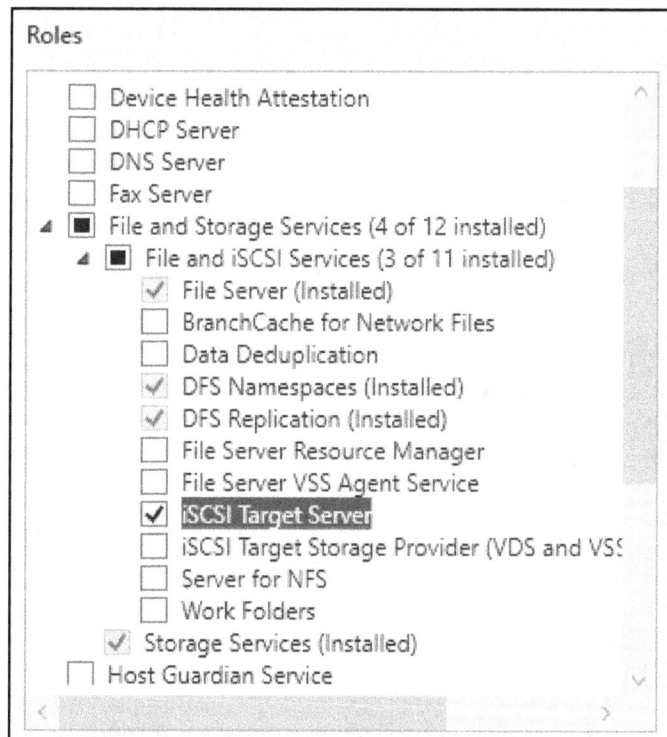

4. Click **Next, Next**, and **Install** to finish putting this new role into place.

5. In the left pane of Server Manager, click on **File and Storage Services**. Then click on **iSCSI**.

6. From the **Tasks** menu located in the far right corner, click on **New iSCSI Virtual Disk...**.

7. Choose a location for this iSCSI target to reside. I am going to utilize my D volume for this storage:

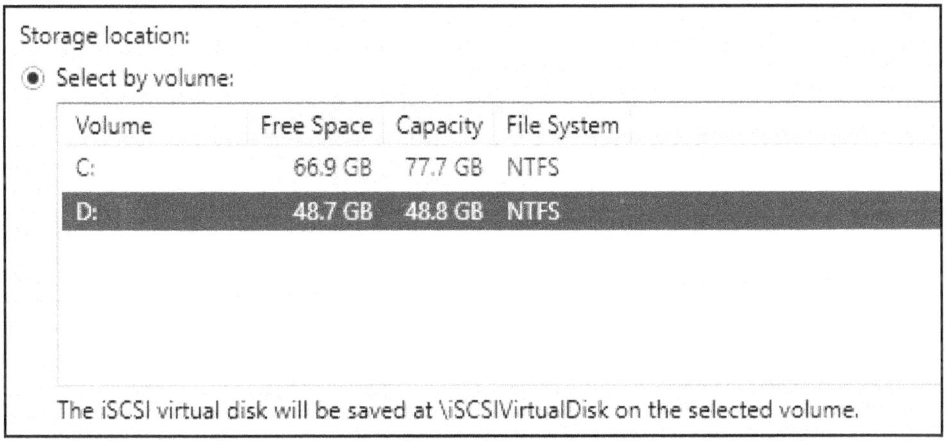

Storage location:

⦿ Select by volume:

Volume	Free Space	Capacity	File System
C:	66.9 GB	77.7 GB	NTFS
D:	48.7 GB	48.8 GB	NTFS

The iSCSI virtual disk will be saved at \iSCSIVirtualDisk on the selected volume.

8. On the next screen, specify a name for your iSCSI virtual disk. You can see that it is going to create and utilize a VHDX file for this storage. Nice!

9. Now we specify the **iSCSI Virtual Disk Size**. Read over the text on this screen so that you understand the different types of disks and sizing available to you. For our recipe, we are setting up a **Fixed size** disk with a size of 10 GB:

Free space: 48.7 GB

Size: `10` `GB  ˅`

◉ Fixed size

This type of disk provides better performance and is recommended for servers running applications with a high level of disk activity. The virtual hard disk is created using the size of the fixed virtual hard disk. It does not change when data is added or deleted.

☑ Clear the virtual disk on allocation

> Note: Un-selecting is NOT RECOMMENDED. Clearing a disk to zero will remove any fragments of data that remained on underlying storage, thus protecting from information leaks.

○ Dynamically expanding

This type of disk provides better use of physical storage space and is recommended for servers running applications that are not disk intensive. The .vhdx file is small when the disk is created and grows as data is written to it.

○ Differencing

This type of disk is associated in a parent-child relationship with another disk that you want to leave intact. You can make changes to this virtual hard disk without affecting the parent disk and easily revert the changes later.

Parent virtual disk path:

`                                                              ` `Browse...`

---

10. Since this is our first iSCSI target on this server, the **New iSCSI target** option should be selected for you. Click **Next**.

11. Create a name for the iSCSI target. This is the name that you will use on the iSCSI initiator server later in order to connect to the storage. I am calling mine `Database1`.

12. Now on the **Access Servers** screen, click the **Add...** button in order to specify which initiators will later connect to this target. We are going to connect to this storage from a server called FILE2, so I am adding that server to the list here:

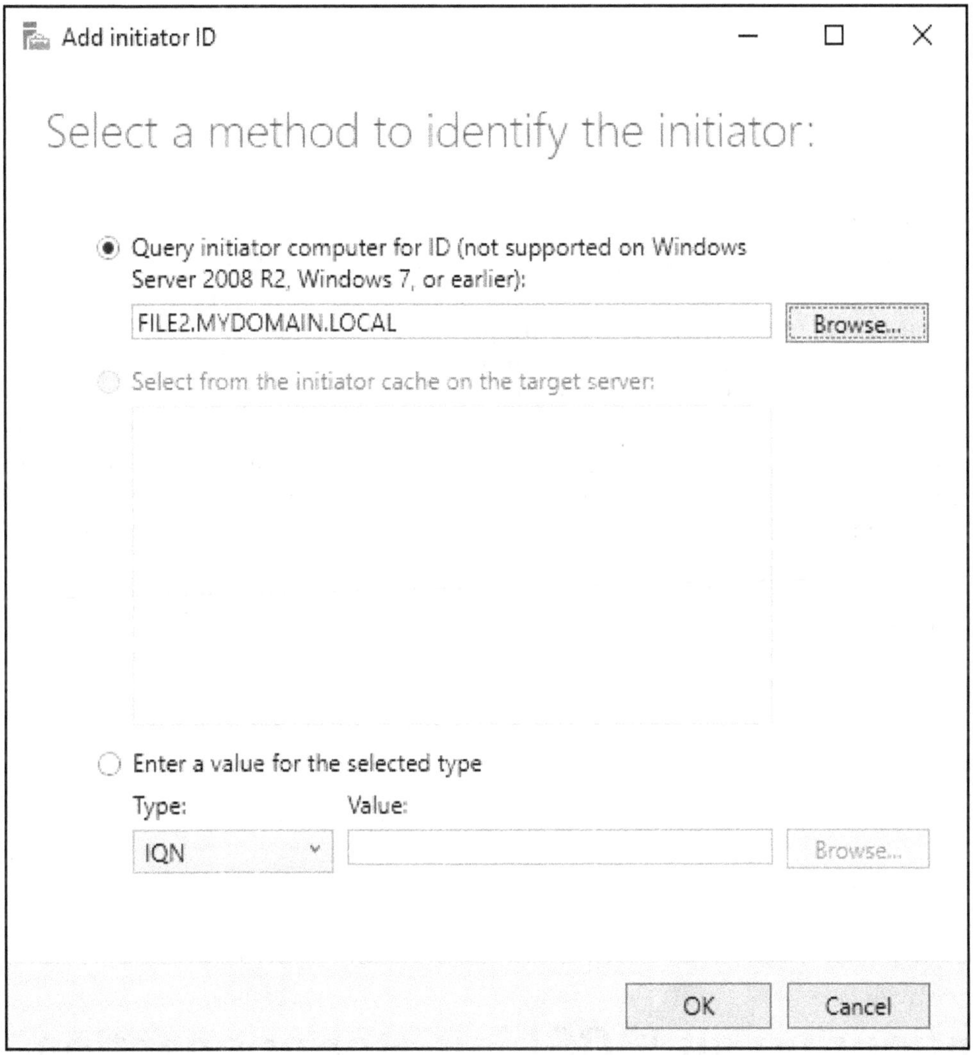

📠 Add initiator ID   —   □   ✕

Select a method to identify the initiator:

◉ Query initiator computer for ID (not supported on Windows
    Server 2008 R2, Windows 7, or earlier):

FILE2.MYDOMAIN.LOCAL	Browse...

○ Select from the initiator cache on the target server:

○ Enter a value for the selected type

Type: Value:

IQN ⌄		Browse...

     OK   Cancel

---

13. When you add a server to this list and click **OK**, you will notice that it is specified on the **Access Servers** screen with an **iSCSI Qualified Name** (**IQN**) value that you did not specify. This is a unique identifier for the server to the iSCSI environment and is a normal behavior. Go ahead and click **Next**.

14. If you would like to utilize CHAP or Reverse CHAP in order to authenticate connections between the initiator and target, you can use the next screen to specify user names and passwords for those authentications. For the purposes of testing this out quickly and in a simple manner, we are not setting anything on this page and are only clicking **Next**.

15. Review the settings and click the **Create** button to finish setting up your iSCSI target. This server is now running as a target and is waiting for a connection to it from our iSCSI initiator server.

How it works...

In this recipe, we are starting to figure out how iSCSI might benefit our environment. In addition to the scenario I discussed, where our database server requires a constant drive letter connection to remote storage, there are some other common utilizations for iSCSI connections. You could use iSCSI connections in order to consolidate storage. For example, take multiple servers that have locally attached storage and map them to iSCSI storage blocks. You could then move the physical storage to your iSCSI target for all application servers involved. They would still access the same data, and the applications running on those servers wouldn't know any different, but the physical storage would now be consolidated into a centralized area for safekeeping and better data management.

iSCSI is also an interesting use case for diskless booting. You could equip diskless computers with NICs that are iSCSI-ready, and those computers could boot over the network, over iSCSI, to virtual disks sitting on the iSCSI target.

See also

Check out the following links for some more great information on iSCSI:

- http://technet.microsoft.com/en-us/library/hh848272.aspx
- http://technet.microsoft.com/en-us/library/dn305893.aspx

Configuring an iSCSI initiator connection

Turning on your first iSCSI target is great, but so far you aren't using that storage for anything. Let's take it a step further and connect a server to that storage so that it can start to be used. The device connecting to an iSCSI target is called an **iSCSI initiator**. We are going to take a file server in our environment and configure it to connect over the network using iSCSI to our target server. When finished, we will have a new hard disk *attached* to our server, even though it is really just block storage from the iSCSI target that is being accessed via the network.

Getting ready

We have already configured one Windows Server 2016 to be an iSCSI target, and are now configuring a second 2016 box as our iSCSI initiator that will be connecting to the target.

How to do it...

Follow along to create the iSCSI initiator connection on our FILE2 server:

1. Launch **Server Manager**. Open up the **Tools** menu and choose **iSCSI Initiator**.
2. If you have never tried using iSCSI on this machine before, you will receive a message that the Microsoft iSCSI service is not running. To start the service and make sure it continues to start on subsequent boots, click **Yes**:

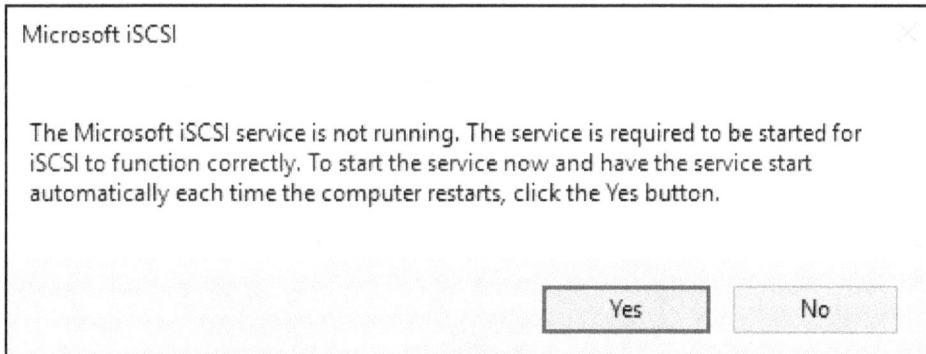

Microsoft iSCSI

The Microsoft iSCSI service is not running. The service is required to be started for iSCSI to function correctly. To start the service now and have the service start automatically each time the computer restarts, click the Yes button.

[Yes]   [No]

---

3. Currently, there is nothing listed in the **Targets** tab, which opens by default. Move over to the **Discovery** tab and click on the **Discover Portal...** button.

4. Type in the name of the server where you have an iSCSI target running and click **OK**. Now move back over to the **Targets** tab of the **iSCSI Initiator Properties** screen:

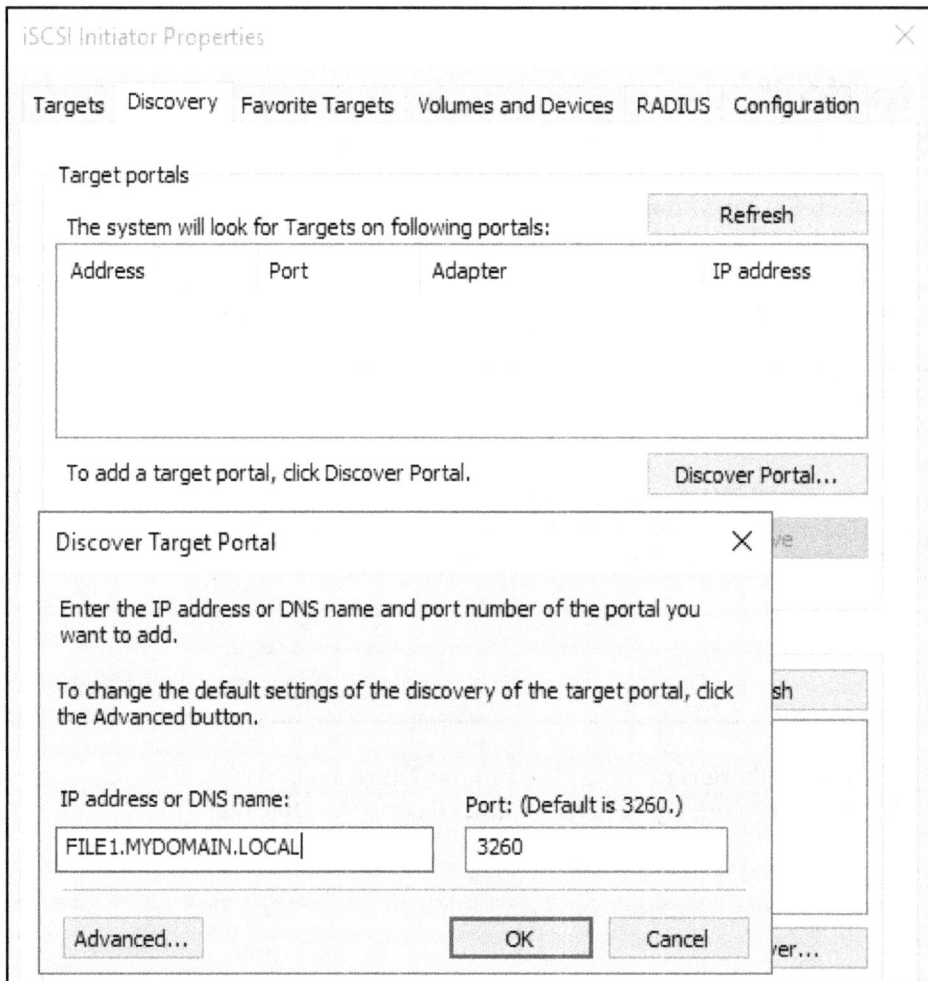

iSCSI Initiator Properties ✕

Targets   Discovery   Favorite Targets   Volumes and Devices   RADIUS   Configuration

Target portals

The system will look for Targets on following portals: Refresh

Address	Port	Adapter	IP address

To add a target portal, click Discover Portal.   Discover Portal...

Discover Target Portal ✕

Enter the IP address or DNS name and port number of the portal you want to add.

To change the default settings of the discovery of the target portal, click the Advanced button.

IP address or DNS name: Port: (Default is 3260.)

FILE1.MYDOMAIN.LOCAL   3260

Advanced...   OK   Cancel

5. The iSCSI connection is now shown on the **Targets** tab by its IQN number. Currently, the status is set to **Inactive**. Select this connection and click on the **Connect** button:

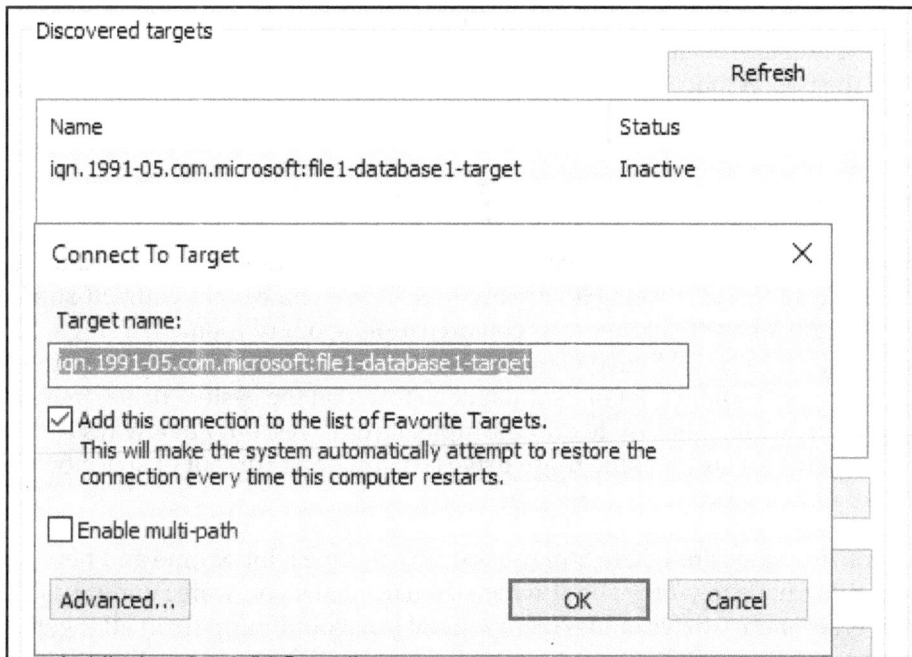

Discovered targets

| | Refresh |

Name	Status
iqn.1991-05.com.microsoft:file1-database1-target	Inactive

Connect To Target   ✕

Target name:

iqn.1991-05.com.microsoft:file1-database1-target

☑ Add this connection to the list of Favorite Targets.
   This will make the system automatically attempt to restore the connection every time this computer restarts.

☐ Enable multi-path

| Advanced... | | OK | Cancel |

6. Click **OK** to finish connecting to this iSCSI target. Make sure to leave the checkbox enabled for **Add this connection to the list of Favorite Targets** so that the connection is persistent and reconnects following server reboots.

How it works...

We have now connected our iSCSI initiator to our iSCSI target, and if you open any of the normal hard disk management tools such as Disk Management on your initiator server, you will see the new *disk* listed and available! You can then manipulate this storage like you would with any other physical storage, including turning it into a permanent drive letter available to the operating system.

It is important to note that an iSCSI initiator is often used without a Windows Server 2016 iSCSI target server being at the other end of the connection. One of the great things about iSCSI is that it doesn't care about what kind of storage you are connecting to, as long as that storage supports being accessed via iSCSI. There are many SAN technologies that you can acquire, or may already have running in your environment, which you can tap into by using the iSCSI initiator on your Windows Server. This gives you the ability to consume storage from the non-Windows SAN device on your Windows application and file servers.

Configuring Storage Spaces

Storage Spaces is an incredibly cool technology that isn't flaunted or marketed on its own; it just does its job and does it well. How many times have you caught yourself stuck between a rock and a hard place because you are running out of room on a single hard drive on one of your servers? I have plenty of times, especially working with technologies like RDS, which may contain a lot of user data all stored on the system drive. In most current server hardware, it is easy to add multiple hard drives, but not always easy to decide how to partition and volume those drives so you don't run out of space on C: while having 200 GB of free space on D:.

These kinds of situations are where Storage Spaces can save a lot of time and headaches. What if you didn't have to worry about what size hard disks you were running as your primary drive, secondary drive, and so on? What if you could lump them all together and utilize the storage out of one big bucket, or pool, as you will? This is exactly what we can accomplish with Storage Spaces in Windows Server 2016. You combine multiple physical hard disks into a storage pool, and then within that pool you can create one or many volumes to consume that storage space. The multiple disks combine storage to behave as one large drive, with options for RAID-style redundancy built into the storage pool configuration. Let's work together to combine a few hard drives together and create a new single volume to be used by the operating system.

Getting ready

We are going to configure Storage Spaces on our FILE2 server, which is running Windows Server 2016.

How to do it…

To enable Storage Spaces on your server use the following steps:

1. Make sure you have hard drives connected that you intend to utilize for your storage pool. On our FILE2 server, I have added three new drives, all of various sizes.
2. Launch **Server Manager** and click **File and Storage Services** from the left window pane.
3. First, click on **Disks** and make sure that we can see the new drives that we are going to combine together to make a storage pool:

	Volumes

Number	Virtual Disk	Status	Capacity	Unallocated	Partition
▲ FILE2 (5)					
0		Online	127 GB	0.00 B	MBR
1		Online	127 GB	127 GB	Unknown
2		Online	50.0 GB	50.0 GB	Unknown
3		Online	30.0 GB	30.0 GB	Unknown
4		Offline	10.0 GB	10.0 GB	Unknown

Disks / Storage Pools / Shares / iSCSI / Work Folders

4. Now that we have confirmed our disks our visible within Windows, go ahead and click on **Storage Pools**.
5. Open the **Tasks** menu and choose **New Storage Pool…**:

Name	Type	Managed by	Available to	
▲ Windows Storage (1)				
Primordial	Available Disks FILE2		FILE2	FILE2

TASKS — New Storage Pool… / Rescan Storage / Refresh

6. Enter something in **Storage Pool Name** and click **Next**.

7. Select the physical disks that you want to be included in this pool. I am going to add all three unused drives on my system:

Physical disks:

	Slot	Name	Capacity	Bus	RPM	Model	Allocation
☐		MSFT Virtual HD (FILE2)	10.0 GB	iSCSI		Virtual HD	Automatic ⌄
☑		Virtual HD (FILE2)	30.0 GB	ATA		Virtual HD	Automatic ⌄
☑		Virtual HD (FILE2)	50.0 GB	ATA		Virtual HD	Automatic ⌄
☑		Virtual HD (FILE2)	127 GB	ATA		Virtual HD	Automatic ⌄

Total selected capacity: 207 GB

ⓘ Selecting these disks will create a local pool.

8. Click **Next**, then click **Create**. Once finished building, you will be taken back to the **Storage Pools** section of Server Manager, where you can now see the new pool listed. The disks are now grouped together in a pool, but are not yet usable by the operating system.

9. Click on the name of your new storage pool in order to select it.

10. Now, down in the **Virtual Disks** section, drop down the **Tasks** menu and choose **New Virtual Disk...**.

11. Select the storage pool from which you want to create a volume and give it a virtual disk name.

12. On the **Storage Layout** screen, you need to choose the method that will be used for storing data on this new virtual disk. Depending on how many physical disks you have in the pool, you may have different options here. For our example, we need as much data storage space as possible and are not worried about redundancy across disks. So I will choose **Simple**:

Select the storage layout

	Layout:	Description:
Before You Begin		
Storage Pool	Simple	Data is striped across physical disks, maximizing capacity and
Virtual Disk Name	Mirror	increasing throughput, but decreasing reliability. This storage layout requires at least one disk and does not protect you from
Enclosure Awareness	Parity	a disk failure.
Storage Layout		
Provisioning		

13. I am going to dedicate the full amount of this storage space to the virtual disk right away, so I will leave the **Provisioning** screen selected for fixed provisioning.

14. On the **Size** screen, it will indicate how much free space exists in the pool. Simply size your new virtual disk to a number that is equal to or below that number. I am going to consume the full space of the pool, so I can either enter 87 GB as indicated, or choose the radio button for maximum size:

Free space in this storage pool: 87.0 GB
○ Specify size:

    87.0   GB ⌄

● Maximum size

15. Finish up the wizard and your new virtual disk will be created! When you finish this virtual disk creation wizard, you will be automatically placed inside **New Volume Wizard**. Walk through these steps or utilize a regular tool such as disk management in order to create your new volume, format it, and assign it a new driver letter. Then you can start using the new volume as you would with any regular volume inside Windows:

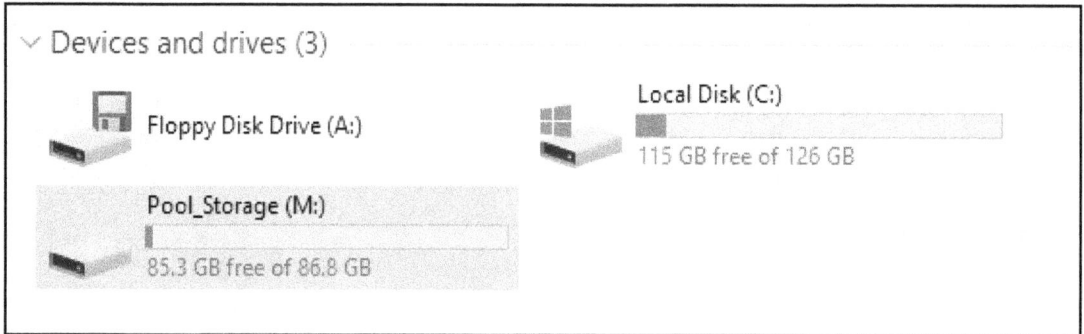

How it works...

By combining these three small hard drives into one storage pool, we can build a single volume that is larger than any one of the hard drives on their own. Storage Spaces can be used like this, or in a myriad of other ways, creating multiple pools and volumes at will, simply by bundling together groups of physical drives on the system.

Hard disk space utilization is something that we have traditionally planned very hard for. What size drives to get? Do they need to match? How large does each of my volumes need to be? Should I use RAID? Should I use dedicated hardware for that RAID? Storage Spaces is a way to bring many of those questions together, package them up, and throw them in the trash can.

See also

If you're interested in Storage Spaces, make sure to check out Storage tiers as well. On a Server 2016, if you combine SSD drives with regular mechanical drives, you can create a storage tier, which is sort of like those hybrid hard drives that come in laptops occasionally. The drives are combined into a single storage unit, but Windows will keep the most commonly accessed items on the SSD, making them faster to access. Here's a link to get you started with looking further into using storage tiers with Storage Spaces:

- http://technet.microsoft.com/en-us/library/dn387076.aspx#bkmk_tiers

Storage Spaces Direct

Expanding on the idea of Storage Spaces and the way that they enable the sharing of hard drives connected to a single system, Storage Spaces Direct is brand new in Windows Server 2016 and enables shared storage across multiple server nodes! In order to utilize Storage Spaces Direct, you need to employ Failover Clustering and will need a cluster of at least two servers. Each of those servers can contain multiple hard drives that can be utilized by Storage Spaces. The beauty of Storage Spaces Direct is that it enables you to utilize directly-connected drives, so we are not limited to expensive, complicated JBOD enclosures. Got a server with a few SATA drives plugged into it? This can be a node in your Storage Spaces Direct cluster! By using Storage Spaces Direct, you can join together up to 16 server nodes containing more than 400 drives in your centralized storage pool! The real beauty to a working Storage Spaces Direct environment is that expanding storage is as easy as adding additional drives into an existing server, or even by adding additional servers into your cluster. As soon as you add new capacity at either the drive or server node level, the storage pool that you have created with Sotrage Spaces Direct will automatically start expanding to include this new storage.

A primary goal for Storage Spaces Direct is to create a very resilient atmosphere for running Hyper-V virtual machines. By utilizing technologies such as SMB3 and the ReFS file system, you can configure Hyper-V to store its virtual machines on top of Storage Spaces Direct to ensure that you always have at least three copies of your data resident and available within the cluster.

The actual configuration of Storage Spaces Direct is not overly complicated, but it does involve more complexity than my simple test lab and the short pages of a cookbook recipe are able to contain. You will interface with Storage Spaces Direct via PowerShell and Failover Cluster Manager, though for best results those of you running SCCM will have the easiest time setting up and managing this new technology, as it is specifically integrated into System Center. Even though we aren't setting it up in this recipe today, if this is a topic that falls into your area of influence, make sure to continue reading with the following link:

- https://technet.microsoft.com/en-us/windows-server-docs/storage/storage-spaces/storage-spaces-direct-windows-server-2016

Storage Replica

Another new storage technology in Windows Server 2016 is Storage Replica. Contrary to Storage Spaces Direct, which is all about sharing storage between nodes, Storage Replica's job is to make sure that data is replicated quickly and securely between servers or clusters of servers. Storage Replica touts the ability to offer synchronous replication across multiple sites, with zero data loss. Another neat feature of Storage Replica is that you can swing workloads from one site to another prior to a disaster event, such as a severe storm warning in the city where your primary datacenter is located, when you want to swing connections to a backup datacenter before the storm hits.

There are three scenarios where Storage Replica can be utilized. First, if you are stretching a cluster across multiple physical sites, you can utilize Storage Replica to keep your cluster synchronized. Second, you can employ Cluster to Cluster replication to keep data up-to-date between two separate clusters that need to replicate together. Third, and perhaps the most important one to the SMB customer, is the Server to Server mode of Storage Replica. This enables synchronous and asynchronous replication between two servers, not necessarily in any kind of cluster scenario.

Given the robust capabilities of Storage Replica, there is a good chance that it may someday replace DFSR as the server administrator's tool of choice for replicating data between servers. One requirement that is important to point out, which does not apply to DFSR, is that we need some pretty low latency between datacenters in order to utilize Storage Replica. As I write this, the current recommendation is under 5ms between the sites. As with any brand new technology, some time will have to pass before large production environments will choose to move over to Storage Replica for handling all of their sensitive and critical data, but I encourage you to look over this additional information and start making use of it now:

- https://technet.microsoft.com/en-us/windows-server-docs/storage/storage-replica/storage-replica-overview

Turning on data deduplication

Deduplication is something that we as people do naturally. Every once in a while, you clean out the refrigerator, right? And if there are seven half-empty bottles of ketchup, you probably deduplicate that and throw some away. Or your closet. If you dig around and find thirty blue shirts, chances are that you can part with a few to save some space. These things make common sense, and so does deduplication when talking about the data that is stored on our servers.

Starting with Windows Server 2012, data deduplication became possible at the filesystem level. When enabled, Windows runs scheduled optimization jobs that search for duplicate files and data, and consolidates them. If you have two copies of the same file, stored in two different locations, all that is doing is consuming extra hard disk space. Data deduplication removes the secondary copy and utilizes the primary whenever that file is called for from either location on the disk.

In Server 2016, we have the ability to extend this deduplication into Hyper-V, specifically for VDI-type deployments. This is huge! Think about all of the different VDI systems that are going to be spun up by that system. With so many similar systems running under the same drive context, there is the potential to have thousands of duplicated files, and all duplicated numerous times. In this recipe, we are going to walk through the steps to enable data deduplication on a server so that you can start trying this out in your own environments.

Getting ready

We will be enabling data deduplication on a single server for this recipe, running Windows Server 2016, of course.

How to do it...

To enable data deduplication on our server, follow these steps:

1. Open up **Server Manager** and click on the **Add roles and features** link.
2. Click **Next** until you get to the **Select server roles** screen.

3. Expand **File and Storage Services | File and iSCSI Services** and check the box next to **Data Deduplication**:

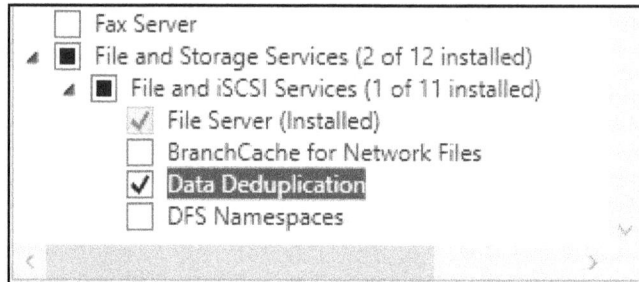

4. Finish the wizard in order to complete the installation of the deduplication role.
5. Now in the left pane of Server Manager, click on **File and Storage Services**.
6. Click on **Volumes**.
7. Right-click on a data volume and choose **Configure Data Deduplication...**:

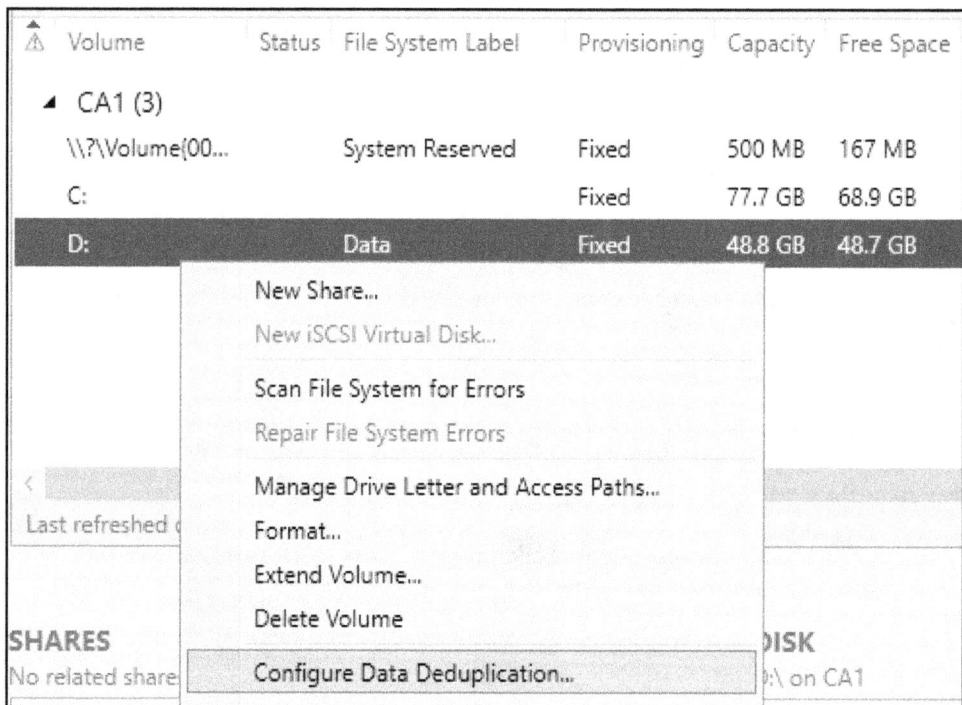

8. Click on the **Data deduplication** drop-down box and specify whether you are intending to run deduplication on a **General purpose file server**, **Virtual Desktop Infrastructure (VDI) server**, or **Virtualized Backup Server**. If you test out selecting one or the other, you will notice that the default list of file extensions to exclude from deduplication changes automatically. These are the file types that Microsoft has determined need to be excluded from deduplication in order for it to run effectively.

9. If there are any specific files or folders that you want the deduplication process to leave alone, you can specify them here as exclusions. There is also a button named **Set Deduplication Schedule...** where you can specify the times of day that the optimization jobs run to consolidate the data:

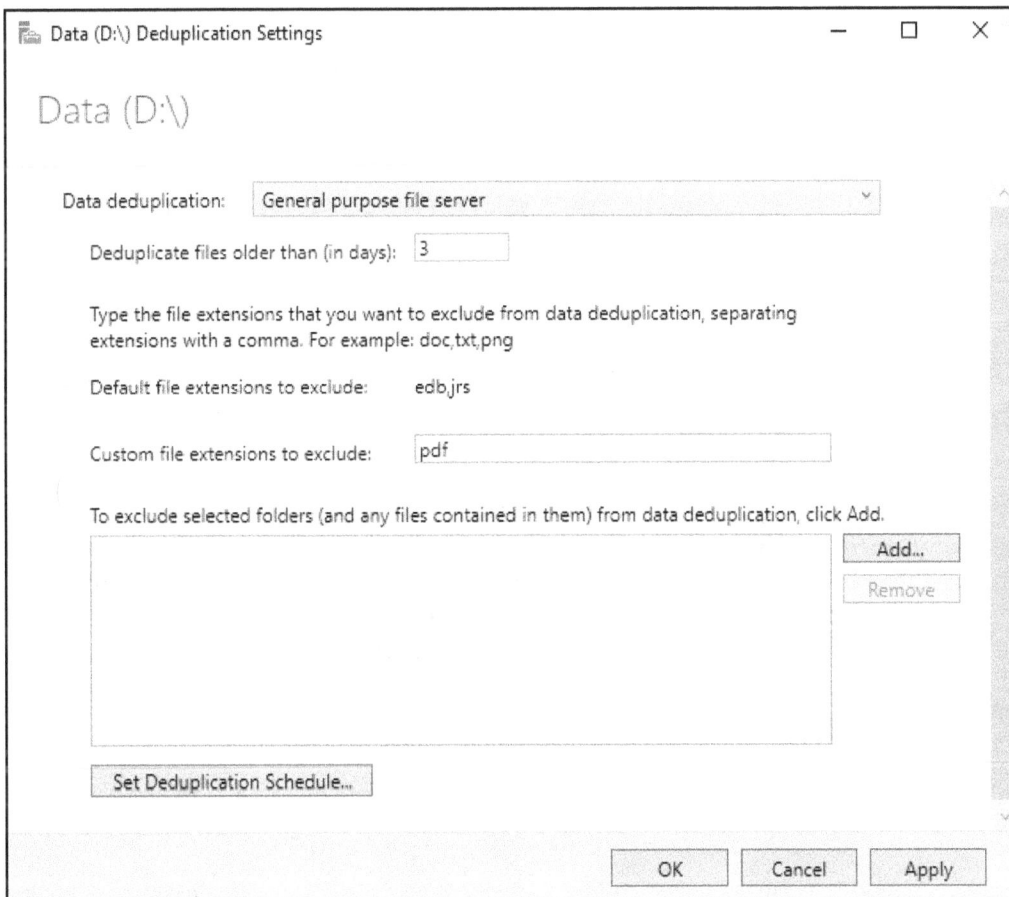

Data (D:\) Deduplication Settings   —   □   ✕

Data (D:\)

Data deduplication:	General purpose file server ⌄
Deduplicate files older than (in days):	3

Type the file extensions that you want to exclude from data deduplication, separating extensions with a comma. For example: doc,txt,png

Default file extensions to exclude: edb,jrs

Custom file extensions to exclude: pdf

To exclude selected folders (and any files contained in them) from data deduplication, click Add.

Add...

Remove

Set Deduplication Schedule...

OK   Cancel   Apply

How it works...

Data deduplication is very easy to enable, but can be a powerful tool for saving disk space on your file servers. A graph available in one of the following links displays Server 2012 R2 deduplication statistics in terms of space-saving percentages for different kinds of data. These numbers are quite a bit larger than I expected to see, around 50 percent for general file shares and over 80 percent for VHD libraries! In Windows Server 2016, we now have support for even larger volumes and files, so the data savings are even greater. We can now support volumes up to 64TB, and individual files up to 1TB! Try data deduplication on some of your own systems and watch your available disk space start to increase.

See also

Check out the following links for additional information on data deduplication in Windows Server 2016:

- `http://technet.microsoft.com/en-us/library/hh831434.aspx`
- `http://blogs.technet.com/b/filecab/archive/2013/07/31/extending-data-deduplication-to-new-workloads-in-windows-server-2012-r2.aspx`

Setting up Windows Server 2016 work folders

Accessing data from wherever you happen to be is becoming more and more important with today's mobile workforce. Given this, it makes sense that more and more technologies are being designed to allow access to this data from more locations, and more device types. This is what Work Folders in Windows Server 2016 is all about. It is a way to publish access to files and folders to multiple device types that the users may be logging in to. These files are accessed via a web listener that is configured on the Work Folders file server, which enables this data to be accessed from inside or outside the corporate network, from both domain-joined and non-domain-joined systems.

Configuring a full-fledged Work Folders environment with all its moving parts and components is far too much data to be contained in a single recipe. Today we will focus on the steps that need to be taken on the file server itself in order to make it ready for hosting Work Folders. Make sure to check out the link provided at the end of this section in order to continue gaining knowledge on this subject. Once you get started with Work Folders and realize the benefits that it can provide, I have no doubt that you will also be tapping into Group Policy in order to roll some of these settings around, and working with a reverse proxy solution like the **Web Application Proxy (WAP)** in order to further enhance the capabilities that Work Folders can bring to the table.

Getting ready

Our work today is happening on a Windows Server 2016 that we use as a file server. Specifically, I am using the FILE1 server in the lab that we have been working with throughout this chapter. To fully configure Work Folders, you will also need the ability to acquire a valid SSL certificate and access to your public DNS environment in order to create a record.

How to do it...

Follow these steps to enable Work Folders in your environment:

1. Log in to your file server and launch Server Manager.
2. Choose the link for **Add roles and features**. Walk through the role installation wizard until you get to the **Select server roles** screen.
3. Navigate to **File and Storage Services** | **File and iSCSI Services**. Then check the box next to **Work Folders**. When you receive a pop-up message about adding the additional IIS feature required, make sure to click on the **Add Features** button.
4. Finish the wizard in order to install the Work Folders role on this server.
5. Once the role has finished installing, head back to Server Manager and navigate to **File and Storage Services** | **Work Folders**.

6. Drop down the **TASKS** menu and choose **New Sync Share...**:

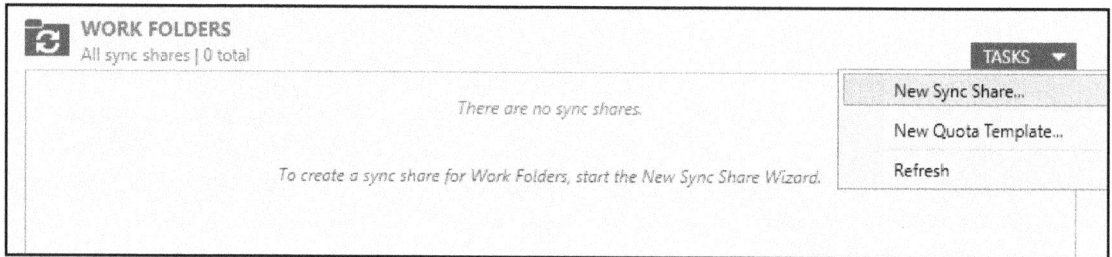

WORK FOLDERS
All sync shares | 0 total

TASKS ▼

| New Sync Share... |
| New Quota Template... |
| Refresh |

There are no sync shares.

To create a sync share for Work Folders, start the New Sync Share Wizard.

7. Choose or enter a path where you want the new Work Folders to be stored. This is the location on our file server that will be populated by folders that are named after our users. If you have already set up a folder and shared it, you will see it in the list to choose from. I have not yet set up any such folder, and so I am going to type in the location where I want the wizard to create a new folder for me:

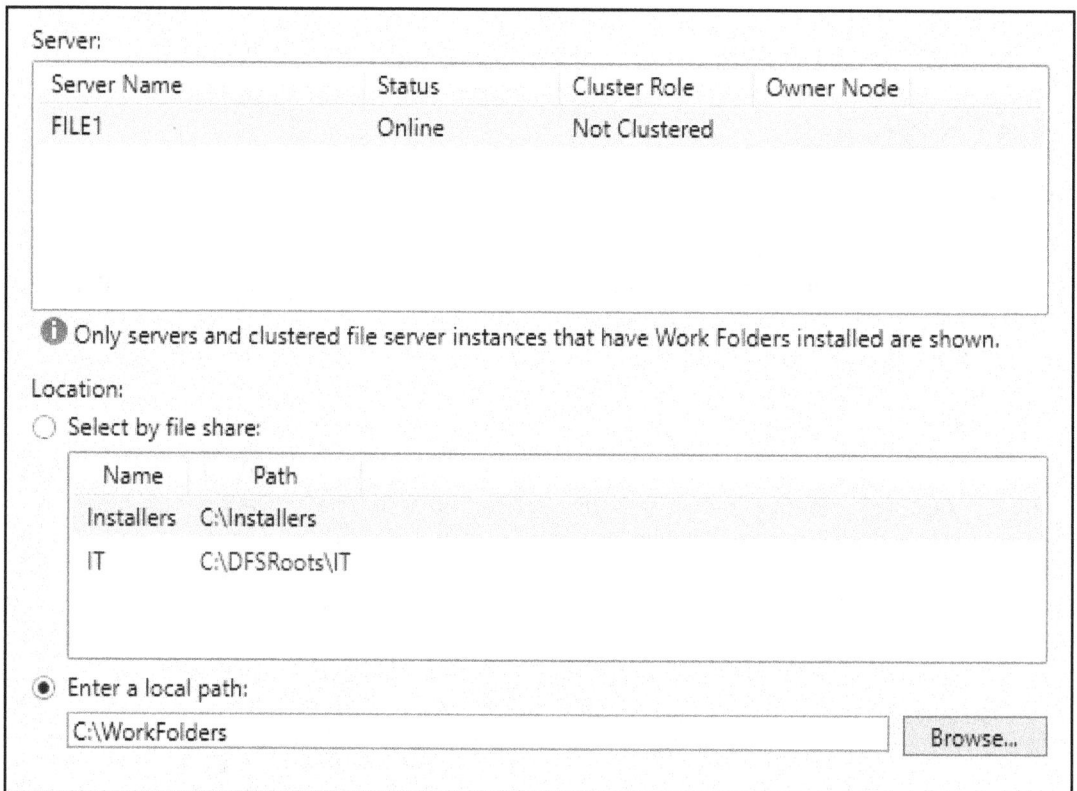

Server:

Server Name	Status	Cluster Role	Owner Node
FILE1	Online	Not Clustered	

ⓘ Only servers and clustered file server instances that have Work Folders installed are shown.

Location:

○ Select by file share:

Name	Path
Installers	C:\Installers
IT	C:\DFSRoots\IT

⦿ Enter a local path:

C:\WorkFolders

Browse...

8. Click **Next**, and if you entered the location of a folder that did not yet exist, you will be prompted with a confirmation box asking whether you want the new folder to be created. Go ahead and click **OK** on that message.

9. On the **User Folder Structure** screen, you choose how the user's folders will be named within our Work Folders sync share. Each user that utilizes Work Folders will get their own folder set up inside our share. These individual username folders will be named via either their username alone, or by their `username@domain`. In a lot of environments, you can get away easily enough with only the username alias. If you have users that will be accessing Work Folders from multiple domains, then you have the potential for conflict between usernames and should choose `alias@domain`. Additionally, on this screen, you can opt to sync only a particular subfolder for the users. For example, if you want their `Documents` folder to be synced across all of their devices but don't care about the other folders such as `Pictures` and `Music`, you could specify only `Documents` on the line here.

10. Specify a name for **Sync Share** and click **Next** again.

11. For the **Sync Access** screen of the wizard, we need to define which users and groups have access to use this sync. I created an Active Directory Security Group called **WorkFolders** and placed my users inside that group. So on this screen, I will simply specify my WorkFolders group:

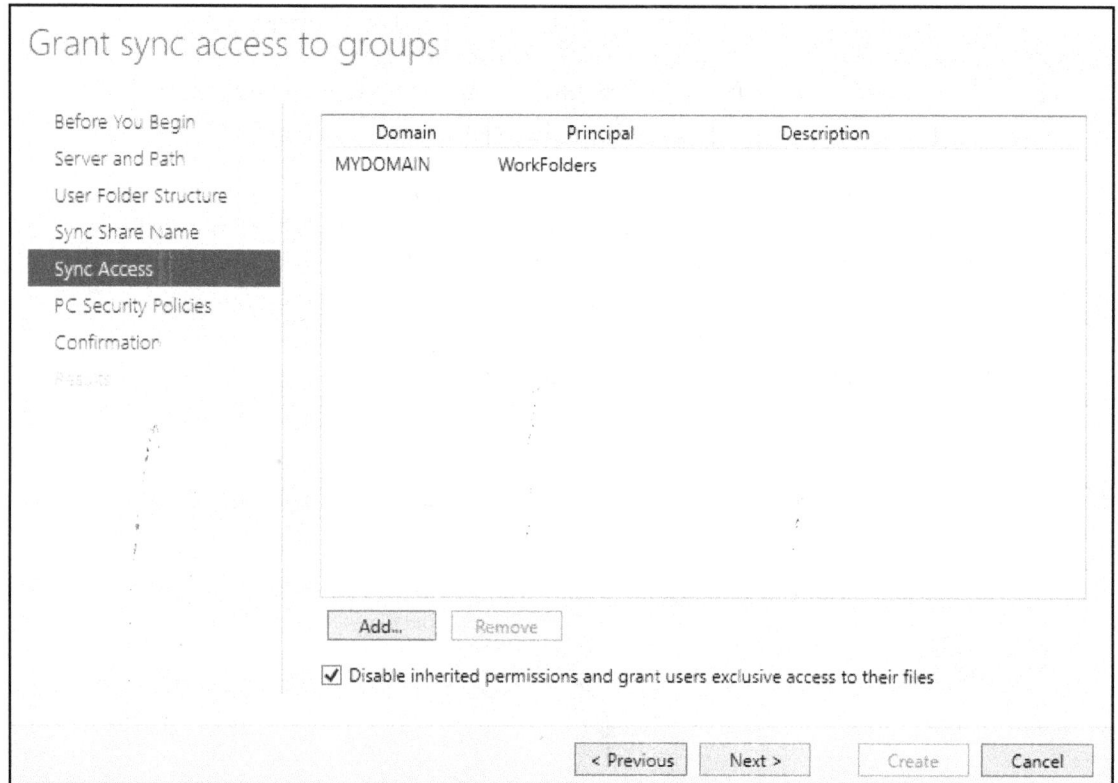

Note the checkbox near the bottom of this screen. If you leave the box enabled for **Disable inherited permissions...** then users will be granted exclusive rights to each of their folders. This means that even administrators will not have access to these folders. If you would like to change that behavior and let the normal file system inherited rights persist, simply uncheck this box.

12. Click **Next, Next,** and then **Create**, and your new WorkFolder Sync Share will be created and ready for use.

13. Client devices will connect to Work Folders on this file server via HTTPS. In order to make that happen successfully, we need to configure a DNS record that points at this file server, and an SSL certificate to be bound to the web listener on the server.

14. On your public DNS, set up the name `workfolders.<yourdomain>` and point it at the IP address that will flow to this file server. For example, the best way to do this is to publish the web listener with a reverse proxy server of some kind; let's say that proxy server is running on the internet IP address 1.1.1.1. You would configure a DNS record for `workfolders.contoso.com` and point it at 1.1.1.1, then let the reverse proxy server bring that traffic inside the network and submit it to the file server where we have Work Folders running.

15. Install an SSL certificate that contains the appropriate `workfolders.contoso.com` name – replacing contoso.com with your domain name, of course – and bind it to the default web site on the Work Folders server. Since the full IIS Management Console is not installed with the Work Folders role, you can utilize the IIS Management tools from another server in your network in order to bind the certificate onto the default website. Alternately, you can use the following netsh command in order to bind the certificate to the site:

```
netsh http add sslcert ipport=<IP address>:443 certhash=<Cert
thumbprint>
    appid={CE66697B-3AA0-49D1-BDBD-A25C8359FD5D} certstorename=MY.
```

> Please note that the previous command should not be run exactly as shown here. There are variables in this netsh command that you need to adjust to your own environment. The IP address of the web server, `certhash`, and `appid` need to be adjusted to match your particulars.

16. Now WorkFolders is configured and listening on our file server. The next step is to configure our client computers to tap into this WorkFolders sync share. The process for accomplishing this is different depending on what client devices you are connecting, but the starting point for Windows 10 and 8.1 machines is **Control Panel | System and Security | Work Folders**.

How it works...

It is pretty easy to overlook Work Folders at first glance, thinking it is just another way to access the same data in a similar way as the folder sharing options that we have had around for years. However, looking more closely shows us that the ability to publish access to files and folders to both domain-joined systems and non-domain-joined systems, working from either the corporate network or from home, can be of enormous advantage. You could utilize Work Folders as a way to grant access to corporate data without needing to issue a company laptop. You could also grant access to file level details without the need to incorporate some form of VPN, which may give more access to a home computer than you are comfortable with handing out. There are numerous situations where a technology such as Work Folders could increase productivity for your users and the security of information within your IT infrastructure. One of the pain points of Work Folders in previous versions of Windows Server was that client computers were not notified of file changes for roughly 10 minutes after the changes were made. This is finally resolved in Windows Server 2016. As long as you are using 2016 on the server side and Windows 10 on the clients, file changes are now reflected as soon as they are generated. Make sure to check it out!

See also

Take a look at the following link for even more detailed information on setting up Work Folders:

- http://technet.microsoft.com/en-us/library/dn528861.aspx

11

Nano Server and Server Core

Anyone working with Windows servers should be familiar with Server Core, or at least the name. As we mentioned back in `Chapter 3`, *Security and Networking*, Server Core is an alternative installation method for Windows Server 2016. It enables you to build a Windows Server with significantly lower amounts of CPU, memory, and hard drive requirements. Nano Server is a new and exciting feature in Windows Server 2016, and also represents a pretty significant shift in the way that we interact with our servers. Nano Server is similar to Server Core, except that Nano Server takes things a step further. A big step further. Nano is almost headless. I say *almost* because, as we will explore together, there is a limited-access console that you can interface with, but the bulk of what is done on both Server Core and Nano Server happens remotely, from another server or from your local workstation. It is around this shift in the management mindset that many of our recipes will be focused today. Let's learn together some of the different ways in which we can take advantage of these smaller and more secure servers. This chapter will cover the following topics:

- Configuring Server Core from the console
- Switching between Server Core and Desktop Experience?
- Building your first Nano Server
- Exploring the Nano Server console
- Managing Nano and Core with Server Manager
- Managing Nano and Core using remote MMC tools
- Managing Nano and Core with PowerShell remoting

Introduction

I feel that this chapter is really important to include, not only because Nano Server is a brand new feature in Windows Server 2016, but also because I have the opportunity to work in new customer environments all the time and to get a feel for the way that they establish their networks and servers. Do you know what I find? That everyone is running their Windows Servers in the full GUI-based Desktop Experience mode. Now, there is nothing inherently wrong with that, but the fact that Server Core has been in existence since Windows Server 2008 and I have yet to encounter a production server in a customer environment that is running Server Core, tells me that either it doesn't work, which I know is untrue, or that people are simply scared of it because they haven't tried it out. I find that to be much more likely. If you haven't done any reading on these technologies, at this point you might be wondering why both Server Core and Nano Server are options. It sounds like they do essentially the same thing, right? Not exactly. Because of the incredibly small nature of Nano Server, there are very few roles that can be installed on it. While Microsoft is working to enable more workloads to run on Nano Server, at the time of writing, there are only a handful of tasks that it can be used for. So it's pretty specialized. If you want a very small, very secure server to provide specific functions in your network, Nano Server can be an incredibly useful way to go. On the other hand, if you need to build a server to host a role or service that is not currently possible with Nano Server, but you still want the lower resource footprint and higher security of a semi-headless server, Server Core fits the bill. You can run essentially anything on Server Core that you can run on Desktop Experience. The big difference is the way that you have to interact with that server for configuration and ongoing management. This is the part that most likely keeps folks away from using it in production. There is always that *what if?* What if something breaks and I can't figure out how to fix it? What if I can't get into it to manage it? I hope that after walking through these recipes today you will feel much more comfortable with building out a Server Core, knowing that you can manipulate it just as extensively as you can with a full Desktop Experience version of Windows Server 2016.

Configuring Server Core from the console

If you remember, we installed our first instance of Server Core in `Chapter 3`, *Security and Networking* but we didn't do much of anything with that server. In one of the screenshots, we displayed how you can flip the default command prompt over to PowerShell, and then run some commands such as the `Rename-Computer` cmdlet in order to set the hostname of the server to CORE1. Beyond that, nothing has been configured and our CORE1 server isn't performing any functions in our network yet. Let's walk through the standard items you can accomplish on any server when you bring it up for the first time in a domain network. Our hostname is already set, but we still need to configure an IP address and join it to our domain before we can really start doing anything with this new server.

Getting ready

I have a new server and have run through the installation of Windows Server 2016. During that install I chose the default selection for the Core version of Windows Server. Following installation, with the same process we used in `Chapter 3`, *Security and Networking*, I am now sitting at the console screen of my new server, wondering what to do next.

How to do it...

Here are some steps we can take to prepare our new Server Core machine for use in the corporate network:

1. Let's set ourselves an IP address on CORE1. I have decided that 10.0.0.15 is going to be the IP address used by this system. Now we simply need to figure out how to put that IP address into place on the NIC. Since PowerShell is available to us within Server Core, we could spend some time digging around in these cmdlets to figure out what our NIC ID is and set the IP address using purely PowerShell, but fortunately Server Core has a special interface which makes this process a little bit easier.

2. From the Command Prompt in the Server Core console, type `sconfig`. You will now be presented with a special set of tools running within the Command Prompt window that allow you to configure various aspects of the operating system.

```
Administrator: C:\Windows\system32\cmd.exe - sconfig                    _ ☐ ✕

======================================================================
                        Server Configuration
======================================================================

1) Domain/Workgroup:                    Workgroup:  WORKGROUP
2) Computer Name:                       CORE1
3) Add Local Administrator
4) Configure Remote Management          Enabled

5) Windows Update Settings:             DownloadOnly
6) Download and Install Updates
7) Remote Desktop:                      Disabled

8) Network Settings
9) Date and Time
10) Telemetry settings                  Enhanced
11) Windows Activation

12) Log Off User
13) Restart Server
14) Shut Down Server
15) Exit to Command Line

Enter number to select an option: _
```

3. Take note that you can even **Shut Down** or **Restart** your server from here. This is important to know, because otherwise there is not a clearly defined way to perform these functions in a Server Core. You could of course use the `shutdown` command, or the `Restart-Computer` cmdlet, which is the way I typically do it, but relying on `sconfig` for these kinds of administrative tasks can make your life a lot easier. We could have even used this to rename our server to CORE1 in the first place!

4. Press the number *8* on your keyboard, and then press *Enter*, in order to enter **Network Settings**.

5. Now type the **Index#** of the network card that you want to manipulate. If your server, like mine, only has one NIC, then you simply press the number 1.

6. You will be presented with the current configuration of that NIC. Now choose option 1 in order to **Set Network Adapter Address**.

```
Available Network Adapters

Index#  IP address      Description

  1     10.0.0.52       Microsoft Hyper-V Network Adapter

Select Network Adapter Index# (Blank=Cancel):  1


------------------------------------
    Network Adapter Settings
------------------------------------


NIC Index              1
Description            Microsoft Hyper-V Network Adapter
IP Address             10.0.0.52          fe80::65f7:942:5efe:7d4b
Subnet Mask            255.255.255.0
DHCP enabled           True
Default Gateway        10.0.0.254
Preferred DNS Server   10.0.0.1
Alternate DNS Server

1) Set Network Adapter Address
2) Set DNS Servers
3) Clear DNS Server Settings
4) Return to Main Menu


Select option:  1
```

7. Press *S* in order to set a **Static** IP address.

8. Type your new static IP address. I will type 10.0.0.15, and press Enter.

9. Continue with the steps to populate your **Subnet Mask** and your **Default Gateway**.

10. Your NIC has now been reconfigured with your new IP address! If you also need to set static DNS server addresses, go ahead and continue on with option number 2 from the prompt. Otherwise, press *4* in order to return to the main sconfig menu.

```
Administrator: C:\Windows\system32\cmd.exe - sconfig
Select option:  1


Select (D)HCP, (S)tatic IP (Blank=Cancel): s

Set Static IP
Enter static IP address: 10.0.0.15
Enter subnet mask (Blank = Default 255.0.0.0): 255.255.255.0
Enter default gateway: 10.0.0.254
Setting NIC to static IP...


----------------------------------
    Network Adapter Settings
----------------------------------


NIC Index                1
Description              Microsoft Hyper-V Network Adapter
IP Address              10.0.0.15          fe80::65f7:942:5efe:7d4b
Subnet Mask             255.255.255.0
DHCP enabled            False
Default Gateway         10.0.0.254
Preferred DNS Server
Alternate DNS Server

1) Set Network Adapter Address
2) Set DNS Servers
3) Clear DNS Server Settings
4) Return to Main Menu


Select option: _
```

11. Now that you are getting comfortable with sconfig, let's also use it in order to join our CORE1 server to the domain. Back at the main sconfig menu, choose option **1) Domain/Workgroup**.

12. Press *D*, which tells the server you want to join it to a domain.

13. Enter the name of your domain and press *Enter*.

14. Type a username. Then type the password into the command window that opens.

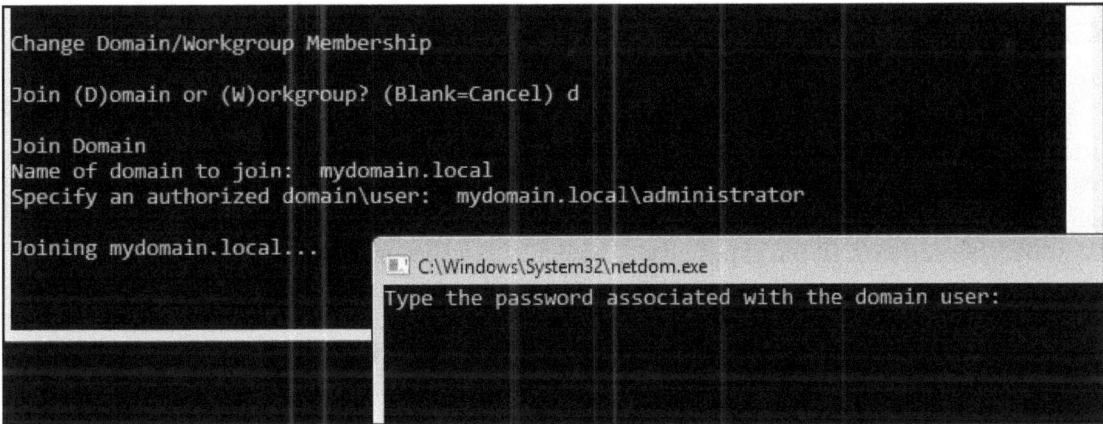

```
Change Domain/Workgroup Membership

Join (D)omain or (W)orkgroup? (Blank=Cancel) d

Join Domain
Name of domain to join:  mydomain.local
Specify an authorized domain\user:  mydomain.local\administrator

Joining mydomain.local...
```

C:\Windows\System32\netdom.exe

Type the password associated with the domain user:

15. You will be prompted to restart the computer. Go ahead and click on **Yes**, and our CORE1 server is now successfully joined to the domain!

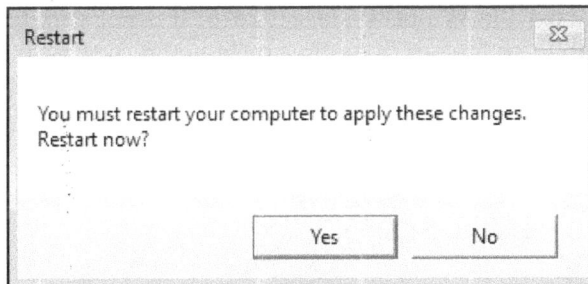

Restart

You must restart your computer to apply these changes. Restart now?

Yes   No

How it works...

There are a variety of ways that you can interface with and manage a Server Core instance, and we will talk about some more of them in upcoming recipes. However, there are certain core—no pun intended—functions that need to be accomplished first, right from the console, before you can start thinking about doing any remote management of your new servers. The sconfig tool is quick to open, very easy to use, and contains some powerful functionality for these initial configuration steps that we all must take on each of our new servers.

Switching between Server Core and Desktop Experience?

At what point do you need to decide whether your brand new server is going to be a Server Core, or a full Desktop Experience version with the traditional Windows graphical interface? It would be common sense to make this decision during the operating system installation process, right? Where you choose from the DVD installer which version of the OS you are putting into place? You are exactly right, except that in previous versions of Windows Server we had the capability to switch a live server back and forth between the two modes. If you had a full graphical version of a server running and wanted to change it over to a Server Core to get some enhanced security benefits, you could run a command and do just that. And the same is true in reverse; if you were running a Server Core and couldn't figure out how to configure something from the command interface, you could run another command which would change it over into the GUI version of the operating system. These commands were essentially just adding or removing some features within the operating system; basically you laid down or removed the graphical shell, which was the interface for Windows Server 2012.

Does that capability still exist in Windows Server 2016? It is not very common for Microsoft to implement new capabilities into an operating system and then yank them back out again later, but you never know until you try. Let's dig up those commands that could do the switching back and forth in the past, and test them out on a Server 2016. You may be surprised at the results.

Getting ready

Using our CORE1 server, which is already online, I am going to attempt to switch it from Server Core over to the Desktop Experience mode of Windows Server 2016, using some cmdlets that I know used to work in previous versions of the Windows Server operating system.

How to do it...

In order to test changing a Server Core into a Desktop Experience version of Windows Server 2016, I am opening up an administrative PowerShell window and going to use the following command:

1. Add-WindowsFeature Server-Gui-Shell, Server-Gui-Mgmt-Infra.

```
Administrator: C:\Windows\system32\cmd.exe - powershell

PS C:\> Add-WindowsFeature Server-Gui-Shell, Server-Gui-Mgmt-Infra
Add-WindowsFeature : ArgumentNotValid: The role, role service, or feature name is not valid:
'Server-Gui-Shell,Server-Gui-Mgmt-Infra'. The name was not found.
At line:1 char:1
+ Add-WindowsFeature Server-Gui-Shell, Server-Gui-Mgmt-Infra
+ ~~~~~~~~~~~~~~~~~~~~~~~~~~~~~~~~~~~~~~~~~~~~~~~~~~~~~~~~~~~~~~
    + CategoryInfo          : InvalidArgument: (Server-Gui-Shell,Server-Gui-Mgmt-Infra:String)
   [Install-WindowsFeature], Exception
    + FullyQualifiedErrorId : NameDoesNotExist,Microsoft.Windows.ServerManager.Commands.AddWin
   dowsFeatureCommand

Success Restart Needed Exit Code      Feature Result
------- -------------- ---------      --------------
False   No             InvalidArgs    {}

PS C:\>
```

2. Uh oh, that's not a very pretty error message to see first thing in the morning. It
   appears my `Add-WindowsFeature` cmdlet is attempting to run, but it cannot find
   the role or features that I am specifying. I know that these cmdlets worked in
   Server 2012, so it's looking like they may have been removed for Server 2016. Just
   to confirm, let us try the other direction. I am logging into one of my Windows
   Server 2016 Desktop Experience servers, and I am going to try changing it over to
   Server Core with the following command:

3. `Remove-WindowsFeature Server-Gui-Shell, Server-Gui-Mgmt-Infra`.

```
Administrator: Windows PowerShell                                    —   □   ×

PS C:\> Remove-WindowsFeature Server-Gui-Shell, Server-Gui-Mgmt-Infra
Remove-WindowsFeature : ArgumentNotValid: The role, role service, or
feature name is not valid: 'Server-Gui-Shell,Server-Gui-Mgmt-Infra'.
The name was not found.
At line:1 char:1
+ Remove-WindowsFeature Server-Gui-Shell, Server-Gui-Mgmt-Infra
+ ~~~~~~~~~~~~~~~~~~~~~~~~~~~~~~~~~~~~~~~~~~~~~~~~~~~~~~~~~~~~~~~~
    + CategoryInfo          : InvalidArgument: (Server-Gui-Shell,Serve
   r-Gui-Mgmt-Infra:String) [Uninstall-WindowsFeature], Exception
    + FullyQualifiedErrorId : NameDoesNotExist,Microsoft.Windows.Serve
   rManager.Commands.RemoveWindowsFeatureCommand

Success Restart Needed Exit Code      Feature Result
------- -------------- ---------      --------------
False   No             InvalidArgs    {}

PS C:\>
```

4. Well, unfortunately that error message looks very similar to the one we received when we tried adding the shell to the Server Core. Let's try just one more thing to make sure we have really lost this ability. In previous versions of Windows Server you could utilize these commands; alternatively, when swinging a server from the full graphical version over to Server Core, you could actually open up the Add/Remove Roles function and see those features listed right inside that screen. Let's walk through that wizard and check over the Features screen to see whether or not the one called **User Interfaces and Infrastructure** is even listed. As you can see in the following screenshot, it is no longer in our list of operating system features. It used to be listed right there, just below the TFTP Client.

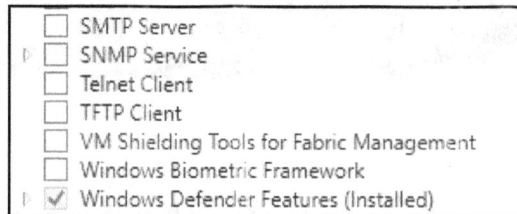

```
    □  SMTP Server
  ▷ □  SNMP Service
    □  Telnet Client
    □  TFTP Client
    □  VM Shielding Tools for Fabric Management
    □  Windows Biometric Framework
  ▷ ☑  Windows Defender Features (Installed)
```

How it works...

As we have proven with this recipe, the ability to change a server between Desktop Experience and Server Core no longer exists inside Windows Server 2016. While it would have been shorter and easier to simply state this fact, taking you through the example proves the point, and it also gives you the commands that you need to switch older versions of Windows Server back and forth, if that is something you were not familiar with in the past.

Building your first Nano Server

Building on the idea of Server Core, Nano Server is a brand new capability in Windows Server 2016 that enables you to create some incredibly small servers. The interface is almost truly headless, meaning that the majority of administration on these servers is going to be done remotely. We will discuss management in just a few minutes with the final recipes in this chapter, but the first thing you need to do in order to start working with Nano Server is to *build* a Nano Server! Putting together your first Server Core or full Desktop Experience machine is as simple as choosing the correct option from the installation DVD, but the process to build a Nano Server is quite different. Let's walk through the steps together to get you started.

Getting ready

Today we are trying to spin up a virtual machine that is running Nano Server 2016. Since there is no installation option for Nano Server on the Windows Server 2016 installation DVD, we will figure out together how to implement this new version of the operating system.

How to do it...

Rather than run through a traditional installation wizard, in order to spin up our first Nano Server we will be taking a few steps to build out a VHD file. This virtual hard disk will be compiled with all the data that it needs to be a Nano Server, and afterwards we can simply boot our new VHD as a virtual machine on any Hyper-V platform. Follow these steps to do it yourself:

1. Copy the Windows Server 2016 installation media onto your computer as an ISO file. Then go ahead and mount this ISO to your computer, which assigns it a drive letter. For example, I downloaded the ISO to my computer and simply double-clicked on it, and now I have a new D: drive on my computer that shows me the data contained within that ISO.

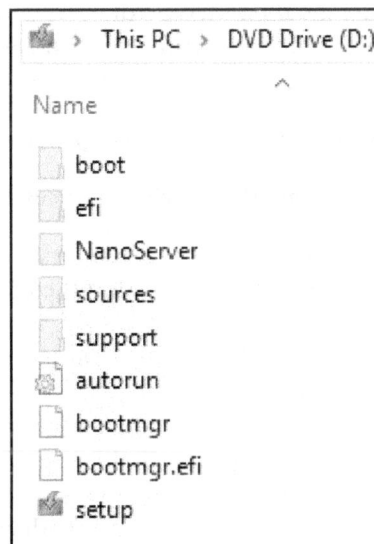

> This PC > DVD Drive (D:)
Name
boot
efi
NanoServer
sources
support
autorun
bootmgr
bootmgr.efi
setup

2. You can see there is a folder in the installer called **NanoServer**. Copy this folder and place it into the C: drive of your computer. You now have a `C:\NanoServer` folder on your machine that contains all the parts and pieces that Nano needs in order to build a VHD file.

3. Now open up an administrative PowerShell session.

4. Import the Generator script into the PowerShell session with the following command: `Import-Module -Name C:\NanoServer\NanoServerImageGenerator\NanoServerImageGenerator .psm1 -Verbose`.

```
Administrator: Windows PowerShell                                    —   □   ×
PS C:\> Import-Module -Name C:\NanoServer\NanoServerImageGenerator\NanoServerImageGe ^
nerator.psm1 -Verbose
VERBOSE: Loading module from path
'C:\NanoServer\NanoServerImageGenerator\NanoServerImageGenerator.psm1'.
VERBOSE: Importing function 'Edit-NanoServerImage'.
VERBOSE: Importing function 'Get-NanoServerPackage'.
VERBOSE: Importing function 'New-NanoServerImage'.
PS C:\> _
```

5. Next we run a single command to build out our VHD file. There are many different ways that this command can be run, with various switches and parameters that can change the outcome of your generated file. I am going to implement a pretty basic standard install of Nano Server to start experimenting with it. Use the following command to output a Nano Server virtual hard disk:

```
New-NanoServerImage -MediaPath D:\ -DeploymentType Guest -Edition
Standard
-TargetPath C:\NanoServer\NANO1.vhd -ComputerName NANO1
```

6. Some of the variables used here are pretty self-explanatory. I need to specify the path of my Windows Server 2016 installation files, which is my D drive, and I need to specify an output location for my new VHD file that is being created. I also have the opportunity right here in the command to give my new Nano Server a hostname, for which I specified NANO1. The last switch I included here was an `Edition`, and I chose `Standard`. If you needed a Nano Server running the Datacenter SKU, you could specify that information right in the command. The item here that is not as self-explanatory is the `DeploymentType` variable. For this you can specify either `Guest` or `Host`. Your decision here depends upon whether you want this Nano server to be running as a virtual machine, or on a physical host server. Most often we will be specifying `Guest` for this option.

7. After pressing *Enter* on the command, you are asked to specify a local administrator password for this new server, and then PowerShell will sit and work for a minute while it compiles and builds your new VHD.

```
Administrator: Windows PowerShell                                    —    □    ×
INFO    : Image 1 selected (ServerStandardNano)...
INFO    : Creating sparse disk...

Dismounting image...
    Processing

INFO    : Windows path (E:) has been assigned.
INFO    : System volume location: E:
INFO    : Applying image to VHD. This could take a while...
INFO    : Image was applied successfully.
INFO    : Making image bootable...
INFO    : Fixing the Device ID in the BCD store on VHD...
INFO    : Drive is bootable.  Cleaning up...
INFO    : Dismounting VHD...
INFO    : Closing Windows image...
INFO    : Done.
```

8. Once finished, you will see inside your C:\NanoServer folder that a brand new NANO1.VHD file exists. Next, simply create a new VM inside Hyper-V just like you would for any other server, and specify this new VHD as the hard disk for your virtual machine.

9. Boot up the server and you will be sitting at an unfamiliar console, which is your entrance into the world of Nano Server.

```
        User name:  _____
        Password:   _____
        Domain:     _____
```

How it works...

In this recipe, we learned how to use PowerShell in order to create a virtual hard disk on our computers, which can then be used to boot into a new instance of Nano Server. This is the first step you will need to take in order to start working with Nano Server and get one up-and-running so that you can start exploring inside the interface. Now that we have a Nano Server running, continue on with this chapter to look further into the administration and management of these servers. You may need to adjust your thinking a little bit as we start figuring out that remote management is a key part in the way that Nano Server works.

See also

If PowerShell isn't your thing, you are not alone, and Microsoft recognizes this. While we should all be striving to become more comfortable with using PowerShell on a daily basis, graphical tools still rule most datacenters. Just released is a new tool that will help you create Nano VHD files, by using your good old color monitor and mouse.

Nano Server Image Builder

Use the Nano Server Image Builder tool in order to create these Nano servers, or even to create a bootable USB installer for placing Nano Server onto physical hardware! Rather than having to explore and remember all of the switches that accompany the `New-NanoServerImage` cmdlet in PowerShell, you can now run this simple graphical tool and walk through a few wizards in order to spin out your new Nano. From what I've seen, the nicest feature of this image builder is the ability to choose which roles will exist on your new Nano server by using check-boxes, just like when you are choosing which roles you want to install on your Server 2016 running full Desktop Experience. For anyone who will be working with Nano Server, this tool is definitely something you are going to want to check out!

Here is a link to some additional information: `https://blogs.technet.microsoft.com/na noserver/2016/10/15/introducing-the-nano-server-image-builder/`. Here is a download link so you can try it for yourself: `https://www.microsoft.com/en-us/downloa d/details.aspx?id=54065`.

Exploring the Nano Server console

After getting your first Nano Server up-and-running, a logical next question to ask is *What now?*. With a traditional server you would set things such as the hostname and IP address, and probably join it to your domain. More than likely, once your Nano Server is established you will be heading down into the final recipes of this chapter to figure out the best ways to remotely administer this new machine, but until you have networking and domain membership established, you aren't going to be able to do much with the remote management tools. So is there any kind of console access on a Nano Server? Yes, but it is very limited. The tool that is presented in the console is called the **Nano Server Recovery Console**, and the capabilities provided by this tool are the focus of our current recipe.

Getting ready

We are going to be working from the console of the new Nano Server we just finished building. This server is plugged into our corporate network, which is running an Active Directory domain. If you remember, when we ran the command to compile our VHD file that is used by NANO1 we were able to set the hostname right there, so we should see that NANO1 name reflected already in the configuration.

How to do it...

Let's explore the Nano Server Recovery Console together:

1. Powering up your new Nano Server brings us to the login screen shown at the end of our previous recipe. Go ahead and login with the local administrator credentials that you specified during the VHD creation process.

2. Now, inside the recovery console we can see that the hostname of our NANO1 was set properly during the VHD creation. That is good news! And it appears we have just a few options available for us to choose from.

```
                         Nano Server Recovery Console
==================================================================================
Computer Name: NANO1
User Name:     .\administrator
Workgroup:     WORKGROUP
OS:            Microsoft Windows Server 2016 Standard
Local date:    Monday, October 17, 2016
Local time:    6:24 PM
- - - - - - - - - - - - - - - - - - - - - - - - - - - - - - - - - - - - - - - - -
> Networking
  Inbound Firewall Rules
  Outbound Firewall Rules
  WinRM




_____
Up/Dn: Scroll  |  ESC: Log out  |  F5: Refresh  |  Ctl+F6: Restart
Ctl+F12: Shutdown  |  ENTER: Select
```

3. We want to set an IP address on the system, so go ahead and choose the **Networking** option.

4. Select the NIC that you want to configure—my system only has one—and press *Enter*.

5. As indicated at the bottom of the screen, you must now press F11 in order to configure **IPv4 Settings** on this network interface.

6. I am currently configured for DHCP, but if I press the *F4* key to **Toggle**, I am able to change to a static IP address and define my own.

```
DHCP              [            Disabled           ]
IP Address        10.0.0.16_____
Subnet Mask       255.255.255.0_____
Default Gateway   10.0.0.254_____
```

7. Press *Enter* twice to save these settings.

8. Use the ESC key to get back to the main menus.

9. This time let's take a look inside **Inbound Firewall Rules**.

```
                              Firewall Rules
================================================================
Select an inbound rule to view
----------------------------------------------------------------
> File and Printer Sharing over SMBDirect (iWARP-In)
  Windows Remote Management (HTTP-In)
  Windows Remote Management (HTTP-In)
  Windows Remote Management - Compatibility Mode (HTTP-In)
  Remote Service Management (RPC)
  Remote Service Management (NP-In)
  Remote Service Management (RPC-EPMAP)
  File and Printer Sharing (NB-Session-In)
  File and Printer Sharing (SMB-In)
  File and Printer Sharing (NB-Name-In)
  File and Printer Sharing (NB-Datagram-In)
  File and Printer Sharing (Spooler Service - RPC)
  File and Printer Sharing (Spooler Service - RPC-EPMAP)
  File and Printer Sharing (Echo Request - ICMPv4-In)
  File and Printer Sharing (Echo Request - ICMPv6-In)
```

10. Looks like we have a good list of pre-defined firewall rules. By navigating into the properties of each of these rules, you will have the option to enable or disable the rule. Even though Nano Server is incredibly locked down right out of the gate, you can further deny the ability to contact this server via methods defined by the individual firewall rules.

11. Other than viewing firewall rules, the only other option you have inside the Nano Server Recovery Console is **WinRM**. Head into that piece of the management tool, and you will see a description that tells you this option is simply to reset the status of WinRM on this server. Since almost all the configuration of Nano Server is intended to be remote, having the WinRM service running and being allowed to communicate with this server is essential to getting your job done. If you have made some firewall tweaks and suddenly you can no longer connect to it with your remote management tools, this section of the recovery console is a quick way to set the WinRM settings and firewall rules back to factory defaults.

How it works...

The Nano Server Recovery Console is very limited, making these servers as close to *headless* as possible. However, there are certain things that you are just going to have to do from a console when starting up a new server, and so those bare minimums are the options presented here. Opening up the console of a Nano Server is going to be an extremely rare task, but it is one that you will most likely have to undertake just after building out a new Nano Server so that you can make those initial configurations.

Managing Nano and Core with Server Manager

So our console access for configuring a Server Core is pretty limited, and making changes at the console to a Nano Server only gives us four little options. Either we're missing something here, or Microsoft intended for us to be managing these servers differently. Queue the drumroll for remote management. Centralized administration of Windows Server operating systems is something that Microsoft really started pushing hard with the release of Server 2012, and it is increasingly important in Windows Server 2016. Tools like Server Manager are now becoming agnostic to the local machine that they are running on. You can use Server Manager on one server to manage a different kind of server halfway across the datacenter, without having to make any adjustments to the way that you are handling that administration. We can even use the RSAT tools to put a copy of Server Manager right on our Windows 8 or Windows 10 computers! Clearly the days of RDPing into every server should be diminishing. We are now technically capable of managing our servers from a single, central pane of glass. The question is—how many server admins are actually taking advantage of this functionality?

Getting ready

We have CORE1 and NANO1 up-and-running in the network. Now we are going to utilize Server Manager on a different server to manipulate these machines. I will be using another Windows Server 2016 for this task, which has the full Desktop Experience version of Windows server installed.

How to do it...

Follow these steps to manage Server Core or Nano Server right from inside Server Manager on another of your servers in the network:

1. Open **Server Manager**, click on the Manage menu near the top-right corner of the screen, and choose the option that says **Add Servers**.
2. When I click the **Find Now** button, I can see a list of my domain-joined servers in the network. Since I was able to join my CORE1 server to the domain from its console, I can see it in the list. Choose CORE1, and move it over to the **Selected** side of the screen.
3. This was easy for CORE1, but I do not see NANO1 in this list. That is because NANO1 is not yet joined to my domain. In order to add NANO1 to Server Manager, I will have to click on the **DNS** tab near the top of my screen, and manually enter the name of this server. Please note that I have already gone into DNS and created a host record for my NANO1 server pointing to the IP address of 10.0.0.16 in order to make this discoverable.

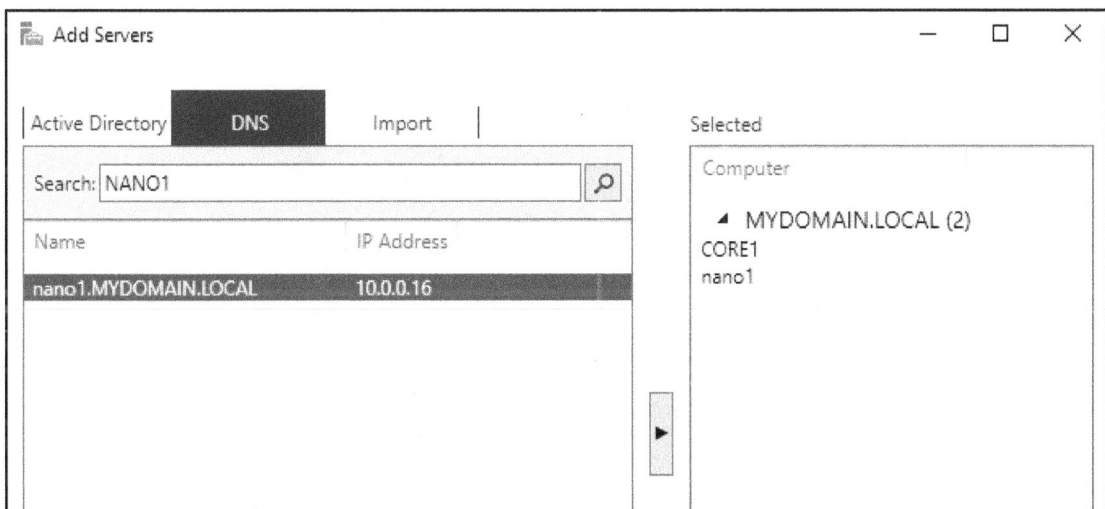

4. Now click **OK**, and both CORE1 and NANO1 are now configurable from within my local Server Manager window. By clicking on **All Servers**, you can see them both listed, and right-clicking on the servers gives me options to do things like openingComputer Management** on them.

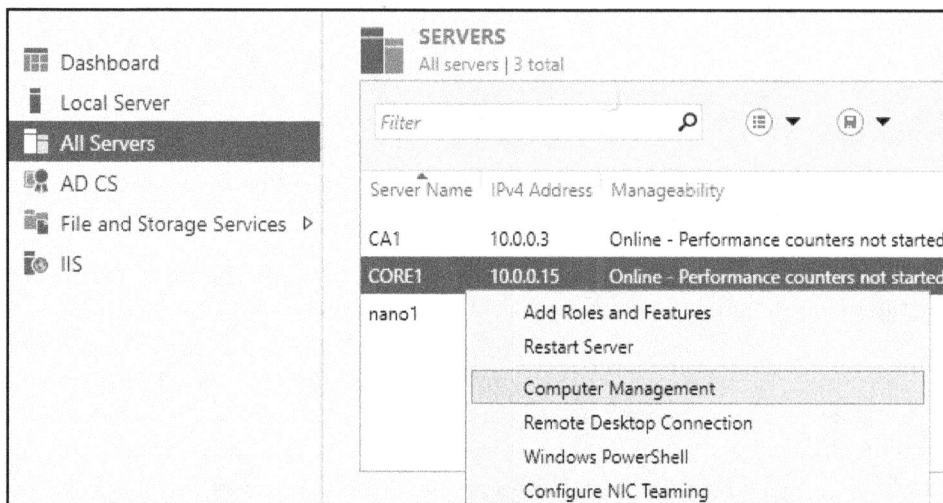

5. In fact, let's try making a change on one of our systems right now. I am using Server Manager on my CA1 server. I didn't choose CA1 for any particular reason, it was just a server that I happened to be logged into. Now that I have added CORE1 into Server Manager, I will right-click on it and choose the option that you can see in the screenshot for **Add Roles and Features**.

6. I am presented with the same**Add Roles and Features Wizard** that I would utilize to install a role on my CA1 server, except that when I walk through the wizard you can see that my default server destination for this new role or feature will be CORE1.

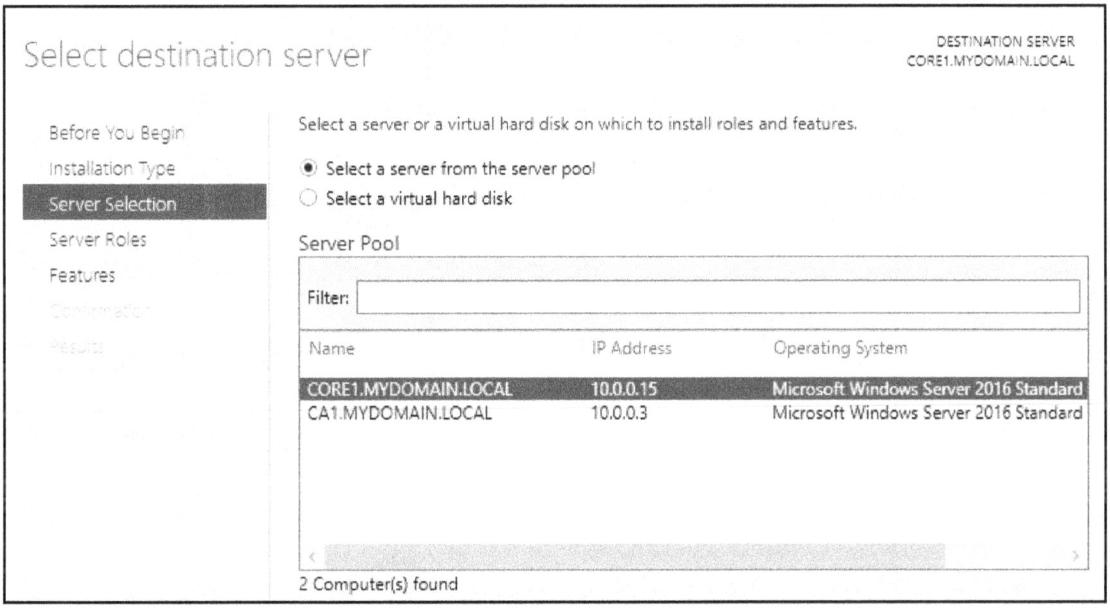

Select destination server

Before You Begin
Installation Type
Server Selection
Server Roles
Features
Confirmation
Results

Select a server or a virtual hard disk on which to install roles and features.

◉ Select a server from the server pool
○ Select a virtual hard disk

Server Pool

Filter:

Name	IP Address	Operating System
CORE1.MYDOMAIN.LOCAL	10.0.0.15	Microsoft Windows Server 2016 Standard
CA1.MYDOMAIN.LOCAL	10.0.0.3	Microsoft Windows Server 2016 Standard

2 Computer(s) found

7. For this example, I am going to use CORE1 to host a website. Therefore, I need to install the **Web Server (IIS)** role onto it. You can see in the following screenshot that our list of available roles is shorter than if we were running this wizard against a traditional server with Desktop Experience. These are the roles available to be installed onto a Server Core:

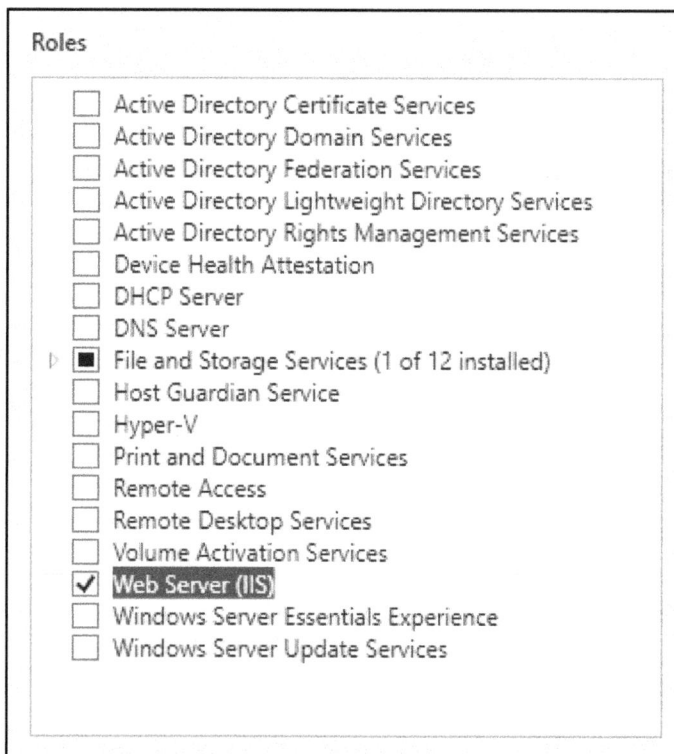

Roles

- [ ] Active Directory Certificate Services
- [ ] Active Directory Domain Services
- [ ] Active Directory Federation Services
- [ ] Active Directory Lightweight Directory Services
- [ ] Active Directory Rights Management Services
- [ ] Device Health Attestation
- [ ] DHCP Server
- [ ] DNS Server
- [▪] File and Storage Services (1 of 12 installed)
- [ ] Host Guardian Service
- [ ] Hyper-V
- [ ] Print and Document Services
- [ ] Remote Access
- [ ] Remote Desktop Services
- [ ] Volume Activation Services
- [✓] Web Server (IIS)
- [ ] Windows Server Essentials Experience
- [ ] Windows Server Update Services

8. Simply run through the wizard, and the Web Server role will be installed remotely onto our CORE1 server.

How it works...

There are certainly some useful configuration options inside Server Manager that you can use to push changes and settings to your headless servers, but it's not the only way. Continue reading through the recipes in this chapter to find some even more powerful options for tapping into your server configuration remotely. As you start navigating around inside Server Manager, you should also be aware that you may bump into some messages about the Windows Firewall rules needing to be adjusted on the remote computers. Server Core and Nano Server are both pretty locked down by default, enough so that even a trusted tool like Server Manager can't always communicate with those servers to the extent that is needed. You will occasionally have to log into the console of those Core and Nano servers in order to permit some firewall rules to be open and to allow Server Manager to do the tasks you are asking it to do.

Managing Nano and Core using remote MMC tools

Another powerful way to interact with servers that you are not logged into, or that you cannot log into in a traditional sense like Nano Server and Server Core, is to make use of the MMC tools from a remote system. By launching MMC and snapping in consoles, or by running the tools straight from the Administrative Tools folder and then specifying which server you want to interact with, you can continue with the centralized management mentality while making changes to systems you are not actively logged into. Let's test this out together.

Getting ready

I just finished using a remote copy of Server Manager to install the Web Server role onto CORE1. Now I want to make some changes to the default website running on CORE1. Because the console of a Server Core isn't going to allow me to simply login and open the IIS Management graphical tools, I am going to use the tools that are already installed onto my CA1 server instead.

How to do it...

It is possible to remotely administer the Web Server role running on CORE1. We will cover two different ways to go about this:

1. Open the **Microsoft Management Console (MMC).** I typically do this by invoking the Run prompt with WinKey + *R*, and then typing MMC.

2. Inside MMC, click the **File** menu and then choose **Add/Remove Snap-in....**

3. Scroll down until you find the snap-in called **Internet Information Services**. Choose that, and click the **Add** button in order to move it over to the **Selected snap-ins**.

4. Press the **OK** button.

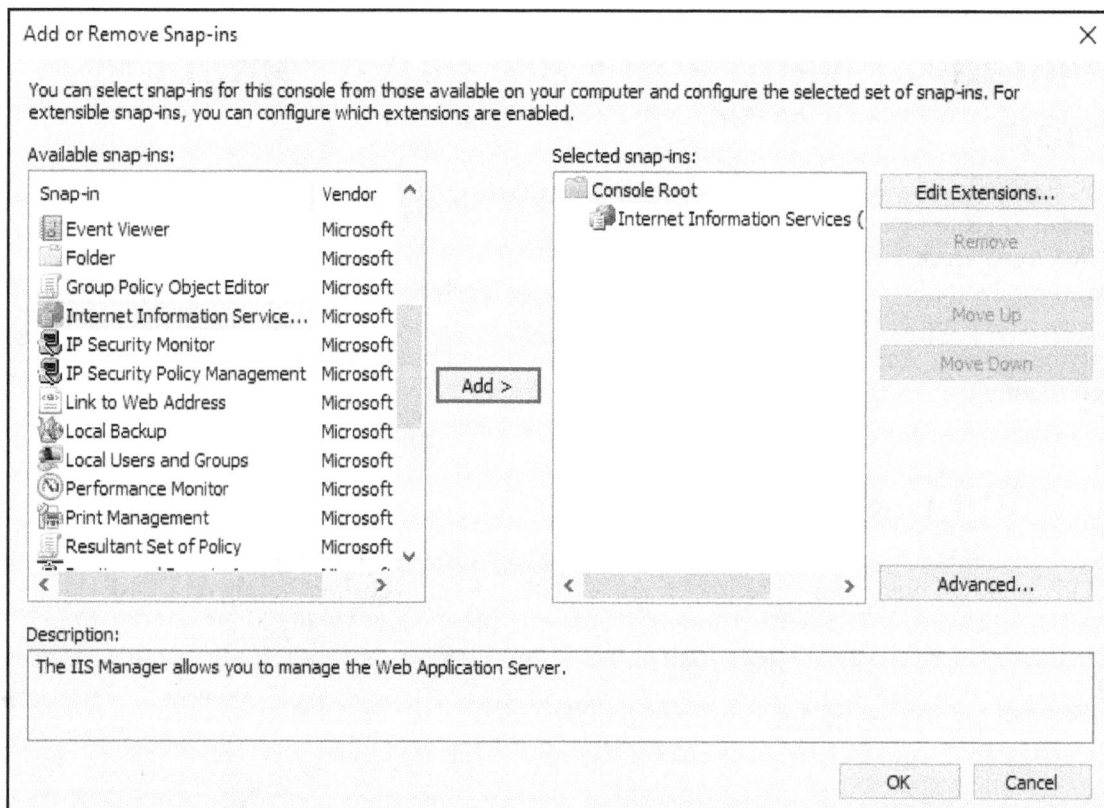

5. By default, MMC opens the IIS console for our CA1 server, which makes sense because so far we have not specified anything about CORE1. Right-click on **Start Page**, and select **Connect to a Server...**

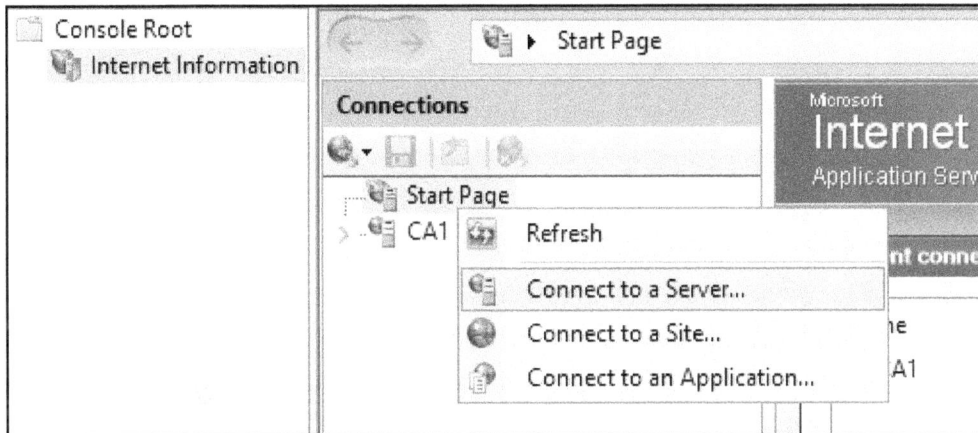

6. Type the name of the server that you want to administer. I want to see the IIS console on CORE1.MYDOMAIN.LOCAL.

> There are many different tools inside MMC that can be launched and then remotely connected to another system. As an alternative to the method we just walked through, you could forego using MMC altogether, and simply open up the IIS console straight from inside the Administrative Tools folder. Once IIS Management is open, follow the same steps outlined earlier in order to connect it remotely to your remote server.

7. In fact, there is one more way that sort of mixes this recipe with the preceding one regarding Server Manager. Now that the Web Server role has been installed onto CORE1, if we go back into **Server Manager** and right-click on our CORE1 server, you will notice that we now have the option to launch **Internet Information Services (IIS) Manager** right from here!

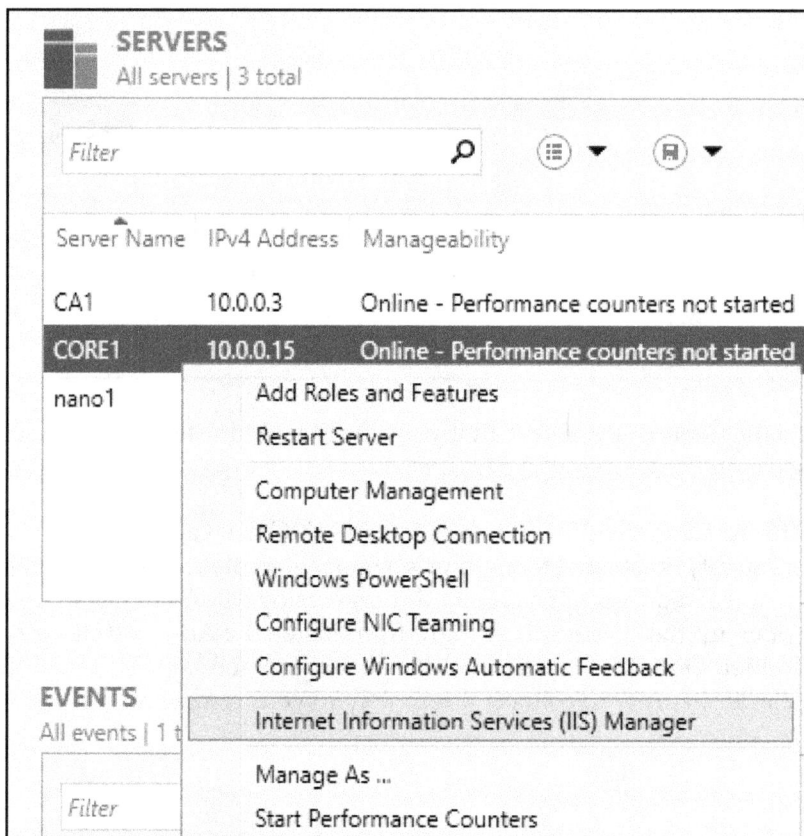

```
  SERVERS
  All servers | 3 total

  Filter                          🔍    (☰) ▼    (📷) ▼

  Server Name   IPv4 Address   Manageability

  CA1           10.0.0.3       Online - Performance counters not started
  CORE1         10.0.0.15      Online - Performance counters not started
  nano1                        Add Roles and Features
                               Restart Server

                               Computer Management
                               Remote Desktop Connection
                               Windows PowerShell
                               Configure NIC Teaming
                               Configure Windows Automatic Feedback
  EVENTS
  All events | 1 t             Internet Information Services (IIS) Manager

                               Manage As ...
  Filter                       Start Performance Counters
```

How it works…

MMC contains snap-ins for most of the tools that you need in order to administer your servers, whether those servers are local or remote to you. I very rarely see administrators using the MMC console to its full potential. It would be quite easy to snap-in all of the management tools that you need for your entire organization, connect them to the servers that are relevant for each role or task, and then have one single MMC console window that was always open on your local computer. This way, any time you need to make a change in IIS, Active Directory, DNS, Group Policy, and so on, you simply open the MMC window on your machine, without the need to log into any of the servers, and make the changes.

Managing Nano and Core with PowerShell remoting

Now we move on to the most powerful way that we can interact with our remote and headless servers, PowerShell. If I've said it once, I've said it a thousand times – PowerShell has the capability to change anything in the operating system; it's just a matter of figuring out the right commands and cmdlets to use. By establishing a remote PowerShell connection to a server, you can manipulate any facet of that machine right from the pretty blue window that is running on your local computer. In this recipe, we will use PowerShell from both a Windows Server 2016 running Desktop Experience and from a Windows 10 client computer.

Getting ready

As we continue to figure out how to remotely manage our new CORE1 and NANO1 servers, we will now be using PowerShell from both our CA1 server and from our Win10 client computer to see what we can or cannot accomplish with these two servers.

How to do it...

Since we are already logged into the CA1 server, let us try to launch a remote PowerShell connection to CORE1 from inside Server Manager. If you are already logged into a server, or if you have installed RSAT to give yourself Server Manager on your local computer, this is a quick and easy way to establish PowerShell remoting:

1. Launch **Server Manager**. We are going to assume that you have already used the **Add Servers** function so that you can see CORE1 inside the **All Servers** screen.
2. Right-click on CORE1, and choose the option for **Windows PowerShell**.

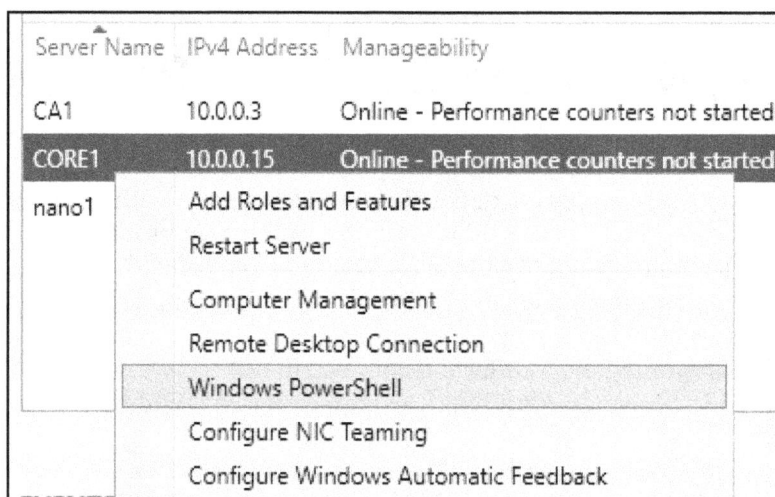

Server Name	IPv4 Address	Manageability
CA1	10.0.0.3	Online - Performance counters not started
CORE1	10.0.0.15	Online - Performance counters not started
nano1	Add Roles and Features	
	Restart Server	
	Computer Management	
	Remote Desktop Connection	
	Windows PowerShell	
	Configure NIC Teaming	
	Configure Windows Automatic Feedback	

3. After a couple of seconds where PowerShell is opening and creating a connection to CORE1, we are presented with a familiar blue PowerShell window. What that doesn't look standard is the fact that, in front of our flashing cursor, you can see the CORE1 server name specified. This indicates that our PowerShell window is actively running against CORE1, and anything that you type into this window reflects CORE1, and not the CA1 server that we are logged into.
4. Let's prove this. As you can see in the following screenshot, I have **System** properties open and you can see that we are currently logged into my CA1 server which is running the full Desktop Experience version of Windows Server 2016. However, when I enter a simple `hostname` command into my remote PowerShell window, it responds that the system hostname is CORE1.

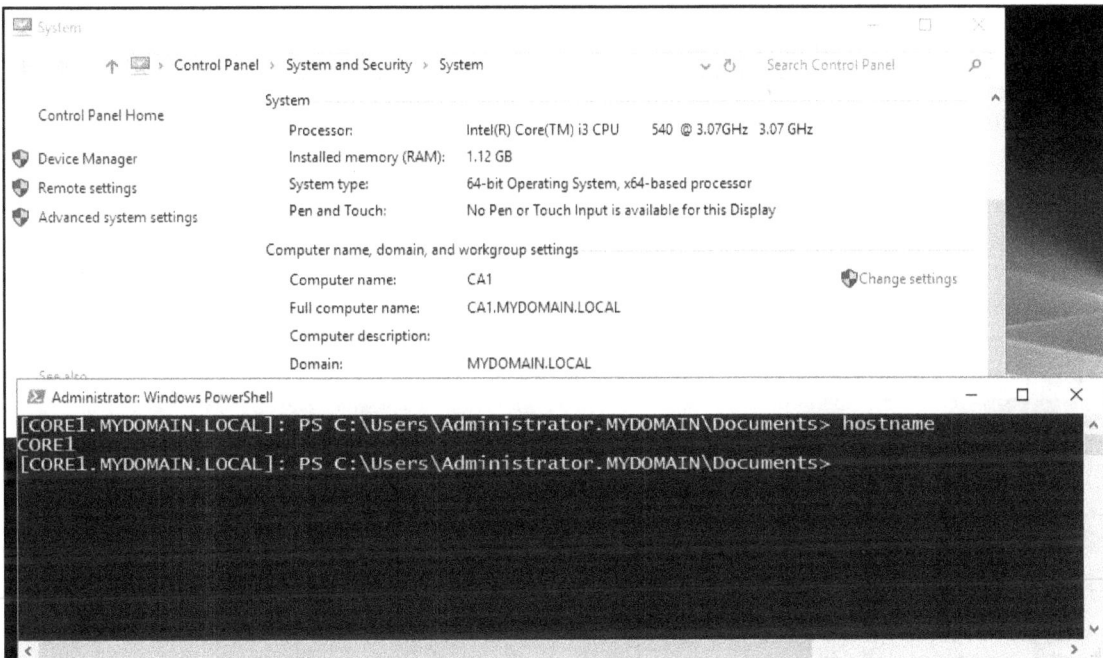

5. One final step here before we move on to our other example: let's try to change something on CORE1. Earlier we installed the Web Server role onto this system, but now I have decided to use this server for a different purpose. Rather than having to launch any graphical tools or wizards, since I already have this remote PowerShell session open I can remove the Web Server role from CORE1 with a single command:

```
Remove-WindowsFeature Web-Server
```

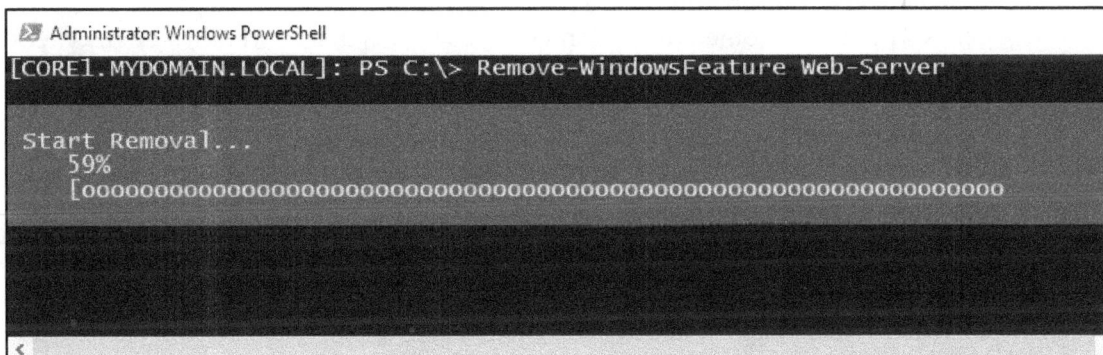

Now let's change gears a little and move away from using a server to remotely manage our system. Instead, I am going to log into a regular Windows 10 client computer, which does not have any of the server tools installed, and use PowerShell right from there to remotely connect to my NANO1 server:

1. Launch an administrative PowerShell session on the Win10 client.

2. Use the following command to attempt connection to NANO1:

   ```
   Enter-PSSession -ComputerName NANO1
   ```

```
Administrator: Windows PowerShell                                        —   □   ×
PS C:\> Enter-PSSession -ComputerName NANO1
Enter-PSSession : Connecting to remote server NANO1 failed with the following
error message : WinRM cannot process the request. The following error occurred
while using Kerberos authentication: Cannot find the computer NANO1. Verify
that the computer exists on the network and that the name provided is spelled
correctly. For more information, see the about_Remote_Troubleshooting Help
topic.
At line:1 char:1
+ Enter-PSSession -ComputerName NANO1
+ ~~~~~~~~~~~~~~~~~~~~~~~~~~~~~~~~~~~~~
    + CategoryInfo          : InvalidArgument: (NANO1:String) [Enter-PSSession
   ], PSRemotingTransportException
    + FullyQualifiedErrorId : CreateRemoteRunspaceFailed

PS C:\> _
```

3. Uh oh, that's kind of a nasty error message. I double-checked the firewall configuration on NANO1, and even ran the process for resetting WinRM to the factory defaults, but I continue to get this message. Wait a minute, I know what's going on. I am running this PowerShell prompt from a domain login, but NANO1 is not yet joined to the domain! This means that PowerShell on my client is not trusting NANO1, because it cannot verify anything with Active Directory.

4. Fortunately, there is a command I can run on my Win10 client that will tell PowerShell to specifically trust NANO1. I will now run this command:

   ```
   Set-Item wsman:\localhost\client\trustedhosts NANO1
   ```

TIP

Note that this will not be required when connecting a remote PowerShell session to a domain-joined system.

5. In addition to setting up the trust, I will also have to adjust my `Enter-PSSession` cmdlet parameters slightly. This is because I am running PowerShell inside my domain login, but NANO1 is not joined to the domain and so it will not yet recognize my domain credentials.

6. In order to connect the remote PowerShell session while specifying local credentials that will actually authenticate to NANO1, try this command instead:

```
Enter-PSSession -ComputerName NANO1 -Credential administrator
```

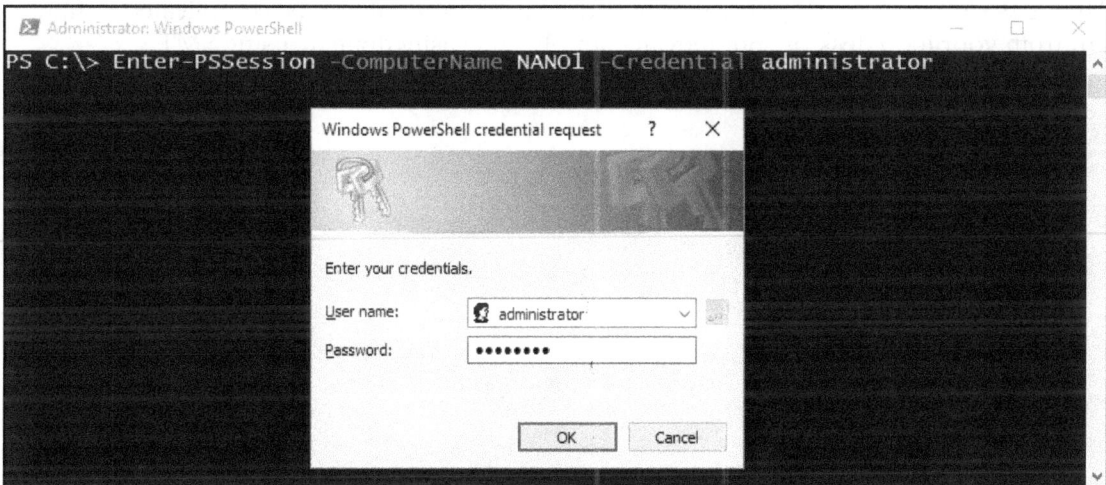

How it works...

We have now explored a variety of ways that you can remotely connect to and manipulate your headless servers such as Server Core and Nano Server. PowerShell is by far the most powerful way to accomplish this, but it is also the most complicated if you are not familiar with using PowerShell cmdlets in your everyday work. While a learning curve is involved, this is the best avenue to pursue as you enhance your IT capabilities.

It is important to note that Nano Server is still brand new, and is still evolving as a technology. The processes and procedures that you use to build and interact with new Nano Servers may change over the coming months as people settle into using Windows Server 2016 and Microsoft makes adjustments to improve it.

See also

If you have any interest in Azure, or even if you don't, make sure you check out the new cloud capability they are providing that helps you manage your servers. The **Server Management Tools** (**SMT**) are a collection of tools, which allow you to interact with all of your servers. You can manage Windows servers running Desktop Experience, or Server Core, or even Nano Server, and you can do it all from your web browser! Yes, this does involve logging into Azure, which means you need an Azure account, but this is one of their free offerings. You can connect both Azure virtual machines as well as your on-premise servers to SMT in order to view data about them and even make changes on them. Things as simple as shutting down or restarting a Nano Server can be complicated to figure out from your local desktop, but they are simply and easily done by using SMT.

12
Working with Hyper-V

Today's server administrators eat, sleep, and breathe virtual machines. They are flooding our computing infrastructure, quickly replacing physical servers in all facets of our technology. Thankfully, entrance into the world of virtualization is quite easy once you know which pieces of the puzzle need to work together in order to start building and hosting virtual machines. I have worked with many server administrators who manage the virtual machines themselves once they are online, but in bigger organizations it is usually someone on the backend who is creating these VMs in the first place. This means that even someone who works with Windows servers every day might not have a lot of experience with using the Hyper-V Management Console, and this is the reason why a chapter about Hyper-V itself is important to include in this book on Windows Server 2016. This chapter will cover the following topics:

- Creating a Windows Server that runs Hyper-V
- Creating a Hyper-V Server
- Networking your VMs
- Building your first virtual machine
- Using the VM Settings page
- Editing virtual hard disks
- Using Checkpoints as rollback points

Introduction

When talking about server virtualization, it is important to note the difference between a virtualization host and a virtual machine. The host server is the big dog, the (usually) physical platform that provides all of the resources to the smaller virtual machines. There are two major players in the virtualization host category. A company called VMware is popular in both personal and enterprise deployments, and of course Microsoft's own Hyper-V. Since I live in the Microsoft world, and this is a Microsoft-centric book, we are going to be focused on the virtualization capabilities provided by Microsoft Hyper-V inside the new Windows Server 2016 operating system. The best part about Hyper-V is that it is available to anyone who is running the Windows Server operating system, so even if you aren't using virtualization technology in your business today, with just a few mouse clicks you probably could be. Furthermore, if you have a VMware shop today, make sure to check out the latest offers from Microsoft regarding your migration to Hyper-V. The release of Windows Server 2016 brings with it some heavy discounts and incentives for companies who are looking to switch to Hyper-V!

Virtualization is an enormous topic and there will certainly be complete books written on all the ins-and-outs of Hyper-V. This chapter will focus on the steps you will need in order to start using it and on the cornerstones of running a virtualized environment. Beyond the scope of the recipes in this book, make sure you read up on topics like Hyper-V Clustering and Replication as you can now build an environment where all of your servers have hot-standby duplicates sitting on the sidelines, waiting to be called into the game. Hyper-V can be a central piece in your disaster recovery plan. Also new in Server 2016 is the idea of nested virtualization, where you can now take a virtual machine that is running inside Hyper-V, and install the Hyper-V role onto that virtual machine itself! Why in the world would you want to do that? "To use containers," is the number one answer to that question, as you start to expand your DevOps capabilities by using Windows Server and Hyper-V Containers to provide tiny, secure, standardized platforms for application development and expansion.

Creating a Windows Server that runs Hyper-V

Before you can start building virtual machines to use in your environment, first you need a virtualization host server on which Hyper-V will run. The first consideration to take into account is hardware. The hardware requirements for a server running Hyper-V depend on how many virtual servers you plan to run on top of this host platform. For example, the server that I am using for the lab environment shown throughout this book is an Intel i3 processor with only 8 GB of RAM. This is not at all conducive to a successful Hyper-V environment. I can only turn on four or five VMs at a time, each of them with very minimal amounts of memory per virtual machine. They all run quite slowly. Multiple Xeon processors with 100 GB of RAM or more will become criteria if you intend to run dozens of servers within your virtualized environment. Or perhaps you can meet somewhere in the middle of those numbers if you are running between one and 10 servers. There's not really a *right* answer here. Just make sure you have enough RAM to assign each VM the amount that it needs, plus an amount dedicated to the host operating system so that it continues to perform properly. Hard drive space is also a good consideration because you need to make sure you have enough physical storage for all of those servers that you plan to spin up.

Once you have decided on the hardware, your next decision is which version of Windows Server 2016 to install on it. If you have run through the installer, you will know that you have options for Server 2016 Standard and Server 2016 Datacenter. One of the most important notes I can give you regarding this topic is that the Standard SKU of Windows Server only allows you to run two virtual machines! If this is not enough to meet your needs, you had better go ahead and install Windows Server 2016 Datacenter. Sneak peek: make sure you check out the next recipe in this chapter for a third option. Spoiler alert: it's much less expensive than the Datacenter SKU!

Getting ready

I have a piece of server hardware upon which I have installed Windows Server 2016 Datacenter edition. This will enable me to spin up an unlimited number of virtual machines from a licensing perspective. Keep in mind that each virtual machine you create that is running Windows Server will also require a server key; there are no freebies here with operating system licenses.

How to do it...

I have already installed Windows Server 2016 Datacenter onto my hardware. I have two NICs on this server, because Hyper-V prefers to have one NIC dedicated to host operating system communications. The second NIC can be used as a bridge between the virtual machines and my physical network. Follow these steps to install the Hyper-V role:

1. Open Server Manager and click on the link for **Add roles and features**. Click **Next** until you see the **Select server roles** screen. Here you simply choose the check-box for **Hyper-V**.

2. Alternatively, and this can be extremely useful if your Hyper-V server is running Server Core, the following PowerShell cmdlet will install the Hyper-V role and its management features:

```
Add-WindowsFeature Hyper-V, RSAT-Hyper-V-Tools, Hyper-V-Tools,
Hyper-V-
PowerShell
```

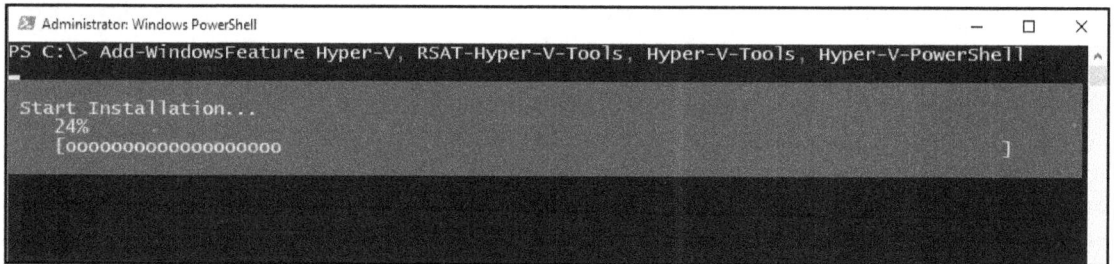

3. Following installation of the role, you must reboot the server. Once it is back online, head into Server Manager and launch **Hyper-V Manager** for the first time from the **Tools** menu.

4. The following screenshot gives you a glance into **Hyper-V Manager**. This is the tool you will most often utilize to interact with the virtual machines that you run on this virtualization host server. As we will discuss in upcoming recipes, there are a variety of ways that you can interact with a server running Hyper-V, and even a number of different ways that you can run the Hyper-V Manager console.

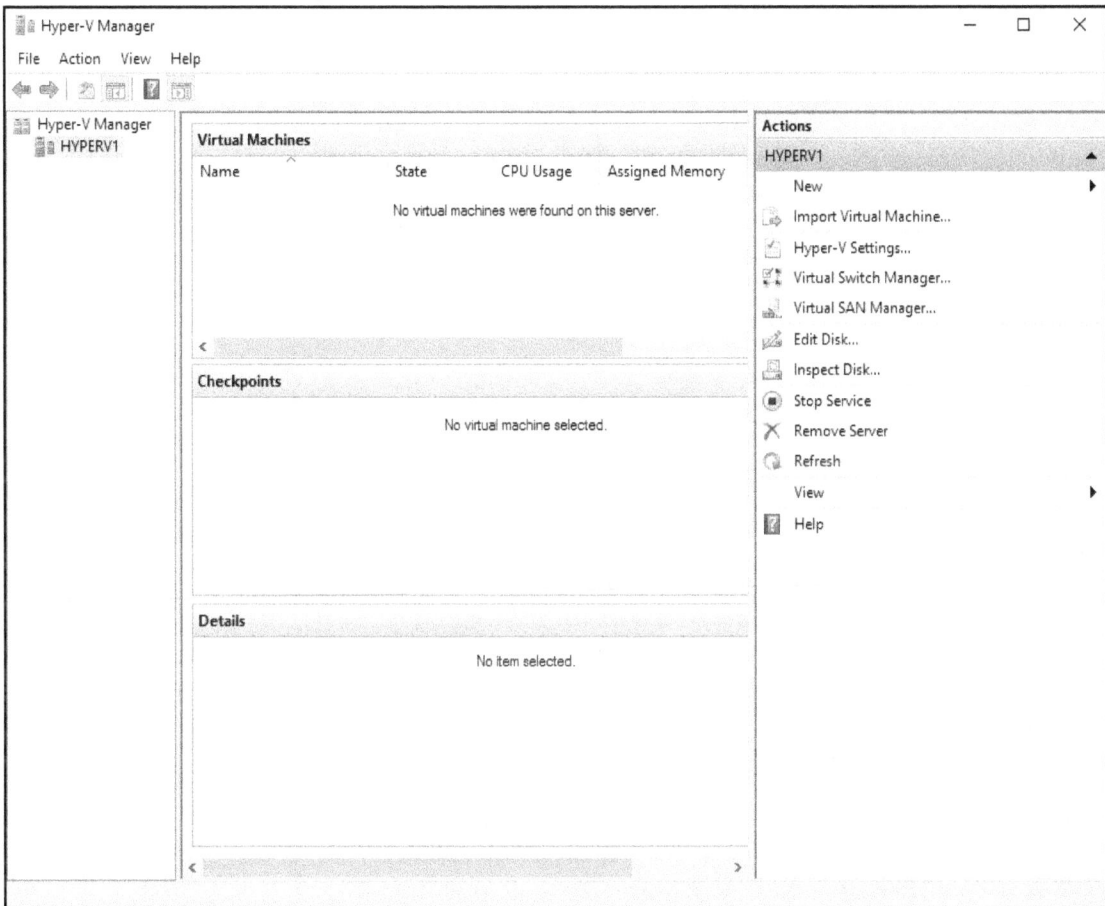

How it works...

Implementing the Hyper-V role onto your new Windows Server 2016 is the first step toward virtualizing your infrastructure. You need to plan for hardware needs carefully, making sure you have wiggle room in case you end up with more servers or bigger servers than you originally planned. Now that our Hyper-V virtualization host is online, has the role installed, and has gone through its initial configuration, it is time to really start making use of the Hyper-V Manager console.

An important item to point out relating to the Hyper-V role installation is that we now have the ability to install the Hyper-V role onto a virtual machine! This is known in the industry as Nested Virtualization. Your virtual servers can host other virtual servers. What is the point of that? This is primarily because of some new functionality in Server 2016 relating to containers, and also for Nano server, but it is an interesting point to spend some time thinking about as you decide on the best way to build out your virtual server environment.

Creating a Hyper-V Server

Wait a minute, didn't we just do this? No, we did not. What we did in our previous recipe was install the Hyper-V role onto a traditional Windows Server 2016. You can implement Hyper-V onto a server running Desktop Experience, a Server Core, or even use a Nano Server to host virtual machines. But an actual Hyper-V Server on the other hand, that is something else altogether.

When you build out a Windows Server 2016 and install the Hyper-V role on it, it is nice and easy to configure and is the way that most admins build their virtualization hosts. But there are a couple of drawbacks, primarily related to cost. As we have already mentioned, if you use Windows Server 2016 Standard as your host, you will only be permitted to run two virtual machines. That is a seriously limiting factor. On the other hand, you can install Windows Server 2016 Datacenter on your host and then run an unlimited number of VMs, but the cost for Datacenter is considerably higher than a Standard server.

This is the importance of Hyper-V Server. It is a completely different installer file that you can download free from Microsoft. Once implemented, this Hyper-V Server has no licensing costs associated with it. For every regular Windows Server that you host on top of your Hyper-V server, there is of course a license fee associated with that. But the Hyper-V Server host machine is totally free. And you can run an unlimited number of VMs on top of it! Given the word "free" you would think that Hyper-V Server would be prevalent inside our data centers, but it really isn't. I believe that is the result of two factors. The first is that many admins may not even know Hyper-V Server exists. Second is the fact that the interface for Hyper-V Server is more like Server Core, and it's not an entirely comforting feeling knowing that the console of your super-important, massive Hyper-V host server is only going to provide you with a command prompt in order to interface with it.

Let's install Hyper-V Server together so you know how to do that, and then we will also take a look at managing VMs on this Hyper-V Server. Trust me, it's not as difficult as you may think.

Getting ready

We have a new server upon which we are going to install Hyper-V Server 2016. We will also be using a Windows Server 2016 that is running Desktop Experience in order to demonstrate the remote management of Hyper-V Server.

How to do it...

Follow these steps to implement and test your first Hyper-V Server:

1. You will need to download the installer ISO from Microsoft. Open up Bing, and search for "Download Windows Hyper-V Server 2016 to find that file.

2. Once downloaded, either burn the ISO file to a DVD or go ahead and use an ISO to USB tool to create bootable media of some kind. Then go ahead and boot your new server hardware to this media.

3. As you can see, the installation wizard looks quite similar to that of our traditional Windows Server 2016 installer. The big difference is that the installer does not pause to ask you which version of the operating system you want to install. After specifying the installation location, it immediately starts installation of Hyper-V Server 2016.

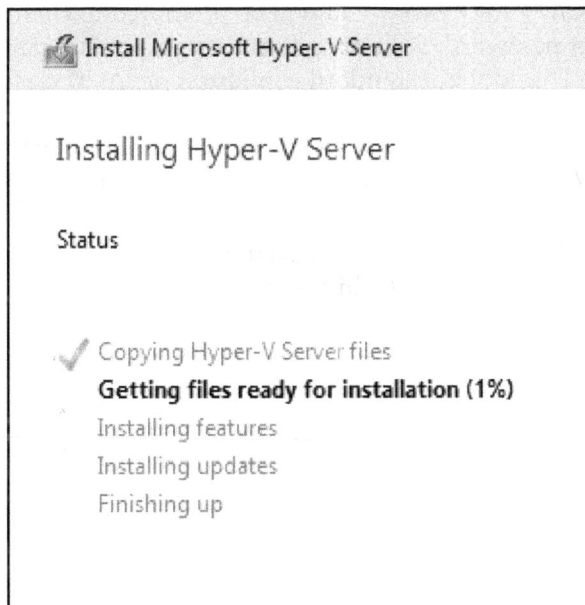

Install Microsoft Hyper-V Server

Installing Hyper-V Server

Status

✓ Copying Hyper-V Server files
Getting files ready for installation (1%)
Installing features
Installing updates
Finishing up

4. Following installation you will be presented with a Command Prompt window that looks incredibly like what we are used to seeing in Server Core.

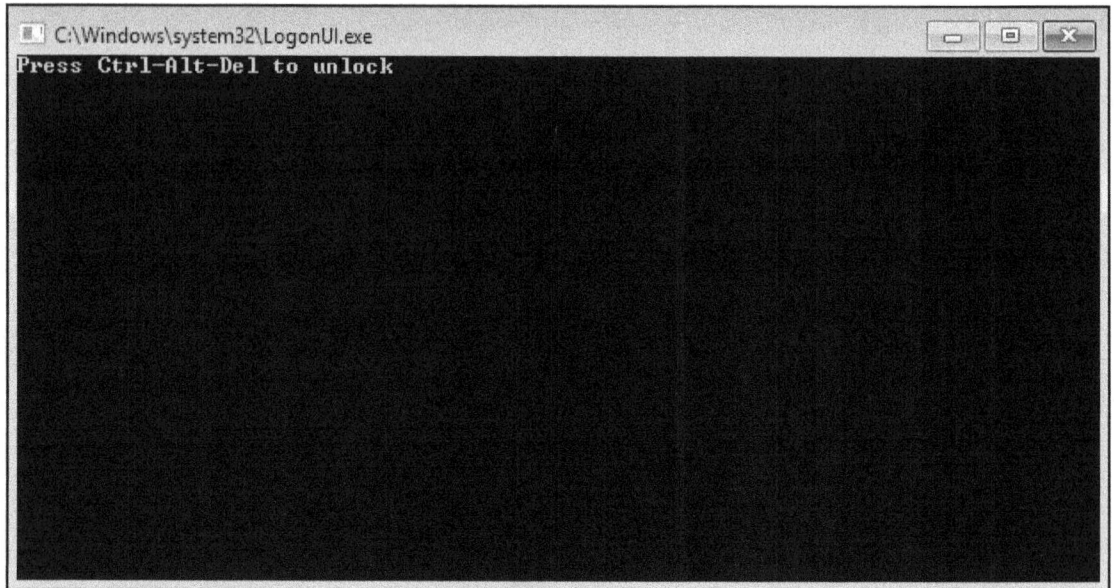

5. If you press *Ctrl + Alt + Delete* you will be prompted to change the local administrator password. Following that change, you are taken directly into the **sconfig** tool. This tool is a standard configuration interface for anyone working with a Server Core, so if you have any experience in that area this will all be familiar to you. As you can see, we have options available here to do things like change the hostname, configure network settings, and join our new Hyper-V Server to the domain.

6. In fact, I just finished walking through those steps in order to set a hostname, IP address, and domain membership on my Hyper-V Server.

```
C:\Windows\System32\cmd.exe - C:\Windows\system32\sconfig.cmd
Microsoft (R) Windows Script Host Version 5.812
Copyright (C) Microsoft Corporation. All rights reserved.

Inspecting system...


================================================================================
                          Server Configuration
================================================================================

1) Domain/Workgroup:                   Domain:  MYDOMAIN.LOCAL
2) Computer Name:                       HYPER-V-SVR
3) Add Local Administrator
4) Configure Remote Management          Enabled

5) Windows Update Settings:             Automatic
6) Download and Install Updates
7) Remote Desktop:                      Disabled

8) Network Settings
9) Date and Time
10) Help improve the product with CEIP  Not participating

11) Log Off User
12) Restart Server
13) Shut Down Server
14) Exit to Command Line


Enter number to select an option:
```

7. Now that Hyper-V Server 2016 is installed and we have accomplished our typical server setup configurations, what's next? Well, the roles and services needed for this box to be a Hyper-V host server are already included with this operating system, so all we need to do at this point is figure out how to get into the Hyper-V Manager console in order to start building VMs. For this, we are going to fall back on our Microsoft remote management mentality.

8. If you want to verify that the Hyper-V role really is installed on our new Hyper-V Server, enter option number 14 into the **sconfig** console. This takes us to the normal Command Prompt. From there type powershell and press *Enter* to bring us into the PowerShell interface.

9. Now inside PowerShell, type `Get-WindowsFeature -name *hyper*` - you can see that the Hyper-V role is already installed.

```
Administrator: C:\Windows\System32\cmd.exe - powershell
5) Windows Update Settings:              Automatic
6) Download and Install Updates
7) Remote Desktop:                       Disabled

8) Network Settings
9) Date and Time
10) Help improve the product with CEIP   Not participating

11) Log Off User
12) Restart Server
13) Shut Down Server
14) Exit to Command Line


Enter number to select an option: 14

PS C:\> powershell
Windows PowerShell
Copyright (C) 2016 Microsoft Corporation. All rights reserved.

PS C:\> Get-WindowsFeature -name *hyper*

Display Name                                        Name                    Install State
------------                                        ----                    -------------
[X] Hyper-V                                         Hyper-V                 Installed
    [ ] Hyper-V Management Tools                    RSAT-Hyper-V-Tools      Available
        [ ] Hyper-V Module for Windows PowerShell   Hyper-V-PowerShell      Available


PS C:\>
```

10. Log in to another server or computer on your network, and use the Hyper-V Manager console from there in order to remotely manage this new Hyper-V Server. You can either log into a Windows Server that has the Hyper-V management tools installed, or you can install those tools right onto your Windows 10 client. As long as you are running Windows 10 Pro or Enterprise, you have the ability to install the Hyper-V tools right onto your desktop computer, and then we can use the tools from there to manipulate this server. I am going to log into my Win10 client, install the Hyper-V tools from the **Turn Windows features on or off** tool inside Control Panel, and then launch Hyper-V Manager from that desktop computer.

11. Once inside, right-click on **Hyper-V Manager** and choose **Connect to Server....**

12. Input the name of your new Hyper-V Server, and press **OK**.

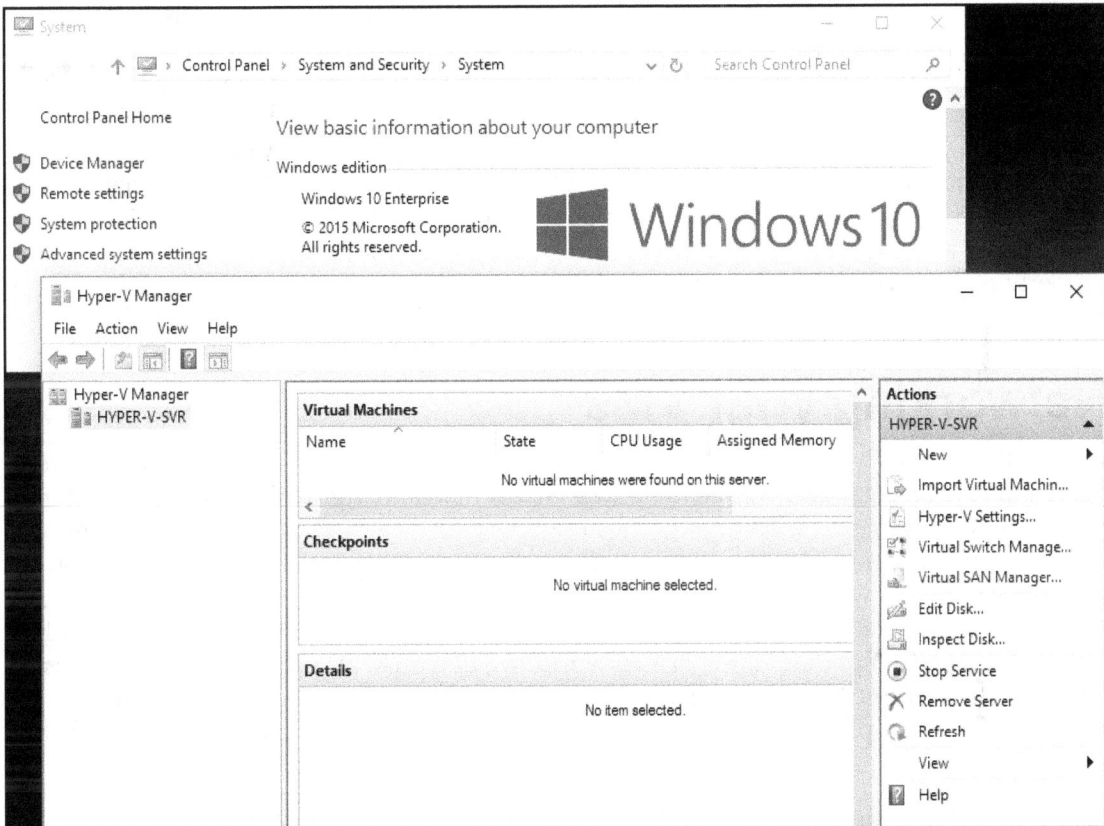

13. You can now see that we are running the Hyper-V Manager console on a Win10 client computer, but are remotely managing the Hyper-V service that is running on that new server. From here we can build new VMs, manipulate VMs, and do anything we would otherwise normally do inside Hyper-V Manager as if it were running right on the Hyper-V Server.

How it works...

Hyper-V Server is essentially a Server Core instance that is preconfigured with the Hyper-V role. The big differences between Hyper-V Server and a traditional Windows Server running the Hyper-V role are cost and the way that you interface with the server itself. By employing remote management tools from another server or directly from your workstation, you can ease the burden of learning a new interface as you start to explore whether or not Hyper-V Server is the right fit for you. For the remainder of our recipes we will utilize Hyper-V installed onto a traditional Desktop Experience version of Windows Server 2016, but knowing that Hyper-V Server exists is very important to be able to properly plan for your virtualization infrastructure.

Networking your VMs

After getting your Hyper-V server up and running, via whichever platform you choose to utilize, the next logical step will be to build a virtual machine, right? So why are we talking about networking? Because setting up the networks that your VMs are going to plug into is an important baseline and it is worth spending some time thinking about this before you start spinning up new VMs. Every virtual machine will have a network interface, sometimes more than one, and those NICs need to be plugged into a switch; just like with a physical server. Except that, in the virtual world, we don't use physical switches, we must tell the VMs which virtual switch to tap into. That means we must build these virtual switches in the first place, before we can start making any network connections possible to our VMs.

Planning the right number of physical NICs to be inside your Hyper-V host server is also important. Each physical NIC can only be plugged into one physical switch, obviously, and so if you plan to host virtual machines on this host server that need to tap into different physical networks, you will need multiple NICs to support that scenario. Each NIC on the physical host server can be plugged into a different switch, flowing traffic to a different area of your network. Then inside the Virtual Switch Manager, we can build virtual switches that correspond to these physical NICs, so that our VMs can be plugged into any piece of the physical network that we choose. As a simple example, think about a DirectAccess server that needs to be connected to both the internal corporate network and into a DMZ. You would need at least three NICs on that physical Hyper-V host server because one gets plugged into the internal network, one into the DMZ network, and also the host operating system on the Hyper-V server itself prefers to have an NIC dedicated to its own communications.

Getting ready

We are using Windows Server 2016 running Hyper-V, which has been hosting the virtual machines throughout this book. This server has just two NICs; unfortunately this is a limitation of the chassis on my test box. It would be much more common for a full-blown Hyper-V server to have more than two physical network interfaces.

How to do it...

Here are the steps you will need to take in order to create and manage the virtual networks on your Hyper-V server:

1. Launch **Hyper-V Manager** from inside the **Tools** menu of Server Manager.
2. You are presented with a list of virtual machines that are installed on this system, and over to the right side of the screen there is an **Actions** pane. Go ahead and click on the link for **Virtual Switch Manager....**

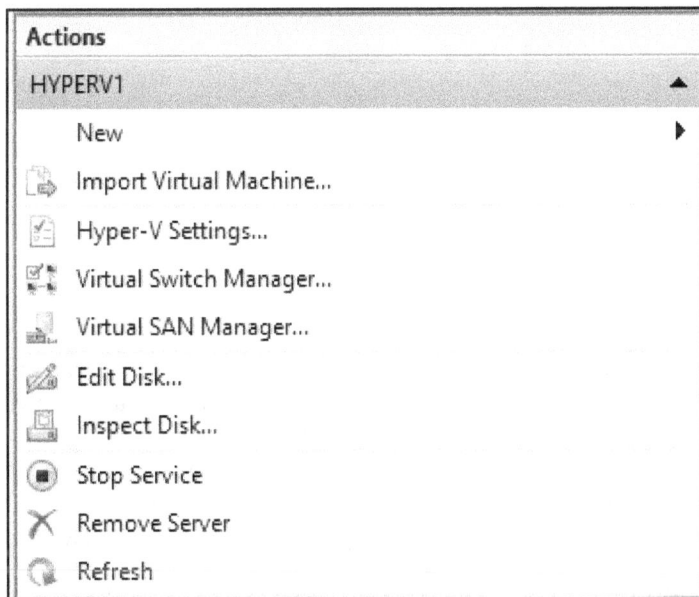

Actions
HYPERV1 ▲
New ▶
Import Virtual Machine...
Hyper-V Settings...
Virtual Switch Manager...
Virtual SAN Manager...
Edit Disk...
Inspect Disk...
Stop Service
Remove Server
Refresh

3. This is the screen where you will define any switches that need to be available for the VM NICs to plug into. As you can see in the following screenshot, a switch is linked to my physical NIC on my Hyper-V host is connected to the corporate network, and this virtual switch was given the name **Physical NIC** when I initially installed the Hyper-V role. I can easily change that name from inside this screen to reflect whatever description I want.

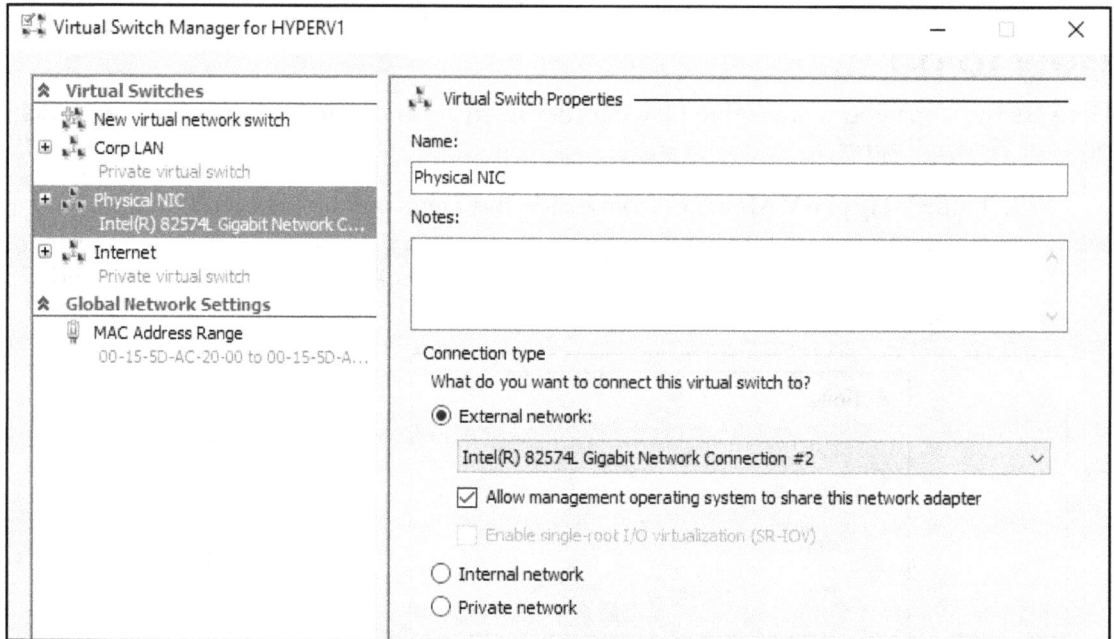

4. There are also two **Private virtual switches** that are currently configured on this server. These are switches I created in order to accomplish the server builds and testing that we have been doing throughout these chapters. As you can see, one is labeled **Corp LAN**, and the other is one I called **Internet**. Neither of these switches is connected to a physical NIC, so they aren't able to communicate outside this host server at all. These kinds of switch are useful for building out segregated test lab environments when you want to test new technologies.

5. If you click on **New virtual network switch**, you see that you have the option of creating three different kinds of virtual switches.

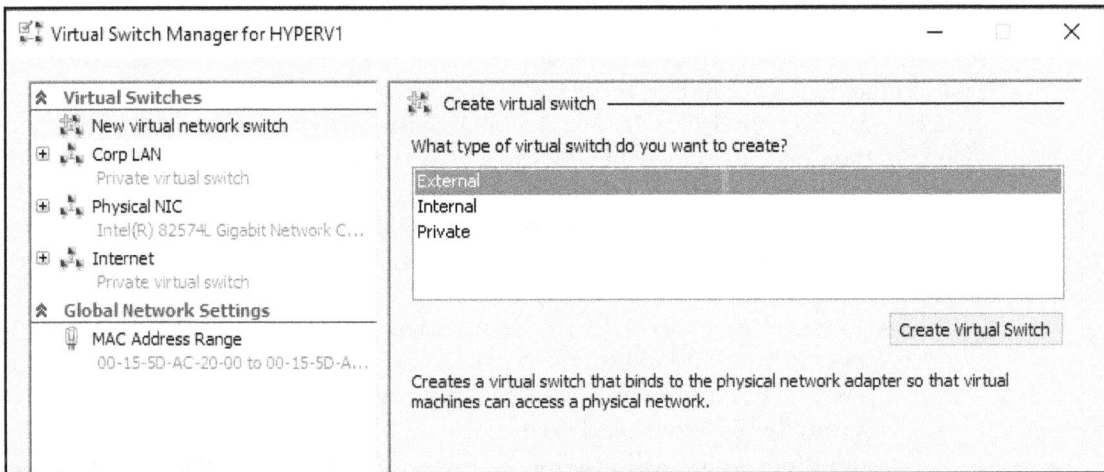

6. Let's take a minute to describe the differences between the three:

- **External**: This kind of virtual switch binds itself to a physical network adapter on the Hyper-V host server. When you connect VMs to an external virtual switch, they have the ability to flow traffic back and forth with that physical network.

- **Internal**: This kind of virtual switch does not bind to a physical NIC, and so the traffic generated in this switch cannot communicate outside the host system. However, the VMs that you connect to these switches are able to communicate with each other, and with the Hyper-V host system itself.

- **Private**: This kind of virtual switch is what I used for the test lab. It is a segregated switch, unable to talk to any of the physical NICs and also unable to communicate back with the Hyper-V host. Any VMs that you plug into a private switch will be able to communicate with each other, such as in the case of my Corp LAN switch, but they will be isolated to each other and nothing else.

7. While I am using a brand new Windows Server 2016 for this recipe and the three standard types of switch are the only ones visible to me in the graphical interface, I would like to point out that there are now two additional types of Hyper-V switch, brand new in Server 2016 and available for us to use. Why are they not visible in the previous screenshot? Because if you want to use the new switch types, you will need to deploy them via PowerShell. Here is the summary information on the two new types of switch available to us on Windows Server 2016 Hyper-V servers that are running the **Software Defined Networking (SDN)** stack:

   - External switch with Switch Embedded Teaming (SET) - SET is brand new in 2016 and allows us to create NIC teams right in a Hyper-V switch, a feature never available in prior versions of Hyper-V. You can group between one and eight physical NICs into virtual network adapters which will provide fault tolerance in the event of a single NIC failure. When using SET, it is important to know that all of the NIC adapters must be installed in the same physical Hyper-V host server, and the NICs must all be identical. You utilize the New-VMSwitch cmdlet combined with the EnableEmbeddedTeaming parameter in order to create a new SET virtual switch.

   - **NAT**: Windows Server 2016 also includes a new Hyper-V switch type called NAT. You would establish this type of virtual switch when you need virtual machines to have a shared internal network, and connect to the external interfaces by using a NAT'd address instead of binding them directly to an external NIC and its own physical IP addressing. NAT is also not available from the graphical console when setting up a new Hyper-V switch; you use the `New-VMSwitch` cmdlet combined with the `-SwitchType NAT` parameter to build one. This new type of switch is particularly useful in a container scenario.

How it works...

From the Hyper-V Virtual Switch Manager, you are able to very quickly create as many different virtual switches as you need to support the different kinds of virtual machines you are planning to create. In most testing environments, it makes the most sense to utilize internal or private switches, to make sure that traffic remains segregated on the host. However, when working with production servers and virtual machines, you will be working mostly with external switches that are bound to physical network cards in your Hyper-V host server. This enables you to assign IP addresses on your VMs and gives them the ability to communicate with your physical network and with places like the real Internet. It is important to have at least some of your virtual switches configured before you start creating a lot of VMs, because, as you will see in our next recipe, one of the options you can configure during the VM creation process is which virtual switch it should be connected to.

Building your first virtual machine

If you haven't worked within Hyper-V Manager before, you are probably chomping at the bit to get your first virtual machine created and running! There are a number of options that you must declare during the virtual machine creation process. Let's take a few minutes and walk through it together so you understand what those options mean and what benefits they can bring to the table.

Getting ready

We are using a Windows Server 2016 with the Hyper-V role and management tools installed. That is the only requirement for this recipe.

How to do it...

Let's walk through the steps to create a brand new virtual machine and install an operating system on that VM:

1. Open **Hyper-V Manager** from the **Tools** menu of Server Manager, or directly from the Administrative Tools folder.
2. Right-click on the name of your Hyper-V server near the top-left portion of the screen, and choose **New** | **Virtual Machine....**

3. This launches the **New Virtual Machine Wizard**,; go ahead and click **Next** to take us into the actual configuration.

4. Specify a **Name** for your new VM. This name does not have anything to do with the actual hostname of the server you are going to build; it is simply the descriptive name that will be visible inside Hyper-V Manager. Whatever name you give the VM here will also be reflected in the folder that is created to house the virtual machine files on the hard drive of our Hyper-V host server.

5. Still on the naming page, make sure to also choose a location within which Hyper-V should store this new virtual machine. Each VM consists of some metadata-type files as well as the virtual hard disk file, and they need to be stored somewhere. I find it is a good practice to specify something other than the default setting here. If you allow Hyper-V to bury these files inside `C:\ProgramData`, that is fine, but it can be confusing to track them down later. I typically have a dedicated drive for my VMs to reside on, and simply create a folder called `VMs`. For example, in the following screenshot I am naming my new virtual machine **DC3**, and I am going to store its file inside `C:\VMs`. The wizard will then create a folder inside that location, giving me a final destination of `C:\VMs\DC3` for this virtual machine.

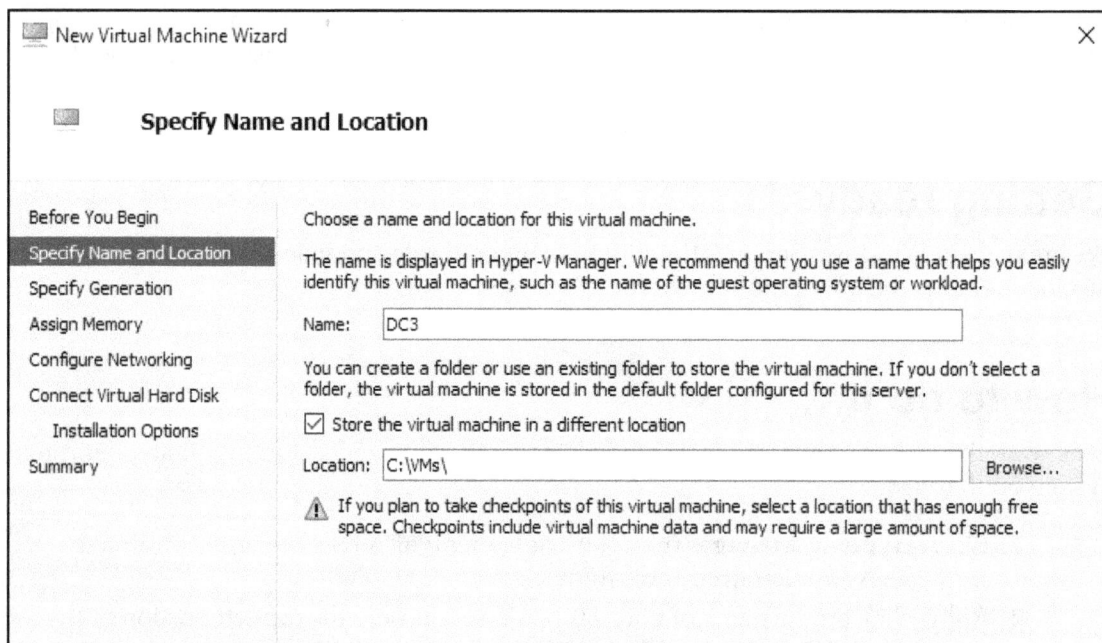

New Virtual Machine Wizard   ✕

Specify Name and Location

Before You Begin	Choose a name and location for this virtual machine.
Specify Name and Location	The name is displayed in Hyper-V Manager. We recommend that you use a name that helps you easily
Specify Generation	identify this virtual machine, such as the name of the guest operating system or workload.
Assign Memory	Name: `DC3`
Configure Networking	You can create a folder or use an existing folder to store the virtual machine. If you don't select a
Connect Virtual Hard Disk	folder, the virtual machine is stored in the default folder configured for this server.
Installation Options	☑ Store the virtual machine in a different location
Summary	Location: `C:\VMs\` Browse...

⚠ If you plan to take checkpoints of this virtual machine, select a location that has enough free space. Checkpoints include virtual machine data and may require a large amount of space.

My new virtual machine could technically serve any purpose within my network, but as you can tell from the name, this guy is going to turn into a domain controller once it is up and running. It is important to note that, when you use virtual machines as domain controllers, there is one special configuration you will probably want to put into place. After building the VM, head into its **Settings** page and disable **Integration Services | Time synchronization**. If you leave time sync enabled, the DCs will get their time from the Hyper-V host, rather than being the time provider themselves, and this can cause problems if time falls out of sync. When using virtual DCs it often works best to disable time sync and push the timekeeping responsibilities elsewhere.

6. Click **Next** and we are now presented with an option to create our virtual machine as a **Generation 1** or **Generation 2** VM. Typically, when you are building VMs on a Hyper-V server, those VMs will also be running a copy of Microsoft Windows Server. Since the last couple of iterations of the Windows Server operating system have only supported 64-bit installations, you will more than likely want to choose **Generation 2** VMs for these servers. This will provide you with all of the latest functionality on the VMs, including the ability to replicate those VMs over to a secondary Hyper-V server. But in case you need to implement a virtual machine that is running a 32-bit operating system, you are still provided with the capability here to choose **Generation 1** and make that possible.

7. Next we have to assign an amount of RAM to the VM. It is quite common for administrators to specify a specific amount that correlates to a real amount of physical RAM, such as 1024 MB, 2048 MB, 4096 MB, and so on. But there is no real reason to do this. You can type any number in here that you want. Take note of the checkbox listed on this screen as well. If you check **Use Dynamic Memory for this virtual machine**, the VM will only consume what it actually needs in order to perform. As an example, my DC1 server that is running on here right now is consuming 1583 MB of RAM. While it seems good in theory to always have lower amounts being utilized than are assigned, when a VM needs to expand dynamic memory it consumes some CPU cycles to do so. This means that if you setup all of your VMs to have dynamic memory you might lower your RAM requirements a little bit, but you'll be working the host server harder in order to keep up with all of the shifting memory requirements.

8. Onwards and upwards. We are now presented with a screen that allows us to **Configure Networking**. This screen is simply a drop-down menu where you can choose to plug your new VM's virtual NIC into one of the virtual switches that we created earlier. If you open that list, you should see each of them available to choose from. I am going to plug DC3 into my **Corp LAN**.

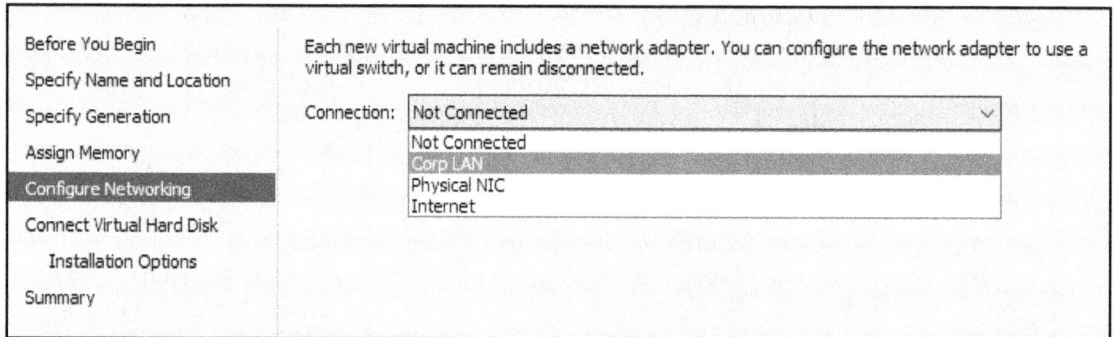

Before You Begin	Each new virtual machine includes a network adapter. You can configure the network adapter to use a virtual switch, or it can remain disconnected.
Specify Name and Location	
Specify Generation	Connection: Not Connected ⌄
Assign Memory	Not Connected
Configure Networking	Corp LAN
Connect Virtual Hard Disk	Physical NIC
Installation Options	Internet
Summary	

9. Now we find ourselves on one of the more important screens: the virtual hard disk specification. As you can see, the default location places the hard disk in a subfolder of C:\VMs\DC3, and much of the time this is an appropriate location because it keeps all of the VMs files together. The most important aspect of this screen, assuming that you are asking the wizard to create a new virtual hard disk for you, is giving it a size. The default is set to 127 GB, which isn't very big compared to today's physical disk size standards. It is a fairly common misconception by new Hyper-V admins to assume that the higher you set this number, the larger the VHDX file is going to be; therefore, if you are only using 50 GB on a 300 GB drive, then you will be wasting 250 GB of your physical disk space. But this is not true!

A virtual machine requires storage so that you can install an operating system. You can specify the storage now or configure it later by modifying the virtual machine's properties.

(●) Create a virtual hard disk

Use this option to create a VHDX dynamically expanding virtual hard disk.

Name: DC3.vhdx

Location: C:\VMs\DC3\Virtual Hard Disks\ Browse...

Size: 250 GB (Maximum: 64 TB)

( ) Use an existing virtual hard disk

Use this option to attach an existing VHDX virtual hard disk.

Location: C:\Users\Public\Documents\Hyper-V\Virtual Hard Disks\ Browse...

( ) Attach a virtual hard disk later

Use this option to skip this step now and attach an existing virtual hard disk later.

After finishing the VM creation wizard, if you seek out the actual VHDX file that was created you will notice that, even though we specified 250 GB, the actual size of this file is only 4 MB! That will grow, of course, as we start to install an operating system onto our new server, but it is important to know that the drive does not automatically consume 250 GB as soon as you create it. Note that it is possible to create a fixed-size virtual disk, which would consume the full amount of space right away, but the default option when using the wizard does not force that to happen.

10. After determining the size of your drive, you need to make a choice on how you plan to lay down an operating system on this drive. For my purposes, I will be installing Windows Server 2016 onto this new VM, and so I can point my new VM at the installation ISO file that I have placed on my Hyper-V server's hard drive. What this does at the VM level is build a virtual DVD drive onto the VM, and then plug this ISO into it as if you were inserting an actual installation DVD. This insures that, when we boot this VM for the first time, it can proceed with the installation of Windows Server 2016.

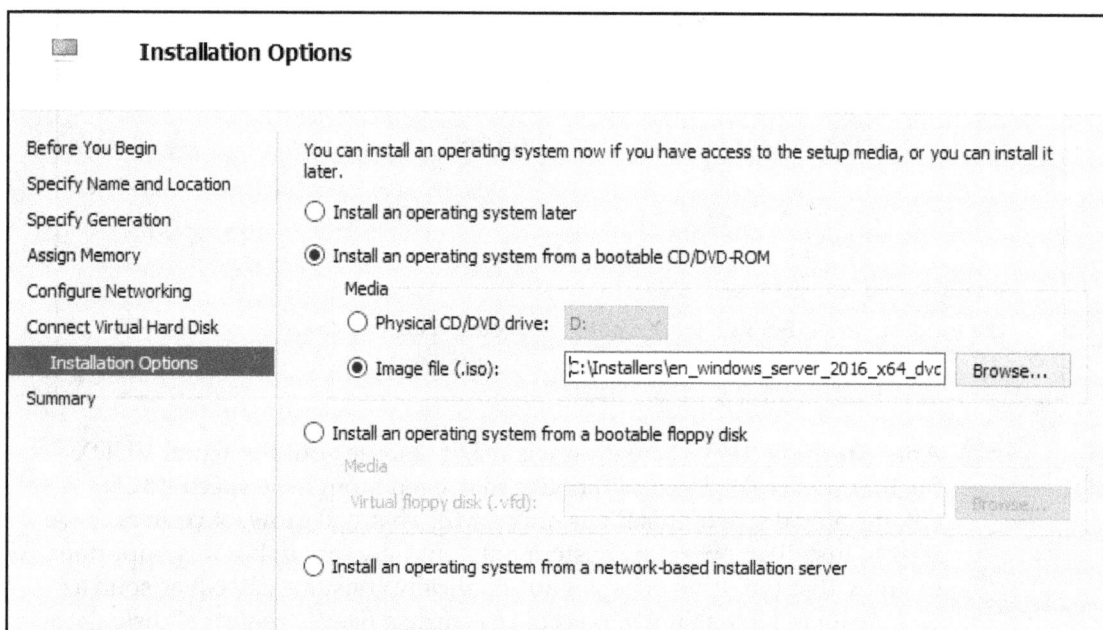

Installation Options

Before You Begin	You can install an operating system now if you have access to the setup media, or you can install it later.
Specify Name and Location	
Specify Generation	⭕ Install an operating system later
Assign Memory	🔘 Install an operating system from a bootable CD/DVD-ROM
Configure Networking	Media
Connect Virtual Hard Disk	⭕ Physical CD/DVD drive: D:
Installation Options	🔘 Image file (.iso): C:\Installers\en_windows_server_2016_x64_dvc [Browse...]
Summary	
	⭕ Install an operating system from a bootable floppy disk
	Media
	Virtual floppy disk (.vfd): [Browse...]
	⭕ Install an operating system from a network-based installation server

11. After pressing **Next** and then **Finish**, your brand new DC3 virtual machine has been created and is ready to be started. Right-click on DC3 from inside Hyper-V Manager, and choose **Connect...**. This will open a window that shows you the console of DC3, just like you were sitting in front of a physical monitor plugged into a physical server.

12. In the top toolbar click on the **Start** button, and watch as your new virtual machine comes to life!

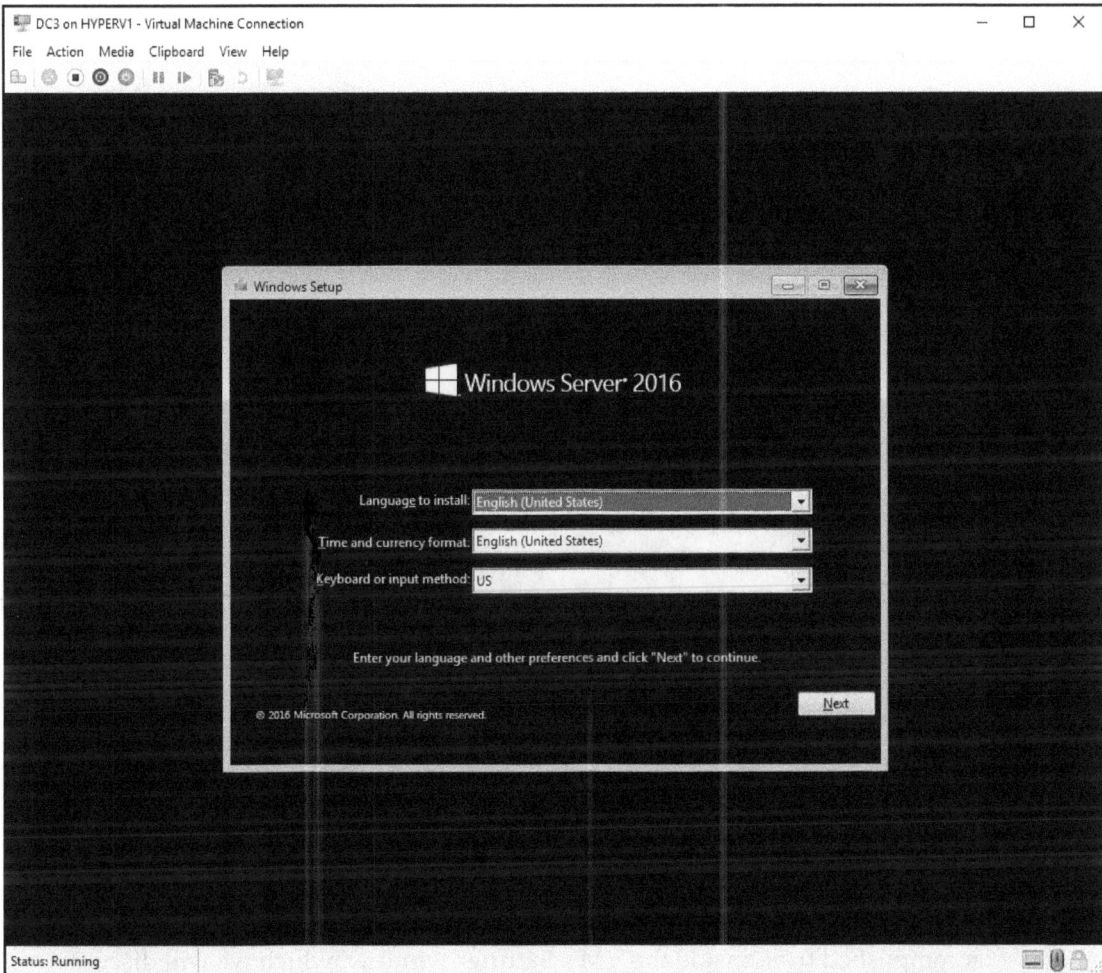

13. It is also possible to spin up a new virtual machine by using PowerShell! Take a look at the following command as an example. As you can see, the parameters specified in our command reflect the options we just walked through in the wizard.

14. Before you run this command, browse to the location on your drive where the VMs are stored. For me, that is `C:\VMs`.

```
New-VM –Name "DC4" –NewVHDPath .\DC4.vhdx –NewVHDSizeBytes 250gb
–MemoryStartupBytes 1024mb
```

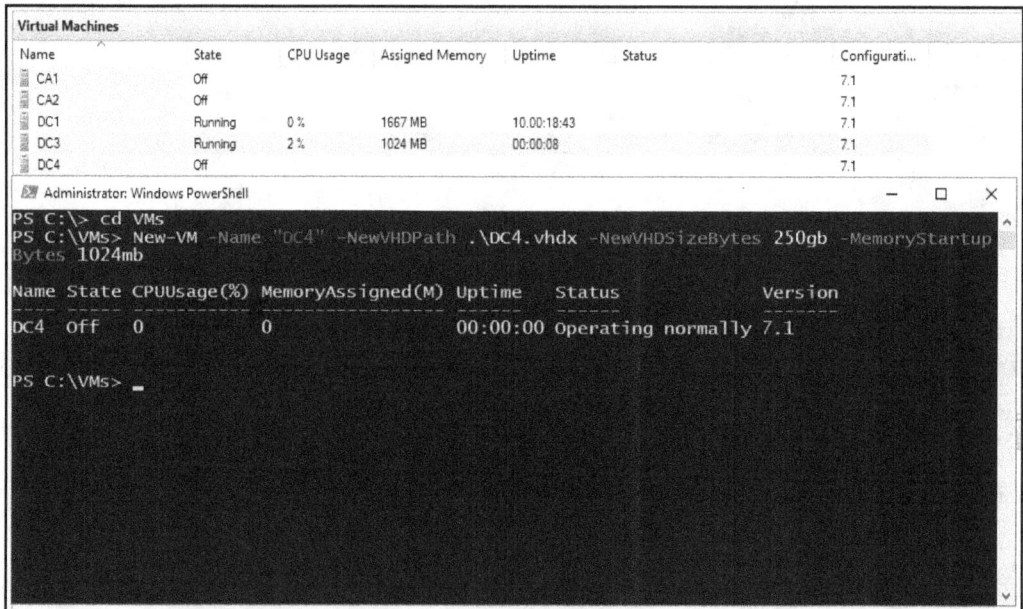

Virtual Machines

Name	State	CPU Usage	Assigned Memory	Uptime	Status	Configurati...
CA1	Off					7.1
CA2	Off					7.1
DC1	Running	0 %	1667 MB	10.00:18:43		7.1
DC3	Running	2 %	1024 MB	00:00:08		7.1
DC4	Off					7.1

```
Administrator: Windows PowerShell                                        —   □   ×

PS C:\> cd VMs
PS C:\VMs> New-VM –Name "DC4" –NewVHDPath .\DC4.vhdx –NewVHDSizeBytes 250gb –MemoryStartup
Bytes 1024mb

Name State CPUUsage(%) MemoryAssigned(M) Uptime    Status              Version
---- ----- ----------- ----------------- ------    ------              -------
DC4  Off   0           0                 00:00:00  Operating normally  7.1


PS C:\VMs> _
```

15. After the command completes, your new VM is ready to go! As you can see, we did not specify which virtual switch to plug into, or which ISO to attach to the virtual DVD drive in order to boot to installation media. These items are easily accomplished from inside the VM's **Settings** window, which we will discuss further in our next recipe.

How it works...

Building virtual machines is one of the core tasks that you will need to accomplish regularly on your Hyper-V servers. There are a number of options to select from as you move through the configuration of your new VMs, so we wanted to take a look at them and explain some of the different options. Having the ability to create VMs from inside PowerShell can be an incredibly powerful tool, especially if you need to create multiple VMs at the same time. Think about the possibilities of automating this so that you simply launch a script and have a dozen new servers running within seconds!

Using the VM Settings page

Once you have some virtual machines up and running, the majority of the configuration that you do to these servers will be from within the operating system running inside the VM. In the case of a VM running Windows Server, you would typically interact with that operating system through either the Hyper-V Connect function, such as the one we have already looked at, or perhaps enable RDP on that new server so you can utilize the Remote Desktop Connection client on your desktop computer to log into this new server. However, whether you are running VMs or physical servers there are some instances where you have to make changes, or configurations to those servers, which cannot be accomplished from inside the operating system: for example, if you need to exchange a hard drive, or add more memory, or add a NIC and plug it into a new network. These are all valid use-case scenarios for both physical servers and virtual servers. The difference is that you don't have a physical piece of hardware to walk up to when using VMs. So how do you make all of these changes? This is where the Hyper-V Settings screens come into play.

Getting ready

We are working inside the Hyper-V Manager console of my Hyper-V host server, where I have a handful of virtual machines up and running.

How to do it...

Follow these steps to open the core settings for one of our virtual machines (we will also discuss some of the more important options listed inside this interface):

1. Once inside Hyper-V Manager, right-click on a VM and take a look at the options available to us in this menu. We will be heading into the **Settings...** menu in just a second, but first note that right-clicking on a VM is a very quick and easy way to do such things as shutting down or powering up VMs. You can even use your *Ctrl* or *Shift* keys to select multiple VMs at the same time, then right-click and start up or shut down a whole batch at once!

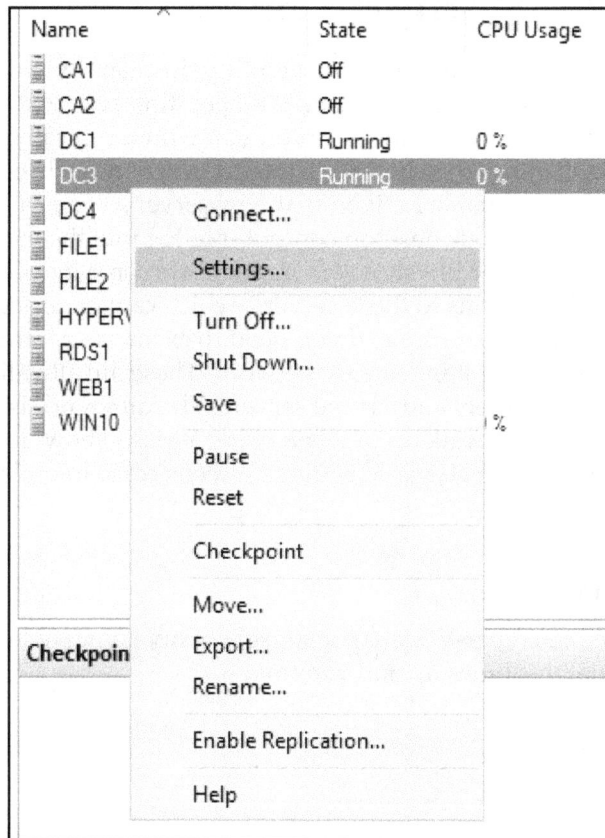

Name	State	CPU Usage
CA1	Off	
CA2	Off	
DC1	Running	0 %
DC3	Running	0 %
DC4		
FILE1		
FILE2		
HYPER\		
RDS1		
WEB1		
WIN10		

Connect...
Settings...
Turn Off...
Shut Down...
Save
Pause
Reset
Checkpoint
Move...
Export...
Rename...
Enable Replication...
Help

Checkpoin

2. Click on **Settings...** and let's bounce around in this screen a little bit to cover some of the options.

3. We land first upon the **Add Hardware** screen. This is the place where you can add components to be connected to your VM. The most common item that I have seen admins select here is **Network Adapter**. There are many reasons why a virtual machine might need more than one NIC, and this screen is exactly the place to accomplish that. You'll notice that some of these options are grayed out; this is because some changes that you want to make to a VM require that the machine be shut down and turned off prior to making those changes. In fact, for Generation 1 VMs you must shut them down before you can add new network cards. Fortunately, I created DC3 as a Generation 2 virtual machine, so we can add new NICs to this VM even while it is running! I will click on the **Add** button right now to test that, and you will see a second **Network Adapter** show up in the list.

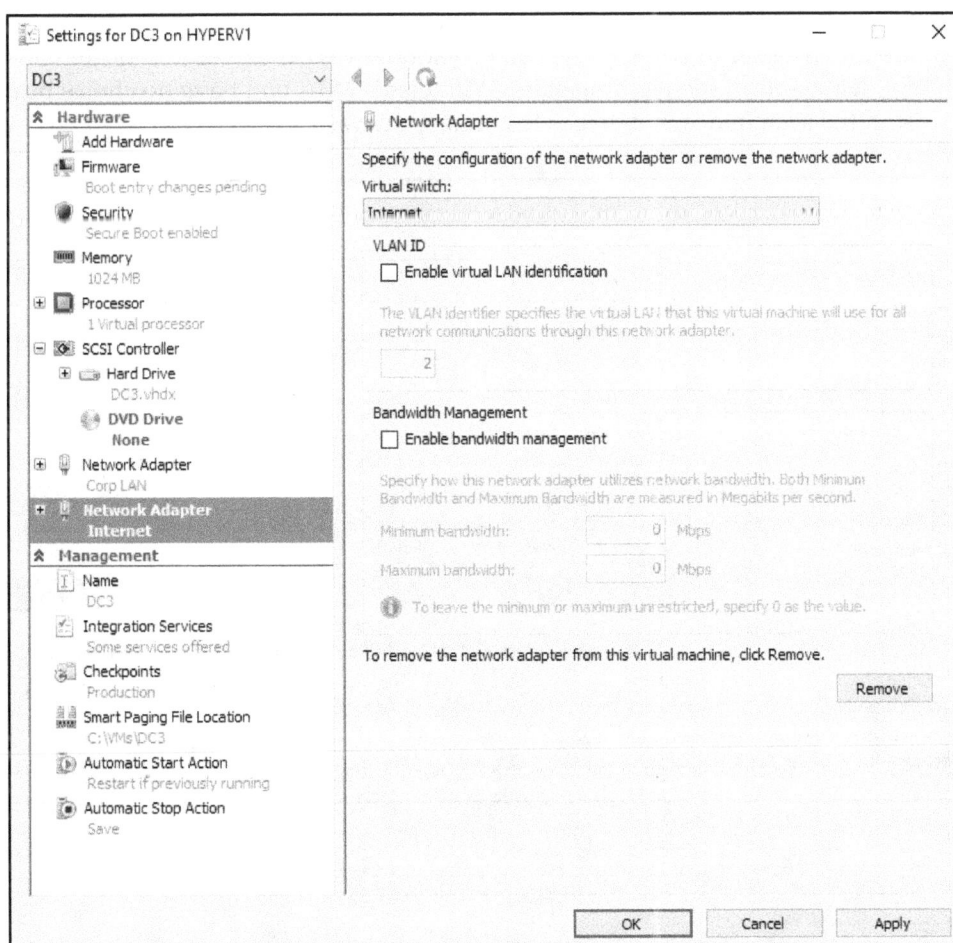

4. This brings us right into another useful and commonly accessed part of the settings interface, the **Network Adapter** screens. Each virtual NIC connected to your VM is listed separately here, and by clicking on each one you have the ability to choose which **Virtual switch** that NIC is plugged into by using the drop-down menu near the top of the screen. I have plugged one of my NICs into the **Corp LAN**, and my other NIC into the **Internet**.

5. A little further down in the list you can see the disk controller options. These settings will be different depending on whether you are running a Generation 1 or Generation 2 VM. Gen1 VMs have IDE controllers listed in settings, but Gen2 VMs have SCSI controllers. In either case, this is the place where you can tap additional hard drives into a VM, and this is also the place you visit in order to plug an ISO file into the virtual DVD drive, which is a very common task when you are building new servers. Over time you will also notice here that Gen2 VMs are much easier to work with. You can add new hard drives to a system on-the-fly, while it is in the running state. With Gen1 VMs, you have no choice but to shut the system down in order to connect a new drive.

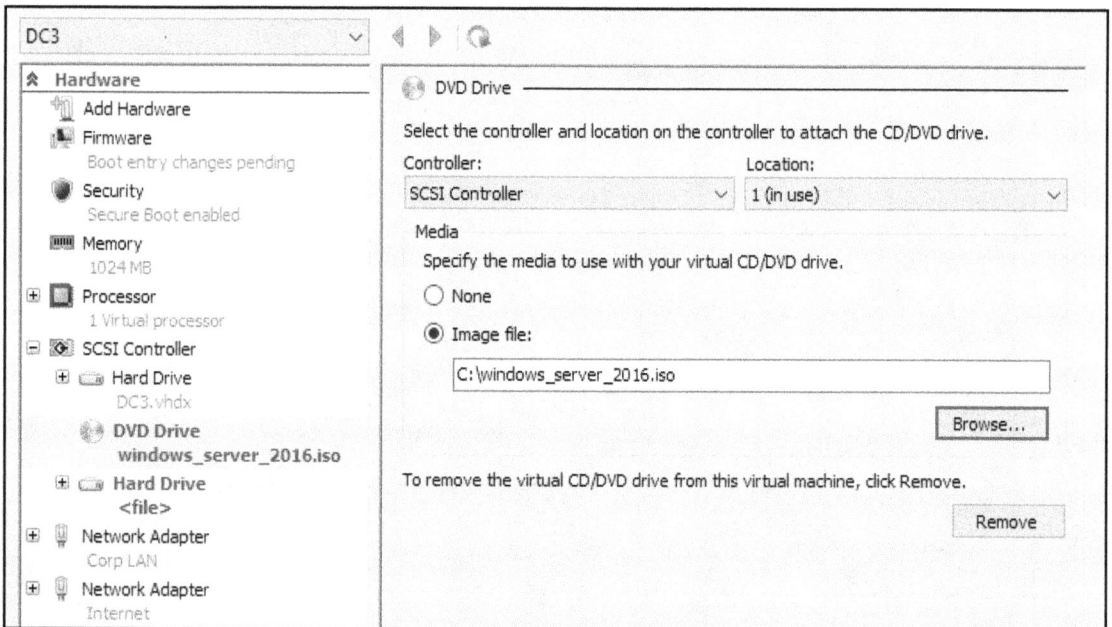

6. As you would expect, you also have the ability to slap additional **Processors** onto a VM. Changing these settings requires that the VM is shut down, whether you are running either Gen1 or Gen2.

7. There are other options in here that are fairly self-explanatory, but one last piece that I wanted to point out is the **Memory** category. While this in itself isn't anything special or fancy (it's just the spot where you define the amount of RAM the system has), we are talking about it here because Windows Server 2016 brings some new functionality to this setting. Historically, we always had to shut VMs down in order to change the amount of RAM they were using. No longer! We can now change this setting and apply it while the VM is running. As you can see in the following screenshot, I just moved my DC3 server from 1 GB to 2 GB of RAM, clicked the **Apply** button, and the change is immediately reflected inside **System** properties of DC3.

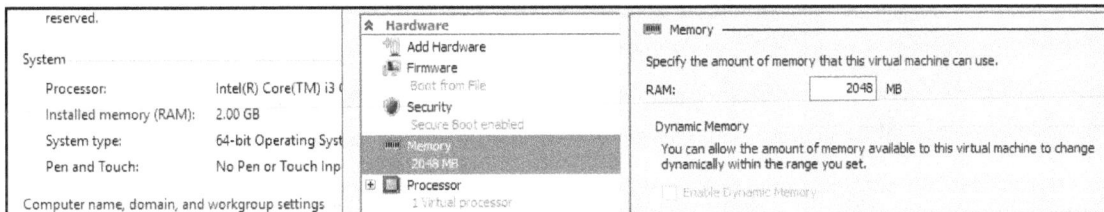

8. The last item that I want to mention inside the **Settings** screen is the drop-down menu at the very top. When you right-click on a VM and head into **Settings...** you are obviously looking at the settings for the virtual machine that you clicked on. Too often I watch people making changes to multiple VMs at the same time, but after each change they click **OK**, which closes the Settings window, and then right-click on the next VM and go right back into that screen. Instead, if you simply click on this drop-down menu near the top, you can navigate between the Settings pages for any of the VMs running on your Hyper-V server. If you have the need to make adjustments on multiple servers, this can definitely save you some time and mouse clicks.

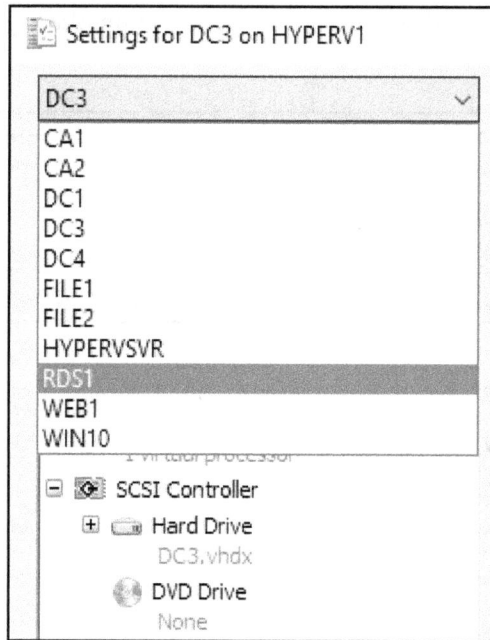

How it works...

As you start administering your Hyper-V servers, the settings screen for your virtual machines is likely the most common place that you will visit on a daily basis. Adjusting hardware and plugging in NICs are tasks that need to be done quickly and easily, so it is important that you are familiar with navigating this portion of Hyper-V Manager. If you are new to the Hyper-V world, I hope this recipe has helped to make this portion of the interface more comfortable for you as you move forward.

Editing virtual hard disks

When we run out of disk space on a physical hard drive, our options are limited. We can replace that drive with something bigger, but then need to worry about moving all of the data over successfully. If we are running some sort of RAID or Storage Spaces, then perhaps we could add a new drive to the array of disks, but that is only possible if we have set up the correct infrastructure to support this in the first place. Thankfully, when working with virtual machines that are running on virtual hard disks, we add a little bit more fluidity to our drive management capabilities. After all, these virtual hard disks are just files, right? So it makes sense that they are a little bit easier to manipulate than a mechanical disk with physical limitations. In this recipe, we are going to explore the options available to us inside the Edit Virtual Hard Disk Wizard. This wizard will allow us to choose a virtual hard disk, and then do one of three things with it. We can compact the disk, expand the disk, or we can convert the disk to a different type.

Getting ready

Our work will be accomplished from inside Hyper-V Manager on a Hyper-V server running in the network. You do not even need a virtual machine inside Hyper-V Manager, as the disk management functions can be performed against any VHD or VHDX file – whether or not they are assigned to a VM.

How to do it...

Here are the steps needed in order to edit your virtual hard disks:

1. Inside **Hyper-V Manager**, take a look at the right side of your screen. Inside the **Actions** pane, click on **Edit Disk...**

2. Click **Next**, and then browse to the location of the VHD or VHDX file that you want to manipulate.

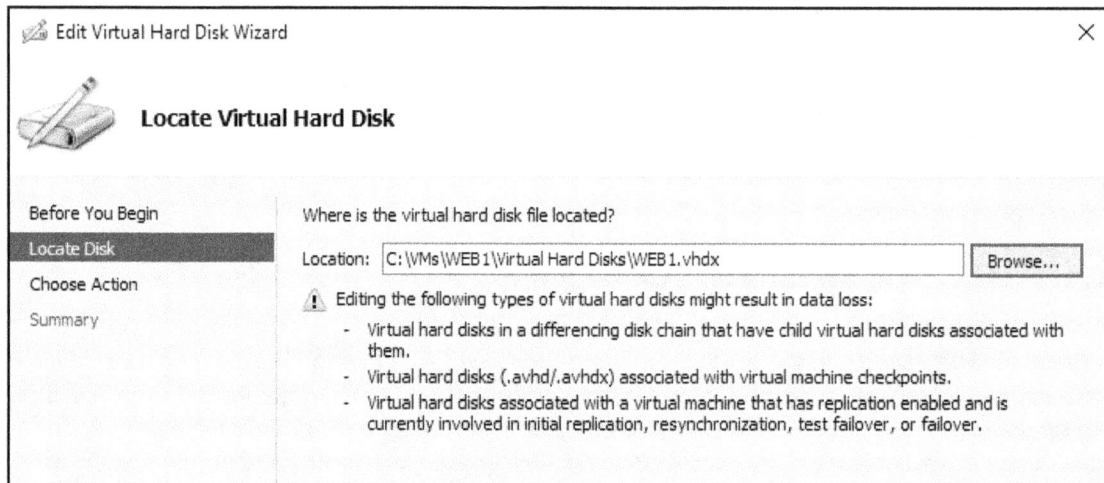

🖉 Edit Virtual Hard Disk Wizard   ✕

Locate Virtual Hard Disk

Before You Begin	Where is the virtual hard disk file located?
Locate Disk	Location: `C:\VMs\WEB1\Virtual Hard Disks\WEB1.vhdx` [Browse...]
Choose Action	⚠ Editing the following types of virtual hard disks might result in data loss:
Summary	- Virtual hard disks in a differencing disk chain that have child virtual hard disks associated with them.
	- Virtual hard disks (.avhd/.avhdx) associated with virtual machine checkpoints.
	- Virtual hard disks associated with a virtual machine that has replication enabled and is currently involved in initial replication, resynchronization, test failover, or failover.

💡 **TIP**

As you can see in the warning presented on this screen, certain types of virtual disks could be negatively affected by editing. Make sure you are not trying to edit a disk in one of those three conditions.

3. Next we need to choose the **Action** that we want to perform against this virtual disk.

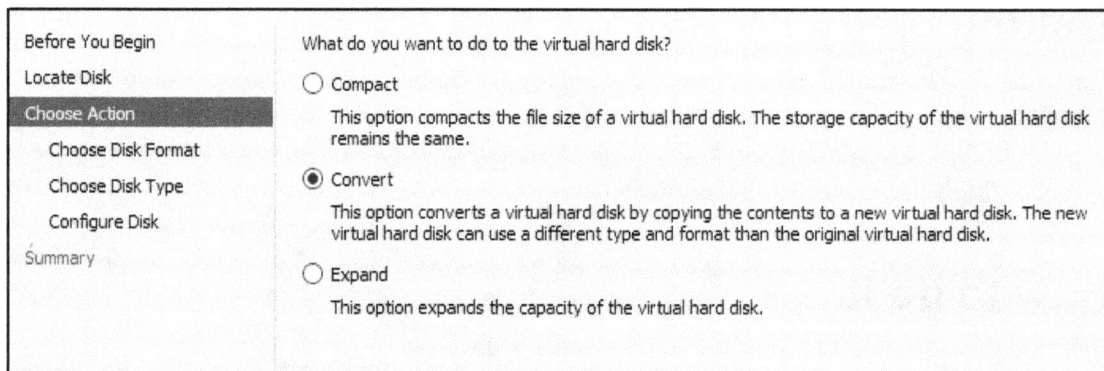

Before You Begin	What do you want to do to the virtual hard disk?
Locate Disk	○ Compact
Choose Action	This option compacts the file size of a virtual hard disk. The storage capacity of the virtual hard disk remains the same.
Choose Disk Format	
Choose Disk Type	◉ Convert
Configure Disk	This option converts a virtual hard disk by copying the contents to a new virtual hard disk. The new virtual hard disk can use a different type and format than the original virtual hard disk.
Summary	○ Expand
	This option expands the capacity of the virtual hard disk.

---

4. **Compact** is pretty self-explanatory; it will renegotiate free space within the disk and compact it to be as small as possible. There are no additional screens you need to run through on this; you simply click **Finish**.

5. **Expand** is also fairly straightforward. Type in a new maximum size for your virtual hard disk, and the file will be expanded to accommodate the larger threshold. This is the most common reason to visit the **Edit Virtual Hard Disk Wizard**.

6. **Convert** is the option we are going to choose in this recipe, because it gives us the opportunity to discuss the different types of virtual disks. After choosing **Convert** and clicking **Next**, you will be asked whether you want this file to be a **VHD** or a **VHDX**. The only reason you would choose a VHD is when you are going to implement an operating system on the virtual machine that doesn't support running on a VHDX disk, such as Windows Server 2008 R2 or earlier. Otherwise, you will always choose VHDX here.

7. Now we choose what type of virtual hard disk to convert to. When you allow the virtual machine creation wizard to set up a new disk for you, it always chooses **Dynamically expanding**. This is most often what is desired by admins, because the VHDX file will start off very small, and it will only grow as it needs to. This keeps physical disk space utilization at a minimum. However, just like with dynamically expanding RAM, it takes resources in order to adjust a hard drive size on the fly. So if you are aiming for a VM that is super-efficient, it will be in your best interests to set that VHDX file to **Fixed size**. Doing so will cause the VHDX file to consume the entire amount of disk space as soon as the disk is created or converted, which takes a toll on the amount of physical space you have available, but it is faster and more useful for workloads that require high disk performance.

8. The VHDX file I am currently editing was configured by the wizard, and so it is currently **Dynamically expanding**. I am going to change it to **Fixed size**, and on the next screen tell it where to store my new VHDX file. This is necessary because, whenever you convert a virtual disk from one type to another, Hyper-V is actually going to create a brand new VHDX file and then copy the entire drive over to the new one.

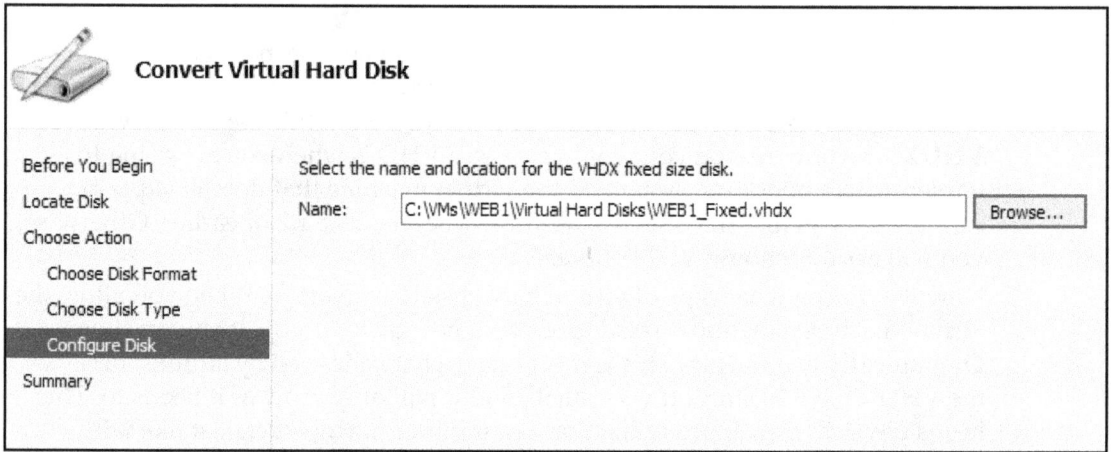

Convert Virtual Hard Disk

Before You Begin

Locate Disk

Choose Action

    Choose Disk Format

    Choose Disk Type

    Configure Disk

Summary

Select the name and location for the VHDX fixed size disk.

Name: `C:\VMs\WEB1\Virtual Hard Disks\WEB1_Fixed.vhdx`   Browse...

How it works...

Editing your virtual disks won't often be necessary, as long as you plan carefully for disk sizes and types during the VM creation process. However, you may come into a Hyper-V environment that was established before your time with a company, and now be tasked with cleaning up and making that Hyper-V server more efficient. Adjusting disk sizes and types can be part of that overall goal to improve the health of your Hyper-V servers.

Using Checkpoints as rollback points

Backing up physical servers and restoring them to previous points in time has always been a little bit tricky in the Windows Server world. When something goes wrong with a server, in most cases it is preferable to fix the issue, rather than to simply rollback to a previous version. If you do want to make the decision to roll back an operating system on a physical server, you are talking about creating downtime. This happens because, whether you are restoring a Windows Backup file, or if you are using some kind of imaging utility that takes a full picture of the hard drive during the backup and is capable of laying that entire image back down in the event of a recovery, you have to stop Windows from running in order to replace its files on the disk. So no matter which technology you have used to take the backup, you must take the server down at least temporarily while you accomplish the restore.

Hyper-V changes everything. When working with our VMs, we have the ability to take and restore Checkpoints whenever we feel the need. This capability was called Snapshots in previous versions of Hyper-V; the term Checkpoints is new in Windows Server 2016. Also new is the choice to create one of two different kinds of Checkpoint – Standard or Production. In this recipe, we will walk through the creation and restoration of both types of Checkpoints to see what benefits each type holds.

Getting ready

All of our backup and restoration work will be accomplished from within Hyper-V Manager on our Windows Server 2016.

How to do it...

We have Hyper-V Manager opened up, and have a number of different VMs running here. Let's explore together the capabilities of Checkpoints:

1. Decide on the VM that you want to Checkpoint. I am going to use my new DC3 server. Find that machine in the list, right-click on it, and choose **Checkpoint**.

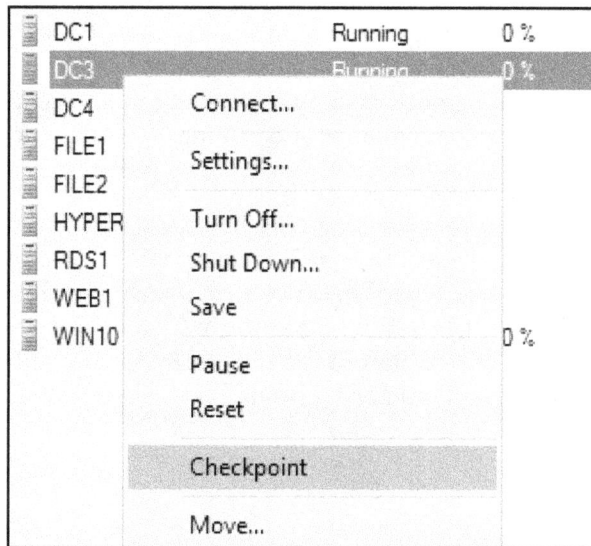

DC1		Running	0 %
DC3		Running	0 %
DC4	Connect...		
FILE1			
FILE2	Settings...		
HYPER	Turn Off...		
RDS1	Shut Down...		
WEB1	Save		
WIN10			0 %
	Pause		
	Reset		
	Checkpoint		
	Move...		

2. As you will notice, we get a message about the fact that a **Production** checkpoint has been created for us. It is important that you understand that the production type of checkpoint is going to be the default mode. You will also notice that the Checkpoints section of Hyper-V Manager has now lit up with an entry under the DC3 server. The currently running virtual machine is listed as **Now**, and you can see a date and timestamp applied above it, which is the Checkpoint we just created.

Virtual Machine Checkpoint	X

Production checkpoint created.

Backup technology in the guest operating system was used to create a production checkpoint. The running application state wasn't included in the checkpoint operation. You can configure checkpoint options under the virtual machine settings.

☐ Please don't show me this again   OK

Checkpoints

⊟ DC3 - (7/5/2016 - 3:27:03 AM)
  ▷ Now

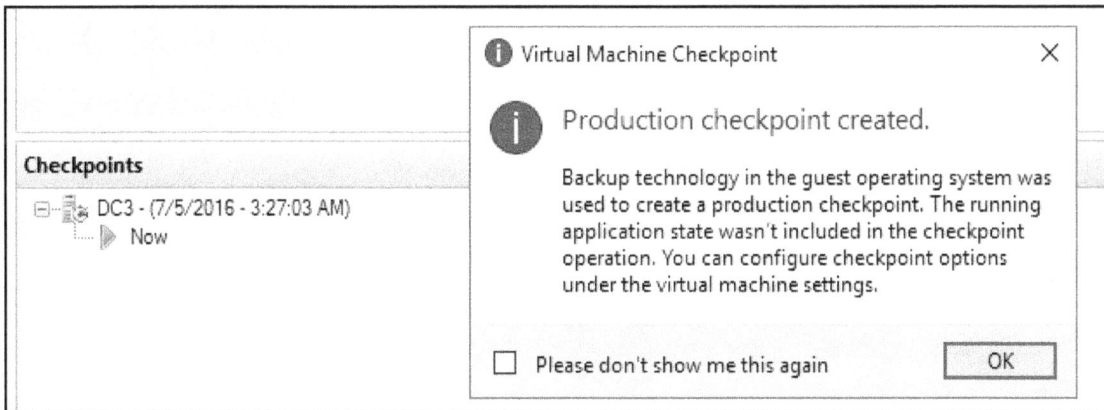

3. The message that presented itself says that backup technology inside the guest operating system was used to create this checkpoint. What does that mean? And more importantly, if we wanted to change back to Standard Checkpoints, where do we accomplish that? Both of these questions can be answered by opening the Settings of your virtual machine. Right-click on DC3, and choose **Settings...**. Once inside, select the heading that says **Checkpoints**.

4. This is the screen where you can choose whether you want to create **Production checkpoints** or **Standard checkpoints**. There is also a good description of each kind. In previous versions of Hyper-V, we could only do Standard checkpoints – called snapshots; we had no other options. Standard checkpoints essentially just create a differencing disk from our VHDX file. When you restore a standard checkpoint, it replaces everything right back to the way it was running, including application level content. Production checkpoints, on the other hand, use backup software inside the guest (VM) operating system. This is more similar to logging into that VM, opening up Windows Backup, and creating a backup file. Except you get to do it in one click, and it only takes a few seconds to accomplish. We will talk about the pros and cons of each type of checkpoint in the *How it works...* section at the end of this recipe.

Settings for DC3 on HYPERV1 — □ ✕

DC3 ∨ ◁ ▷ ↻

Hardware
- Add Hardware
- Firmware
  - Boot from File
- Security
  - Secure Boot enabled
- Memory
  - 2048 MB
- ⊞ Processor
  - 1 Virtual processor
- ⊟ SCSI Controller
  - ⊞ Hard Drive
    - DC3_E34870A8-CEDC-46FB-9...
  - DVD Drive
    - None
- ⊞ Network Adapter
  - Corp LAN
- ⊞ Network Adapter
  - Internet

Management
- Name
  - DC3
- Integration Services
  - Some services offered
- Checkpoints
  - Production
- Smart Paging File Location
  - C:\VMs\DC3
- Automatic Start Action
  - Restart if previously running
- Automatic Stop Action
  - Save

Checkpoints

You can configure options for checkpoint for this virtual machine.

Checkpoint Type

☑ Enable checkpoints

Select the type of checkpoint that will be created when users choose to checkpoint this virtual machine.

◉ Production checkpoints

Use backup technology in the guest operating system to create data-consistent checkpoints that don't include information about running applications.

☑ Create standard checkpoints if it's not possible to create a production checkpoint.

Take a checkpoint with full application state if it is not possible to use backup technology inside the guest operating system.

○ Standard checkpoints

Create application-consistent checkpoints that capture the current state of applications.

Checkpoint File Location

Choose where to store the checkpoint configuration and checkpoint saved state files for this virtual machine.

C:\VMs\DC3

Browse...

⚠ The checkpoint file location cannot be changed because the virtual machine has at least one checkpoint.

OK   Cancel   Apply

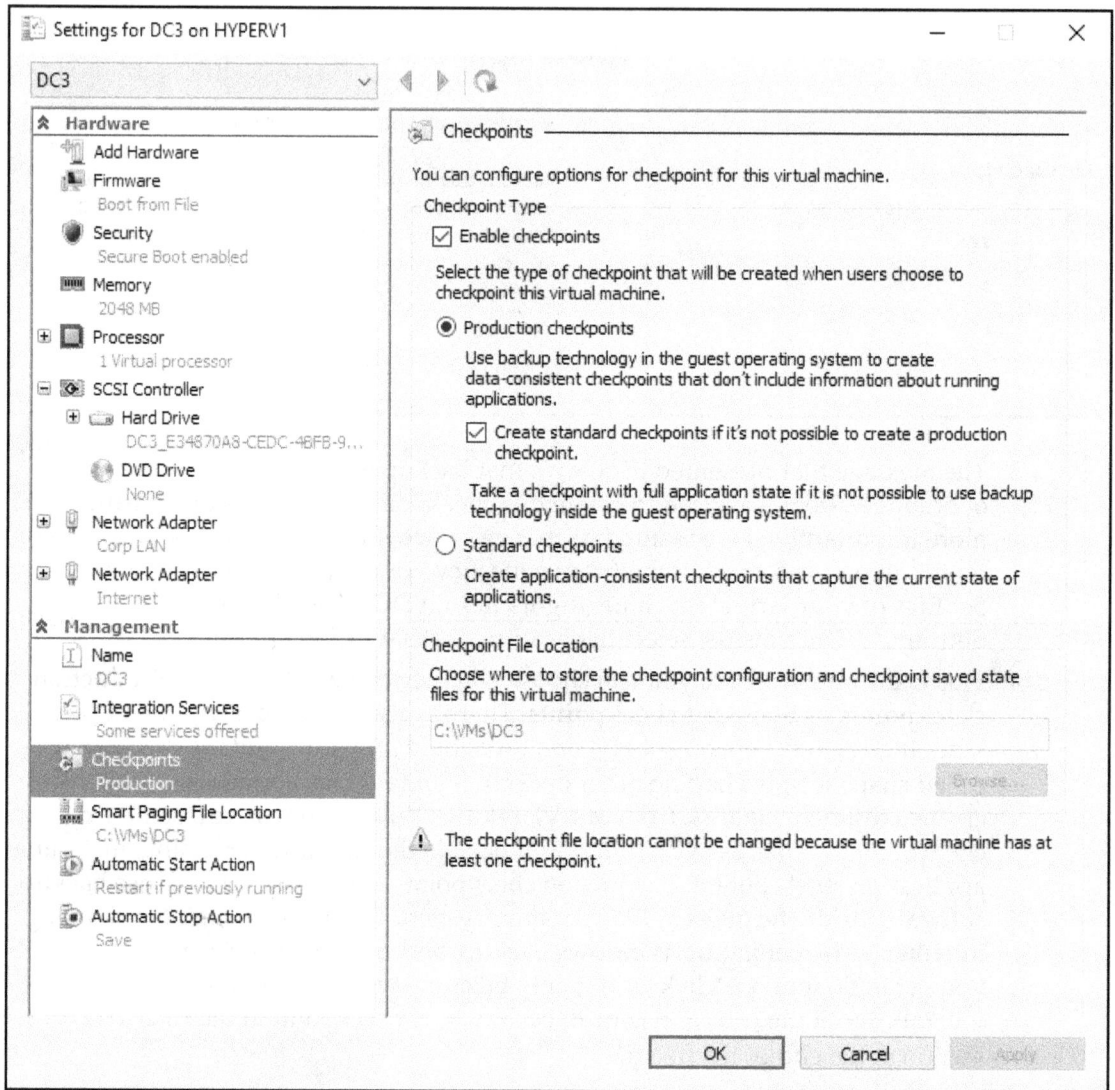

5. Go ahead and change **Checkpoint Type** to **Standard checkpoints**. Then right-click on your VM and choose **Checkpoint** again. This will create a second checkpoint for us, this one being the Standard type.

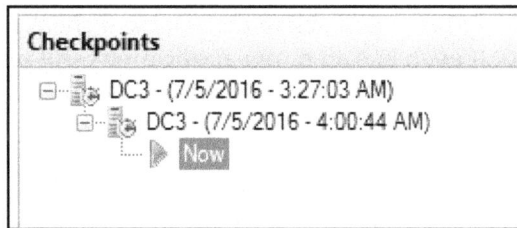

6. As you can see, there is really nothing distinguishable between the two different checkpoints we have taken, other than the timestamp. Other than our own knowledge, we would not be aware that the 3:27a.m. checkpoint was a production checkpoint, while the 4:00a.m. checkpoint was of the standard variety. If you think you will be taking snapshots of both kinds, it may be helpful to rename these checkpoints, by simply right-clicking on them, to reflect their checkpoint type somewhere in the name of the checkpoint itself.

7. Now we want to try restoring these checkpoints, bringing our DC3 server back to those particular moments in time. If you want to test the fact that these rollbacks are really working, you could go make some changes in the operating system at this time. Maybe create some files on the hard drive so that you can verify after accomplishing the rollback that those files have been removed.

8. To rollback a VM to a previous checkpoint, simply right-click on the checkpoint that you want to recover, and choose **Apply....**

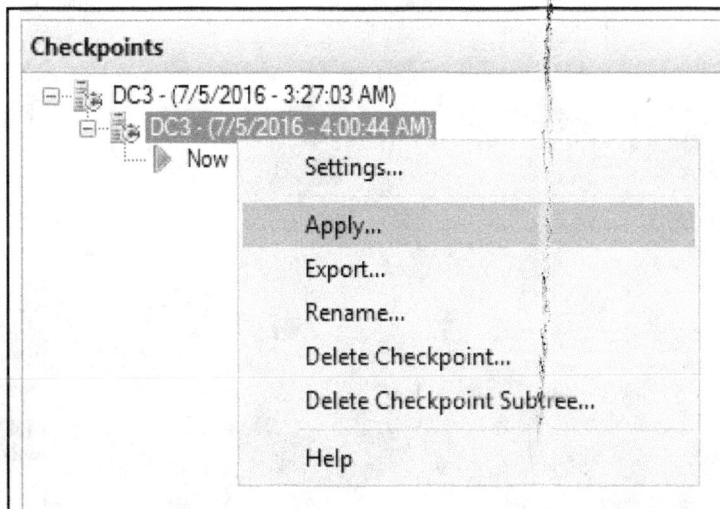

9. DC3 is immediately reverted back to the standard checkpoint that we created a few minutes ago. It even has all of my applications still up and running on the screen, exactly as the machine was the moment that I created that checkpoint image.

> **TIP**
>
> Make sure to read the *How it works...* section of this recipe carefully. While the Standard Checkpoint may seem like the better approach because of the immediate restores, it comes with some caveats that you need to be aware of!

10. Now that we have successfully restored a standard checkpoint, let's try restoring the first checkpoint that we created, which was the new Production type. Our procedure is the same: right-click on the checkpoint file and choose **Apply....**

11. This time, however, you will notice that the DC3 virtual machine has turned itself **OFF** when we chose to restore the checkpoint.

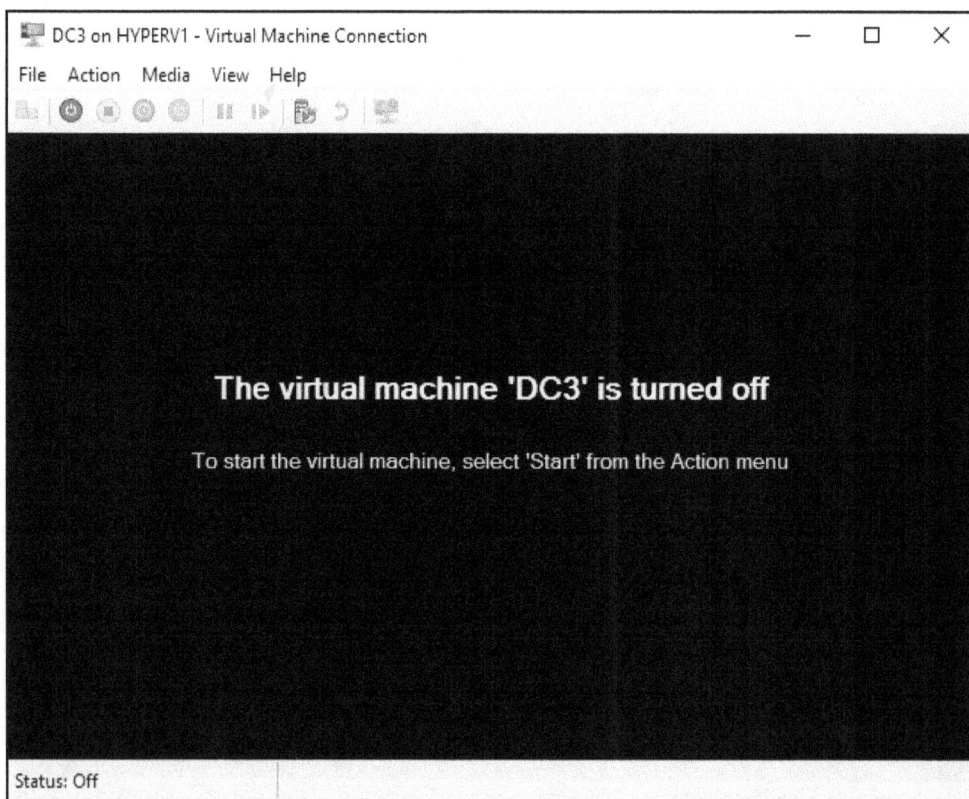

12. Click the **Start** button to bring DC3 back to life, and it boots right up. But this is a fresh boot, not the immediate application-aware restore that happened with our first checkpoint rollback. The VM has now been restored back to that initial Production checkpoint we took. As you have seen, the major difference with our procedure here was that we had to turn the server back on following the restore process.

How it works...

The capability in Windows Server 2016 Hyper-V to create Checkpoints is a very powerful one. Previous versions of Windows Server called this feature Snapshots, and for the most part Checkpoints work in exactly the same way. The major difference is that we now have two different types of images that we can create when we choose to Checkpoint our virtual machines.

Standard checkpoints are the same as our previous-generation snapshots—they allow for immediate rollback to an image file, keeping the VM online and running, and remembering even application-specific information when the rollback is finished. There is one major problem that has existed with snapshots, and will continue to be a problem with standard checkpoints. This is the issue where certain kinds of servers will fall out of sync with other servers when you apply standard checkpoints. You see, when you create standard checkpoints of servers like domain controllers or database servers, the file that is created is a simple snapshot from the Hyper-V Manager's level—it is supremely uninterested in what is going on inside the virtual machine or its own operating system at that moment in time. This means that, when you restore a standard checkpoint, it just lays the data back down exactly how it was before, with no consideration for the server or what function it performs. This often results in domain controllers falling out of sync with other DCs in your network, and data being skewed after the restore. This causes big problems for companies.

Production checkpoints are the new kid on the block, and are the default option for a reason. Even though they are slower to restore and your VM will shut itself down following the rollback of a production checkpoint, which results in downtime for this server, production checkpoints make use of backup and recovery tools like VSS inside the guest operating system. This means that those checkpoint files will be more comprehensible to the VM itself, and will recover more smoothly in a production environment.

Index

www.ingramcontent.com/pod-product-compliance
Lightning Source LLC
Chambersburg PA
CBHW080124220326
41598CB00032B/4942